2221066

D1715958

German Expansionism, Imperial Liberalism, and the United States, 1776–1945

This book traces the importance of the United States for German colonialism from the late eighteenth century to 1945, focusing on American westward expansion and racial politics. Jens-Uwe Guettel argues that, from the late eighteenth century onward, ideas of colonial expansion played a very important role in liberal, enlightened, and progressive circles in Germany, which, in turn, looked across the Atlantic to the liberal-democratic United States for inspiration and concrete examples. In the early years of the twentieth century, this America-inspired and -influenced imperial liberalism dominated German colonial discourse and practice. Yet following this pre-1914 peak of liberal political influence on the administration and governance of Germany's colonies, the expansionist ideas embraced by Germany's far right after the country's defeat in World War I had little or no connection with the German Empire's liberal imperialist tradition. *German Expansionism, Imperial Liberalism, and the United States, 1776–1945* therefore shows that, for example, Nazi plans for the settlement of conquered Eastern European territories were not directly linked to pre-1914 transatlantic exchanges concerning race and expansionism.

Jens-Uwe Guettel is Senior Lecturer in the Department of History and Religious Studies at the Pennsylvania State University.

German Expansionism, Imperial Liberalism, and the United States, 1776–1945

JENS-UWE GUETTEL

The Pennsylvania State University

CAMBRIDGE
UNIVERSITY PRESS

CAMBRIDGE UNIVERSITY PRESS
Cambridge, New York, Melbourne, Madrid, Cape Town,
Singapore, São Paulo, Delhi, Mexico City

Cambridge University Press
32 Avenue of the Americas, New York, NY 10013-2473, USA

www.cambridge.org
Information on this title: www.cambridge.org/9781107024694

First published 2012

Printed in the United States of America

A catalog record for this publication is available from the British Library.

Library of Congress Cataloging in Publication Data

Guettel, Jens-Uwe, 1974–
German expansionism, imperial liberalism and the United States, 1776–1945 /
Jens-Uwe Guettel, Pennsylvania State University.
    pages cm
Includes bibliographical references and index.
ISBN 978-1-107-02469-4
1. Germany – Territorial expansion.   2. United States – Territorial
expansion.   3. Germany – Colonies – History.   4. Germany – Relations –
United States.   5. United States – Relations – Germany.   6. Imperialism –
History.   7. Race – Political aspects – Germany – History.   8. Political
culture – Germany – History.   9. Liberalism – Germany – History.
10. Germany – Politics and government.   I. Title.
DD118.5.G84 2013
325′.343–dc23   2012036770

ISBN 978-1-107-02469-4 Hardback

Contents

Acknowledgments	*page* vii
Abbreviations	ix
Introduction	1
The Great War and the Question of German Historical Continuities	18
Liberalism, Imperialism, and Imperial Liberalism	27
A Note on Sources	41
1 Soil, Liberty, and Blood: Germans and American Westward Expansion Before 1871	43
Freedom and Empire	44
Progress, Social Control, Land, and Race	55
Visions of Unity and American Colonies	69
2 From Theory to Practice: German Colonialism and American Westward Expansion before World War I	79
Nineteenth-Century German Colonial Discourse, Indians, and American Expansion	82
Expansion and Empire: Indians, America, and German Colonial Discourse after 1866	87
Native Americans, American Expansion, and German Southwest Africa	111
3 The American South and Racial Segregation in the German Colonies	127

Racial Segregation in German Colonial Practice and
   Metropolitan Discourse, 1905–1914   130
"So that he doesn't become slothful": The United
   States, Racial Control, and German Colonialism   133
Jim Crow and Mixed-Race Marriage Bans in the
   German Colonies from 1905 to 1912   140
Jim Crow in Berlin: Parliamentary Miscegenation
   Debates, the RKA, and the American South   145
A Liberal American Solution?   151

4 America, Race, and German Expansionism from
   the Great War to 1945   161
   German Liberals and the United States during the
      1920s   175
   "Yes, yes, America, you're better off. But, please, keep
      your benevolence to yourself": Nazi Expansionism
      and America   182
   Against "Liberalist" Imperialism: Nazi Lebensraum
      Visions as Antiliberalism and Anticolonialism   189
   "The United States under a Jewish Dictatorship" –
      Nazi Anti-Americanism after 1933   197
   From the American West to the German East?   207

Conclusion: Imperial Liberalism, Nazi Expansionism,
   and the Continuities of German History   217

Bibliography   233
Index   265

Acknowledgments

It would have been impossible for me to complete this book without the help and scholarly advice of many supporters. First, I would like to thank my dissertation advisor Jon Butler for letting me conceive of the beginnings of this project under his supervision, although, ultimately, my topic had little to do with his own research. I would also like to thank Frank Turner, who is missed, and Ute Frevert for their input and criticism. In addition, I wish to thank Ben Kiernan and Benjamin Madley. Their interest in my research shaped the argumentative trajectory of my work once it came to the task of revising the dissertation. In respect to the latter undertaking I cannot thank Andrew Zimmerman enough for his support and engagement with my work. I would also like to thank Erik Grimmer-Solem and Bradley Naranch for reading portions of the manuscript, and Lora Wildenthal for her kind comments on parts of this project that, ultimately, have become the basis for a separate article and new project.

I am also deeply indebted to my mother, Sigrid Güttel, for her tireless research assistance. Although I live in the United States, far from German archival materials, I could always rely on her willingness to go to various archives in Berlin and seek out the documents I needed. I was thus able to engage in archival research, even when I could not be in the archives myself. She was even willing to transcribe Wilhelm Solf's handwriting for me, which was quite a task. The same holds true for my mother-in-law, Sarah Paulu Boittin. Her patient and repeated editing of the text has ironed out many Germanisms, grammatical mistakes, and rhetorical imprecisions. The book would not be what it is without her. I also wish to thank Peter Prüfert, who is missed, and Waltraut Prüfert for helping me to find the book's cover image.

Last but certainly not least, I would like to thank my partner Jennifer Anne Boittin. Without her piercing criticism, scholarly input and advice, and willingness to repeatedly help me edit my writing, this book would not exist. I cannot thank her enough.

Abbreviations

BArch	Bundesarchiv Berlin/Koblenz (German Federal Archives Berlin/Koblenz)
DDP	Deutsche Demokratische Partei (German Democratic Party, 1918–30)
DFP	Deutsche Fortschrittspartei (German Progressive Party, 1861–84)
DVP	Deutsche Volkspartei (German People's Party, 1918–33)
FSVP	Freisinnige Volkspartei (Liberal People's Party, 1893–1910)
FVP	Fortschrittliche Volkspartei (Progressive People's Party, 1910–18)
GEA	German East Africa (Tanzania, Rwanda, Burundi)
GSWA	German Southwest Africa (Namibia)
NLP	Nationalliberale Partei (National-Liberal Party, 1867–1918)
NSDAP	Nationalsozialistische Deutsche Arbeiterpartei (National-Socialist German Workers' Party, 1920–45)
Reichstagsdebatte	*Verhandlungen des Reichstages / Stenographische Berichte / Anlagen. Berlin: 1871–1939*

RKA   Reichskolonialamt (Imperial Colonial
                Department, 1907–19)
RKA-B   Reichskolonialabteilung (Imperial Colonial
                Office, 1890–1907. Part of the Foreign
                Office until 1907)
SPD   Sozialdemokratische Partei Deutschlands
                (Social-Democratic Party of Germany,
                1875–)

Introduction

"Even those of us who feel completely liberated from the German original sin of adoring everything foreign just because it is foreign still have much to learn from the measures the Americans have taken to solve the Native problem."

Alexander Kuhn, *Zum Eingeborenenproblem in Deutsch-Südwestafrika* [Regarding the Native Problem in German Southwest Africa] (1905)

"[While it is] a trite saying that 'the pen is mightier than the sword,' it is equally true that the bullet is the pioneer of civilization."

Buffalo Bill's Wild West: "The Rifle" (1886, 1893)[1]

"The history of the colonization of the United States, clearly the biggest colonial endeavor the world has ever known, had as its first act the complete extermination of its native peoples." Thus spoke Bernhard Dernburg, the German left-liberal ex-banker and new head of the German Colonial Office in January 1907, during a speech meant to fire up pro-colonialist German voters for the upcoming national elections. Present-day readers, German or American alike, may be startled by Dernburg's mention

---

[1] Cited in Richard Slotkin, "Buffalo Bill's 'Wild West' and the Mythologization of the American Empire," in *Cultures of United States Imperialism*, ed. Amy Kaplan and Donald E. Pease (Durham: Duke University Press, 1993), 171.

I

of genocide and his labeling the expansion across the continent of the fledgling American republic a "colonial endeavor," analogous to nineteenth-century European imperialism no less. Although Dernburg did not approve of genocidal violence as a colonialist tool, seeing the United States as the biggest colonial endeavor in the world nevertheless recommended America both for close scrutiny and for emulation in Germany's own colonies. Nor did the importance of America for Germany's colonial ventures go unnoticed on the other side of the Atlantic: Historian Frederick Jackson Turner, author of the famous essay, "The Significance of the Frontier in American History," thus remarked, "American colonization has become the mother of German colonial policy."[2]

By 1907, these ideas were no longer new. During a speech at a meeting of the German National-Liberal Party in September 1884, the year in which the German Empire began to acquire overseas possessions, Friedrich Ratzel, an influential geographer and one of Imperial Germany's most fervent proponents of overseas expansion, remarked that "if we had had the option 200 years ago, we too would have preferred to carve a New Germany out of North America.... However, today we do not have this choice and it would be foolish to turn down black bread just because we did not reach the white bread in time." In no uncertain terms Ratzel described American westward expansion as colonialism and used the impossibility of creating a "New Germany" on American soil, represented positively by the image of refined, high-quality white bread, as an argument for German imperialist endeavors in Africa. Of course, the term "black bread" Ratzel used to depict Africa just happened to include an adjective often employed to describe race, a clear reminder that colonial expansion and race went hand in hand.[3]

---

[2] Bernhard Dernburg, "Speech in front of the Kolonialpolitisches Aktionskomité," in *Reichstagsauflösung und Kolonialpolitik*, ed. Gustav Schmoller (Berlin: Wedekind, 1907), 7–8. Turner cited in Peter Bergmann, "American Exceptionalism and the German 'Sonderweg' in Tandem," *The International History Review* 23, no. 3 (2001): 516.

[3] Friedrich Ratzel, *Wider die Reichsnörgler: Ein Wort zur Kolonialfrage aus Wählerkreisen* (München: 1884), 23.

This book traces America's role within German expansionism from its intellectual origins in the late eighteenth century to its murderous and bitter end in 1945. Throughout the nineteenth century and until 1914, German observers attributed the impressive and unmatched success of America's westward expansion to laissez-faire principles and the country's liberal political system. These conclusions made American colonization practices especially attractive for liberal German expansionists – and it was German liberals, together with the social groups traditionally supportive of liberal ideas, such as entrepreneurs, merchants, and academics, who during the late nineteenth century provided much of the public pressure and support for German overseas expansion. America thus occupied an important position in nineteenth- and early twentieth-century German expansionist discourse and practice. The following analysis highlights the significance of German liberalism for German colonialist discourse and overseas expansion before and after 1884, the year in which the German Empire began to acquire colonies. Ideas of empire and colonialism deeply permeated liberal and progressive segments of German society from the late eighteenth century until 1914, fueled by transatlantic German-American exchanges on matters of territorial expansion and race.[4]

This book thus dissects and contests preconceived notions of German and, at least indirectly, American exceptionalisms: German perspectives on the American frontier reveal that pro-colonialist sentiments in nineteenth-century Germany grew as much from transatlantic exchanges on expansionism and race as from domestic and national contexts. German admiration for the United States was never exclusively rooted in America's supposedly exceptional status as the world's biggest and most successful republic. Instead, from the perspective of German observers, the United States' attractiveness was inseparable from its westward expansion. The experience of the United States appeared to

---

[4] Dieter Langewiesche, *Liberalismus in Deutschland*, 1. Aufl. ed., *Neue historische Bibliothek* (Frankfurt am Main: Suhrkamp, 1988), 218–19; Horst Gründer, *Geschichte der deutschen Kolonien* (Paderborn: Schöningh, 1985), 54.

demonstrate that empire and the development of a political system based on liberal principles had to go hand in hand, because both seemed to be invariably connected to continuous colonization. Moreover, although it was indeed perceived as the land of exceptional freedom and opportunity, the United States also offered intriguing examples of social exclusion, expulsion, and extinction – necessary byproducts of colonialism in the minds of nineteenth-century Germans (and Americans for that matter). German observers discerned (sometimes with and sometimes without regret) that the many advantages America offered to its white inhabitants were linked to various forms of disfranchisement of the country's ethnic minorities, most obviously blacks and Native Americans. Ultimately, these approaches were all at least potentially applicable in Germany's colonies as well.[5]

German views of America thus became key components not only of nineteenth-century colonial discourse but also of real-life conditions in the German colonies. Germany's main (and for all practical intents and purposes only) settler colony was German Southwest Africa, where American-style settlement policies and mixed-race marriage prohibitions were explored. In addition, in German East Africa and German Samoa, the introduction of race codes was justified against the backdrop of American segregation statutes. Soon after 1776, Germans began to identify the United States as an exemplary, yet unexceptional (and hence replicable) empire. In other words, American expansionism and racial policies were seen as models that European colonizers could and should reproduce elsewhere in the world – in particular in Germany's own colonies. Contrary to popular and scholarly belief, eighteenth-, nineteenth-, and twentieth-century Germans were therefore neither necessarily sympathetic to America's Indians nor did they always accept romanticized depictions of them. Instead, German expansionists frequently viewed both American reservation policies and sometimes the outright

---

[5] In the following, the terms "Native Americans," "Indians," and "Amerindians" are used interchangeably. See Colin G. Calloway, *The World Turned Upside Down* (Boston: Bedford Books, 1994), vii.

extermination of Amerindians as unavoidable side effects of successful colonization policies. This perspective was by no means uniquely German, but rather shared by the Western world: For example, Buffalo Bill Cody's Wild West shows, which ran successfully in Germany and Europe during the 1890s, but had initially been equally if not more popular in the eastern United States, aimed not only to entertain audiences with spectacular scenes from "the West" but were also geared to emphasize the "moral truth" of the frontier experience, namely "that violence and savage war were the necessary instruments of American progress" and that "the bullet is the pioneer of civilization." In turn, during the 1890s Americans applied practices and terminology related to the frontier in an overseas context – for example during the Spanish-American War, when Cody proposed a "Wild West" approach and Theodore Roosevelt's First Volunteer Cavalry regiment took on the name, "The Rough Riders," a term generally applied to Western horsemen and made famous by Cody's shows.[6]

---

[6] Slotkin, "Buffalo Bill's 'Wild West' and the Mythologization of the American Empire," 171–79; Susanne Zantop, "The Beautiful, the Ugly, and the German: Race, Gender and Nationality in Eighteenth-Century Anthropological Discourse," in *Gender and Germanness* (Providence: Berghahn, 1997); Susanne Zantop, *Colonial Fantasies: Conquest, Family, and Nation in Precolonial Germany, 1770–1870* (Durham: Duke University Press, 1997); Susanne Zantop, "'Der Indianer' im Rasse- und Geschlechterdiskurs der deutschen Spätaufklärung," in *Das Subjekt und die Anderen: Interkulturalität und Geschlechterdifferenz vom 18. Jahrhundert bis zur Gegenwart*, ed. Viktoria Schmidt-Linsenhoff (Berlin: 2001); Hartmut Lutz, "German Indianthusiasm: A Socially Constructed German National(ist) Myth," in *Germans and Indians. Fantasies, Encounters, Projections*, ed. Colin G. Calloway, Gerd Gemünden, and Susanne Zantop (Lincoln: University of Nebraska Press, 2002); H. Glenn Penny, "Elusive Authenticity: The Quest for the Authentic Indian in German Public Culture," *Comparative Studies in Society and History* 48, no. 4 (2006); H. Glenn Penny, "Illustrating America. Images of the North American Wild West in German Periodicals, 1825–1890," in *I like America: Fictions of the Wild West*, ed. Pamela Kort and Max Hollein (Munich: Prestel, 2006); Kate Flint, *The Transatlantic Indian* (Princeton: Princeton University Press, 2009), 5. On the so-called *Drang nach Osten* see most recently David Blackbourn, *The Conquest of Nature: Water, Landscape and the Making of Modern Germany* (London: Jonathan Cape, 2006), 282; Mark Mazower, *Hitler's Empire. Nazi Rule in Occupied Europe* (London: Penguin Books, 2008), 20–27.

This study underlines the liberal impact on German colonialism from the late eighteenth to the early twentieth century and traces the divide that existed between German expansionism before and after the Great War. Although continuities persisted as well, after 1918 the vanishing importance of liberal ideas was more than matched by the ascendance of radically new notions of how and why Germany needed to expand again after the Versailles Treaty had forced the country to relinquish its colonies and to cede around 20 percent of its contiguous European territory to France, Belgium, Denmark, Poland, Czechoslovakia, and Lithuania. This new expansionism was enunciated, for example, by Nazi ideologues such as Alfred Rosenberg. Understanding the important roles played by liberal German colonialists before 1914 and the significance of the United States for them highlights the differences and ruptures between pre–World War I colonialism and Nazi expansionism.

German colonialism has traditionally been viewed as hardly more than a sideshow, a mere distraction from Imperial Germany's many (and allegedly more important) domestic developments and problems. Moreover, according to this view, nineteenth-century German liberals were not so much the originators of German expansionist sentiment as they were distracted by it. According to historian Hans-Ulrich Wehler's famous analysis, German imperialism was thus a "social imperialism" that "amounted to a conservative 'taming' policy which sought to divert abroad reform attempts which found their expression in the emancipatory forces of liberalism." The classic post-1945 German exceptionalism argument – Sonderweg – held that, instead of being "distracted," "diverted," or "tamed" by Otto von Bismarck, German liberals should have directed their attention to liberal-democratic reform at home, as did (allegedly) their counterparts in Britain, the United States, and France, and not focus on pointless colonial adventures. This interpretation, put forth in various ways by scholars such as Wehler and other German historians during the 1960s and 1970s, reinforced the impression that imperialism and colonialism were not substantial elements of nineteenth- and early twentieth-century German history, because Germany's true problems were to be found at home and not in overseas ventures.[7]

7 Until the 1990s, only a small group of German-speaking historians, among them most prominently Hans-Ulrich Wehler, Klaus Bade, Pogge von Strandmann, and Hans Fenske, engaged with German imperialism in a sustained fashion. Among English-speaking historians, only A. J. P. Taylor stands out in this respect. Although colonial specialists such as Horst Gründer, Helmut Bley, and Horst Drechsler published important and detailed accounts of German colonialism, only the aforementioned historians attempted to analyze and explain German expansionism, imperialism, and colonialism against the broad backdrop of nineteenth-century German history. Wehler's influential evaluation of German overseas expansion as a "distraction," a "social imperialism" meant to project domestic tensions overseas, has traditionally been the most influential explanation for Germany's acquisition of colonies. Other historians of Wehler's generation, most prominently Thomas Nipperdey and Lothar Gall, have paid little attention to German imperialism. Ralf Dahrendorf, *Society and Democracy in Germany* (Anchor Books, 1969), 46; H. Pogge von Strandmann, "Domestic Origins of Germany's Colonial Expansion under Bismarck," *Past and Present* 42, no. 1 (1969); Hans Ulrich Wehler, *Bismarck und der Imperialismus* (Köln, Berlin: Kiepenheuer u. Witsch, 1969); A. J. P. Taylor, *Germany's First Bid for Colonies 1884–1885: A Move in Bismarck's European Policy* (New York: W. W. Norton & Co., 1970); Hans Ulrich Wehler, *Imperialismus* (Köln: Kiepenheuer & Witsch, 1970); Hans-Ulrich Wehler, *The German Empire, 1871–1918* (Dover, N.H.: Berg Publishers, 1985 [1973]), 173; Klaus J. Bade, *Fabri und der Imperialismus in der Bismarckzeit* (Freiburg: Atlantis-Verlag, 1975); Wolfgang J. Mommsen, "Wandlung der Liberalen im Zeitalter des Imperialismus," in *Liberalismus und imperialistischer Staat. Der Imperialismus als Problem liberaler Parteien in Deutschland*, ed. K. Holl and G. List (Göttingen: Vandenhoeck & Ruprecht, 1975); Hans-Ulrich Wehler, "Bismarck's Imperialism," in *Imperial Germany*, ed. James Sheehan (New York: Franklin Watts, 1976), 180–222; Horst Drechsler, *Let us die fighting: The struggle of the Herero and Nama against German imperialism (1884–1915)* (Zed Press, 1980); Horst Drechsler, *Aufstände in Südwestafrika* (Berlin (East): Dietz, 1984), Gründer, *Geschichte der deutschen Kolonien*, Klaus Hildebrand, *Deutsche Außenpolitik 1871–1918*, vol. II, *Enzyklopädie Deutscher Geschichte* (München: R. Oldenbourg Verlag, 1989); Hans-Ulrich Wehler, "Sozialimperialismus," in *Escape into War? The Foreign Policy of Imperial Germany*, ed. Gregor Schöllgen (Berg, 1990), 8; Thomas Nipperdey, *Deutsche Geschichte 1866–1918. Vol. II – Machtstaat und Demokratie* (München: C. H. Beck, 1992); Wolfgang J. Mommsen, *Das Ringen um den nationalen Staat. Die Gründung und der innere Ausbau des Deutschen Reiches unter Otto von Bismarck 1850 bis 1890* (Berlin: Propyläen Verlag, 1993); Klaus Hildebrand, *Das Vergangene Reich: Deutsche Außenpolitik von Bismarck bis Hitler 1871–1945* (Stuttgart: Deutsche Verlags-Anstalt, 1995); Helmut Bley, *Namibia under German Rule* (Münster: LIT Verlag, 1996); Lothar Gall, *Europa auf dem Weg in die Moderne, 1850–1890* (München: Oldenbourg Verlag, 1997);

Horst Gründer, "Zum Stellenwert des Rassismus im Spektrum der deutschen Kolonialideologie," in *Rassenmischehen – Mischlinge – Rassentrennung. Zur Politk der Rasse im deutschen Kolonialreich*, ed. Frank Becker (Stuttgart: Franz Steiner, 2004). Already in the 1970s, Hans Fenske demonstrated that expansionist sentiment was not merely a product of German nationalism after the founding of the German Empire. Although his work traced German colonial discourse to the eighteenth century, his findings never led to a revision of the "Wehlerian paradigm." In fact, Fenske claimed that his findings supported Wehler's thesis, which they did not. See Hans Fenske, "Imperialisitische Tendenzen in Deutschland vor 1866: Auswanderung, überseeische Bestrebungen, Weltmachtsträume," *Historisches Jahrbuch* 97/98 (1978): 378–79. Only in the 1990s did scholars begin to engage more seriously and in sustained fashion with Germany's expansionist past; this group of scholars includes, most prominently, Susanne Zantop, Jürgen Zimmerer, Pascal Grosse, Birthe Kundrus, and John K. Noyes. In the first years of the twenty-first century, several important works on this subject have been published, including Jürgen Conrad's *Globalisierung und Nation im Deutschen Kaiserreich*, Andrew Zimmerman's *Alabama in Africa*, Lora Wildenthal's *German Women for Empire*, Dirk van Laak's *Imperiale Infrastruktur*, and Matthew Fitzpatrick's *Liberal Imperialism in Germany*. See Zantop, *Colonial Fantasies: Conquest, Family, and Nation in Precolonial Germany*; Frank Lorenz Müller, "Imperialist Ambitions in Vormärz and Revolutionary Germany: The Agitation for German Settlement Colonies Overseas, 1840–1849," *German History* 17, no. 3 (1999); Lora Wildenthal, *German Women for Empire, 1884–1945* (Durham: Duke University Press, 2001); Jürgen Zimmerer, *Deutsche Herrschaft über Afrikaner* (Münster: Lit, 2001); Birthe Kundrus, "Die Kolonien – 'Kinder des Gefühls und der Phantasie," in *Phantasiereiche. Zur Kulturgeschichte des deutschen Kolonialismus*, ed. Birthe Kundrus (Frankfurt/New York: Campus Verlag, 2003); Birthe Kundrus, "Von Windhoek nach Nuernberg? Koloniale 'Mischehenverbote' und die nationalsozialistische Rassengesetzgebung," in *Phantasiereiche. Zur Kulturgeschichte des deutschen Kolonialismus*, ed. Birthe Kundrus (Frankfurt a. M.: Campus Verlag, 2003); Benjamin Madley, "Patterns of Frontier Genocide 1803–1910," *Journal of Genocide Research* 6, no. 2 (2004); Dirk van Laak, *Imperiale Infrastruktur: Deutsche Planungen für eine Erschließung Afrikas 1880 bis 1960* (Paderborn: Schöningh, 2004); Pascal Grosse, "What Does German Colonialism Have To Do With National Socialism? A Conceptual Framework," in *Germany's Colonial Pasts*, ed. Eric Ames (Lincoln: University of Nebraska Press, 2005); Benjamin Madley, "From Africa to Auschwitz: How German Southwest Africa Incubated Ideas and Methods Adopted and Developed by the Nazis in Eastern Europe," *European History Quarterly* 35, no. 3 (2005); Sebastian Conrad, *Globalisierung und Nation im Deutschen Kaiserreich* (München: C. H. Beck, 2006); John K. Noyes, "Commerce, colonialism, and the globalization of action in late Enlightenment Germany," *Postcolonial Studies* 9, no. 1 (2006); Matthew P. Fitzpatrick, *Liberal Imperialism in Germany. Expansionism and Nationalism, 1848–1884* (New York: Berghahn Books, 2008); Andrew Zimmerman, *Alabama in Africa: Booker T. Washington, the German Empire, and the Globalization of the New South* (Princeton: Princeton University Press, 2010).

During the decades immediately following World War II, the political atmosphere in West Germany strengthened the tendency of a new generation of German historians to dismiss the phenomenon of German imperialism as secondary, as part of an authoritarian and antiliberal past that needed to be erased. The ideological needs of the young, West German republic thus reinforced scholarly propensities to create a history of liberalism that was untainted by expansionist tendencies. Similar leanings can be observed in the United States during the Cold War. After 1945, the face-off with the Soviet Union, which had just extended its hegemony over almost all of Central and Eastern Europe, helped generate the idea that America's own imperialist and colonialist past was positively exceptional. According to this notion, the United States, unlike most European states, never (or at the most only peripherally) engaged in the so-called New Imperialism of the late nineteenth and early twentieth centuries during which Europeans divided up much of the world. As a result, late nineteenth-century American imperialism, peaking with the conquest of the Philippines, Puerto Rico, and Guam in 1898, was presented as an unfortunate and brief "aberration" from American liberal and republican principles (the Philippines gained independence in 1946). More important, America's westward expansion before the 1890s was typically entirely absolved of ties to imperialism. Despite having been debunked by scholars, the notion that the United States was never an imperialist nation still permeates American political discourse today.[8]

---

[8] Fitzpatrick, *Liberal Imperialism in Germany. Expansionism and Nationalism, 1848–1884*, 4. Use of the term "empire" in respect to eighteenth- and nineteenth-century American continental expansion (as opposed to American imperialism after 1898) remains infrequent and quasi-heretical to this day. The geographer Neil Smith, author of one of the most recent books on American imperialism, thus distinguishes American imperialism after 1898 from American westward expansion. In his classic study *The Rising American Empire*, Robert W. Van Alstyne argues that, through the middle of the nineteenth century, Americans used the term "empire" and conceived of the United States as an ever expanding "empire." After the Civil War, this particular characterization began to fall out of favor and, from 1898 onward, was used by critics of U.S. overseas expansion. After World War I, "imperialism" ceased to

Nineteenth- and early twentieth-century German expansionists saw a different history. The United States was immensely important for them because they viewed America as an expanding empire even before it acquired overseas colonies. After all, during the nineteenth century, two issues that became more and more critical for German expansionists existed conjointly along the American frontier and in the American South: Acquiring space prompted the need to manage people(s), and this management was often carried out through race. For German expansionists, the U.S. experience thus became especially important with respect to questions of settler colonialism and the "handling" of native and other allegedly racially inferior peoples.

In recent years, German colonial activities in the late nineteenth and early twentieth centuries have attracted the attention of a number of scholars. This scholarly interest has resulted in the publication of many exciting new works on the German Empire, German imperialism, and German liberalism. Sebastian Conrad's *Globalisierung und Nation* reinterprets Imperial German history against a global and transnational backdrop. Andrew Zimmerman's *Alabama in Africa* expertly demonstrates that concrete economic and intellectual connections between Germany, Germany's African colonies, and the American South shaped this transnational framework. In addition, Matthew Fitzpatrick's *Liberal Imperialism* outlines nineteenth-century German liberalism's relationship to expansionist discourse and shows how colonialist visions played a key role for German liberals in their attempt to construct a German national identity between 1848

be a positive categorization in any way, and after World War II, maintaining America's nonentanglement in the history of European imperialism became a common exercise. Richard Koebner, "The Concept of Economic Imperialism," *The Economic History Review* 2, no. 1 (1949): 5; William Appleman Williams, "The Frontier Thesis and American Foreign Policy," *Pacific Historical Review* 24 (1955); R.W. Van Alstyne, *The Rising American Empire* (Oxford: Basil Blackwell, 1960), 6–7; Amy Kaplan, "'Left Alone with America': The Absence of Empire in the Study of American Culture," in *Cultures of United States Imperialism*, ed. Amy Kaplan and Donald E. Pease (Durham: Duke University Press, 1993); Neil Smith, *American Empire: Roosevelt's Geographer and the Prelude to Globalization* (Berkeley: University of California Press, 2003), xiii.

and 1884. Heeding criticism recently leveled by historian Alison
Games against the field of "New Atlantic History" for not being
much more than "an expanded history of the colonial Americas,"
my study turns the tables and focuses on the German reaction
to American westward expansion and U.S. race questions. Its
results illuminate the impact of transatlantic phenomena such as
American slavery and the settlement of the American continent
on metropolitan Germany and its colonial peripheries over the
course of well over 150 years.[9]

Sebastian Conrad has perceptively argued that "around 1900
globalization and the institutions of the nation state were not

[9] Sebastian Conrad and Jürgen Osterhammel, *Das Kaiserreich transnational.
Deutschland in der Welt 1871–1914* (Vandenhoeck & Ruprecht, 2004); Laak,
Imperiale Infrastruktur; Conrad, *Globalisierung und Nation im Deutschen
Kaiserreich*, 316. See also Sven Beckert, "From Tuskegee to Togo: The Problem
of Freedom in the Empire of Cotton," *The Journal of American History* 92, no.
2 (2005); Andrew Zimmerman, "A German Alabama in Africa: The Tuskegee
Expedition to German Togo and the Transnational Origins of West African
Cotton Growers," *American Historical Review* 110 (2005); Fitzpatrick, *Lib-
eral Imperialism in Germany. Expansionism and Nationalism, 1848–1884*;
Bradley Naranch, "Made in China: Austro-Prussian Overseas Rivalry and the
Global Unification of the German Nation," *Australian Journal of Politics and
History* 56, no. 3 (2010); Zimmerman, *Alabama*.; Erik Grimmer-Solem, "The
Professors' Africa: Economists, the Elections of 1907, and the Legitimation
of German Imperialism," *German History* 25, no. 3 (2007); Helmut Walser
Smith, "The Talk of Genocide, the Rhetoric of Miscegenation: Notes on the
Debates in the German Reichstag Concerning Southwest Africa, 1904–14,"
in *The Imperialist Imagination: German Colonialism and its Legacy*, ed. Sara
Friedrichsmeyer, Sara Lennox, and Susanne Zantop (Ann Arbor: University
of Michigan Press, 1998); Helmut Walser Smith, "The Logic of Colonial Violence: Germany in Southwest Africa (1904–1907); the United States in the
Philippines (1899–1902)," in *German and American Nationalism: A Comparative Perspective*, ed. Hartmut Lehmann and Hermann Wellenreuther (New
York: Berg, 1999). In addition, *German Expansionism, Imperial Liberalism,
and the United States* extends Susanne Zantop's path-breaking *Colonial Fantasies*, which ends in 1884. Zantop argues that German "colonial fantasies"
(specifically regarding the role American Indians played in them) were not
transnational, but rather peculiarly German. See also Allison Games, "AHR
Forum: Atlantic History: Definitions, Challenges, and Opportunities," *The
American Historical Review* 111, no. 3 (2006): 18. In addition Shelley Baranowski's *Nazi Empire* (New York: Cambridge University Press, 2010) offers a
synthesis of the existing scholarship on German imperialism from 1884 until
1945.

in competition with each other. On the contrary: Global inter-dependence ... did not lead to the dissolution of national affiliations ... but supported their assertion worldwide." My study shows that the linkage of German nationalism and liberal visions of global expansion did not arise in the late nineteenth century, but reached all the way to the eighteenth century. Moreover, although Conrad terms colonialism a "cross-European project with many common features and parallels," German colonialism was also transatlantic and America-focused. To be sure, Germans, at least until 1884, remained onlookers with respect to the "Atlantic world." Yet for nearly a century before then, their political, economic, and social concepts corresponded with and reacted to transatlantic and often American phenomena.[10]

For example, in 1788, the Göttingen professor Christoph Meiners, who lived in the small Duchy of Hannover and had no personal connections to slavery or the slave trade, turned his assessment of the benefits of America's colonization into a genocidal pro-slavery argument: "Yet even if it were proven that in the American possessions ... one hundred thousand Negroes died every year ..., it would only demonstrate that the slave trade and the labor for which the Negroes are bought are detrimental to the black race, but not that they constitute a disadvantage for humankind as a whole." In 1827, the outspoken proponent of Germans' settling the American West, Gottfried Duden, justified the expulsion of Indians by stating that "nothing is more lop-sided than quixotic rants against the [westward] expansion of people of European origin based on overly sentimental praise of Indians."[11]

In 1862, Karl Andrée, publisher of the widely read geographic journal *Globus*, in referencing the potential abolition of

---

[10] Conrad, *Globalisierung und Nation im Deutschen Kaiserreich*, 316; Sebastian Conrad, *Globalisation and the Nation* (New York: Cambridge University Press, 2010), 137.

[11] Christoph Meiners, "Über die Bevölkerung von America," *Göttingisches Historisches Magazin* 3 (1788): 409; Gottfried Duden, *Bericht über eine Reise nach den westlichen Staaten Nord-Amerikas und einen mehrjährigen Aufenthalt am Missouri* (Elberfeld: Lucas, 1829), 104–06.

slavery in the American South because of the Civil War, remarked sardonically, "In hot climates it is impossible to make Negroes work in regular fashion without the use of force. In these regions emancipation, about which an unclear and unctuous pseudo-philanthropy loses so many senseless words, equals brutalization." Seven years later, the geographer and pro-colonialist Friedrich Ratzel made a similar statement in the same journal: "Should slavery be abolished altogether or can it be maintained in principle and scientifically legitimated, these were the questions that were discussed on beer benches ... in our pure white Central European homeland, where an actual Negro is a rare attraction, without any sign of true enlightenment concerning such matters." At least in part, both Andrée and Ratzel were assessing the impact of the abolition of American slavery on the economic viability of European colonialism: If natives could not be enslaved, other ways of forcing them to work had to be explored.[12]

During the early years of the twentieth century, colonizers in German Southwest Africa were inspired by Southern Jim Crow provisions and pointed out that in the American South, "marriages between whites and blacks are prohibited." They also argued for American Indian reservations as models for similar institutions in German colonies, stating that Germans had "much to learn from the measures the Americans have taken to solve the Native problem." Finally, before German expansionism ran its course with Nazi Germany's defeat in World War II, Hitler affirmed in 1941 that "the Volga must be our Mississippi," concluding that "there is only one task [in the East]: To set about the Germanization of the land ... and to regard the indigenous inhabitants as 'Indians.'"[13]

---

[12] Karl Andrée, "Unsere schwarzen Brüder," *Globus* 1 (1862): 314. Ratzel quoted in Bradley Naranch, "Global Proletarians, Uncle Toms, and Native Savages: The Antinomies of Black Identity in Nineteenth-Century Germany" (Conference paper presented at Black Diaspora and Germany Across the Centuries, German Historical Institute, Washington, D.C., 2009), 1.

[13] Bundesarchiv Berlin, R 1001/5423, pp. 68–69. Alexander Kuhn, *Zum Eingeborenenproblem in Deutsch-Südwestafrika* (Berlin: Dietrich Reimer (Ernst Vohsen), 1905), 3. Hitler quoted in Blackbourn, *The Conquest of Nature*, 280, 86.

Of course, the function of the United States within German debates over colonialism and race changed over time. No straight trajectory led from late eighteenth-century views on Indians and the role of slavery in the young American republic to Hitler's equation of Eastern European resistance fighters with Native Americans. In fact, my study argues explicitly against works that directly trace the lineage of Nazi imperialism to the German Empire's African colonies or the American West. Moreover, the United States was not the only backdrop against which German expansionists formulated their colonialist visions and policies: The British Empire loomed large in German colonialist discourse and so did the French colonies, albeit often as negative examples. Yet ever since the founding of the United States, Germans had looked westward across the Atlantic. Older literature on nineteenth-century German perceptions of the United States often explains the German fascination with America by pointing out that, before German unification in 1871, the U.S. federal system was perceived to be a good model for a future German nation-state. Yet Germans were equally (if not more) fascinated by the apparently obvious connections between America's continental expansion and the steadily increasing global importance of this new country, a fascination that reached all the way into the eighteenth century.[14]

---

[14] Horst Dippel, "Die Wirkung der amerikanischen Revolution auf Deutschland und Frankreich," *200 Jahre amerikanische Revolution und moderne Revolutionsforschung. Geschichte und Gesellschaft* Sonderheft, no. II (1976); Horst Dippel, *Germany and the American Revolution* (Wiesbaden: Steiner, 1978); Horst Dippel, *Die Amerikanische Verfassung in Deutschland im 19. Jahrhundert* (Goldbach: Keip Verlag, 1994). Works that argue for direct links between Nazi imperialism and German overseas colonialism and/or American westward expansion include, but are not limited to, David Furber, "Near as Far in the Colonies: The Nazi Occupation of Poland," *International History Review* 26, no. 3 (2004): 542; Jürgen Zimmerer, "Holocaust und Kolonialismus: Beitrag zu einer Archäologie des genozidalen Denkens," *Zeitschrift für Geschichtswissenschaft* 51, no. 12 (2003); Jürgen Zimmerer, "Von Windhuk nach Warschau. Die rassische Privilegiengesellschaft in Deutsch-Südwestafrika, ein Modell mit Zukunft?," in *Rassenmischehen - Mischlinge - Rassentrennung. Zur Politk der Rasse im deutschen Kolonialreich*, ed. Frank Becker (Stuttgart: Franz Steiner Verlag, 2004); Jürgen Zimmerer, "The Birth

The traditional Sonderweg thesis argues that, because of the failures of nineteenth-century German political liberalism and the social class that fashioned it – the German bourgeoisie – Imperial Germany took a special historical path that ultimately led to (or at the very least made possible) the Nazis' seizure of power. This notion has lost much of its persuasiveness since the 1984 publication of David Blackbourn and Geoff Eley's *The Peculiarities of German History*. However, the recent resurgence of scholarly interest in German colonialism has renewed the "German exceptionalism" notion: A number of historians have pointed to the existence of peculiarly German continuities between its colonial empire before 1914 and the Nazis' racial policies after 1933. Recent studies on the so-called German push eastward [*Drang nach Osten*] – German formal and informal imperialism in Eastern Europe during the nineteenth and twentieth centuries – have concluded that "the German frontier was in the east," whereas historian Mark Mazower has argued that the liberal and democratic United States "provided the settlement model" for the Nazis' "living space"-inspired expansionism in Eastern Europe between 1939 and 1945.[15]

of the Ostland out of the Spirit of Colonialism: A Postcolonial Perspective on the Nazi Policy of Conquest and Extermination," *Patterns of Prejudice* 39, no. 2 (2005); Madley, "From Africa to Auschwitz: How German Southwest Africa Incubated Ideas and Methods Adopted and Developed by the Nazis in Eastern Europe."

[15] Josef Anker, "Paul Rohrbach," in *Allgemeine Deutsche Biographie* (Berlin: Rohmer – Schinkel, 2005); Kundrus, "Von Windhoek nach Nuernberg? Koloniale 'Mischehenverbote' und die nationalsozialistische Rassengesetzgebung," 119. See also Isabel V. Hull, "Military Culture and the Production of 'Final Solutions' in the Colonies," in *The Specter of Genocide*, ed. Robert Gellately and Ben Kiernan (Cambridge: Cambridge University Press, 2003); David Furber, "Near as Far in the Colonies: The Nazi Occupation of Poland," *The International History Review* 26, no. 3 (2004): 542; Gründer, "Stellenwert;" Isabel V. Hull, *Absolute Destruction: Military Culture and the Practices of War in Imperial Germany* (Ithaca, N.Y.: Cornell University Press, 2004), 1; Zimmerer, "Von Windhuk nach Warschau. Die rassische Privilegiengesellschaft in Deutsch-Südwestafrika, ein Modell mit Zukunft?;" Grosse, "What Does German Colonialism Have To Do With National Socialism? A Conceptual Framework;" Madley, "From Africa to Auschwitz: How

These three interpretations fall short of presenting a complete picture of both German imperialism before World War I and Nazi visions and colonialist practices in the East. Most important, before 1914, German colonialists who admired the American frontier did not automatically "push eastward." Moreover, as historian Robert L. Nelson has pointed out in respect to German eastward expansion, "German reference to the Wild West is only a metaphor.... It is the fantasy of the Wild West... to which the German Wild East is compared. As such, comparing these two frontiers... is deeply problematic." As my account shows, before 1914 the American West had a different, much more concrete function within the context of overseas expansion, as views of America as a model empire (often based on firsthand knowledge of the United States and "scientific" analysis of American expansionism by scholars and liberal politicians such as Ratzel and Bernhard Dernburg) powerfully underwrote both longings for and the practice of German colonialism. In addition, from the vantage point of supporters of German territorial expansion, the East was simply not enough. According to Friedrich List, one of the major proponents of German expansionism before 1848, despite the potential benefits of "inner colonization" in the East, overseas colonies remained essential for Germany's demographic and economic progress. Forty years later, the German Empire's best-known colonialist, Carl Peters, went even further. In his view, overseas possessions inspired and attracted German settlers, whereas plans to "Germanize the east," a notion that Peters sardonically referred to as "a truly exquisite little phrase,"

German Southwest Africa Incubated Ideas and Methods Adopted and Developed by the Nazis in Eastern Europe;" Zimmerer, "The Birth of the Ostland," Blackbourn, *The Conquest of Nature*, 280–96 (esp. 82); Matthew P. Fitzpatrick, "The Pre-History of the Holocaust? The Sonderweg and Historikerstreit Debates and the Abject Colonial Past," *Central European History* 41 (2008); Mazower, *Hitler's Empire*, 15, 584; Matthew P. Fitzpatrick, "The Threat of 'Woolly-haired Grandchildren': Race, the Colonial Family and German Nationalism," *The History of the Family* 14 (2009); Robert Gerwarth and Stephan Malinowski, "Hannah Arendt's Ghosts: Reflections on the Disputable Path from Windhoek to Auschwitz," *Central European History* 42, no. 02 (2009): 299.

were a waste of time: Prussia's eastern regions were simply too unappealing for Germans, who therefore left in droves.[16] Germany's pre-1914 colonialism, like that of its European counterparts, was to a large degree sustained by liberal politics. Yet many German political liberals, who had embraced America as a model for German overseas expansion during the nineteenth century and eventually prompted the German Empire to adopt their brand of colonial politics in the decade preceding World War I, were immediately marginalized after the Nazi seizure of power in 1933. Consider the example of Paul Rohrbach: Although he was one of the most racist proponents of American-style settler colonialism in German Southwest Africa, he actively opposed the Nazis' ascendancy to power before 1933. Frequently, colonialism and race simply did not mean the same thing to liberals and Nazis.[17]

Indeed, Nazi ideologues and expansionists found it impossible to ignore American "liberalist" republicanism, as their main newspaper *Der Völkische Beobachter* called it. The Nazis were unable to divorce memories, myths, and accounts of the settlement of the American West from their liberal, democratic, and republican backdrop. Despite scattered references to "vanishing" Indians, the Nazis could not use America as a model for their settlement and extermination plans and practices in the East. Although the United States had an impressive (and partially genocidal) settler-colonialist past and many American states had race codes in their law books, America remained a liberal, democratic republic, at least for its white citizens. The Nazis could not negate this all too obvious fact and thus detested the United States. Recent arguments for the importance of the American West for Nazi visions of living space in the East often depend on over-interpretations of scattered and exclusively metaphorical references to an imagined America by Nazi leaders. In fact,

---

[16] Robert L. Nelson, "The 'Archive for Inner Colonization,' the German East and World War I," in *Germans, Poland, and Colonial Expansion to the East*, ed. Robert L. Nelson (New York: Palgrave MacMillan, 2009), 66.

[17] See Jennifer Pitts, *A Turn to Empire: The Rise of Imperial Liberalism in Britain and France* (Princeton: Princeton University Press, 2005), 19–21, 247–54.

Nazi ideologues also often explicitly denied parallels between (Nazi-) German and American measures (for example, between the Nuremberg race laws and American segregation provisions) simply because the latter were American and hence suspicious.[18]

The Great War and the Question of German Historical Continuities

My study takes us from the late eighteenth century all the way to the end of World War II. It touches on many often contested issues, including questions about the historical relationship between the German Empire and the Third Reich, and, more precisely, the problem of how to evaluate the impact of the Great War on developments that either connect or separate Imperial Germany from Nazi Germany. Over the past forty years, historians' understandings of the social, cultural, and political relationship between the Second and the Third Reich have changed significantly. Initial assumptions of fairly direct sociocultural continuities were complicated by David Blackbourn and by Geoff Eley in the late 1970s and early 1980s. Eley in particular delineated the profound changes the German Empire's sociocultural and political structures underwent between 1871 and 1914. Nevertheless, even for Eley, important (albeit nuanced and complicated) continuities existed between pre- and post-World War I Germany: In his view, changes in the structure of right-wing

---

[18] Mazower, *Hitler's Empire*, 587–88, "Abraham Lincoln und das Rasseproblem Amerikas," *Völkische Beobachter* 04-16-1935. See also the discussion of liberalism, Nazism, and German historical continuities in the conclusion of this volume. Compare Eric Kurlander, *The Price of Exclusion: Ethnicity, National Identity, and the Decline of German Liberalism, 1898–1933* (New York: Berghahn Books, 2006), 2–3. Among those who argue for direct links between the "American West" and the "German East" are, most importantly, Alan E. Steinweis, "Eastern Europe and the Notion of the 'Frontier' in Germany to 1945," *Yearbook of European Studies* 13 (1999); Mazower, *Hitler's Empire*, Shelley Baranowski, *Nazi Empire: German Colonialism and Imperialism from Bismarck to Hitler* (New York: Cambridge University Press, 2011); Caroll P. Kakel, *The American West and the Nazi East. A Comparative and Interpretive Perspective* (Basingstoke: Palgrave Macmillan, 2011).

politics in Germany shortly before the outbreak of the Great War provided "the vital condition for the emergence of a German fascism" after 1918. In 1913, the increasing importance placed on mass popular support by, for example, the Pan Germans and the unifying power of radical-nationalist ideology made a new and broad if uneasy right-wing alliance possible – the Cartel of the Productive Estates, which, while attempting to be populist, was also antidemocratic, antiliberal, and, naturally, antisocialist. According to Eley, this alliance and the expansionist and "völkische" (meaning racially and nationally essentialist) ideology it embraced and promoted not only challenged the imperial government from the right before and during the Great War but also continued to attack the legitimacy of the Weimar Republic after 1918. Although the Nazis did not emerge directly out of this grouping, it nevertheless helped prepare the ground for their eventual success.[19]

In the wake of Eley's magisterial *Reshaping the German Right* (1980), other studies began to emphasize that if there were continuities to be discerned between the German Empire and the Third Reich, one should seek them not in the empire's overall structure, but rather in specific right-wing movements and ideologies that emerged during the time of the empire's existence. In his *The Ideological Origins of Nazi Imperialism* (1986), historian Woodruff Smith analyzes the increasing prominence of Ratzel-inspired Lebensraum notions within the framework of both the radical right (especially the Pan-German League after 1905) and German colonialist circles. Smith recognizes that Lebensraum expansionism (i.e., a racialized settler colonialism) acquired its overarching dominance within right-wing, government, and army circles only in late 1917. Nevertheless, in his view the ideology had been fully articulated before the outbreak of the Great War, and thus the war itself had only a limited impact on existing ideological patterns. It broadened their appeal, but it

---

[19] Geoff Eley, *Reshaping the German Right: Radical Nationalism and Political Change after Bismarck* (New Haven & London: Yale University Press: 1980), 321, 357, 358, 361.

did not create them. In Smith's view, neither Germany's impressive (albeit short-lived) territorial gains in the East nor the country's eventual defeat at the Western Front "fundamentally altered the structure of German imperialist ideology." Roger Chickering's study of the Pan-German League argues along similar lines. Chickering posits that "whatever the forms of mediation, the Pan-German League had served as a chief provider of practically all the elements that went into the ideological turbidity of the Nazis' program and Hitler's *Weltanschauung*."[20]

Eley's, Smith's, and Chickering's 1980s works, all authoritative in their own right, have in common that they make the case for the durability of pre-1914 structural and ideological configurations within the framework of German radical right-wing politics. Not only did these patterns survive World War I but they also, either directly or indirectly, had an important impact on the later development of German fascism and the Nazi movement. Because all three studies are nuanced and make fine distinctions, they acknowledge the significance of the Great War for the emergence of a new kind of radical right within the framework of the young Weimar Republic after 1918, although they do not analyze the nature of this impact.[21]

Very recently, historians Peter Walkenhorst, Stefan Frech, and Heinz Hagenlücke have taken fresh looks at the phenomenon of German radical nationalism before and during World War I. Although their studies partially confirm older views on the Pan Germans, or the Deutsche Vaterlandspartei, they nevertheless present us with a more complex picture of radical nationalism and right-wing expansionism before 1914. Most important, these studies make it harder to view Pan-German expansionism as the clear and sole precursor to the obsession of Hitler, Heinrich Himmler, Alfred Rosenberg, or Richard Walther Darré with

---

[20] Woodruff D. Smith, *The Ideological Origins of Nazi Imperialism* (New York: Oxford University Press, 1986), 110–11, 187, 189, 195, 204, 256–258.

[21] Roger Chickering, *We Men Who Feel Most German: A Cultural Study of the Pan – German League, 1886–1914* (Boston: George Allen & Unwin, 1984), 299–300. See also David Blackbourn and Geoff Eley, *The Peculiarities of German History* (New York: Oxford University Press, 1984), 22–28.

"living space in the East." Pan-Germans like Ernst Hasse and Theodor Reismann-Grone did indeed pioneer racialized-völkisch ideas of continental imperialism, yet the Nazis' exclusive and fanatical focus on Eastern Europe is absent from their writings and publicly expressed views. Instead, Hasse envisioned continental expansion both in the West and East, whereas Reismann-Grone preferred annexations in Western Europe. Moreover, the Pan-German Eduard von Liebert, the ex-governor of German East Africa, criticized Reismann-Grone and defended Germany's colonial activities overseas. In addition, historian Peter Walkenhorst argues that, although the embarrassing and unsatisfactory outcome of the First Morocco Crisis in 1905 prompted some Pan-German expansionists to focus increasingly on Lebensraum aims in Europe, this very openly promoted emphasis on continental expansion was in fact designed to distract Great Britain from the continued build-up of the German Navy, an undertaking that became one of the Pan Germans' main obsessions after 1905. Once this build-up would be completed, more traditional imperialist plans to acquire overseas territories (both settler colonies and naval outposts, still preferably in Morocco) were to be put back on the Pan-German agenda. The conventional narrative of the increasing triumph of continental and Eastern-Europe-focused living space ideas even before 1914 therefore looks somewhat less convincing today than it did in the 1980s. At the very least it needs to be balanced with an acknowledgment of the volatility, complexity, and variety of expansionist ideas embraced and promoted by the radical right before 1914.[22]

---

[22] Theodor Reismann-Grone and Eduard von Liebert, "Überseepolitik oder Festlandspolitik?" (paper presented at the Alldeutscher Verbandstag, Worms, 1905), 20–21; Stefan Frech, *Wegbereiter Hitlers? Theodor Reismann – Grone. Ein völkischer Nationalist (1863–1949)* (Paderborn: Ferdinand Schöningh, 2009), 413; Heinz Hagenlücke, *Deutsche Vaterlandspartei: Die nationale Rechte am Ende des Kaiserreiches* (Düsseldorf: Droste Verlag, 1997), 408–09; Peter Walkenhorst, *Nation – Volk – Rasse. Radikaler Nationalismus im Deutschen Kaiserreich 1890–1914* (Göttingen: Vandenhoeck & Ruprecht, 2007), 216; Ernst Hasse, *Deutsche Politik*, vol. 2 (München: J. F. Lehmann's Verlag, 1908), 65. Compare Baranowski, *Nazi Empire: German Colonialism*

Several recent studies do link the German Empire and German pre-1914 imperialism directly to Nazi expansionism. Historians Benjamin Madley and Jürgen Zimmerer argue for straight connections between German colonialism and both the Holocaust and Nazi conquests in Eastern Europe, whereas David Furber explains German eastward expansion during World War II from the perspective of European colonialism. Finally, Mark Mazower in his magisterial *Hitler's Empire* (2009) combines these scholars' perspectives into his complex narrative of the Nazis as "heirs" of the European imperialist tradition, who then "tried to build their empire in Europe itself." In turn, these imperialism- and colonialism-based continuity perspectives have been contested by studies that reevaluate the impact of World War I on social, political, ideological, and cultural developments in both pre- and postwar Germany. Robert L. Nelson argues that the Great War did not merely provide prewar expansionist concepts with a refreshed impetus; instead, "in the radicalized moment of war, anything could be rationalized." Nelson therefore posits that World War I created new, much more uncompromising attitudes toward both expansionism and "population management;" attitudes that by and large had been unacceptable even in radical-nationalist circles before 1914. In addition, Vejas Liulevicius focuses on the impact of the German Army's occupation of large swaths of Eastern European territory during World War I. In his view, these activities brought about a radicalized colonialist mindset that eventually provided fertile grounds for Nazi visions of living space in the East.[23]

and Imperialism from Bismarck to Hitler, 44; Smith, *The Ideological Origins of Nazi Imperialism*, 110–11.

[23] Vejas Gabriel Liulevicius, *War Land on the Eastern Front* (Cambridge: Cambridge University Press, 2000), 278–81; Furber, "Near as Far," Zimmerer, "Von Windhuk nach Warschau. Die rassische Privilegiengesellschaft in Deutsch-Südwestafrika, ein Modell mit Zukunft?;" Zimmerer, "The Birth of the Ostland;" Madley, "From Africa to Auschwitz: How German Southwest Africa Incubated Ideas and Methods Adopted and Developed by the Nazis in Eastern Europe;" Mark Mazower, *Hitler's Empire. Nazi Rule in Occupied Europe* (London: Penguin Books, 2009); Nelson, "The 'Archive for Inner Colonization,' the German East and World War I," 82,

Nelson's and Liulevicius' points are confirmed by a fresh look at Heinrich Class's infamous *Wenn ich der Kaiser wär'* [If I were Emperor, 1912], a publication that has at times been viewed as a proto-Nazi text. Class was chairman of the Pan-German League when he wrote this book. Because of this position and because the ideas outlined in the work were extremely radical compared even to those espoused by other Leaguers, the book was initially published under the pseudonym Daniel Frymann. There can be no question that many positions outlined by Class and colored by extreme anti-Semitism sound like rough, albeit slightly less callous and murderous drafts for Nazi visions and actual policies – most obviously his suggestion that any territories gained by Germany after a successfully concluded war should be vacated by their original population to make room for German settlers. The book was sharply criticized, especially by the Emperor and Chancellor Bethmann-Hollweg. Both men strongly disapproved of Class's extreme anti-Semitism and, more important, his implicit suggestion that only a governmental coup could bring about the constitutional changes he desired. Class himself admitted that his ideas were "alien" and unthinkable in the context of German imperial politics – unless war broke out: "In other words we should not contemplate a war of aggression for the purpose of annexing foreign lands.... A predatory war contradicts our values. But a ruthless attack justifies us in exerting punishment, even when it takes on this harshest of all forms [the annexation of cleared lands]."[24]

Class was correct: In pre-1914 Germany his ideas were intolerable. Yet the Great War – which a broad majority of Germans

---

86–88; Kakel, *The American West*. On Imperial-Nazi continuities see also Shelley Baranowski's essay in Volker Langbehn and Mohammad Salama, *German Colonialism: Race, the Holocaust, and Postwar Germany* (New York: Columbia University Press, 2011). On World War I as a transformative moment see also Dirk Bönker, "Ein German Way of War? Deutscher Militarismus und maritime Kriegsführung im Ersten Weltkrieg," in *Das Deutsche Kaiserreich in der Kontroverse*, ed. Sven Oliver Müller and Cornelius Torp (Göttingen: Vandenhoeck & Ruprecht, 2009), 309–10, 22.

[24] Heinrich Class, *Wenn ich der Kaiser wär': Politische Wahrheiten und Notwendigkeiten* (Leipzig: Dieterich, 1912), 140–41.

from the left to the right perceived as a defensive war, one that
was forced on Germany by the Entente – changed the situation.
Historian Ian Kershaw sums up the German Empire's situation in
1914 as follows: "On the eve of the First World War, Germany
was certainly a state with some unattractive features.... But
nothing in its development predetermined the path to the Third
Reich. What happened under Hitler was not presaged in Imperial
Germany. It is unimaginable without the experience of the First
World War and what followed it." Historian Margaret Lavinia
Anderson makes a similar point regarding the deeply rooted and,
in the early years of the twentieth century, dominant presence
of a parliamentary and democratic culture in Imperial Germany
before the Great War. Anderson is able to make this argument so
convincingly because her study clearly highlights the marginality
of the extreme right before 1914. Directly contesting Wehler and
to some degree also Eley, Blackbourn, and Chickering, Anderson argues that the German Empire's political culture did not
weigh heavily on the Weimar Republic. Instead, "it was war that
turned ethnocentric nationalism into mass pathology. It was war
that made paranoid styles of reasoning cogent."[25]

On a broad sociocultural level, historian Ute Frevert also
makes the case for deep divides and changes brought about
by the experience of World War I. In her view, before 1914
both Germany's influential liberal-bourgeois circles and its semi-
autocratic government could acknowledge other nation-states
and their citizens as equals. Transnationalism is therefore not
merely a vantage point of late twentieth- and early twenty-first-
century historiography, but was actually lived before 1914. Yet
among many other things, World War I destroyed the prewar

---

[25] Ibid. Chickering, *We Men Who Feel Most German: A Cultural Study of
the Pan-German League, 1886–1914*, 287; Ian Kershaw, *Hitler, 1889–1936:
Hubris* (New York: Norton, 1999), 80; Margaret Lavinia Anderson, *Practicing Democracy: Elections and Political Culture in Imperial Germany* (Princeton: Princeton University Press, 2000), 428–29, 436–37; Helmut Walser
Smith, *The Continuities of German History. Nation, Religion, and Race
Across the Long Nineteenth Century* (New York City: Cambridge University Press, 2008), 206.

faith and trust in the traditional European nation-state. In its place, "Europe emerged as an autonomous concept, a notion of its own." This notion was so powerful that the Nazis could use it to attract both West and East European volunteers: "The Europeanist rhetoric, drawing on a short but lively tradition since the 1920s, quite evidently helped to facilitate collaboration between Germany and the occupied countries." Most important, part of the attractiveness of "Europe as a notion of its own" was that only Europe was believed to be strong enough to prevent the European nations from being squeezed between the "American menace" in the West and Soviet Russia in the East. Anti-American sentiment ran rampant in 1920s Germany and in Europe at large, and it also found its way into the nascent Nazi ideology. Other scholars who have analyzed German imperialism before and after 1918 – among them Lora Wildenthal, Pascal Grosse, Birthe Kundrus, Robert Gerwarth, Stefan Malinowski, and Matthew Fitzpatrick – therefore argue both for the importance of the lost war for expansionist and/or colonialist ideas after 1918 and for the existence of significant ruptures between pre-1914 and post-1918 imperialist concepts. Fitzpatrick, Gerwarth, and Malinowski have leveled especially piercing criticisms against colonialism-focused continuity theses.[26]

Although a number of historians of domestic developments in nineteenth- and early twentieth-century Germany – most prominently Kershaw, Anderson, and Frevert – have demonstrated that

---

[26] Ute Frevert, "Europeanizing Germany's Twentieth Century," *History and Memory* 17, no. 1–2 (2005): 95–98, 100–01; Pascal Grosse, "From Colonialism to National Socialism to Postcolonialism: Hannah Arendt's Origins of Totalitarianism," *Postcolonial Studies* 9, no. 1 (2006); Grosse, "What Does German Colonialism Have To Do With National Socialism? A Conceptual Framework;" Kundrus, "Von Windhoek nach Nuernberg? Koloniale 'Mischehenverbote' und die nationalsozialistische Rassengesetzgebung." See also Fitzpatrick, "The Pre-History of the Holocaust? The Sonderweg and Historikerstreit Debates and the Abject Colonial Past;" Robert Gerwarth and Stephan Malinowski, "Der Holocaust als "kolonialer Genozid"? Europäische Kolonialgewalt und nationalsozialistischer Vernichtungskrieg," *Geschichte und Gesellschaft* 33 (2007); Gerwarth and Malinowski, "Hannah Arendt's Ghosts."

the importance of World War I and the ruptures and changes it produced cannot be underestimated for German historical trajectories after 1918, this perspective is still very much contested when it comes to the question of potential continuities between pre-1914 German colonialism and Nazi expansionism. My analyses (especially in Chapter 4) are situated within the framework of debates over continuities and ruptures between the Second and the Third Reich. Because of my study's double focus on the United States' importance and presence in German expansionist discourse and practice and on the links between German liberalism and imperialism, it highlights and confirms the many deep rifts between the situation before and after World War I. Of course, taking this perspective does not mean denying the continuities between the pre-1914 radical right and the Nazis' activities and eventual successes after 1918. Yet it does mean emphasizing the importance of World War I for creating the framework in which radically expansionist and eastward-focused ideas took on new meanings that enabled them to become incorporated in an ideology that presented itself as a fanatic alternative not only to the weak Weimar Republic but also to the German Empire's failed liberal imperialism.

Especially after 1933, the Nazis could not escape their own antiliberal, antidemocratic, and anti-American concepts and propaganda. Using the United States as an example for expansionist plans, race laws, or any other measures was not something that leading Nazis did often, even during the 1920s. Yet after 1933 making positive references to the United States became almost impossible. To be sure, the Nazis were indeed "heirs" to the European (and German) imperialist tradition. But because of its generality, this conclusion is neither particularly meaningful nor does it help us understand why, then, Nazi ideology came into being in Germany and not in countries with much stronger imperialist traditions. Both Wildenthal and Grosse perceptively argue that it was Germany's forced decolonization in 1919 that provided the necessary precondition for the Nazis' frenzied focus on a racialized hyper-expansionism in the East, not the country's imperialist and colonialist activities before its defeat. Nazi ideologues emphatically denied that their goals were a continuation of what they saw as Imperial Germany's liberal imperialism; indeed they viewed their expansionism as the polar opposite to the German Empire's colonialist activities. For Nazi ideologues Eastern-Europe-focused living space visions were a kind of anti-colonialism, which in turn also meant that they repudiated the strong focus on America of Germany's pre-1914 expansionism.[27]

Liberalism, Imperialism, and Imperial Liberalism

Some scholars have suggested that it is impossible to find a definition of liberalism that truly covers all aspects of this protean and fluid ideology. However, historian James Sheehan argues that, despite its regional, chronological, and political differences, it is possible to view German liberalism as a single tradition, as "a 'family' of ideas and behavior patterns" throughout the nineteenth century and later. To a certain degree, the focus of the following analysis on liberalism's expansionist dimensions validates Sheehan's approach. According to the sociologist Ralf Dahrendorf, the core values of this "family" of views and modes of conduct "have clear and simple guidelines for political action: It is paramount to do everything possible to improve and widen every individual's chances in life. The more people have more chances in life, the more liberal is a society." Dahrendorf's definition certainly captures important elements of both European and German liberalism. From this core stemmed demands, in different contexts and forms, for constitutional and limited government, equality before the law, social and political progress, and, at least in the German case, national unity. However, the last two tendencies also led many liberals to both develop and easily embrace racialized worldviews. Already during the late

---

[27] Grosse, "What Does German Colonialism Have To Do With National Socialism? A Conceptual Framework," 118–19; Wildenthal, *German Women for Empire*, 173, 176; Kakel, *The American West*, 35, Mazower, *Hitler's Empire*, 584; Steinweis, "Eastern Europe and the Notion of the 'Frontier'." See also the introduction to Langbehn and Salama, *German Colonialism. Race, the Holocaust, and Postwar Germany*, "Introduction."

eighteenth century (and increasingly during the nineteenth), racism was at the cutting edge of the blossoming sciences and therefore by definition progressive. Because of Dahrendorf's openly expressed philo-liberalism, his definition of this ideology does not include this and other "dark undersides" of nineteenth-century liberalism. Although these undersides are highly problematic from a current-day perspective, they were never fringe phenomena. Instead, racism, rationalizations of colonialism, imperialism, and related issues such as methods of social and political exclusion not only belonged to but also undergirded and determined the creed of many nineteenth- and early twentieth-century liberals just as much as ideas of (white, and, for the most part, male) equality, civil liberties, and limited government. Of course, being liberal did not automatically lead one to embrace imperialist and ethnicist/racialized sentiments. However, many if not the majority of nineteenth- and early twentieth-century liberals, in Germany and elsewhere, actively engaged in visions and practical politics of empire and contemplated exclusionary policies vis-à-vis colonials, domestic out-groups, or both.[28]

During the 150 years covered in this book, liberal groups and parties considered some of liberalism's core demands, whether universal or exclusionary, more important than others. True, Immanuel Kant and Thomas Jefferson would not have used the term "liberal" to describe themselves, yet both were nevertheless dedicated to a set of values that were at the core of the liberal tradition: human equality, freedom, and the rule of law. From a present-day perspective, both men also embraced less positive sentiments, seemingly contradictory to the aforementioned universal notions, including the belief in white racial superiority, an at best ambiguous stance on race-based slavery (white slavery

---

[28] Sheehan cited in Geoff Eley, "James Sheehan and the German Liberals: A Critical Appreciation," *Central European History* 14, no. 3 (1981): 273, 279. On the "dark sides" of liberalism in general see of course Horkheimer and Adorno's famous *Dialectic of the Enlightenment*, and for German left-liberalism in particular see Andrew Zimmerman, "Decolonizing Weber," *Postcolonial Studies* 9, no. 1 (2006). Dahrendorf quoted in Langewiesche, *Liberalismus in Deutschland*, 7. See also Dahrendorf, *Society and Democracy in Germany*, 13–14, Pitts, *A Turn to Empire*, 4–5, 242.

was unacceptable for both), and, at least as far as Jefferson was concerned, a clear commitment to the necessity of territorial expansion. Whereas Kant was nominally opposed to colonialism (although his disdain for black Africans nevertheless left some wiggle room for practical exertions of white superiority in colonial contexts), his colleague at the University of Göttingen, Christoph Meiners – a fellow philosopher, admirer of the French Revolution, and liberal-minded reformer – unabashedly supported it.[29]

My study tracks the reciprocal relationship between universal and exclusionary-oppressive liberal sentiments from the late eighteenth through the twentieth century. Within German liberalism, much changed during these more than 150 years, but the link between liberalism and expansionism remained, at least until 1918. To be sure, the nature of this connection and its preeminence in liberal circles varied. For example, during the revolution of 1848–49, a radically democratic segment of German liberalism played an important political role, especially in respect to German-American connections. Its most famous representatives, among them Carl Schurz, Friedrich Hecker, Lorenz Brentano, and Gustav Struve, were eventually forced to flee Germany and subsequently found their way to the United States. There, they became involved in the antislavery movement, the young Republican Party, and eventually the American Civil War.[30]

My study does not deny this grouping's importance for German revolutionary politics in 1848–49. It also does not question this faction's impact on German liberalism in general,

[29] See Chapter 1.
[30] Fenske, "Imperialisitische Tendenzen," Hans Fenske, "Ungeduldige Zuschauer: Die Deutschen und die europäische Expansion, 1815–1880," in *Imperialistische Kontinuität und nationale Ungeduld im 19. Jahrhundert*, ed. Wolfgang Reinhard (Frankfurt am Main: Fischer, 1991); Müller, "Imperialist Ambitions in Vormärz and Revolutionary Germany;" Fitzpatrick, *Liberal Imperialism in Germany. Expansionism and Nationalism, 1848–1884*. On these radically democratic, revolutionary liberals see most recently Andrew Zimmerman, "The German Empire, the Atlantic Revolutions of the Nineteenth Century, and the Colonial Construction of the Precolonial" (paper presented at the Conference: German Post-Colonial History in a Global Age, Free University Berlin, 2011).

particularly on the ideas embraced by their late nineteenth-century left-liberal heirs, among them Eugen Richter and Ludwig Bamberger. Yet the following pages are not about them. Radically democratic and antiimperialist liberals did not represent liberalism any more fully than their imperialist counterparts. In fact, they were usually in the minority. The following analysis thus focuses on those who were not as radically democratic as Hecker, Struve, or Brentano or as anti-imperialist as Richter or Bamberger in the late nineteenth century; it focuses on those who in 1848, before a German nation-state had even been created, backed the (premature, as it turned out) acquisition of a German navy and contemplated the need for Germany's future overseas expansion instead of first securing their domestic revolutionary gains. These German standard- bearers of imperial liberalism in the middle years of the nineteenth century passed on their colors to those – Friedrich Ratzel, Max Weber, Friedrich Naumann, Bernhard Dernburg and many others – who after German unification in 1871 and after Germany's acquisition of overseas colonies in 1884 turned their liberal political creed into a blueprint for "liberal colonialism."[31]

In 1861, the liberal-reformist Progressive Party was founded. The terms "liberal" and "progressive" can thereafter be used interchangeably, although the latter term would eventually become more closely associated with left-liberals than with liberalism in general. The Progressive Party grew out of various national- and liberal-minded clubs. For a few years it united German or, to be more precise, Prussian liberals in a single political party that embraced the central claims of political liberalism in Germany: national unity under Prussian leadership, a free economy unfettered by state control, the rule of law, and the expansion of political and civil rights. In 1866, however, Otto von Bismarck's policies split Prussian and German liberals. Right-liberals founded the National-Liberal Party (NLP), which tended to prioritize national demands more highly than other liberal values. In contrast, left-liberals – whose various factions, despite a number of long-standing differences, united in 1910 and formed the Progressive People's Party – incorporated ideas of social and political reform into their brand of liberalism, which at times led them to be more critical of government policies than their national-liberal counterparts.

Within both wings of German liberalism, perceptions about government, society, the economy, and even ideas about "the nation" continued to change after the 1866 split. Geoff Eley thus perceptively points out that "static" approaches to the history of German liberalism (i.e., methodologies that focus too much on a single, meta-historical ideal-type of liberalism), risk glossing over important breaks and discontinuities. In addition, Eley forcefully demonstrates that from the 1890s onward the German right underwent a process of reorientation away from traditional, elite power structures in Prussia toward attempts to gain popular legitimacy. Both older and newer studies argue that during the second half of the nineteenth century German liberalism paralleled this development by moving away from alleged "classically" liberal ideas of universally applicable individual rights toward a heightened sense of nationalism and exclusionary ethnicism.[32]

More recently, Eric Kurlander posits that, beginning in the last decade of the nineteenth century, ethnicist sentiments made increasing inroads into liberal political structures, thereby moving German liberalism (to various extents in different regions) from its assumed universal essence toward racialized and exclusionary political visions of German society. Once the National Socialist German Workers Party embraced and promoted these ideas in a much more direct way than the liberal parties ever did, voters defected en masse and voted for the Nazis. This development was supposedly peculiar to German (and Central

---

[32] Geoff Eley, "Review: James Sheehan and the German Liberals: A Critical Appreciation," *Central European History* 14, no. 3 (1981): 279; Eley, *Reshaping the German Right*, 351–55; Woodruff D. Smith, "Friedrich Ratzel and the Origins of 'Lebensraum'," *German Studies Review* 3, no. 1 (1980): 57; Smith, *The Ideological Origins of Nazi Imperialism*, 21, 26, 28, 30, 48–50; Kurlander, *The Price of Exclusion*, 5.

European) liberalism and did not occur in France, Great Britain, or the United States. My analysis traces developments within liberalism that challenge this evaluation of German liberalism before the Great War: From its beginnings in the seventeenth century – and certainly within the chronological framework of my study – liberalism was an imperial ideology. Imperialism was therefore a constitutive part of liberalism and not merely the result of developments that undermined the ideology's "true" core, or, within the German context, resulted in liberalism's eventual permeation by ethnicist ideas. In fact, racialist forms of imperial liberalism had a long history in the United States and Great Britain, and in both countries, just as in the German Empire, the 1890s witnessed powerful manifestations of these sentiments in the public sphere: In Britain, the liberal politician and later secretary of state Edward Grey embraced and promoted them just as strongly as the progressive Theodore Roosevelt in the United States. According to historian Paul Kramer, by the late nineteenth century, liberal and progressive racism was directed

against a multitude of opponents on innumerable violent frontiers. British Anglo-Saxons had contended with Normans, colonized Celts, enslaved Africans, conquered Indians, and challenged Latins for world dominance. American Anglo-Saxons had defended African slavery, conquered Native Americans, confronted Latin empires, wrenched land away from Mexicans, and struggled to fend off waves of immigrants.

Accounts that sharply differentiate between allegedly normative, meaning universal, and undermined, meaning ethnicist and exclusionary, liberalisms therefore do not tell the whole story, from either a German or a transnational perspective. Of course, because of the long shadow of the idea of a German Sonderweg, this chronological splicing has a long tradition in German historiography. Conventionally, historians have separated pre- from post-1848 liberalism, but the demarcation line has also been moved forward in time. Most famously, Hans-Ulrich Wehler's version of the Sonderweg thesis rests at least partially on the assumption that German liberalism "lost" not only in 1848 but also during the 1860s when the Prussian and German bourgeoisie "sold out" by accepting national unification as a substitute for liberal constitutionalism. German liberalism thus ingratiated itself to Bismarck and Prussia's "old" and "feudal elites" and became a hollow, de facto illiberal shell. Wehler's view has lost its paradigmatic status, but the idea that at some point during the second half of the nineteenth century liberalism turned "bad" is still very much alive.[33]

Exclusionary definitions of ethnicity or expansionist tendencies did not suddenly appear among liberals at some point in the late nineteenth century. Instead, these sentiments had been an integral part of this ideology since its inception – and not only in Germany. One does not have to follow Max Horkheimer and Theodor Adorno's thesis about the "dark undersides" of the Enlightenment or exclusively abide by Edward Said's postcolonial axioms to arrive at this conclusion. Historians of French and British imperialism, and increasingly also scholars of American expansionism, have analyzed the links between liberalism and colonialism for the past three decades. They have clearly demonstrated that liberalism's universal claims were consistently flanked by justifications for the suppression and exploitation of peoples deemed culturally or racially inferior and by rationalizations not only supportive of already existing empires but also of additional expansion. France has thus been termed an "imperial nation state," and the same phrase, possibly with even greater justification, can also be applied to the American republic – at least the United States' nineteenth- and early twentieth-century German observers thought so. Liberals involved in the politics of empire in Britain, France, and, most important from the

[33] James J. Sheehan, *German Liberalism in the Nineteenth Century* (Chicago: University of Chicago Press, 1978), 123–24; Wehler, *The German Empire, 1871–1918*, 21–25; Langewiesche, *Liberalismus in Deutschland*, 9; Michael Geyer and Charles Bright, "World History in a Global Age," *The American Historical Review* 100, no. 4 (1995); Paul Kramer, "Empires, Exceptions, and Anglo-Saxons: Race and Rule between the British and United States Empires, 1880–1910," *The Journal of American History* 88, no. 4 (2002): 1321; Kurlander, *The Price of Exclusion*, 5, 12, 344. On racialized thought among British imperialists see also Tony Ballantyne, *Orientalism and Race: Aryanism in the British Empire* (New York: Palgrave, 2002), 55.

vantage point of my study, the United States were willing (with more, less, or no scruples) to accept that different levels of rights were given to different ethnic groups within the areas controlled by their respective governments. John Locke, arguably one of the earliest sources of what would eventually be termed liberal thought, thus easily paired ideas of popular sovereignty and a God-given, rights-based individualism with justifications for slavery and the expulsion of Indians from their lands. Less than a hundred years later, Thomas Jefferson undergirded his republicanism with deeply held racist sentiments and the perceived need of the young United States to constantly expand westward. In Germany, Immanuel Kant simultaneously argued for the racial superiority of white Europeans based on his uncritical acceptance of Anglo-American pro-slavery texts as valid sources for his anthropological inquiries. A half-century later, Alexis de Tocqueville not only accepted Jefferson's idea that the United States needed to expand westward, thereby pushing Indians out of the way of white settlers, but also vehemently backed France's conquest of Algeria, interpreting the battle of the French military against indigenous resisters as a conflict "between races." During its first three decades, the French conquest of Algeria cost the lives of between 500,000 and one million Algerians. Furthermore, during the 1860s John Stuart Mill, who is often held up as the poster child of nineteenth-century liberalism's individual-rights-based universalism, defended and promoted British imperialism by drawing on racialized views of the inferiority of Britain's colonial subjects (in Europe and overseas) and stated, "I myself have always been for a good stout despotism, for governing Ireland like India."[34]

[34] Eileen P. Sullivan, "Liberalism and Imperialism: J. S. Mill's Defense of the British Empire," *Journal of the History of Ideas* 44, no. 4 (1983): 606; Alice L. Conklin, "Colonialism and Human Rights, A Contradiction in Terms? The Case of France and West Africa, 1895–1914," *The American Historical Review* 103, no. 2 (1998): 422, 23, 33, 34, 37, 38, 41; Max Horkheimer and Theodor Adorno, *Dialectic of Enlightenment: Philosophical Fragments*, ed. Gunzelin Schmid Noerr (Stanford: Stanford University Press, 2002), 138–39; Robert Bernasconi, "Kant as an Unfamiliar Source of Racism," in *Philosophers on Race: Critical Essays*, ed. Julie K. Ward and Tommy Lee Lott

The following analysis thus argues that perceptions of German liberalism as exceptional because of its embrace of expansionist sentiments and racialized ethnicist concepts are problematic in several ways. First, such perceptions emerged from a Germany-centric historiography that viewed racist and imperialist liberals in the late nineteenth or early twentieth century as an exclusively German phenomenon without taking into account that their counterparts in France, Great Britain, or the United States often held similar views. Second, such perspectives rest on the acceptance of a sanitized image of liberalism created after 1945. After World War II, the legacies of Nazi Germany's genocidal military expansionism and the perceived threat of the Soviet Union prompted a rewrite of the history of liberalism: Before 1914, liberals, in Germany as well as elsewhere, openly and proudly promoted expansionism and racialized views. After 1945, scholars, including Hannah Arendt, Louis Hartz, Richard Hofstadter, and (indirectly) Hans-Ulrich Wehler, began to focus exclusively on liberalism's universal tenets, thereby overlooking the ideology's oppressive, racist, and expansionist dimensions. Wolfgang Mommsen's seminal scholarly biography of Max Weber (1959) is testimony to the power of this new Cold War liberal paradigm. Mommsen's study highlighted Weber's racism, expansionism, and nationalism (and was harshly criticized for doing so). Yet instead of probing the allegedly normative notion that "true" liberalism was neither racist nor expansionist, Mommsen questioned Weber's liberalism. This perspective, motivated both by the ideological needs of the Cold War and the conviction that the Western democracies were (and had to be) the polar sociopolitical opposite to Nazi Germany, saw Germany's lack of a strong liberal tradition as the reason for the country's negative historical peculiarities. In turn, the ideology's assumed all-pervasive

(Oxford: Blackwell, 2002), 148–49, 58–59, 63 (note 16), 64 (note 18); Pitts, *A Turn to Empire*, 213–14, 42; Gary Wilder, *The French Imperial Nation State: Negritude and Colonial Humanism Between the Two World Wars* (Chicago: University of Chicago Press, 2005), 3–4; Ben Kiernan, *Blood and Soil. A World History of Genocide and Extermination from Sparta to Darfur* (New Haven: Yale University Press, 2007), 243, 314, 65.

presence in the history of the United States turned liberalism into the source of America's alleged positive (republican, democratic, and hence anticommunist) exceptionalism.[35]

Nineteenth-century German observers of the United States agreed that liberalism was all pervasive in America and revealed their own liberal leanings when admiring the importance of individualist, bourgeois, and republican tenets in American politics. Yet they also pointed out the significance of America's continuous expansion for these precepts. Imperialist and colonialist outlooks thus shaped German liberals' reflections on the history and the continuities of their political creed and movement. In 1884, the national-liberal Friedrich Ratzel could therefore view his calls for German colonies as a legacy of the 1848 revolution, clearly linking his political views to that of the preceding generation of liberal revolutionaries. Moreover, during the last decade before the outbreak of World War I, colonialism was a topic that enabled liberal parties to attract voters. In 1907, during the

[35] On liberalism as a global, transnational, yet nevertheless cohesive phenomenon see also Jürgen Osterhammel, *Liberalismus als kulturelle Revolution: Die widersprüchliche Weltwirkung einer euroäischen Idee* (Stuttgart: Stiftung Bundespräsident-Theodor-Heuss-Haus, 2003), 15. On the United States as a quintessential liberal society see the classic accounts of Louis Hartz and Richard Hofstadter: Richard Hofstadter, *The American Political Tradition and the Men Who Made It* (Vintage Books, 1948); Louis Hartz, *The Liberal Tradition in America: An Interpretation of American Political Thought Since the Revolution* (Harcourt Brace, 1955). See also Hannah Arendt's *On Totalitarianism* for a "cleansed" view of nineteenth-century liberalism. Hannah Arendt, *The Origins of Totalitarianism* (San Diego: Harcourt Inc., 1968), 194; Wehler, *The German Empire, 1871–1918*, 21–25; Wolfgang J. Mommsen, *Max Weber and German Politics: 1890–1920* (Chicago: University of Chicago Press, 1984 [1959]). On the importance of both German National Socialism and the Soviet Union for the liberal "consensus school" of American history after 1945 see Bergmann, "American Exceptionalism and the German 'Sonderweg' in Tandem," 528. For one of the latest "traditionalist," nontransnational explanations of German colonialism that argues both for Bismarck's towering importance for German colonialism and for the exceptional violence of German colonialism in Africa (especially compared to French colonialism) see H. Pogge von Strandmann, "The Purpose of German Colonialism, or the Long Shadow of Bismarck's Colonial Policy," in *German Colonialism: Race, the Holocaust, and Postwar Germany*, ed. Volker Langbehn and Mohammad Salama (New York: Columbia University Press, 2011), 201.

"Hottentot elections," which were dominated by colonial questions, the two left-liberal parties made significant gains compared to the 1903 elections, with the more right-leaning National-Liberal Party following closely behind. In addition, ideas of individual self-determination, hopes for social and economic spheres free from privileged entrenched interests and burdensome bureaucracies, and expectations of social and economic independence not only permeated writings and public debates about the colonies but also guided the actions taken by liberal administrators such as Bernhard Dernburg and Wilhelm Solf, or expansionists like Carl Peters.

Traditionally, Peters has been viewed as one of the main proponents of the emerging radical right in late nineteenth-century Germany or, even worse, as somebody who, according to Wehler, had been justifiably appropriated by Nazi propaganda because of his "Pan-German, antisemitic, and openly racist ideas." Yet Peters was no anti-Semite, on the contrary. In addition, against the backdrop of a definition of liberalism that takes seriously the ideology's imperialist and exclusionary dimensions, Peters' liberalism becomes clearly apparent. He surely was a racist, an imperialist, and a nationalist, but within the broad framework of nineteenth-century political liberalism these characteristics did not move him out of the liberal fold. Instead, borrowing a phrase from political scientist Jennifer Pitts that will be used throughout this study, his views fit comfortably within the margins of "imperial liberalism," a set of liberal beliefs that embraced the ideology's racist, nationalist, and expansionist as well as universal aspects (at least vis-à-vis other white Europeans and Americans). Peters shared this dimension of liberalism with his contemporaries Cecil Rhodes and Theodore Roosevelt, among others.[36]

---

[36] Wehler, *Bismarck und der Imperialismus*, 338; Eley, *Reshaping the German Right*, 47; Richard Parry, "'In a Sense Citizens, but Not Altogether Citizens...': Rhodes, Race, and the Ideology of Segregation at the Cape in the Late Nineteenth Century," *Canadian Journal of African Studies* 17, no. 3 (1983): 380–81; Smith, *The Ideological Origins of Nazi Imperialism*, 97; Walter LaFeber, *The American Search for Opportunity, 1865–1913* (Cambridge: Cambridge University Press, 1993); 57–59.

Carl Peters is important for this study because his activities and political views show that it is difficult to readily connect liberal imperialism and pre-1914 German colonialism with Nazi expansionism. Not only did Peters dislike the Pan-German League's anti-Semitism but during World War I he also did not follow the German radical right's path toward a progressively more racialized and Eastern-Europe-centered expansionism. Instead, in "good" liberal fashion, he argued for a renewed German commitment to its African colonies, while at the same time rejecting calls for large-scale annexations in the East. Peters posited that the demise of the Russian Empire would result in the emergence of numerous independent nation-states that would be friendly toward Germany. As a consequence, after the successful conclusion of the war the German Empire would finally be able to decrease the size of its military and therefore lift a huge burden from German taxpayers and the German economy. These anti-expansionist sentiments (at least regarding Eastern Europe) had little in common with the views promoted at the same time by the Pan-German League and the German Fatherland Party. This ultraright milieu, further radicalized by the war and Germany's eventual defeat, has often been viewed as a direct precursor of the Nazis and their radical, eastward-oriented living-space fantasies. Although recent scholarship has added nuance to this perception, Peters' ideological distance from both the Pan-German League, of which he was nevertheless still a member, and the Fatherland Party in 1918 indicates that the war in fact confirmed Peters' lifelong commitment to colonialism and imperial liberalism. In 1917, Peters argued that if Germany had been more dedicated to overseas expansion during the 1880s, it would have been welcomed into the global circle of white colonizers, which, in turn, would have resulted in peaceful, growth-oriented policies between Germany, Great Britain, and other colonizing nations. In Peters' view, a true devotion to liberal imperialism by the German Empire would have prevented the outbreak of war. Unlike other studies of Peters, my analysis therefore takes seriously his frequent claims to being liberal and his political activities on behalf of the National-Liberal Party. This perspective is not designed to rehabilitate Carl Peters – far from it; rather, it aims to move analyses of pre-1914 imperialism away from normative and often presentist understandings of the complex nature of nineteenth- and early twentieth-century liberalism.[37]

In my study, German imperialism and colonialism are treated not as separate phenomena, but as intertwined with German liberalism in general and with imperial liberalism in particular. Traditionally, the term "imperialism" has been used to describe the indirect rule of foreign territories for mostly economic purposes, whereas colonialism has denoted the direct administration of lands designated for settlement. Even though individual proponents of imperialist and colonialist policies were at times more interested in one than in the other, contemporaries did not see these two ways of projecting the metropole's power across the globe as mutually exclusive, but as two sides of the same coin. This study's liberalism-focused vantage point cannot claim to highlight all aspects of nineteenth-century imperialism, but its perspective demonstrates that imperialism, colonialism, and liberalism belong together. Both imperialism and colonialism projected exclusionary and ethnicist practices across the globe; even Enlightenment notions of cultural uplift (the notorious "civilizing mission") moved the eventual inclusion of natives into a community of equals far off into the future – a future that never came before the advent of decolonization. As Christoph Meiners

[37] Carl Peters, *Carl Peters gesammelte Schriften*, ed. Walter Frank, 3 vols., vol. 3 (München & Berlin: C. H. Beck'sche Verlagsbuchhandlung, 1944), 431–32, 98–99, Peters, *Schriften (Vol. 1)*, 474–76; Arne Perras, *Carl Peters and German Imperialism, 1856–1918* (Oxford: Clarendon Press, 2004), 183, 222. My definition of "imperialism" and "colonialism" relies heavily on Andrew Zimmerman's characterization of these two terms. *Alabama in Africa*'s analysis of the transatlantic and transnational connections between Imperial Germany, the United States, and Africa makes his perspective on these phenomena especially relevant for my analysis. See Alice L. Conklin, *European Imperialism, 1830–1930: Climax and Contradiction* (Houghton Mifflin Co., 1999); George Steinmetz, "Return to Empire: The New U.S. Imperialism in Comparative-Historical Perspective," *Sociological Theory* 23, no. 4 (2005); Zimmerman, "Decolonizing Weber," 75 (note 5); Fitzpatrick, *Liberal Imperialism in Germany. Expansionism and Nationalism, 1848–1884*, 22 (note 61).

explicitly and Thomas Jefferson, Alexis de Tocqueville, and John
Stuart Mill implicitly acknowledged, domestically a "liberal"
society of equal individuals only became possible by excluding
colonial natives and/or African-American slaves and by building
it on their backs. Imperial liberalism thus was supposed to create
inclusion through exclusion. In his 1895 inaugural speech at the
University of Freiburg, Max Weber recognized this connection
as well. Acknowledging bourgeois fears of the German working
class, Weber attempted to allay apprehensions of the German
proletariat's revolutionary potential by pointing out its political
immaturity. However, Weber did not argue that German workers should be excluded from political power in Germany; on the
contrary, he was hoping for their full democratic inclusion. In
classically liberal fashion he posited that once the proletariat had
reached the necessary level of education and experience it could
justifiably demand its share of political power:

And why is England's and France's proletariat partially different [from
Germany's]? . . . Primarily because of a political factor: It is the impact of
these countries' world power position that forces their governments to
continuously deal with the task of power-politics, which in turn imposes
an incessant learning process on the individual. . . . It will also be decisive
for our development whether doing big politics will enable us to focus
on great power-political questions. We have to understand that German
unification was merely a youthful escapade . . . if it does not become the
starting point for German world power politics [Weltmachtpolitik].[38]

Hence projecting German power abroad would create the necessary preconditions for a more integrated and equal society at
home. What the self-proclaimed "proud bourgeois" Weber called
for in his Freiburg speech thus stands in sharp contrast to Hans-
Ulrich Wehler's classic "social imperialism" thesis, although the
historian Wehler relied heavily on Weber's sociological analyses
of Imperial Germany's problems: Weber, who even according to
Wehler was one of the sharpest critics of Imperial Germany's

38 Max Weber, *Der Nationalstaat und die Volkswirtschaftspolitik: Akademische
Antrittsrede* (Freiburg i. B. & Leipzig: Akademische Verlagsbuchhandlung von
J.C.B. Mohr, 1895), 12.

autocratic structure, forcefully demanded Weltmachtpolitik and called for German imperialism. Imperialism therefore in no way "distracted" Weber from domestic concerns. The philosopher Georg Lukács believed that Weber's liberal-democratic domestic reformism fulfilled merely a technical function "for the purpose of a better functioning imperialism." Yet it was actually the other way around: For Weber, imperialism was an engine of progress, a catalyst for liberal domestic change. Yet – and this set imperial liberalism fundamentally apart from Nazism – for Weber and other progressives, at least within their envisioned Weltpolitik- and imperialism-based society, hierarchies and political exclusions would eventually be reduced to a minimum. In contrast, Nazi ideologues equated societies not ordered according to a strict leadership principle [Führerprinzip] and purged of any dissent with weakness and decay.[39]

A Note on Sources

This book is based on a range of sources including archival materials and published texts, among them both periodicals and monographs. The first source group I worked with comprised Enlightenment periodicals of which the *Berlinische Monatsschrift* is the best known. I also consulted many other late eighteenth- and early nineteenth-century serial publications; most were in various libraries in Berlin, most prominently the Berliner Staatsbibliothek. However, missing copies were often found in the Bundesarchiv in Berlin-Lankwitz. Newspapers and other

---

[39] Fitzpatrick, *Liberal Imperialism in Germany. Expansionism and Nationalism, 1848–1884*, 22 (note 61); Wehler, *The German Empire, 1871–1918*, 176. Georg Lukács quoted in Cornelius Torp, *Max Weber und die preußischen Junker* (Tübingen: Mohr Siebeck, 1998), 83. In his *German Empire*, Wehler heavily relies on Weber's analyses. Although Wehler does recognize Weber's "liberal imperialism," he assumes that it was Weber and other "liberal imperialists" who were attracted to the German government's imperialist distractions like moths to a flame, because his arguments rest on his interpretation of the German Empire as an almost completely top-down state. In Wehler's view, agency thus rests entirely with the "old elites;" liberal imperialists merely "lent their support" to the measures taken by the administration.

periodicals printed from the late eighteenth century to 1945 comprise another major part of the sources. I surveyed many titles in toto, including *Die Gartenlaube, Das Ausland, Globus, Petermann's Mittheilungen, Beiträge zur Kolonialpolitik und Kolonialwirtschaft, Zeitschrift für Kolonialpolitik, Kolonialrecht und Kolonialwirtschaft, Deutsche Kolonialzeitung, Der Völkische Beobachter* (1932–45), and Alfred Rosenberg's *Nationalsozialistische Monatshefte* (1933–44).

Because the links between the general topic of "America" and questions of race and expansion became obvious early on, I expanded my research to include monographs on U.S. and German colonization in general, an increasing number of which were published in the 1830s and 1840s. For the revolutionary years 1848–49, the *Stenographischer Bericht über die Verhandlungen der deutschen constituirenden Nationalversammlung zu Frankfurt am Main* was indispensable, as were, for the years between 1884–85 and 1933, the published proceedings of the German parliament (*Verhandlungen des deutschen Reichstages*). Most archival sources used for this book, among them the files of the Reichskolonialabteilung (RKA-B) and, after 1906, the Reichskolonialamt (RKA), are located in the Berlin branch of the Bundesarchiv. Probably because a number of the RKA's materials were written by hand and in Kurrentschrift (the traditional German script in use until 1941), the series of files that provide the bulk of the source materials used in Chapter 3 have, to my knowledge, never been analyzed before.

I

Soil, Liberty, and Blood

Germans and American Westward Expansion before 1871

"Amerika, du hast es besser" [America, you are better off].
Johann Wolfgang von Goethe made this oft-quoted statement
in 1827. Why was America "better off?" For most of his life
Goethe was not particularly interested in the United States. In the
end, the two events that did attract his attention were connected
more to perceptions of America as a space for travel, exploration, and expansion than with the United States as a political
phenomenon. Goethe's interest in America was first stimulated
by Alexander von Humboldt's return from his travels in 1804.
About two decades later, Goethe was again inspired, this time
by the journey to the United States of Duke Bernhard, the son of
Goethe's patron.[1]

Goethe's attitude is typical of late eighteenth- and early
nineteenth-century Germans (and Europeans in general, for that
matter): They did not think the United States was "better off"
simply because the country was the world's largest – and, in
1827, to all intents and purposes, only – republic. Although they
recognized, commented on, and approved of the United States'
exceptional status as a republic, in their eyes America was even
more fascinating because it was a vast space, much larger than

---

[1] Goethe quoted in Horst Dippel, *Germany and the American Revolution* (Wiesbaden: Steiner, 1978), 48, 49.

Western and Central Europe combined. It had to be discovered, explored, and, most important, settled. America had the potential to become a vast "empire of liberty," as Thomas Jefferson termed it. Yet this empire was also a republic, founded on the principles of popular sovereignty, individual freedom, and social and political progress. As a result, America was living proof that empire and liberty were by no means mutually exclusive. Indeed, during the first half of the nineteenth century, especially for Germans of a liberal political persuasion, the United States appeared to demonstrate that colonialism and territorial growth were inextricably linked to the establishment of a nation-state based on liberal principles. In consequence, the United States and American westward expansion were of continuing importance for these Germans' hopes of creating a liberal and nationally unified Germany. At the same time, the ever growing American republic inspired them to ponder the benefits and necessity of expansion from a German perspective.[2]

Freedom and Empire

Thomas Jefferson believed that political liberty could not exist without easily available land. For him, farmers constituted the cornerstone of the young United States. Their economic situation made them autonomous from landlords and moneyed individuals, thus making them ideal citizens for the American republic. Because it freed farmers from any kind of outside influence, their economic situation also enabled them to disinterestedly ponder the needs of their country. Yet only continuous westward expansion would allow the number of virtuous farmer-citizens to multiply. Moreover, the availability of land ensured that the American republic would not become as densely populated as the European states: Europe simply did not have enough land for all of its inhabitants to become or remain independent farmers. The old continent's states and nations had therefore become

---

[2] See Matthew P. Fitzpatrick, *Liberal Imperialism in Germany: Expansionism and Nationalism, 1848–1884* (New York: Berghahn Books, 2008), 50.

"corrupt" and oppressive. Because of its westward-moving frontier, America, unlike Europe, could combine freedom with power and become an "empire of liberty." If this empire did not continue to grow, however, the social and economic preconditions for its liberty would fall apart. The United States was thus both destined and doomed to expand and thereby come into potentially violent contact with those dwelling on the lands into which it expanded.[3]

Jefferson made this line of reasoning explicit to those on the other side of the Atlantic. During the War of 1812 against Great Britain, Thomas Jefferson, in a letter to Alexander von Humboldt, whom he met during the last leg of Humboldt's travels through South and North America in the early years of the nineteenth century, argued that because so many Native Americans had allied themselves with England, the United States could do "whatever necessary" to secure itself against "their savage and ruthless warfare." Although Jefferson blamed England's "unprincipled policy" for the Indians' involvement in the war, he nevertheless made it clear that reprisals against Native Americans would not be limited to the duration of the current conflict. Indeed, because of his belief in the inseparable links between liberty and land, any "future effects" of Native American hostility against the United States would also have to be curbed, and because of the United States' steady westward expansion such "effects" were bound to occur. This process, as Jefferson admitted to Humboldt, would inevitably lead to the "confirmed brutalization, if not extermination of this race in our America."[4]

Viewed from a European perspective, Jefferson's sentiments made a lot of sense. European observers of the young United

---

[3] Gordon S. Wood, *Empire of Liberty: A History of the Early Republic, 1789–1815* (Oxford: Oxford University Press, 2010), 357. Jefferson was by no means the only Founding Father who referred to the young American republic as an empire. See R. W. Van Alstyne, *The Rising American Empire* (Oxford: Basil Blackwell, 1960), 1–2.

[4] Helmut de Terra, "Alexander von Humboldt's Correspondence with Jefferson, Madison, and Gallatin," *Proceedings of the American Philosophical Society* 103, no. 6 (1959): 793–94.

States understood that empires needed to expand. Less than three decades after Jefferson wrote this letter to Humboldt, the Frenchman Alexis de Tocqueville, who was both amazed and somewhat frightened by American freedom and democracy, recognized that, although American westward expansion was certainly awe inspiring, the American frontier was by no means exceptional. Indeed, because of France's recent expansion into North Africa, the American West could serve as a "model" for French Algeria. In Tocqueville's eyes, in 1841 the city of Algiers thus looked like "Cincinnati transported onto the soil of Africa." Tocqueville too understood that expansion would inevitably lead to conflict, and although he often displayed sympathy for the fate of America's indigenous population, he nevertheless refrained from fundamental criticism of American expansionism. Like Jefferson, he believed American expansion to be vital for the country's existence. In the end, for Tocqueville as for so many nineteenth-century German and other European observers of the United States, the demise of America's Indians was the tragic but inevitable outcome of the encounter between civilized colonizers and "savage" natives. Viewed from a European perspective, the American example showed that the issues of liberty, expansion, and race were inextricably connected.[5]

Unlike France, the German states could not muster the resources to obtain overseas colonies before German unification in 1871. Yet this fact did not prevent Germans from participating in debates about expansion, nor did the German states lack concrete experience in the area. For example, Prussia acquired several Polish territories between 1772 and 1795, and even in the late eighteenth century, America was inspirational when it came to governing those newly acquired lands: Prussia's king Fredrick II compared the territories' Polish inhabitants to the Iroquois, and settlements in these areas were named Florida, Philadelphia, and Saratoga. However, although some

---

[5] Jennifer Pitts, *A Turn to Empire: The Rise of Imperial Liberalism in Britain and France* (Princeton: Princeton University Press, 2005), 196–97; Jennifer Pitts and Alexis de Tocqueville, *Writings on Empire and Slavery* (Baltimore: Johns Hopkins University Press, 2001), xiv, xv.

Germans were fascinated with settlement opportunities in the East, Prussia's activities in Poland never provided the main focus of German debates about expansion before 1884. The East was important, but settlement activities in this region needed to be augmented if not fully replaced by the acquisition of overseas colonies. Sometimes, die-hard colonialists even made fun of German expansionist designs for Eastern Europe, instead extolling the superior virtues of overseas colonies modeled on Anglo-American examples. American westward expansion thus prompted them, as it prompted Tocqueville, to look overseas and to perceive expansion as a worldwide process – a process that would require Germany to develop the capacities to reach out globally.[6]

To be sure, Enlightenment thinkers such as Immanuel Kant, Christoph Meiners, or, a little later, Alexander von Humboldt approached things from very different vantage points than did scientists like Friedrich Ratzel or expansionists like Carl Peters a century later. First and foremost, Germany as a unified and powerful nation-state did not yet exist when the former thinkers pondered colonial questions. Yet during the first decades of the nineteenth century – and even more so before, during, and after the 1848 revolution – concerns about the future of continental Europe and ideas of a unified Germany increasingly began to seep into more general discussions about America, empire, and race. Especially after the Napoleonic Wars, debates about the benefits and necessity of global expansion, which often simultaneously reflected on Germany's future and the settlement of

---

[6] David Blackbourn, *The Conquest of Nature: Water, Landscape and the Making of Modern Germany* (London: Jonathan Cape, 2006), 290. See also David Furber, "Near as Far in the Colonies: The Nazi Occupation of Poland," *International History Review* 26, no. 3 (2004). For colonialist criticisms of eastward expansionism, see Carl Peters' essay "Alltagspolemik und Kolonialpolitik" (1884), in Carl Peters, *Carl Peters gesammelte Schriften*, ed. Walter Frank, 3 vols., vol. 1 (Munich: C. H. Beck'sche Verlagsbuchhandlung, 1943), 338. The state of Brandenburg did "dabble" in colonialism in the late seventeenth and early eighteenth centuries. Yet the "Brandenburgisch-Afrikanische Compagnie," which owned a small number of fortified outposts along Africa's Gold Coast (Ghana) and, because of a treaty with Denmark, was also allowed to use the Caribbean island St. Thomas, only existed between 1682 and 1711.

the United States, were steeped in Enlightenment universalism; throughout the course of the nineteenth century they often continued to be conducted within the broad framework of German political liberalism.

As avid observers of the spectacle they began to see unfolding on the other side of the Atlantic after 1776, even late eighteenth-century Germans thus pondered America's future in conjunction with questions of race and expansion, because America's liberty and republicanism seemed to be entangled with both issues. Therefore discussions of racial difference, which abounded in the (proto-) anthropological treatises of the late Enlightenment, often focused on the United States, frequently against the backdrop of debates about the necessity and benefits of colonialism. In his third anthropological essay, entitled "On the Use of Teleological Principles in Philosophy" (1788), Immanuel Kant thus argued that Indians ranked "far beneath even the Negro, who is actually supposed to occupy the lowest of all other gradations, which we have pointed out to be racial differences." Thinking about questions of racial superiority and inferiority, Kant focused on both Native Americans and Africans, in the earlier quote slightly elevating the latter by juxtaposing them with the former. In Kant's view, there existed a linkage between Africa and America because both continents were home to supposedly racially inferior native populations. To support his inferiority thesis, in his 1788 essay Kant added a lengthy footnote that quoted from the German translation of a pro-slavery tract (the same publication also contained a translation of an antislavery essay he chose to ignore), which argued that both "Negroes" and Indians possessed fixed racial traits that made them lazy and shiftless. Kant's ideas about race were thus rooted in the transnational intellectual framework surrounding slavery, the slave trade, and European colonialism in America and Africa, despite the fact that at least in theory he opposed all three institutions.[7]

---

7 Immanuel Kant, "Über den Gebrauch teleologischer Prinzipien in der Philosophie," *Der Teutsche Merkur* 1 (1788): 117–21 and "Anmerkungen über Ramsays Schrift von der Behandlung der Negersklaven in den Westindischen Zuckerinseln," *Beiträge zur Völker- und Länderkunde* 5 (1786): 267–92; Robert

Christoph Meiners, a professor at the University of Göttingen and contemporary of Kant, was even more acutely aware of the links between race and colonial expansion. Although Meiners is barely known today, he was an important, widely published, and widely read contributor to the public sphere in late eighteenth- and early nineteenth-century Germany. His works were translated into both English and French, and they were positively received abroad. He concurred with Kant's views on the racial inferiority of Native Americans, asking his readers whether "the inhabitants of the New World, who can achieve so much less and are much inferior [to Europeans], should be granted the same rights and freedoms we enjoy." For Meiners, the answer was a resounding no. In his view, both American Indians and black Africans belonged to the same "strain" of humanity, the Mongolian race, and the inferiority of both predestined them to serve their white superiors. Inspired by the question of slavery, Meiners easily jumped from America to Africa and back again, linking the issues of racial inferiority, slavery, and America's settlement by Europeans.[8]

Meiners' most direct vindication of slavery as a necessary precondition for the colonization of America appeared as a journal article titled "On the Lawfulness of the Negro Trade" (1788). Meiners was steeped in the international discourse surrounding slavery and colonialism; he had read and cited French, Dutch, and American authors. Yet one of his favorite writers was the English slave holder Samuel Estwick, who, like Meiners, linked slavery to the successful colonization of America and to the benefits England had derived from these colonization efforts.

Bernasconi, "Kant as an Unfamiliar Source of Racism," in *Philosophers on Race: Critical Essays*, ed. Julie K. Ward and Tommy Lee Lott (Oxford: Blackwell, 2002), 148, 149, 158, 159, 163 (note 16), 164 (note 18).

[8] Nell Irvin Painter, "Why White People Are Called 'Caucasian'" paper presented at the Fifth Annual Gilder Lehrman Center International Conference: Collective Degradation: Slavery and the Construction of Race, Yale University, November 7–8, 2003; Britta Rupp-Eisenreich, "Choses occultes en histoire des sciences humaines: le destin de la 'science nouvelle' de Christoph Meiners," *Ethnographie* 90–91 (1983); Christoph Meiners, "Zweyte Abhandlung über die Natur der Americaner," *Göttingisches Historisches Magazin* 2 (1790): 209–11, 229.

Meiners broadened Estwick's argument and maintained that all white Europeans had the right to force their will on less capable groups of human beings. In doing so, Meiners espoused a racialized form of bourgeois utilitarianism. Just as from his vantage point it was fair and necessary that the ruling nobility in Europe should share political power with well-educated and capable members of the bourgeoisie, so those who could never be expected to fulfill any higher social and political functions could be oppressed and exploited. Meiners based his pro-slavery argument on a completely racialized credo: "Yet even if it were proven that in the American possessions of the Europeans yearly there died one hundred thousand Negroes more than there were born, it would only demonstrate that the slave trade and the labor for which the Negroes are bought are detrimental to the black race, but not that they constitute a disadvantage for humankind as a whole."[9]

In Meiners' view, white racial superiority provided sufficient validation of slavery. There was no need to argue for its civilizing or Christianizing dimension. The benefits that whites derived from slavery and the slave trade were twofold: (1) The forced labor of racially inferior human beings created much coveted wares, goods, and amenities, and (2) without slavery, colonial expansion was impossible. Meiners therefore not only presented himself as a defender of slavery but also as a supporter of colonialism. Moreover, although Meiners' arguments had essentially no real-life consequences for late eighteenth-century Germany, he nevertheless pursued concrete political objectives. He wanted the European states, most importantly the German lands, to engage in processes of liberal political reform. In Meiners' view, England and its recent offspring, the United States, demonstrated two basic political truths. On the one hand, the history of these

[9] Samuel Estwick, *Considerations on the Negroe Cause Commonly So Called, Addressed to the Right Honourable Lord Mansfield, Lord Chief Justice of the Court of King's Bench* (London: J. Dodsley, 1773), 82, 85; Christoph Meiners, "Über die Rechtmässigkeit des Negern-Handels," *Göttingisches Historisches Magazin* 2 (1788): 409; Christoph Meiners, "Ueber die Ursachen des Despotismus," *Göttingisches Historisches Magazin* 2 (1788): 197–98.

states showed that political systems based on the inalienable rights of their citizens were more successful than nations that relegated their population to subject status. On the other, the British Empire and America revealed that territorial expansion and colonization (and the exploitation of inferior races) were connected to these nations' political liberties and, in the case of the British Empire, its global might. Meiners hoped that political reform and the acquisition of overseas colonies would put the states of continental Europe on a path that would eventually enable them to create both internally and externally similarly successful political structures.[10]

Even during the 1790s, when the French Revolution had descended into bloody turmoil, Meiners argued for liberal reform in the German lands and elsewhere. Yet how to make this case when France was clearly incapable of carrying out this process without plunging the country into chaos? For Meiners, recognizing the innate and unchangeable distinctions between different groups of human beings provided the answer to this question. As a result, Meiners connected the topics of colonization, white superiority, race-based slavery, and liberal reform. For the German professor, social progress and political freedom were underwritten and supported by the economic advantages produced by colonialism in general and by the settlement of America in particular. Whereas Jefferson projected American republicanism onto the geography of the North American continent, thus connecting political freedom with westward expansion, Meiners went two steps further. Because Europe lacked contiguous territories readily available for colonization (Meiners did not look eastward), he projected the (pre-) conditions of political reform in Europe onto both the whole globe and the human body. Without

---

[10] Susanne Zantop, "The Beautiful, the Ugly, and the German: Race, Gender and Nationality in Eighteenth-Century Anthropological Discourse," in *Gender and Germanness* (Providence: Berghahn, 1997), 31; Susanne Zantop, *Colonial Fantasies. Conquest, Family, and Nation in Precolonial Germany, 1770–1870* (Durham: Duke University Press, 1997), 236; Christoph Meiners, *Geschichte der Ungleichheit der Stände unter den vornehmsten europäischen Völkern*, 2 vols. (Hannover: Im Verlage der Helwingischen Buchhandlung, 1792), 4–5.

colonial settlements (in America and elsewhere), Europeans and white Americans lacked the material prerequisites for progress, civilized life, and the political reform process advocated by self-proclaimed Enlightenment thinkers like himself:

> Without Negroes, all plantations would have to close, because neither Americans nor Europeans can endure the hard labor that is connected with the planting, maintenance, and crushing of the sugar cane.... It is therefore Negro hands alone which supply us with the rest of the precious goods of the New World and which create the livelihood and affluence of all the millions of white and nobler people.... Never has there been ... the founding of any kind of colony without ... many people losing their health or life. Yet when one examines the utility or perniciousness of such enterprises, one looks not only at the accidental or unavoidable ills that they produce, but also at the positive consequences which are connected with them; and one also has to look at the Negro trade in this way.[11]

Meiners also argued that despotism "solely and necessarily arises ... from an *inherited* [my emphasis] meanness of spirit on the part of whole nations ... on the other hand, despotism is only a passing illness among the nobler peoples of our part of the globe; it vanishes immediately when its random and changing causes cease to be." For Meiners, political maturity was an innate characteristic of whites, both European and American. Political reform in "white" countries was therefore a safe process, at least in the long run. Meiners never retracted this point, not even during the Terror in France. For him, racial attributes determined human intellectual capability. In turn, these inherited features established a natural gradation among humans – one that should not and could not be abolished, despite demands to the contrary. For Meiners, progress and Enlightenment meant replacing the social hierarchies that had determined the political structure of medieval Europe with geographical ones: Whereas Europe's rigid social order had to be abolished, Africa offered naturally inferior peoples in abundance. A more pleasant and politically mature life for white Europeans and Americans could and should therefore be constructed on the backs of racially inferior slaves:

[11] Meiners, "Über die Rechtmässigkeit des Negern-Handels," 409–10.

"[D]espite the cruelties it causes, for humankind as a whole the Negro trade has been more salutary than pernicious." There can be no question that Meiners' extreme racism and advocacy of colonialism and race-based slavery made him an outlier within the German intellectual and political context. His closest intellectual peers were thus not his German colleagues but those English slave holders, such as Samuel Estwick and Edward Long, who attempted to justify their plantation businesses by publishing pro-colonialist and pro-slavery tracts. However, Meiners' concerns – to demonstrate the necessity, usefulness, and, ultimately, safety of liberal domestic reform while delineating both these changes' natural limits and their obligatory connection to colonialism – would remain constant features in the thought of imperial liberals throughout the nineteenth century, determining their anxious, ambivalent and often negative attitudes toward the process of democratization. Political scientist Jennifer Pitts thus shows that, forty years after Meiners penned the earlier quoted essay, for Alexis de Tocqueville "colonial expansion was instrumentally valuable for French liberal democracy. . . . The development of a stable and liberal regime might require the exploitation of non-European societies, might legitimate suspending principles of human equality and self-determination abroad in order to secure . . . stable liberty at home in France." The same was true for John Stuart Mill and other mid-nineteenth-century British liberals, who "consistently conceived the case for extending the franchise at home in terms of contrast with colonial subjects whose incapacity for participation in political power they deemed self-evident."[12]

[12] Although Meiners' racialized worldview was far more vulgar and crass than Kant's off-hand remarks on the racial inferiority of Indians, both men espoused similarly negative evaluations of Native Americans. The closeness of their views reveals that supremacist perceptions of Amerindians had an established place even within the German Enlightenment's "humanitarian tradition." Meiners, "Ueber die Ursachen des Despotismus," 196, 197; Meiners, "Über die Rechtmässigkeit des Negern-Handels," 410; Kant, "Teleologischer Prinzipien," 121; Meiners, "Zweyte Abhandlung," 209–11, 229; Meiners, *Geschichte der Ungleichheit*, 1–2, 4–5; Peter J. Brenner, *Reisen in die Neue Welt* (Tübingen: Niemeyer, 1991), 216; Pitts, *A Turn to Empire*, 248–49.

To be sure, many German observers criticized the United States for condoning slavery on its territory. Nevertheless, Meiners was not the only eighteenth-century German who understood that slavery, in addition to producing economic benefits, also had important sociopolitical ramifications. In a very widely read late eighteenth-century monthly, the *Berlinische Monatsschrift* (the same journal that in 1784 had published Immanuel Kant's famous essay "What Is Enlightenment"), Dr. Bollmann, a physician who traveled to the United States, wrote an open letter about the function of slavery in the American South in 1796:

> The latter [northern] states are dependent upon commerce and have no or at least only very few slaves, but they have white trash; therefore they are less democratic. The inhabitants of the southwestern states are almost all owners of land, while the better part of the workers are slaves: as a consequence there is no white rabble because there [in the southern states] slaves, like horses and cows, are not part of society; and in their present state pose as little danger for public safety as the latter; this is the reason why these states are more democratic.[13]

Bollmann's remarks about the role slavery played in American society were perceptive and indeed foreshadowed arguments of two of the most prominent twentieth-century works on American slavery, David Brion Davis's *The Problem of Slavery in the Age of Revolution* (1975) and Edmund Morgan's *American Slavery, American Freedom* (1975). Unlike Meiners, Bollmann was not a defender of slavery, but he nevertheless accepted it, at least for the time being. Even more important, and this time in line with Meiners' idea of racial superiority as a prerequisite for a more liberally organized society, Bollmann recognized that the absolute control the white planter class exercised over its black slaves contributed decisively to the abundance of liberal ("democratic") political rhetoric in the American South. Moreover, at least indirectly,

Compare Susanne Zantop, "'Der Indianer' im Rasse- und Geschlechterdiskurs der deutschen Spätaufklärung," in *Das Subjekt und die Anderen: Interkulturalität und Geschlechterdifferenz vom 18. Jahrhundert bis zur Gegenwart,* ed. Viktoria Schmidt-Linsenhoff (Berlin: 2001), 133.
[13] "Auszug eines Schreibens von Doktor Bollmann aus Philadelphia, d. 20 Juni 1796," *Berlinische Monatsschrift* (1796), 448–49.

Bollmann also confirmed Jefferson's linkage of land, liberty, and westward expansion when referencing "the West" as a point of orientation in his description of Americans living in the South: These people were not merely Southerners, but were the "inhabitants of the southwestern states." Northerners, in contrast, did not deserve the geographic designation of the West. The North was urban and "dependent on commerce," whereas "almost all" white Southerners owned land – and if they wanted more land, they went westward. This fact, in combination with the South's reliance on slavery, resulted in a more equal, homogeneous, and "democratic" (white) population.[14]

Already during the late years of the eighteenth and early years of the nineteenth centuries, the German fascination with the United States was thus also grounded in an understanding of the socially and politically important links among questions of race, race control, and expansion. To be more precise, German observers denied, as Jefferson attempted to do as well, the political, social, and philosophical tensions inherent in American expansionism. According to Jefferson, westward expansion was necessary for the preservation of America's liberal and republican political system, yet it was often undertaken with the help of slavery and made conflict with Native Americans inevitable. The universal liberties that westward expansion was meant to secure were thus inseparably tied to exclusionary national-imperialist and racialized contexts.

Progress, Social Control, Land, and Race

Historian Gordon Wood has argued that the "Early Republic" – the United States before the War of 1812 – cannot be understood without considering the importance of republican-democratic views for this era's sociopolitical developments (it can be argued that the same holds true later in the nineteenth century). During this period, German observers' analyses of the American republic also addressed questions of race and expansion.

[14] Ibid.

Did travelers like Bollmann or intellectuals like Humboldt (or Tocqueville) therefore misunderstand the United States in its early years? Did they fail to pay enough attention to America's republican principles? Were they instead too fascinated by America's continuous growth? Sources like Bollmann's open letter in the *Berlinische Monatsschrift* indicate that Europeans were very aware that honest appreciations of America had to acknowledge the clear connections between political ideals and questions of race and expansion. However, this realization did not mean that the links between the country's fast-paced development and the topics of expansion and race negatively affected perceptions of the United States. Even Alexander von Humboldt, who detested slavery and abhorred the brutal treatment of native populations worldwide, conveniently ignored his firsthand knowledge of Jefferson's exterminatory attitudes toward Indians when describing the benefits of the settlement of North America for humankind as a whole.[15]

Between 1800 and 1850, literacy rates jumped from 5 percent to approximately 80 percent in the state of Prussia. In response to the expansion of the German reading public during the first half of the nineteenth century, an increasing number of travelogues and emigration brochures were printed, many of which were distributed and read widely (most famously Gottfried Duden's publication, which is analyzed later). These texts, although written by Germans, repeated American viewpoints that justified or at least accepted the expulsion and disappearance of Native Americans because they stood in the way of American westward expansion. The eminent philosopher Georg Friedrich Wilhelm Hegel thus argued that the Indians' ultimate fate, after they were pushed westward again and again by the growing American republic, would be marginalization, if not extinction: "In the North American free states all citizens are descendants of Europeans with whom the first inhabitants could not mix and [thus the Indians] were pushed back. The aboriginals have adopted certain arts from Europeans, among others the

---

[15] Wood, *Empire of Liberty*, 718.

consumption of brandy, which has had a destructive effect on them.... The inferiority of these individuals is visible in every way, even in regards to their body size." In the eyes of (Euro-) American, European, and German observers it was the physical inferiority of Native Americans that appeared to make their disappearance inevitable.[16]

As Indians were pushed westward, ever increasing swaths of land became available, inviting white Americans and European immigrants to settle there. During the early years of the nineteenth century, this expansion secured the existence of the American republic, at least from Jefferson's viewpoint. Simultaneously it began to inspire the first German plans for establishing a German colony on American soil. In 1817, Hans Christoph von Gagern, the father of Heinrich von Gagern, the first president of the 1848 Frankfurt parliament, sent his cousin to the United States to explore the possibility of establishing German settler colonies in the American West. Although the Netherlands, France, and Great Britain all had their own colonies, it was the American colonization of the West that was most inspirational for a well-educated, liberal statesman from Hesse like von Gagern. During the years immediately after the Napoleonic Wars, liberal-nationalist calls for a united Germany had become increasingly frequent. After having read Malthus and his dire predictions, von Gagern was deeply concerned about Germany's future (Malthus in fact had had a similar impact on Jefferson, deepening his concerns about the vitality of American republicanism.). Von Gagern believed that without continuous emigration, Germany's "social question" (i.e. pauperism, famine, and other consequences of the end of feudalism and early industrialization) could not be solved. However, if there were no colonies under German control and the emigrants had to settle in other areas, they would eventually shed their nationality and become

[16] Ben Kiernan, *Blood and Soil: A World History of Genocide and Extermination from Sparta to Darfur* (New Haven: Yale University Press, 2007), 310–64; David Blackbourn, *The Long Nineteenth Century* (New York: Oxford University Press, 1998), 35; Georg Friedrich Wilhelm Hegel, *Vorlesungen über die Philosophie der Geschichte* (Stuttgart: Reclam, 1961), 140–41.

part of their new host societies. Thus, although such emigration might help solve Germany's social question, it would be
unacceptable from a nationalist viewpoint. A "German America" appeared to offer a solution, albeit only until von Gagern's
cousin returned from the United States, having ascertained that
the country would not tolerate non-U.S. settlements in the American West. Von Gagern came to the realistic conclusion that a
"New Germany" on American soil was impossible. Yet the lure
of expansion into the American West remained irresistible for
German colonialists for a long time to come. Thirty years after
von Gagern abandoned such plans, some German liberals still
believed that German settler colonies could be established in "the
West," and after 1871, the impossibility of German settlements
in America would be used to argue for the acquisition of German
colonies elsewhere.[17]

Colonialism and the United States were twin topics in German
publications after the Napoleonic Wars. The widely traveled
Alexander von Humboldt, perhaps because of his personal contacts with Jefferson, spoke highly of American westward expansion while simultaneously criticizing the establishment of European colonial outposts along the coast of Africa. In Humboldt's
view, Africa was a continent whose population showed no sign of
"vanishing." In contrast, in North America, as he noted in 1826,
natives "usually withdrew when the whites approached."[18]

Yet although the natives' disappearance both justified and
facilitated colonization, it also created problems. In Humboldt's
view, the low population density in America resulted in a "need
for labor." Together with "the preference given to culturing
sugar, indigo, and cotton," these factors necessitated the introduction of "the despicable slave trade." Humboldt detested slavery, yet his rejection of forced labor was inconsistent with his
uncritical acceptance of the "vanishing native" topos. After all,

[17] Hans Fenske, "Imperialisitische Tendenzen in Deutschland vor 1866:
Auswanderung, überseeische Bestrebungen, Weltmachtsträume," *Historisches Jahrbuch* 97/98 (1978): 344–47.
[18] Alexander von Humboldt, "Über die zukünftigen Beziehungen von Europe
und Amerika," *Morgenblatt für gebildete Stände*, no. 33–34 (1826): 130.

thirteen years earlier Jefferson had told him that the ultimate disappearance of America's natives would be the result of war and
"extermination," not of the Indians' voluntary "withdrawal."
Moreover, the introduction of slavery to North America was,
in Humboldt's own view, a natural (albeit regrettable) result of
the vanishing of the natives. Ultimately, for Humboldt, both the
Indians' disappearance and slavery were therefore side effects
of an overall positive development, namely the global spread of
civilization:

It is in the nature of civilization that it strides forward.... Because of
the immeasurable progress in the art of navigation, one is tempted to say
that the water basins of the seas appear to have narrowed. The Atlantic
Ocean presents itself to us in the form of a narrow channel, which no
more distances the European mercantile states from the New World than
in the childhood of navigation the water basin of the Mediterranean Sea
separated the Peloponnesian Greeks from the inhabitants of Ionia, Sicily,
Syria.

Humboldt thus linked the establishment of progressive societies
to the colonization of America and the transatlantic connected-
ness of the Old with the New World. Regrettably, the spreading of civilization westward across the Atlantic and then, again,
westward across the North American continent through settler
colonialism resulted in the "withdrawal" of native peoples.[19]

Although Humboldt's 1826 remarks repeated the myth of a
quasi-voluntary vanishing of America's Indians, within the next
two decades the tone of German reports about the situation of
Native Americans in the United States began to change. The writings of Gottfried Duden, one of the most widely read proponents
of German emigration to America in the late 1820s and 1830s,
exemplify this development. Before publishing his widely read
Account of a Journey to the Western States of North America
(1829), Duden had lived in Missouri for three years, where fellow frontiersmen related to him many negative characterizations
of Amerindians. Because of his personal experience of living in

the West and his vivid prose, Duden became one of the primary vectors for the introduction of frontier attitudes toward
Native Americans to early nineteenth-century Germany. Duden
recounted gruesome stories about Amerindians, among them an
account of an Indian attack on a settler family in Missouri. In
one account the only survivor (albeit not for long) is a five-year-
old boy who is found by his grandfather. Before the boy dies, he
whispers, "Grand-daddy, the Indians did scalp me." In his works,
Duden used this and other frontier tales to explicitly reject the, in
his words, "quixotic" notion that Europeans should refrain from
settling the American West so as to avoid displacing America's
native population. After all, how could one possibly lament the
disappearance of a people who, according to Duden, indulged
in "abominable aberrations of the sex drive," such as bestiality
and homosexual fornication with boys, or who ate their own
children?[20]

In 1829, Duden's *Account* made frontier sentiments available
to German readers, and during the 1830s and 1840s, scientific
journals such as *Das Ausland* [Foreign Lands], which would
become extremely important several decades later, published
reports that corroborated Duden's negative assessment of Indians (and of African Americans, too). These accounts fit the times.
The little more than two decades between Humboldt's optimistic
assessment of the progress of civilization in Europe and America
in 1826 and the revolutionary events of 1848 were years of anx-
iety and upheaval – not only in the German states and France,
two countries that would witness revolutions in 1848, but also
in England and the United States. In Great Britain, the Chartist
and anti-Corn Law movements aroused apprehension among the
ruling elites. In the United States, the first stirrings of working-
class activism, the success of Andrew Jackson's Democracy Party,
and the founding of many often religiously motivated reform

---

[20] Gottfried Duden, *Bericht über eine Reise nach den westlichen Staaten Nord-
Amerikas und einen mehrja"hrigen Aufenthalt am Missouri* (Elberfeld: Lucas,
1829), 104–06. On Duden's reception in Germany see Horst Dippel, "Gustav
Körner," in *Neue deutsche Biographie* (Berlin: 1980), 384.

associations accompanied America's transition from an elitist republic to a democratic mass society that was rife with sectional tension between North and South. In the German states, the French July Revolution of 1830 stirred up domestic political activity that found its most famous expression in the "Hambacher Fest" of 1832, the participants of which were representatives of Germany's liberal and nationalist opposition to the forces of restoration in the governments of the German Confederation.

For many contemporary observers, whether German, French, English, or American, the issue of the day was therefore control – controlling one's life as an individual and citizen as well as controlling broader sociopolitical developments. In his introduction to the first volume of *Democracy in America*, Alexis de Tocqueville described his "religious terror" in the face of the historical changes he believed to be occurring in the United States and the countries of Western Europe. America faced these monumental developments earlier than the European nations. In consequence, Tocqueville feared that, although at the moment the European states still held their political fates "in their own hands;...they may lose control" very soon. Tocqueville believed that the perceived unstoppable process of social leveling and democratization could and must be controlled lest it again produce events like the Terror of the French Revolution. The United States offered examples of how such a task could be accomplished. After traveling in the United States, Tocqueville believed that colonialism provided a means of gaining control of these sociopolitical developments. This conviction, combined with France's renewed imperialist enterprises in North Africa and Asia, prompted him to write extensively on territorial expansion and empire. For Tocqueville and, as we see later, his German contemporary Friedrich List, the question of how to deal with the massive sociopolitical challenges of the times was thus connected to the acquisition of new territories.[21]

---

[21] Alexis de Tocqueville, *Democracy in America* (New York: Random House, 1981), 7–8; Pitts and Tocqueville, *Writings on Empire and Slavery*, xi–xii.

During the 1830s, the rapidly increasing population in the eastern U.S. states and the changes and problems that accompanied this increase prompted Lewis Cass, Andrew Jackson's secretary of war, to give a concrete answer to the question of who, ultimately, deserved to be in control of the North American continent. Unsurprisingly, the answer was Americans of European stock and not the land's native peoples. Germans took note. Germany's best known and most widely read geographic journal at the time, *Das Ausland*, offered the most comprehensive coverage of the topic of Indian removal and in 1831 printed an extensive series titled "The Political Situation of the Indians in the United States of America," largely based on Lewis Cass's *North American Review* essay, "Removal of the Indians." Cass's argument, as translated by *Das Ausland*, was simple: "What once was an immense hunting ground for barbaric hordes has quickly grown into a mighty empire in which freedom and moral education are sprouting the most magnificent blossoms." In Cass's view, America's native population had brought about its own demise, because the Indians had not recognized that their life as hunters "was destined to perish." If the Indians did not want to abandon their doomed culture, their way of life had to be "protected" by removing them as far away as possible from the advancing (white) civilization. If white Americans and settlers of European stock wanted to continue building the American republic and remain in control of its sociopolitical development, Native Americans had to relinquish their land claims – initially only east of the Mississippi river, but soon also to the west of it. More and more land was opened up for white settlement and colonization, which in turn promised to guarantee America's sociopolitical progress and stability.[22]

---

[22] *Das Ausland*, No. 107/110 (April 17/20, 1831), 425–26, 437–39; Lewis Cass, "Removal of the Indians," *North American Review* (1830): 62–121; Joshua David Bellin, "Apostle of Removal: John Eliot in the Nineteenth Century," *New England Quarterly* 69, no. 1 (1996): 9–10; Mary Hershberger, "Mobilizing Women, Anticipating Abolition: The Struggle against Indian Removal in the 1830s," *Journal of American History* 86, no. 1 (1999): 18–19.

During the 1820s, 1830s, and early 1840s, the German economist Friedrich List closely followed the developments that were occurring in the United States. Driven into exile by the oppressive restoration policies in Germany after the Napoleonic Wars, List lived in America between 1825 and 1834 and became a U.S. citizen. Seven years after his return to Europe, List published his most famous work, *The National System of Political Economy* (1841). Although List has not traditionally been linked to pro-colonialist sentiment in nineteenth-century Germany, his ideas nevertheless played a key role in shaping German liberal imperialist views. List believed that historical and economic alterations continually changed the patterns of social life. Like Tocqueville, he wanted "a new science of politics" that would be able to analyze, understand, and direct this inevitable process of social alteration. Moreover, like Tocqueville, List was interested in the spatial dimension of social control and therefore proposed what he called "inner colonization" as a means to direct problematic social and demographic processes.[23]

No united German nation-state existed during List's lifetime, and the German states were unable to acquire overseas possessions before 1884. List's "inner colonization" concept therefore aimed to direct German emigrant streams from the United States or Canada to sparsely populated regions of Central and Eastern Europe. This slightly realistic proposal was List's only effort to turn his American-inspired acceptance of the need to colonize and expand into potentially practical advice for German readers. Other German liberals had much more far-fetched (and even more America-focused) colonial fantasies than List. Ultimately, despite his advocacy for "inner colonization," List too came to envision a future German nation-state that would expand globally. In the end, Eastern Europe was not Germany's equivalent to the American West, because increased

---

[23] Tocqueville, *Democracy in America*, 8; Woodruff D. Smith, *The Ideological Origins of Nazi Imperialism* (New York: Oxford University Press, 1986), 25; Woodruff D. Smith, *Politics and the Sciences of Culture in Germany, 1840–1920* (New York: Oxford University Press, 1991), 31; Fitzpatrick, *Liberal Imperialism*, 57–59.

settlement in the East did not eliminate the need for overseas colonies.[24]

There can be no question that List's years in the United States were formative for his intellectual development. In America, he observed firsthand how important the abundant availability of arable land was for industrial development and growth: "Now the demand for the manufactured products of the Atlantic states increases simultaneously with their consumption of the raw materials supplied by the west. Now the population of these states, their wealth, and the number and extent of their towns increase in equal proportion with the cultivation of the western virgin lands." Like the geographer Friedrich Ratzel fifty years later, List believed that both land and a growing industrial sector were necessary for the economic progress of a nation: The United States provided the strongest proof of this assumption. For List, settler colonialism, in the American West and elsewhere, was not meant to preserve an agricultural society. Instead, territorial expansion was necessary for the creation of a modern, industrialized state. Unlike Jefferson, who saw westward expansion as offering a way out of the trappings of modernization and providing the United States with the means to maintain its republican and agrarian status quo, List believed that America's westward expansion and simultaneous industrialization pointed toward the future. In List's view, the United States was thus, along with the British Empire, the most important sociopolitical model for German emulation.[25]

During the 1830s and 1840s, a host of German publications on America made clear that the topic of expansion was inseparably linked to racial questions. During the late eighteenth century, a number of Germans, among them Immanuel Kant, Christoph Meiners, Samuel Thomas Sömmering, and Johann Friedrich Blumenbach, had made important contributions to the international debates about race. In the two decades preceding the 1848

---

[24] Fitzpatrick, *Liberal Imperialism*, 57–59.
[25] Friedrich List, *The National System of Political Economy* (New York: Kelley, 1966), 101–02, 105–06; Fitzpatrick, *Liberal Imperialism*, 57–59.

revolution, racial questions again acquired a prominent position in German publications. This time, however, the debates were often sparked by foreign publications, most notably by the writings of the University of Pennsylvania professor Samuel George Morton. As so often when it came to the distribution of allegedly scientific information about America, it was *Das Ausland* that made these texts available to German readers. Morton was one of the pioneers of what is now termed "scientific racism." He was a self-styled objective empiricist who had amassed the world's largest pre-Darwinian collection of human skulls. Termed "the American Golgotha," it was housed at the Academy of Natural Sciences in Philadelphia. In Morton's view, his craniological studies proved the racial superiority of whites. Native Americans were situated below whites, and blacks ranked lowest.[26]

During the 1840s, *Das Ausland* kept track of Morton's publications and reviewed them positively. Conveniently for both apologists of slavery and those Americans and Europeans who were settling the American West, Morton's findings provided justifications for southern slavery and federal Indian removal measures. Most important, and in contrast to Lewis Cass's arguments for the displacement of the remaining eastern Native American tribes, Morton's publications came with the aura of scientific certainty. As a result, their authenticity was rarely questioned. Morton was highly esteemed by his academic peers, both in the United States and in Germany, where Alexander von Humboldt applauded his work for "the profundity of its anatomical views" and "the numerical detail of the relations of organic confirmation, and the absence of those poetical reveries which are the myths of modern physiology." Humboldt approved of Morton's empirical method and admired the large quantity of data on which his findings were supposedly based. In Humboldt's view, such an approach seemed to promise the most accurate results

[26] *Das Ausland*, No. 107/110 (April 17/20, 1831), 425–26, 437–39; "Amerikanische Schädel," *Das Ausland* (1841): 701–02; "Über die Neger als primitive Race," *Das Ausland* (1842): 1221; "Die schwarze Race in Amerika," *Das Ausland* (1844): 1389.

and add the most to humankind's knowledge of nature and itself. The more one knew, the better one's conclusions were bound to be – and during the 1830s and 1840s, Germans heard and read more and more about America.[27] During the same decade in which Morton's racist inquiries were published in Germany, the first book by the German traveler, novelist, and committed political liberal Friedrich Gerstäcker appeared in print. Widely read in Germany and beyond, Gerstäcker had traveled the United States from 1837 to 1843. He returned to America two more times: as a prospector in California during the 1849 Gold Rush and as a traveler in the late 1860s. During his first sojourn in the United States, Gerstäcker was impressed with the expansion of the American republic and with its achievements (fast-growing cities, steamboats, extensive farming). His meetings with Indians happened randomly. He ran into individual Indians while hunting or met them on their way "West," without asking why they were being relocated. Gerstäcker mixed positive portrayals of Native Americans with patronizing and negative descriptions, often implying that, despite their many admirable features, Indians were, regrettably, inferior to whites.[28]

To Gerstäcker the Indians' disappearance was natural. It could be witnessed and lamented by white observers, but not halted – a view that simultaneously blamed and exculpated white Americans and Europeans. For Gerstäcker, the American West was a zero-sum game. On the one hand, America in general and the West in particular allowed whites to take control of their own lives, a process that had a clear spatial dimension. The United States offered white men and women the opportunity to carve out their private niches in the country's thinly spread social fabric,

---

[27] Humboldt cited in Stephen Jay Gould, "Morton's Ranking of Races by Cranial Capacity," *Science* 200, no. 4341 (1978): 503–04; John S. Michael and Stephen Jay Gould, "A New Look at Morton's Craniological Research," *Current Anthropology* 29, no. 2 (1988).

[28] Christof Mauch, "Indianer und Schwarze aus deutscher Perspektive: Sichtweisen des 19. Jahrhunderts," *Amerikastudien* 40, no. 4 (1995): 621–22; Fitzpatrick, *Liberal Imperialism*, 195.

by claiming forested lands and building their own wooden houses in the vast backwoods. On the other hand, America's native population was deprived of the possibility to control its own destiny. Speaking about California Indians, Gerstäcker thus observed, "They go down the path that all wild peoples follow; some slowly, some more quickly, yet they all march inevitably towards their certain doom." Gerstäcker realized the injustice inherent in this development, but did not see an alternative to it: "Therefore, the demise of the Indians is also unavoidable, because civilization spreads out further and further and cannot be held back." For him, European expansion was necessary and inevitable, and the victims of this global process were to be pitied but could not be helped.[29]

Since 1776, Germans had discussed the United States of America in debates about political progress, reform, race, and settler colonialism. During the 1830s and 1840s, the last two issues became increasingly prominent as growing numbers of accounts of German travelers to or settlers in the United States and its western territories were published in Germany. Friedrich List's perspectives and observations were much broader than those of "mere" travelogue writers like Duden or Gerstäcker, but all of them reached a wide German audience and linked American expansion to increased social and economic opportunities for both white Americans and newly arriving settlers. Whereas List described the progress of civilization and industrialization in the United States, Lewis Cass pointed out (to both American and German audiences) that this process was necessarily accompanied by the displacement and "vanishing" of America's natives.

---

[29] Friedrich Gerstäcker, *Streif- und Jagdzüge*, 2 vols. (Dresden: in der Arnold-schen Buchhandlung, 1844), 124–25, 156–57; Friedrich Gerstäcker, *Reisen*, 4 vols. (Stuttgart: J. G. Cotta'scher Verlag, 1853), 320, 369–73; Friedrich Gerstäcker, *California Gold Mines* (Oakland: Biobooks, 1946), 81; Friedrich Gerstäcker, *Neue Reisen*, 3 vols. (Jena: Hermann Costenoble, 1876), 200–01; Jeffrey L. Sammons, "Nineteenth-Century German Representations of Indians from Experience," in *Germans and Indians* (Lincoln: University of Nebraska Press, 2002), 188–90.

The flipside of the spread of white Americans and European immigrants over the North American continent was thus the active removal of Native Americans from the territories coveted by whites. For the readers of geographical journals such as *Das Ausland* or the writings of Friedrich List, thinking about America increasingly meant pondering the connected issues of sociopolitical opportunity and space, on the one hand, and questions of race, in particular the disappearance of allegedly racially inferior Indians and, as Morton's studies suggested, the justified exploitation of black slaves, on the other. During the 1830s and 1840s, German debates about the United States very clearly suggested that in America, the continuous creation of social, political, and economic opportunities for white Americans and European immigrants depended on settling the West and controlling allegedly inferior races: in the case of most African Americans through enslavement or, for Native Americans, through expulsion and sometimes extinction.

Yet views that either embraced or at least accepted slavery, negative perceptions of Amerindians, and U.S. Indian removal policies were by no means dominant in German debates, especially before 1848. Sharp criticism of these phenomena existed as well. It is hardly surprising that Germans held more than one viewpoint in respect to the United States and American westward expansion. However, just how multifaceted America-related debates were in early nineteenth-century Germany has often been ignored. Instead, scholars have painted the picture of an all-pervasive (and naïve) German infatuation with Native Americans and of a lofty rejection of slavery especially by German liberals. This simplistic analysis of nineteenth-century German perceptions of the United States as well as of German liberalism was then used to construct an allegedly clear chronological divide between "good" (albeit not politically savvy) German liberals until 1848 and "bad" liberals after 1866 – the year in which the Prussian Progressive Party split into a right-nationalist faction that supported Bismarck's aggressive unification policies, and a left-liberal faction that opposed them. Yet the topics of empire, expansion, and America demonstrate that such a separation between pre–1848–49 and postrevolutionary liberals is at the very least partially arbitrary.[30]

Visions of Unity and American Colonies

As in much of continental Europe, in the German lands the social and political tensions underlying public debates during the 1830s and 1840s finally resulted in more than a year of social unrest and revolution between March 1848 and the summer of 1849. During this period liberals had the chance not only to debate German politics but also to shape them. From May 18, 1848, until May 31, 1849, the first freely elected German parliament met in Frankfurt. Along with the all-important question of national unity, the National Assembly discussed economic and social problems, as well as questions of empire. All these topics were linked. As historian Matthew Fitzpatrick argues, for Frankfurt parliamentarians

---

[30] On this phenomenon, see James J. Sheehan, *German Liberalism in the Nineteenth Century* (Chicago: University of Chicago Press, 1978); Geoff Eley, "Review: James Sheehan and the German Liberals: A Critical Appreciation," *Central European History* 14, no. 3 (1981): 279–80; David Blackbourn and Geoff Eley, *Mythen deutscher Geschichtsschreibung. Die gescheiterte bürgerliche Revolution von 1848* (Ullstein Taschenbuchverlag, 1986), 75; Dieter Langewiesche, *Liberalismus in Deutschland,* in *Neue historische Bibliothek* (Frankfurt am Main: Suhrkamp, 1988). On liberal German views on America, Native Americans, and slavery around 1848, see Horst Dippel, "Die Wirkung der amerikanischen Revolution auf Deutschland und Frankreich," *200 Jahre amerikanische Revolution und moderne Revolutionsforschung. Geschichte und Gesellschaft* Sonderheft, no. II (1976); Dippel, *Germany and the American Revolution*; Horst Dippel, *Die Amerikanische Verfassung in Deutschland im 19. Jahrhundert* (Goldbach: Keip Verlag, 1994); Mauch, "Indianer und Schwarze"; Susanne Zantop, *Colonial Fantasies: Conquest, Family, and Nation in Precolonial Germany, 1770–1870* (Durham: Duke University Press, 1997); Volker Depkat, *Amerikabilder in politischen Diskursen* (Stuttgart: Klett-Cotta, 1998); Willi Paul Adams, "The Declaration of Independence in Germany," *Journal of American History* (1999): 62–75; Hartmut Lutz, "German Indianthusiasm: A Socially Constructed German National(ist) Myth," in *Germans and Indians. Fantasies, Encounters, Projections,* ed. Colin G. Calloway, Gerd Gemünden, and Susanne Zantop (Lincoln: University of Nebraska Press, 2002); H. Glenn Penny, "Elusive Authenticity: The Quest for the Authentic Indian in German Public Culture," *Comparative Studies in Society and History* 48, no. 4 (2006).

"expansionism offered a mechanism for constructing, uniting, and identifying a new liberal German nation." Deputies viewed overseas expansionism as a solution for, not a deflection of, the "social question" – a term denoting the many problems (migration, dislocation, and poverty) created by the beginnings of industrialization in Germany. Because over the previous decades German writers had increasingly identified U.S. policies as exemplary when it came to solving these problems, America was never far from the Frankfurt parliamentarians' minds.[31]

The deputies scrutinized the United States as a potential model for the yet-to-be-created German federal state. Yet because of the "social question," the topics of emigration and colonization always loomed in the background. In June 1848, the economic committee of the National Assembly received a petition from the German Association in Le Havre asking for assistance for the many German emigrants to the United States who filled this French city; after all, German monarchical authorities had already provided aid: "The royal consul of Wuerttemberg has been empowered by his government to cover the costs of sending the subjects in question to America." Simultaneously, the committee collected a host of petitions that demanded the establishment of German colonies abroad. The members of the National Assembly were thus forced to ponder concurrently the questions of emigration, colonization, and America.[32]

There can be no question that the liberal deputies of the first national and freely elected German parliament believed the acquisition of overseas territories to be of paramount importance for a future German nation-state. Various continents and countries were envisioned as possible venues for German overseas expansion, including Asia, South Africa, and South America. Yet the

[31] Fitzpatrick, *Liberal Imperialism*, 28.
[32] Dippel, "Wirkung"; Willi Paul Adams, *Deutschland und Amerika* (Berlin: Colloquium Verag, 1985); Werner Conze and Wolfgang Zorn, *Die Protokolle des Volkswirtschaftlichen Ausschusses der deutschen Nationalversammlung 1848/49* (Boppard am Rhein: Harald Boldt Verlag, 1992), 457, 461; Dippel, *Amerikanische Verfassung in Deutschland*; Adams, "Declaration of Independence."

American West was by far the most popular focus of liberal German colonial fantasies during the 1840s. In 1848, German liberals appeared to be even more enchanted with America than Hans Christoph von Gagern had been in 1817. Few sentiments underscore the allure of American westward expansion for German liberal imperialists better than these entirely unrealistic ideas. The United States was so inspiring in respect to questions of empire and expansion that many of those lobbying for the establishment of German overseas territories wanted the future German colonies to be on American soil, despite the obvious impracticality of such plans (which at least some colonialist writers pointed out). After all, Germans were increasingly aware of the United States' exclusive territorial claims in North America's western regions. However, the American West was simply too tempting for German colonialists to give up the idea of a New Germany on American soil.[33]

During the 1840s, one of the most important national-liberal newspapers, Baron von Cotta's *Augsburger Allgemeine Zeitung*, repeatedly recommended the United States not only as the best destination for German emigrants but also endorsed it as the best location for German colonies. Other publications did so as well, among them Ernst Ludwig Brauns' *Neudeutschland in Westamerika* [A New Germany in Western America (1847)] and Hermann Blumenau's *Deutsche Auswanderung und Colonisation* [German Emigration and Colonization (1846)]. The latter work was a short pamphlet aimed at popularizing the idea of German colonization projects. Blumenau's main point was that "the emigration question is the most important question [Lebensfrage] for Germany's future." To underscore the nationalist allure of a German colonial empire, Blumenau asked his readers to imagine how important "the 5,000,000 Germans in the Union would be if

---

[33] On the popularity of the American West within colonial debates during the *Vormärz* years, see Fenske, "Imperialisitische Tendenzen," 347 and Frank Lorenz Müller, "Imperialist Ambitions in Vormärz and Revolutionary Germany: The Agitation for German Settlement Colonies Overseas, 1840–1849," *German History* 17, no. 3 (1999): 354. See also Fitzpatrick, *Liberal Imperialism*, 10.

they only had their own state or lived in a contiguous territory." Barely more realistic than other liberal advocates for German colonies on American soil, Blumenau concluded his pamphlet with the prospect of a New Germany in California, which he believed to be protected from Anglo-American settlers by the Rocky Mountains. In Blumenau's view, a "Germanization" of "Ober-Californien" would be even better for German settlers than the establishment of German colonies in South America.[34]

During the revolutionary years of 1848–49, the ground was thus well prepared for voicing these ideas in the Frankfurt parliament. For a fleeting moment, the prospect of a liberal, united Germany appeared to provide these America-focused colonial fantasies with an aura of possibility. On March 15, 1849, in a long speech about the need for German overseas expansion, the liberal Friedrich Schulz thus argued for the acquisition of colonies in the American West by the yet-to-be-established united Germany:

It would not be difficult for the national government to procure spacious territories from the United States on friendlier terms than any individual.... Across the great ocean a powerful, magnificent New Germany can blossom, which will make the natural friendship between us and the United States even stronger. But if we do not hurry, we will also come too late in Western America, at least for extensive colonies.

Schulz was not the only Frankfurt deputy who looked toward the United States when pondering German colonialism. Johann Tellkampf, who was one of the most vocal proponents of overseas expansion in Frankfurt, argued that the newly established German government should actively "protect" German immigrants in the United States so as to create a German quasi-colony there: "If we watch over our German emigrants ... they will be more willing to support trade measures through the influence of their votes; such measures would be equally valuable for the United States and Germany." Similar concepts prevailed for a

<hr>

[34] Hermann Blumenau, *Deutsche Auswanderung und Colonisation* (Leipzig: J. E. Wappäus, 1846), 2, 99, 103 and Müller, "Imperialist Ambitions in Vormärz and Revolutionary Germany," 354.

long time in German discussions of America and also found their way into popular magazines such as *Die Gartenlaube* [The Gazebo], which reported "that it truly appears to be no illusory hope that the future of the great trans-Atlantic republic will be won for the Germans."[35]

Moreover, Germans not only talked about colonizing the American West; they tried to do it too. Between 1842 and 1853, the Mainzer Adelsverein [Aristocrats' Association] attempted to organize a German colonial settlement in Texas. Its colonization efforts eventually failed because of organizational incompetence and lack of funds. Yet the American West's allure was so strong for German colonialists that visions of German colonies on American soil died hard. Thirty-five years later, when the united Germany was (finally, from the vantage point of German liberals) beginning to acquire overseas territories, right-liberal colonial enthusiasts like Friedrich Ratzel were still referencing the idea of a New Germany on North American soil.[36]

The revolution of 1848–49 failed to create a German nation-state. Because of this failure, the twin topics of expansion and America remained a focus of German liberals even after 1849, although their discussion was necessarily moved from the open political arena of the Frankfurt parliament to the realm of intellectual discourse. The ever expanding United States was

---

[35] Franz Wigard, *Stenographischer Bericht über die Verhandlungen der deutschen constituirenden Nationalversammlung zu Frankfurt am Main*, vol. 8 (Frankfurt am Main: 1849), 5721; Franz Wigard, *Stenographischer Bericht über die Verhandlungen der deutschen constituirenden Nationalversammlung zu Frankfurt am Main*, vol. 2 (Frankfurt am Main: 1848), 1057; *Die Gartenlaube* (1869), 809.

[36] Fenske, "Imperialisitische Tendenzen," 370–71 and Müller, "Imperialist Ambitions in Vormärz and Revolutionary Germany," 356. Compare also Brian Vick in Michael Perraudin and Jürgen Zimmerer, eds., *German Colonialism and National Identity* (Milton Park: Routledge, 2011). Vick attempts to refute historians who argue for the importance of concepts of overseas expansion in the Paulskirche debates, yet Vick does not address Matthew Fitzpatrick's work and thus does not consider the impressive amount of evidence compiled by him.

inspirational: America's increasing size and success demonstrated not only that ideas of a liberal German nation-state were viable but also that their eventual implementation was a necessity. Only as an expanding, globally active nation could Germany ever aspire to reach American heights. These sentiments were thinly veiled criticisms of the reactionary atmosphere in the German states during the 1850s. The cause of liberal German nation-alism had been temporarily defeated, a development that made the German states move backward, not forward, at least in the view of German liberals. The American republic represented the future. In 1853, the co-editor of the popular liberal journal *Die Gartenlaube*, Ferdinand Stolle, thus opined that in Wash-ington, DC, "quiet anticipation is dawning that this is the place where eventually the fate of the whole world will be decided." In Stolle's view, America's bright future was also linked to its terri-torial expansion: "[F]or a long time already, star upon star has been added to the Union's banner." As Stolle admitted, it was sad to see that the American republic was erected on the graves of the continent's original inhabitants, yet observers could take comfort in the fact that America was on course to "become a Hercules among nations" – a prospect that made the Native Americans' "vanishing" meaningful. The editor of the *Gartenlaube* had no doubts: The United States was both a liberal republic and at the same time a "mighty empire." As a result, the nation's "vitality and growth" had "*no* [italics in original] historical rival, either in ancient times or today."[37]

Liberal journals such as *Die Gartenlaube* and more scientific publications such as *Das Ausland* or *Petermann's Mittheilungen* reported often and in detail on the United States and on thriv-ing German settlements in America. Unlike in Germany, in the "Free States" of America Germans prospered and contributed in important ways to the advancement of this "mighty [American]

---

[37] Ernst Keil, the journal's main editor, was in prison at the time because of his (too) liberal publications. See *Die Gartenlaube* (1853), 550–51; *Die Garten-laube* (1854), 40. On the importance of *Die Gartenlaube* within liberal milieus in post-1848 Germany, see Fitzpatrick, *Liberal Imperialism*, 178.

empire.'" Yet at the same time, at least according to *Gartenlaube* reports, the establishment of informal German "colonies" on American soil also underwrote liberal hopes for a united German nation-state. *Die Gartenlaube*'s features on America argued that through the activities of German immigrants "Germany has risen greatly in esteem." Long before German unification and its acquisition of colonies, the *Gartenlaube* conveyed the impression that there existed a positive feedback effect between German settlements on American soil and the rise of Germany's standing in the world. For the liberal *Gartenlaube*, German greatness and unity were issues with clear transatlantic and, ultimately, global dimensions. German settlements abroad and the achievements of their settlers (even within another nation's territory) helped the cause of German nationalism at home: Colonialism was portrayed as an integral part of the liberal quest to achieve German national unity, and viewed from a liberal vantage point German "colonies" in the "American Free States" highlighted the positive correlation between overseas expansion and national unity exceptionally well. During the 1850s the *Gartenlaube*'s authors painted distorted pictures of German immigrant communities in America, which greatly downplayed their "Americanness," while at the same time stressing their independent, colonial character.

These sentiments pointed to the future: Naturally, the *Gartenlaube* would have preferred to report on "real" German colonies, and after 1884 it would finally be able to do so. The American historian Frederick Jackson Turner recognized the connection between fantasies of German colonies in the American West and Germany's eventual acquisition of colonies in Africa and Asia. In 1893, nine years after the German Empire had become a colonial power, Turner remarked that "[r]ecent events make it worthwhile considering whether the attempt [to create German colonies on American soil] did not succeed!" Turner went on to explain that it was only natural that the unofficial and "spontaneous" German colonization of the American West had left a legacy that eventually "compelled the German government to develop a colonial policy of its own, in order to divert the stream into lands politically dependent upon Germany."[38]

Jefferson believed that the United States depended on virtuous farmer-citizens to remain a republic, and as long as they were provided with western lands for continuous colonization, Americans would remain independent and republican-minded farmers who – in contrast to European wage laborers who were dependent on their employers and therefore could not make free decisions – could control their destinies. As late as 1848, this expansion-focused republicanism seemed to find echoes in the speeches of Germany's liberal revolutionaries. These Germans did not repeat Jefferson's sentiments exactly, but they certainly linked expansion with ideas of societal rejuvenation. Johann Tellkampf thus argued that colonies strengthened a country's youth, because "in the territories that are to be cultivated it finds unlimited elbowroom in order to release its energies." Two decades earlier, Alexander von Humboldt and Friedrich List outlined the connections between both global and American westward expansion and the dawning of a new era in which not only American cities were connected to their western hinterland but the world at large had also become a place where, as Humboldt put it, oceans were no longer obstacles but had turned into "channels" that facilitated trade and "civilization." However, whereas Jefferson's view of the American West was based on the belief that expansion would arrest America's development and would maintain the country's agricultural purity and virtue, German observers, even as early as 1826, clearly felt that America's constant reach beyond the frontiers of its current settlements did not signify stasis but rather positive change.

Lewis Cass's argument for Indian removal was that Native Americans were incapable of changing and hence had to leave:

---

[38] *Die Gartenlaube* quoted in Fitzpatrick, *Liberal Imperialism*, 180; *Die Gartenlaube* (1853), 551; Frederick Jackson Turner, "American Colonization," in *The Eloquence of Frederick Jackson Turner*, ed. Ronald H. Carpenter (San Marino: Huntington Library, [1893] 1983), 190. See also Matthew Fitzpatrick's analysis of the links between domestic perceptions of Germans abroad and liberal reform at home. Fitzpatrick, *Liberal Imperialism*, 193–94.

Expansion equaled progress and progress necessitated expansion and, as far as Native Americans were concerned, expulsion and/or extinction. During the 1820s, 30s, and 40s, in Germany the emerging liberal and nationalist movement strongly embraced these views. For several reasons its proponents' gaze became fixed on the United States. Although Britain and France were also constantly on the minds of German liberals, these countries were not as directly relevant for the still-to-be-created Germany as the United States. Both America and Germany were still "becoming," and their respective potentials were not yet fulfilled, although the United States was many steps ahead of Germany. Moreover, in respect to the "vanishing" of America's native population, at least the *Gartenlaube* believed that the very fact of the United States' immense potential offered comfort and solace: "There is always woefulness around a dying nation [the *Gartenlaube* was referring to the "Indian nation"]; yet here there's comfort in the fact that on the grave of the former there stands the cradle of another which promises to become a Hercules among nations."[39]

Germans were determined to catch up to the United States. In 1848, some German liberals believed that Germany's territorial "catching up" could be done on American soil: It was the United States and not the British or the French Empire that set the example regarding expansion. Around the middle of the nineteenth century a number of conservative European politicians embraced a similar view that colonial empires as maintained by France and Britain were a thing of the past. In 1852, Benjamin Disraeli referred to Britain's colonies as "millstones around our necks." As late as 1868 Bismarck concurred and viewed the alleged advantages of colonial expansion as "illusory." However, both leaders were forced to change their minds. In the end, even Bismarck, who has traditionally been portrayed as a quasi-omnipotent controller and manipulator of politics in the German Empire, had to respond to popular, liberal-bourgeois

---

[39] *Die Gartenlaube* (1853), 551 and Wigard, *Stenographischer Bericht über die Verhandlungen der deutschen constituirenden Nationalversammlung zu Frankfurt am Main*, 1057.

pressure to develop "a politically resonant Kolonialpolitik." Liberals like Tellkampf, Schulz, or the editors of the *Gartenlaube* never shared Bismarck's or Disraeli's (temporary) disdain for colonial expansion, partially because they looked in a different direction than did these conservative diplomats. Unlike the British Empire, American western expansion was a harbinger of things to come. After all, as the *Gartenlaube* so clearly discerned in 1853, "as an empire" the United States remained unrivaled by any other state, and it was on American soil where, again according to the *Gartenlaube*, "Germandom would accomplish its mission first."[40]

During the middle years of the nineteenth century, for German liberals the settlement of America, German national unity, and German colonialism formed a single discursive field. American westward expansion inspired colonialist dreams in Germany that, ideally, were supposed to become reality in America itself. Yet even if these dreams did not come true, the presence of German "colonies" (i.e., regions with many German immigrants and German Americans) within the United States inspired hope for progress and national unity at home. Under the auspices of America's liberal and progressive political system, German settlers showed their true and potent selves. From the perspective of German liberals, this interpretation of German mass emigration to the United States was entirely self-serving because it inextricably linked the topics of colonialism, political progress, and national unity with liberal political ideas.

---

[40] *Die Gartenlaube* (1856), 111; Hendrik L. Wesseling, *Teile und herrsche. Die Aufteilung Afrikas 1880–1914* (Stuttgart: Franz Steiner Verlag, 1999), 37, 105. On Bismarck responding to pressure from the National-Liberal Party, see Fitzpatrick, *Liberal Imperialism*, 122–23. See also H. Washausen, *Hamburg und die Kolonialpolitik des Deutschen Reiches, 1880 bis 1890* (Hamburg: H. Christians, 1968), 142.

2

From Theory to Practice

German Colonialism and American Westward Expansion before World War I

Not Quebec but Boston became the trading center of the westerly waters. Although France bought wood from Canada at prices that were much too high, it was not the woods around the St. Lawrence that were thinned out. Rather, field after field was cleared between the Hudson and the St. John's River. In short, although French-Canada basked in the full sun of government attention, it remained a dead edifice; English North America, which received only one merciful gift from its mother country, namely that its development would be disturbed as little as possible, blossomed in the liveliest fashion: the sturdy child which in its adulthood would become the North American giant. From this historic fact of world-wide importance one can deduce an eternally valid program for practical colonialism.[1]

Carl Peters, the author of these lines, was Imperial Germany's most notorious colonialist. Peters traveled the United States extensively in 1893 and was full of admiration for that country's successful settlement of much of the North American continent. Like other German colonialists he was most impressed with the apparent relationship between "self-government" and America's successful westward expansion. And he was quite willing to admit that American-style "liberal colonialism," as Peters put

---

[1] Carl Peters, *Carl Peters gesammelte Schriften*, ed. Walter Frank, vol. 1 (Munich: C. H. Beck'sche Verlagsbuchhandlung, 1943), 378.

it, had led to the expulsion and/or extermination of the native population. He therefore upbraided his critics for believing "that colonies with independent administrations are distinguished by a particular softheartedness towards aboriginal tribes" and advised them to take a look at "how the free English settlements in North America treated the Indians."[2]

Sentiments like these were neither new nor a feature of Peters' eccentric personality alone. In 1884, Friedrich Ratzel regretted that it was too late for Germany to colonize North America – and expressed his view that the United States' successful settlement of the continent should be an inspiration for Germany to colonize Africa. Twenty-three years after Ratzel, and ten years after Peters, the director of the colonial office in Berlin, Bernhard Dernburg, proclaimed that the United States in general and American west-ward expansion in particular were important reference points for German colonization efforts. After all, the United States was "the biggest colonial endeavor the world has ever known," although it had, unfortunately yet inevitably, begun with the "complete extermination" of America's native population. These and simi-lar perceptions about the United States and American westward expansion, though not uncontested, were so widely shared in the early years of the twentieth century that, during and after Lothar von Trotha's murderous campaign against the Herero and Nama in German Southwest Africa (GWSA), colonial administrators and proponents of colonialism in both GSWA and the German mainland viewed American westward expansion and Indian poli-cies as worthy of emulation in Germany's only settler colony. In fact, the United States was omnipresent in German colonial dis-course, as colonialists also attempted to import American cotton cultivation methods from the American South to German-Togo, or, as explored in Chapter 3, justified the implementation of race decrees in GSWA, East Africa, and German Samoa against an American backdrop.[3]

[2] Ibid., 393, 406–07.
[3] Friedrich Ratzel, *Wider die Reichsnörgler: Ein Wort zur Kolonialfrage aus Wählerkreisen* (München: 1884), 23 and Bernhard Dernburg, "Speech in Front

By 1914, many Germans were familiar with representations of America as a nation destined to grow and in doing so to educate, dominate, and sometimes exterminate other races. Many German imperialists, scholars, and writers therefore viewed the extinction of Amerindians at the very least as inevitable, and some even saw it as necessary. Over the course of the nineteenth century German proponents of colonialism increasingly identified American expansionism and racial policies as models that colonizers could replicate elsewhere in the world – in particular in German Southwest Africa. Of all the German colonies, only Southwest Africa had a sizable settler population. By 1903, slightly less than 5,000 Europeans lived in the colony, but the number tripled within a decade. As a result, the settlement of the American West was viewed as especially relevant for GSWA. Moreover, German observers attributed the success of America's westward expansion to laissez-faire principles and the United States' liberal political system. These reflections made American colonization practices especially attractive for liberal German expansionists. Because of the United States' impressive growth and developing world-power status, the draw of the American model transcended the sphere of German political liberalism, eliciting the appreciation of colonial enthusiasts from nationalist and conservative backgrounds. Yet even they acknowledged that liberal, laissez-faire attitudes underwrote America's successful expansionism in the most powerful way.[4]

of the Kolonialpolitisches Aktionskomité," in *Reichstagsauflösung und Kolonialpolitik*, ed. Gustav Schmoller (Berlin: Wedekind, 1907), 7–8.

4 Paul Rohrbach, *Die deutschen Kolonien* (Dachau: Der Gelbe Verlag Mundt & Blumtritt, 1914), 23; Paul Rohrbach, *Buch der deutschen Kolonien*, (Leipzig: Wilhelm Goldmann Verlag, 1937), 115; Christof Mauch, "Indianer und Schwarze aus deutscher Perspektive: Sichtweisen des 19. Jahrhunderts," *Amerikastudien* 40, no. 4 (1995): 625; Susanne Zantop, *Colonial Fantasies: Conquest, Family, and Nation in Precolonial Germany, 1770–1870* (Durham: Duke University Press, 1997), 2–16; Woodruff D. Smith, "'Weltpolitik' und 'Lebensraum,'" in *Das Kaiserreich transnational: Deutschland in der Welt 1871–1914* (Göttingen: Vandenhoeck & Ruprecht, 2004), 36–37; Sebastian Conrad, *Globalisierung und Nation im Deutschen Kaiserreich* (München: C. H. Beck, 2006), 104–05, 117, 118, 236–37; Lora Wildenthal et al., "German Colonial Imagination," *German History* 26, no. 2 (2008). On the usage

Nineteenth-Century German Colonial Discourse, Indians, and American Expansion

A number of scholars have argued for the importance of American frontier imagery for Nazi imperialism in Eastern Europe, a perspective that is further explored in Chapter 4. In contrast, the significance of the American frontier and American westward expansion within nineteenth- and early twentieth-century German colonial discourse has so far gone largely unnoticed. Moreover, although there exists a broad literature on the popularity of romanticized images of American Indians in Germany, the important role played by "ignoble savage" perceptions of Amerindians in debates linked to German expansionism has garnered little scholarly interest.[5]

Using the popularity of Karl May's Western novels in late nineteenth- and twentieth-century Germany as a starting point, the literary scholar Susanne Zantop has argued that, from the eighteenth to the mid-twentieth century and later, "enthusiasm for things Indian... has particularly flourished in the German lands." For a variety of political, social, and cultural reasons – for example, the craving for political freedom or a sense of inadequacy vis-à-vis France or Great Britain – Germans, much more

of the term "Indian" see Colin G Calloway, *The World Turned Upside Down* (Boston: Bedford Books, 1994), vii.
[5] Benjamin Madley, "Patterns of Frontier Genocide 1803–1910," *Journal of Genocide Research* 6, no. 2 (2004): 183; H. Glenn Penny, "Elusive Authenticity: The Quest for the Authentic Indian in German Public Culture," *Comparative Studies in Society and History* 48, no. 4 (2006): 798–99; David Blackbourn, *The Conquest of Nature: Water, Landscape and the Making of Modern Germany* (London: Jonathan Cape, 2006), 280–96; Caroll P. Kakel, *The American West and the Nazi East: A Comparative and Interpretive Perspective* (Basingstoke: Palgrave Macmillan, 2011). Compare Mauch, "Indianer und Schwarze aus deutscher Perspektive"; Alan E. Steinweis, "Eastern Europe and the Notion of the 'Frontier' in Germany to 1945," *Yearbook of European Studies* 13 (1999); Erik Grimmer-Solem, "The Professors' Africa: Economists, the Elections of 1907, and the Legitimation of German Imperialism," *German History* 25, no. 3 (2007): 325; George Steinmetz, *The Devil's Handwriting: Precoloniality and the German Colonial State in Qingdao, Samoa, and Southwest Africa* (Chicago: University of Chicago Press, 2007), 238–39.

than other Europeans, empathized, sympathized, and identified with American Indians. Historian H. Glenn Penny, who
has traced the German fascination with Native Americans from
the nineteenth to the late twentieth century, reinforces Zantop's
assessment. There is no doubt that romanticized images of Native
Americans were fashionable in late nineteenth-century Germany.
After the German Empire's founding in 1871, a national mass
market for cheap and widely available publications emerged,
and Indian fiction became increasingly popular. Yet the fact
that romanticized views of Native Americans were stock features of widely sold pulp westerns does not tell us whether
nineteenth-century Germans were more or less fascinated by Indians than were other Europeans. When German perceptions of
Native Americans are viewed against a European backdrop, German fascination with and interest in Native Americans seem less
exceptional. For example, recent studies show the British fascination with Indians and comparisons of late eighteenth- and early
nineteenth-century French and German perceptions of Amerindians demonstrate how views of Indians functioned in similar fashion in both French and German discourses about Europe's aristocracy during the first half of the nineteenth century.[6]

---

[6] Compare Penny, "Elusive Authenticity," 798–99. See also Christian F. Feest,
"The Indian in Non-English Literature," in *History of Indian-White Relations*,
ed. Wilcomb E. Washburn (Washington, DC: Smithsonian Institution, 1988);
Peter J. Brenner, *Reisen in die Neue Welt* (Tübingen: Niemeyer, 1991), 212–18;
Mauch, "Indianer und Schwarze aus deutscher Perspektive"; Zantop, *Colonial
Fantasies*, 3, 7, 9, 14, 90; Susanne Zantop, "The Beautiful, the Ugly, and the
German: Race, Gender and Nationality in Eighteenth-Century Anthropologi-
cal Discourse," in *Gender and Germanness* (Providence: Berghahn, 1997), 23;
Harry Liebersohn, *Aristocratic Encounters: European Travelers and North-
American Indians* (Cambridge: Cambridge University Press, 1998), 5, 166–
70; Susanne Zantop, "'Der Indianer' im Rasse- und Geschlechterdiskurs der
deutschen Spätaufklärung," in *Das Subjekt und die Anderen: Interkultur-
alität und Geschlechterdifferenz vom 18. Jahrhundert bis zur Gegenwart*, ed.
Viktoria Schmidt-Linsenhoff (Berlin: 2001), 133; the following chapters in
Germans and Indians: Fantasies, Encounters, Projections, ed. Colin G. Cal-
loway, Gerd Gemünden, and Susanne Zantop (Lincoln: University of Nebraska
Press, 2002): Hartmut Lutz, "German Indianthusiasm: A Socially Constructed
German National(ist) Myth," 167; Christian F. Feest, "Germany's Indians in a
European Perspective," 36, 37; and Zantop, "Close Encounters: Deutsche and

Nonetheless, Karl May was widely read in early twentieth-century Germany, and his popularity raises several questions. Does May's attractiveness for (mostly male) teenagers at the turn of the century tell us anything about his overall cultural impact? Moreover, although May himself was not politically active on behalf of Native Americans and other aboriginals worldwide, were his readers so involved? Regarding these questions, Jeffrey L. Sammons, one of the most prominent in a long line of literary scholars dealing with Karl May, believes "that the [May] phenomenon escapes final analysis, because it is over-determined and, perhaps, to some degree accidental. I draw no conclusion about the 'German mind' from it." Opinions differ widely regarding both Karl May's influence on his German readers and how accurately he expressed fin-de-siècle German attitudes toward Native Americans, with Sammons representing one end of the spectrum and Zantop the other. Debates about May's sway over his readers and the importance of romanticized images of Native Americans for Germans help us understand the colonial imaginary in nineteenth- and early twentieth-century Germany. They also provide vital elements of this study's social, cultural, and historical backdrop. However, the subjects of this chapter – among others Dernburg, Hermann Müller, Paul Rohrbach, and Theodor Leutwein – were unaffected by both May and the general German enthusiasm for American Indians because they were interested in successful models of settler colonialism. Romanticized perceptions were thus by no means the only perspectives on Amerindians that can be located in Germany during this period. Influential antithetical views existed. Because of their explicitly pro-expansionist overtones, these perceptions of Indians as

Indianer," 4, 13 (note 8); Pamela Kort, "'The Unmastered Past of the Indians' Murder,'" in *I like America: Fictions of the Wild West*, ed. Pamela Kort and Max Hollein (Munich: Prestel, 2006), 45; Penny, "Elusive Authenticity," 798 (note 1); H. Glenn Penny, "Illustrating America. Images of the North American Wild West in German Periodicals, 1825–1890," in *I like America: Fictions of the Wild West*, ed. Pamela Kort and Max Hollein (Munich: Prestel, 2006); Kate Flint, *The Transatlantic Indian* (Princeton: Princeton University Press, 2009).

ignoble savages belonged to transnational discussions surrounding the subject of settler colonialism and existed separately from romanticized images of Native Americans.[7]

Germans, like Americans, had held pro-expansionist and at times exterminatory attitudes vis-à-vis Native Americans ever since the late eighteenth century. German immigrants moved westward along with Americans and other Europeans, embracing negative frontier attitudes toward Indians, which then found their way back to Germany. In nineteenth-century American debates about the continent's native peoples, "ignoble savage" takes on Indians coexisted with popular "noble savage" perceptions. After all, James Fenimore Cooper's *Last of the Mohicans* was selling very well when Lewis Cass, Andrew Jackson's secretary of war, published his infamous "Indian removal" essay in 1831 and when, a half-century later, Theodore Roosevelt stated, "I don't go so far as to think that the only good Indians are dead Indians, but I believe nine out of ten are, and I shouldn't like to inquire too closely into the case of the tenth." Because the settlement of the West was not only an American but also a transatlantic enterprise that included many first-generation European settlers, German deliberations about Native Americans displayed similarly dual characteristics.[8]

Viewed from the perspective of historians of the American West, Karl May therefore does not so much appear to be particularly German as European or transatlantic: Although perhaps the most successful, he was merely one of a number of nineteenth-century authors writing novels about the "Wild West," including James Fenimore Cooper (the genre's creator), the French

---

[7] Karl May, *Winnetou I* (Bamberg: Bayerische Verlagsanstalt, [1892] 1950), 5–6; Jeffrey L. Sammons, *Ideology, Mimesis, Fantasy: Charles Sealsfield, Friedrich Gerstäcker, Karl May, and Other German Novelists of America* (Chapel Hill: University of North Carolina Press, 1998), 229; Viktor Otto, *Deutsche Amerika-Bilder. Zu den Intellektuellen-Diskursen um die Moderne 1900–1950* (Munich: Wilhelm Fink, 2006), 89–109 (esp. 96–97), 143–85. See also Matthew P. Fitzpatrick, *Liberal Imperialism in Germany: Expansionism and Nationalism, 1848–1884* (New York: Berghahn Books, 2008), 197–98.

[8] Hermann Hagedorn, *Roosevelt in the Badlands* (Boston: Houghton Mifflin, 1921), 355.

Gustave Aimard (who, as historian Ray Allen Billington recounts, could only keep up with demand for his books by publishing one a month), or the Englishman Percy St. John.[9]

The nineteenth-century German fascination with Native Americans was therefore not a national peculiarity but rather a transnational regularity. In consequence, the question of the role and place of negative assessments of Amerindians within German discussions of America deserves close scrutiny. By the last third of the nineteenth century, Germans had long been discussing Indians within the context of American and European colonial expansion and in so doing had often displayed little sympathy for America's indigenous population. Throughout the nineteenth century, negative perceptions of Native Americans were part of discussions about the geopolitical role of the progressively more important United States. This debate was closely linked to ideas about the position of the German states and, after 1871, that of the German Empire in a world increasingly shaped by European imperialism.

The "ignoble native" topos had a clear function within the broader context of German imperialist aspirations. Because the successful acquisition of territory in North America by the United States, or Great Britain before 1776, had always been connected with encountering and controlling aboriginal peoples, and sometimes with their demise, German colonizers would do well to take a close look at native policies in North America. Instead of viewing themselves as better colonizers than other Europeans or North Americans, many German imperialists accepted the Anglo-American colonial experience as normative and urged their compatriots to follow the examples set by English-speaking colonizers in America and elsewhere. The links between German perceptions of the American frontier and German debates about what to do in GSWA indicate that nineteenth- and early twentieth-century German imperialism was embedded in a transnational

[9] Ray Allen Billington, "The Plains and Deserts through European Eyes," *Western Historical Quarterly* 10, no. 4 (1979): 467–72; Ray Allen Billington, *Land of Savagery / Land of Promise* (New York: Norton, 1981), 139–41, 144–45; Flint, *The Transatlantic Indian*; Roger L. Nichols, "Western Attractions: Europeans and America," *Pacific Historical Review* 74, no. 1 (2005): 1, 2, 9.

network of intellectual and practical processes of exchange. This transatlantic set of connections was by no means solely focused on the United States, yet within this framework America played an important and so far largely ignored role.[10]

Expansion and Empire: Indians, America, and German Colonial Discourse after 1866

During the first half of the nineteenth century, intellectuals on both sides of the Atlantic believed America to be different from the Old World. In Europe, G. W. F. Hegel and Alexis de Tocqueville arrived at this conclusion precisely because of the existence of the American frontier. Hegel presented the idea of American exceptionalism in a nutshell when he argued that "North America will be comparable to Europe only after the measureless space which this country affords is filled." Tocqueville held similar beliefs, positing that "God himself gave them [the Americans] the means of remaining equal and free, by placing them on a boundless continent." Despite the fact that Tocqueville felt sincere regret when he witnessed Indian removal, he never indicted American expansion. On the contrary – anticipating some of Friedrich Ratzel's and Carl Peters' arguments, Tocqueville actually believed America to be a model for French Algeria. In Tocqueville's view, France's prestige and authority would increasingly rely on colonial possessions. As a result, he deemed "a wide range of colonial actions" to be justified.[11]

---

[10] Alexander Kuhn, *Zum Eingeborenenproblem in Deutsch-Südwestafrika* (Berlin: Dietrich Reimer (Ernst Vohsen), 1905), 3; Raymond F. Betts, "Immense Dimensions: The Impact of the American West on Late Nineteenth-Century European Thought about Expansion," *Western Historical Quarterly* 10, no. 2 (1979): 154; Zantop, *Colonial Fantasies*, 6–8; Sven Beckert, "From Tuskegee to Togo: The Problem of Freedom in the Empire of Cotton," *Journal of American History* 92, no. 2 (2005); Andrew Zimmerman, "A German Alabama in Africa: The Tuskegee Expedition to German Togo and the Transnational Origins of West African Cotton Growers," *American Historical Review* 110 (2005).

[11] Georg Wilhelm Friedrich Hegel, *Lectures on the Philosophy of World History* (Cambridge: Cambridge University Press, 1975), 170; Alexis de Tocqueville, *Democracy in America* (New York: Random House, 1981), 172, 173; David

Although America's westward expansion was important for Germans during the first half of the nineteenth century and inspired Germans to ponder the issues of progress, national unity, and colonialism, after 1850 individual travelers and members of the German scientific community increasingly noted that settlers along the American frontier implemented, in Tocqueville's words, "a wide range of colonial actions" that resulted in twin processes of expansion and extinction. As white Americans and Europeans settled more and more territory, America's indigenous peoples disappeared. This outcome linked the American frontier to other areas colonized by Europeans such as Australia and Africa. German perceptions of "vanishing Indians" therefore normalized and globalized the American experience, because they challenged two core assumptions of the idea of U.S. exceptionalism: the distinctiveness of the American frontier and the uniquely benign nature of the United States. For many German observers of the United States during the second half of the nineteenth century, America's frontier was extremely fascinating, but it was not a national singularity and not exceptional. Instead, it was an example of a global phenomenon, which was a good thing: Because the United States was a typical colonial empire – in Dernburg's words, the "biggest" the world had ever known – its remarkably successful expansionist policies could and should be emulated in other colonial settings.[12]

M. Wrobel, *The End of American Exceptionalism* (Lawrence: University Press of Kansas, 1993), 4–5; Jennifer Pitts and Alexis de Tocqueville, *Writings on Empire and Slavery* (Baltimore: Johns Hopkins University Press, 2001), xiv–xv.

[12] Friedrich Gerstäcker, *Reisen*, 4 vols. (Stuttgart: J. G. Cotta'scher Verlag, 1853), 320, 369–73; Ida Pfeiffer, *Reise in die neue Welt: Amerika im Jahre 1853* (Wien: Promedia, 1994), 38–39, 132–33; Friedrich Gerstäcker, *Neue Reisen*, 3 vols. (Jena: Hermann Costenoble, 1876), 200–01; Ernst Haeckel, *Natürlich Schöpfungsgeschichte*, 10 ed., vol. 1 (Berlin: Georg Reimer, [1868] 1902), 242; Mark Bassin, "Turner, Solov'ev, and the 'Frontier Hypothesis,'" *Journal of Modern History* 65, no. 3 (1993): 473; Philipp Gassert, "'Without Concession to Marxist or Communist Thought': Fordism in Germany, 1923–1939," in *Transatlantic Images and Perceptions: Germany and America since 1776*, ed. David E. Barclay and Elisabeth Gläser-Schmidt (Cambridge: Cambridge University Press, 1997), 222–23.

In 1869, two years before the unification of Germany under Prussian hegemony, *Das Ausland*, a scientific journal edited by the Darwinist geographer Oscar Peschel, reviewed the latest book by the German traveler and popular novelist, Friedrich Gerstäcker. Peschel's review praised all of Gerstäcker's books for delivering "vivid" descriptions of life in America. For Gerstäcker, both American westward and European global expansion were "unavoidable" processes, the victims of which, whether Native American or African, were to be pitied but could not be helped. Peschel agreed, accepting the inevitability of European and (white) American expansion. Gerstäcker's depictions of the American expansion process were one of the reasons why Peschel promoted his publications, along with works by members of the scientific community and by other popular writers. Under his guidance, *Das Ausland* therefore occupied a key position in disseminating information in mid-nineteenth-century Germany on the American frontier and on other regions colonized by Europeans. *Das Ausland*'s first issue appeared in 1828, and the journal's publication ceased almost exactly seventy-five years later. Its focus and profile reflected the growing self-confidence of the German scientific community during the nineteenth century. *Das Ausland*'s reports and articles testify to the increasing importance of "hot" new scientific fields and disciplines from the 1850s on; for example, ethnography, biology, and geography.[13]

Because of its editors' prestige, *Das Ausland* was among the most important and well-respected popular scientific publications in nineteenth-century Germany. This elite group included the earlier mentioned Peschel, the ethnographer Friedrich Hellwald, and Friedrich Ratzel – all towering presences in their respective academic fields and all proponents of applying Darwinist approaches to their disciplines. Moreover, they and other scientists believed Darwinist principles to be all-purpose solutions for humankind's problems: Darwinism could be used to judge human behavior, to ground ethics and morality

---

[13] Gerstäcker, *Reisen*, 369–73, 320, Gerstäcker, *Neue Reisen*, 200–01. See also *Das Ausland* (1869): 149, *Das Ausland* (1863): 1103–04.

scientifically (as opposed to religiously or metaphysically), and, last but not least, to understand the rules underlying domestic and international politics. Unsurprisingly, these men also interpreted and advocated German, European, and (white) American expansion against a Darwinist backdrop. The evolutionary principle was a scientific verity; its workings had to be accepted, with or without regret. These sentiments are summed up in this passage by Friedrich Hellwald:

> [C]ontact with the culture of the higher race is a fatal poison for the lower race and kills them.... Equipped with knowledge of these laws, the spreading of civilization in the [North American] colonies can be satisfactorily explained. Native Americans were thus reduced to nothing... their race vanishes and civilization strides across their corpses. Therein lies once again the great doctrine that the evolution of humanity and of individual nations does not progress through moral principles, but rather by dint of the right of the stronger.[14]

According to *Das Ausland*'s editors Peschel, Hellwald, and Ratzel, Darwinist science had enormous ethical, moral, and therefore political implications. The journal thus took it on itself to analyze the state of politics and civilization around the globe. In so doing *Das Ausland* purposefully infused political commentary with the aura of scientific certainty. Its editorials applied Social Darwinist doctrine to world affairs in general, and to European and American colonial expansion in particular. In a 1860 article, Peschel commented that American expansion had always been accompanied by massacres, "which even today are still being committed by European pioneers, fur traders, and scalp hunters on the nearside and (in even worse fashion) the far side of the Rocky Mountains." Eventually, according to Peschel, this process would lead to the "disappearance" of all indigenous peoples in many parts of the globe. Peschel also praised the construction of a transcontinental railway line that would "cut the red man's lifeline and that of the big bison herds." For Peschel, this development was no reason to pity Native Americans: "We

---

[14] Friedrich von Hellwald, *Kulturgeschichte in ihrer natürlichen Entwicklung bis zur Gegenwart*, vol. IV (Leipzig: Friesenhahn, 1898), 615–16.

are not among those who believe the extermination of an ancient human race to be a crime committed by American society." Historian and anthropologist George W. Stocking Jr. has demonstrated how nineteenth-century British ethnologists reinterpreted the slaughter of Tasmania's native peoples by British settlers by labeling it either "decline" or "degeneration," a view that exonerated British settlers. In similar fashion, the German geographer Peschel believed the "extermination" of Native Americans not to be a "crime." Instead, it was a natural consequence of the global expansion of the white race.[15]

A year after Peschel voiced these thoughts, the Darwinist biologist Ernst Haeckel published the first edition of his massively popular *Natürliche Schöpfungsgeschichte* [Natural History of Creation]. In it, Haeckel gave his own explanation of the demise of Native Americans and other nonwhite races around the globe. He viewed the exterminatory consequences of European and white North American colonial expansion as a simple biological necessity: "While the European tribes are spreading out all over the world, others are perishing. . . . This holds especially true for the redskins in America and also for the black-reddish aboriginals of Australia." Haeckel's popularity in Germany demonstrates not only that pitiless views of Amerindians existed side-by-side with empathetic ones but also that they were read by a broad public.[16]

Haeckel and Peschel made abundantly clear that sympathy for the disappearance of "weaker" human races was unnecessary. Reports about Native Americans in popular German magazines like *Die Gartenlaube* [The Gazebo], which had a circulation of 380,000 copies at its peak in 1876, at times displayed a

[15] *Das Ausland* (1855): 387, 424; *Das Ausland* (1860): 393; *Das Ausland* (1867): 1225; George W. Stocking Jr., *Victorian Anthropology* (London: Collier Macmillan, 1987), 281; Richard Weikart, "Progress through Racial Extermination: Social Darwinism, Eugenics, and Pacifism in Germany, 1860–1918," *German Studies Review* 26, no. 2 (2003): 278–79; Richard Weikart, *From Darwin to Hitler: Evolutionary Ethics, Eugenics, and Racism in Germany* (New York: Palgrave Macmillan, 2004), 8, 24–25, 34.

[16] Haeckel, *Natürlich Schöpfungsgeschichte*, 242; Peter J. Bowler, *Evolution: The History of an Idea* (Berkeley: University of California Press, 1989), 202, 290.

smug faith in white European superiority that went even further than the racialized views of these two scientists. *Die Gartenlaube*'s feature on the Battle at Little Big Horn in 1876 thus expressed the hope that it would be "one of the first tasks of the republic during the second century of its existence to cleanse the lands from the Indian pest that has already...claimed so many thousands of precious human lives." In fact, despite the popularity of Karl May's "noble savage" hero Winnetou, supposedly an Apache chief, late nineteenth-century ethnographical publications consistently offered negative representations of the Apache. Friedrich Hellwald's *Amerika in Wort und Bild* [America in Word and Image] hence stated that the Apache's "foot is less flat than that of the Negro...their facial expression is ugly and revolting.... The Apache possesses no personal courage... in everything; he merely displays the characteristics of a coyote.... These hordes, roaming around on a territory as big as Germany, occupy the lowest cultural rank, and are estimated to be 14,280 heads strong." Rudolf Cronau, a frequent traveler in the United States, whose reports were printed in *Die Gartenlaube* and who is usually remembered for his positive attitudes toward Native Americans, made similar statements about this southwestern tribe. Cronau described the Apache as "cruel as hyenas." In his view, they were "a veritable scourge" for Arizona and New Mexico.[17]

Such statements, which implied that the undeserving Apache had too much land at their disposal, were by no means particularly German. According to historian Ray Billington, they reiterated British and Scandinavian outlooks on Native Americans, because these European countries and regions (like the German states) had contributed "so largely to the immigrant stream then flowing toward the frontiers." They also echoed

[17] Friedrich von Hellwald, *Naturgeschichte des Menschen*, vol. 1 (Stuttgart: W. Spemann, 1882), 337–38; Friedrich von Hellwald, *Amerika in Wort und Bild. Eine Schilderung der Vereinigten Staaten*, vol. 2 (Leipzig: Heinrich Schmidt & Carl Günther 1885), 502, 504–05. Cronau quoted in Undine Janeck, *Zwischen Gartenlaube und Karl May. Deutsche Amerikarezeption in den Jahren 1871–1913* (Aachen: Shaker Verlag, 2003), 205–06.

American frontier attitudes, of course. For example, in 1851, California's first civilian U.S. governor, Peter Burnett, publicly declared "that a war of extermination will continue to be waged... until the Indian race becomes extinct" and warned that what he called "the inevitable destiny of the race is beyond the power or wisdom of man to avert." In the end, Peschel's and Haeckel's evaluation of the ultimate fate of Native Americans was little more than a reflection of this sentiment, especially given that *Das Ausland* had keenly followed the American debate about what to do with the continent's native peoples ever since the journal had published Lewis Cass's Indian removal essay in 1831. The *Gartenlaube*'s feature on the need to "cleanse" the West of the Apache also echoed American frontier viewpoints. As a "solution" to the perceived "Apache problem" in 1864 the *Arizona Miner*, a weekly newspaper based in Prescott, Arizona, had declared that "[e]xtermination is our only hope, and the sooner the better." Twelve years later, the *Gartenlaube* presented similarly cruel positions to a broad, nonacademic German audience.[18]

German colonialists were impressed by American expansionism and envied the United States for the easily available ("empty") lands in "the West." In fact, Friedrich Ratzel was so impressed that he changed his career after visiting the United States as a journalist in 1874–75. Back in Germany, Ratzel immersed himself in the new scientific field of geography and in 1886 became professor at the University of Leipzig. In his first book, a travelogue entitled *Sketches of Urban and Cultural Life in North America* (1876), his fascination with both the question of race control and the immense space available for westward expansion was already apparent, and America featured prominently in most of his subsequent publications. In the early 1890s,

---

[18] *Das Ausland* (1831): 425–26, 437–39; Billington, *Land of Savagery*, 139–40; Benjamin Madley, "California's Yuki Indians: Defining Genocide in Native American History," *Western Historical Quarterly* 39, no. 3 (2008); Karl Jacoby, "'The Broad Platform of Extermination': Nature and Violence in the Nineteenth-Century North American Borderlands," *Journal of Genocide Research* 10, no. 2 (2008): 252.

Ratzel's impressions of and thoughts on American expansion helped him develop his concept of geopolitics. This intellectual development also found expression in his praise for Fredrick Jackson Turner's "frontier thesis," although unlike the historian Turner, the geographer Ratzel believed that the frontier was not an exclusively American but rather a global phenomenon. Frontiers were places where indigenous peoples were pushed aside by white settlers. In his widely read *Political Geography* (1897), Ratzel therefore linked the perceived problem of racial conflict with his views on modern agricultural developments and territorial expansion. In 1901, Ratzel subsumed many of the questions he had already addressed in his *Political Geography* under the concept "Lebensraum" [living space], a scientific premise that described the space needed to sustain a species or a people; it posited that, to survive, plants, animals, and nations had to expand their living space by migration, colonization, and/or conquest.[19]

---

[19] Ratzel, *Wider die Reichsnörgler: Ein Wort zur Kolonialfrage aus Wählerkreisen*, 8; Friedrich Ratzel, "Über allgemeine Eigenschaften der geographischen Grenzen und über die politischen Grenzen," *Berichte über die Verhandlungen der Königlich Sächsischen Gesellschaft der Wissenschaften zu Leizpig, Philologisch-Historische Klasse* 44 (1892): 65, 74–75, 99; Friedrich Ratzel, Dr. *A Petermanns Mitteilungen aus Justus Perthes Geographischer Anstalt* 41 (1895): 122; Friedrich Ratzel, *Politische Geographie* (München: R. Oldenbourg, 1897), 1–14; Murray Kane, "Some Considerations on the Frontier Concept of Frederick Jackson Turner," *Mississippi Valley Historical Review* 27, no. 3 (1940): 398–99; Friedrich Ratzel, *Der Lebensraum: Eine biogeographische Studie* (Darmstadt: Wissenschaftliche Buchgemeinschaft, [1901] 1966), 45, 55–56, 67; Woodruff D. Smith, "Friedrich Ratzel and the Origins of 'Lebensraum,'" *German Studies Review* 3, no. 1 (1980); Robert H. Block, "Fredrick Jackson Turner and American Geography," *Annals of the Association of American Geographers* 70, no. 1 (1980): 40; Helmut Walser Smith, *The Continuities of German History: Nation, Religion, and Race across the Long Nineteenth Century* (New York: Cambridge University Press, 2008), 183–89. Ratzel's works on the United States, in order of publication date: *Städte und Culturbilder aus Nordamerika*, 2 vols. (Leipzig: F. A. Brockhaus, 1876); *Die Vereinigten Staaten von Nord-Amerika*, 2 vols. (Munich: R. Oldenbourg, 1878); *Physikalische Geographie und Naturcharakter der Vereinigten Staaten von Nord-Amerika* (Munich: 1878); *Culturgeographie der Vereinigten Staaten von Nordamerika unter besonderer Berücksichtigung*

Ratzel's conviction that the need for expansion could be scientifically proven also shaped his politics. During a speech at a meeting of the National-Liberal Party in Munich in September 1884, he argued for German overseas expansion and criticized "colonial skeptics." He also made clear that North America was the place ideally suited for European colonization, although Germany never had the opportunity as a nation-state to participate in the continent's settlement. Ratzel backed his call for German overseas expansion by arguing that his and the National-Liberal Party's support of colonial expansion was directly linked to notions that had been discussed by the revolutionary National Assembly in Frankfurt in 1848–49. Back then, as he recounted, liberal revolutionaries had stipulated that the (still to be established) German national government should protect international commerce and emigration. Ratzel clearly believed that the German Empire's colonial endeavors in 1884 fulfilled demands voiced by liberal revolutionaries thirty-six years earlier.[20]

As late as 1884, Ratzel thus still had faith in political tenets that dated back to German political liberalism's revolutionary past. His entirely positive descriptions of life in the United States in his first major publication, *Sketches of Urban and Cultural Life in North America* (first published in the second half of the 1870s), also speak to the durability of Ratzel's progressive convictions. This early publication by Ratzel does not merely stress the importance of westward expansion for the development of the United States but also focuses on the significance of America's big cities for the country's growth. In 1876, we therefore find Ratzel not fetishizing pioneer life along the frontier but rather praising the modernity of American city life: "North America, this amazing country of modern culture, has also overtaken the old world

der wirtschaftlichen Verhältnisse 2 vols. (Munich: 1880); *Politische Geographie der Vereinigten Staaten von Amerika*, 2 vols. (Munich: R. Oldenbourg, 1893).

[20] Ratzel, *Wider die Reichsnörgler: Ein Wort zur Kolonialfrage aus Wählerkreisen*, 8, 23; Peters, *Schriften (Vol. 1)*, 318.

in respect to these two developments [growth of cities; leveling of differences between city and country life]. Every cultural seed that here has to strenuously free itself from the brittle and twisted undergrowth . . . – there it thrives in the fresh, unspoiled, youthful prairie soil like corn or wheat." To be sure, Ratzel's use of the western prairie as metaphor, although it referred to the progressive developments he witnessed in America's cities, indicates his fascination with the American West. Yet for him, this was not a nostalgic perspective. Neither in his *Sketches* nor in his later publications did Ratzel ever posit that colonial expansion (be it the "winning" of the American West or Germany's acquisition of colonies in Africa) helped maintain traditional rural societies. Instead, colonialism was an engine of social, political, and cultural progress, just as it had been for those revolutionary liberals in 1848 who called for colonies before the revolution's achievements had even been secured.[21]

In Ratzel's 1884 pro-colonialist speech on behalf of the NLP, his affirmative references to Germany's failed liberal revolution pointed toward the important role that his positive views of the United States' liberal political system would later play in shaping the premises of his most influential works, most prominently his *Political Geography*. For Ratzel, "space" shaped character. He therefore argued that the ready availability of land for the ever expanding United States had beneficial effects for Americans as individuals and for the stability of their republican government:[22]

In the United States . . . the greatness of space has counteracted decay . . . the will and the power to colonize that enliven so many individuals have time and again enlarged the national economic sphere. . . . The draining and dissipating effects of the vast space have contributed to the

---

[21] Ratzel, *Städte- und Culturbilder aus Nordamerika*, 3–4.
[22] Smith, "Friedrich Ratzel and the Origins of 'Lebensraum'," 57; Woodruff D. Smith, *The Ideological Origins of Nazi Imperialism* (New York: Oxford University Press, 1986), 21, 26, 28, 30, 48–50.

wonderful stability of the American constitution, which for 100 years has suffered fewer changes than any European constitution.[23]

Ratzel was well aware of the attractiveness to German audiences of such a reading of American history. His praise for American expansion and America's republican constitution harkened to the many pro-American sentiments expressed by liberal revolutionaries in 1848–49 and in periodicals such as *Die Gartenlaube* during the 1850s: The United States was exemplary and impressive because of its political system and its steady growth – and the former feature was closely linked to the latter phenomenon. American westward expansion had much more relevance during the last two decades of the nineteenth century than in the time of the revolution: In 1884 the German Empire had become a colonial power, and colonialism either already was or quickly became appealing to various sociopolitical groups. Progressives like Max Weber and Friedrich Naumann argued for the necessity of expansionist "big politics," because Germany's global engagement would educate its citizenry at home and make democratic reform possible and inevitable. Conservatives and right-wing liberals like Johann von Miquel or to a lesser extent Friedrich Meinecke hoped that colonialism would have the opposite effect. They believed that colonialism would act like a stabilizing steam valve, with settler colonies minimizing domestic pressures for social change.

Ratzel's depiction of America and his related colonialist arguments catered to all of these diverse political perspectives, although it is clear that, despite his support for the National-Liberal Party, he leaned more toward Weber's and Naumann's reform-oriented imperial liberalism. Ratzel's expansionism was therefore worlds apart from that of NLP right-wingers such as Ernst Hasse. Throughout his life, Ratzel's progressive inclinations remained apparent, especially when he wrote about the United States. For him as for other German liberals, liberal

---

[23] Ratzel, *Politische Geographie der Vereinigten Staaten von Amerika*, 95.

political systems were supposed to provide individuals with the necessary protection to successfully engage in their particular entrepreneurial endeavors. Despite its autocratic government, the German Empire was therefore such a system, at least in the eyes of most German liberals (whether right- or left-leaning), because it respected and protected its citizens' private spheres and economic interests.[24]

According to Ratzel, the white settlement of North America was the best example of both why and how Germans should engage in policies of colonial expansion. The United States demonstrated that the availability of land for settlement both stabilized domestic politics and energized economic and cultural development. In addition, America's liberal (barely regulated) expansionism explained why the Anglo-American colonization of North America had been triumphant, whereas French efforts had failed, although they had

> led to mild policies towards the Indians. . . . Yet the very qualities that made them [the French] better neighbors for the Indians influenced their failure as settlers who tilled the soil. . . . They [the English] then left it to the settlers to acquire individual stretches of land from the Indians. . . . The English left the energetic colonization of their emigrating families unfettered, while the Spanish conquest of Peru protected the Indians and their separate economies.

In this explanation Ratzel sounded eerily similar to Tocqueville, who regretted that the French in North America "had failed to plant the roots of civilization," in contrast to the English who,

---

[24] Max Weber, *Der Nationalstaat und die Volkswirtschaftspolitik: Akademische Antrittsrede* (Freiburg: Akademische Verlagsbuchhandlung von J. C. B. Mohr, 1895), 12; Ernst Hasse, *Deutsche Politik*, vol. 1.3 (Munich: J. F. Lehmann's Verlag, 1906), 167ff.; Hans-Ulrich Wehler, *Bismarck und der Imperialismus* (Köln: Kiepenheuer u. Witsch, 1969), 454–503; James J. Sheehan, *German Liberalism in the Nineteenth Century* (Chicago: University of Chicago Press, 1978), 276–78; David Blackbourn and Geoff Eley, *The Peculiarities of German History* (New York: Oxford University Press, 1984), 146–55; Smith, *The Ideological Origins of Nazi Imperialism*, 21, 26, 28, 30, 48–50; Dieter Langewiesche, *Liberalismus in Deutschland*, in *Neue historische Bibliothek* (Frankfurt am Main: Suhrkamp, 1988), 219–20; Conrad, *Globalisierung und Nation im Deutschen Kaiserreich*, 85.

because of their laissez-faire attitude toward their colonists, had succeeded. A multitude of decentralized Indian policies carried out independently by numerous white pioneers had thus resulted in the permanent Anglo-American settlement of most of North America.[25]

According to Ratzel, this pattern of lasting liberal, laissez-faire expansion had been practiced first in North America, and during the late nineteenth century it was being repeated on a global scale. Europeans, especially the British and the Germans, valued "the soil" more highly than native peoples in North America or Africa. In his *The State and Its Soil* (1896), Ratzel therefore argued that "the colonial efforts of a state that espouses a higher appreciation of the soil will always be easily successful in a country whose inhabitants have not yet progressed to such estimation. Initially, this state pushes . . . into the numerous gaps between the widely dispersed political settlements of the Negroes, Indians, etc., until the incursions onto tribal territories cause disputes." Given Imperial Germany's overseas expansion after 1884, the process of the growth of states that Ratzel described was well anchored in German political reality. By 1901, when Ratzel published *Der Lebensraum*, Southwest Africa had become Germany's most populous dependency abroad.[26]

During the 1890s, Ratzel's French colleague Camille Vallaux accused him of merely cloaking German imperialist aspirations in scientific garments. The tensions between France and the German Empire after 1871 explain Vallaux's concerns about the scientific validity of Ratzel's work. However, Ratzel received an entirely different reception on the other side of the Atlantic. The Harvard professor Nathaniel S. Shaler introduced Ratzel's ideas to American readers in his *Nature and Man in America*, coupling them with his own brand of extreme scientific racism with its proposals of a variety of resolutions to America's "ethnic

---

[25] Friedrich Ratzel, *Der Staat und sein Boden geographisch betrachtet* (Leipzig: S. Hirzel, 1896), 97, 98; Pitts and Tocqueville, *Writings on Empire and Slavery*, xv.

[26] Ratzel, *Der Staat und sein Boden*, 86; Ratzel, *Der Lebensraum: Eine biogeographische Studie*, 45, 55–56, 67.

questions," including eugenic control and immigration restriction. In fact, during the 1890s, Ratzel's ideas found a second home among Harvard geologists and geographers. Shaler was steeped in them, and so were William Morris Davis and Isaiah Bowman. In particular, Bowman's influence was not limited to academic circles. During the first half of the twentieth century, his views shaped American foreign policy objectives on more than one occasion.[27]

The most important American admirer of Ratzel, however, was the historian Frederick Jackson Turner, whose famous frontier thesis posited that American westward expansion, which had officially come to an end in the early 1890s, had made the United States exceptional. Turner quoted the German geographer at length in his 1896 paper, "The West as a Field for Historical Study," and cooperated with Ratzel's influential American devotee Ellen Churchill Semple. In his 1905 review of Semple's *Geographical Interpretations of American History*, Turner commented on Ratzel's death and the German's importance for the study of American history: "Miss Semple is a student of Ratzel, whose recent death is lamented by American scholars. He was a forerunner in the path that American historians must follow who view their problems as those arising from the study of the evolution of society in the American environment."[28]

Ratzel's work was inextricably linked to German imperialism, and his American admirer Turner was not only aware of this fact

[27] William Coleman, "Science and Symbol in the Turner Frontier Hypothesis," *American Historical Review* 72, no. 1 (1966): 40; Ronald H. Carpenter, *The Eloquence of Frederick Jackson Turner* (San Marino: Huntington Library, 1983), 190; David N. Livingstone, "Science and Society: Nathaniel S. Shaler and Racial Ideology," *Transactions of the Institute of British Geographers, New Series* 9, no. 2 (1984): 190; Neil Smith, *American Empire: Roosevelt's Geographer and the Prelude to Globalization* (Berkeley: University of California Press, 2003), 38–39, 334–35; Conrad, *Globalisierung und Nation im Deutschen Kaiserreich*, 61.

[28] Frederick Jackson Turner, "Geographic Influences in American History (Book Review)," *Journal of Geography* 4 (1905): 34; Ray Allen Billington, *The Genesis of the Frontier Thesis* (San Marino: Huntington Library, 1971), 96–97, 268; Bassin, "Turner, Solov'ev, and the 'Frontier Hypothesis,'" 480.

but also approved of the German geographer's colonial agitation, in part because he felt that German colonialism was modeled after the best possible example. Turner observed that "American colonization [by which Turner meant American westward expansion] has become the mother of German colonial policy." Indeed, the United States played such an important role in Ratzel's thought that many Americans readily absorbed his arguments. During the 1890s the imperialist subtext of Ratzel's ideas was a perfect match for the frenzied American debate about the necessity of further "postfrontier" expansion. In Germany, in contrast, Ratzel's analysis of the American frontier confirmed views of the United States as a "normal" expansionist state. According to Ratzel and other contributors to German discussions about North America, the American West was just one frontier region among many, albeit certainly the most impressive one.

Ultimately, Americans agreed with this analysis. After the Spanish-American War, which ended with the United States acquiring Guam, Puerto Rico, and the Philippines, Wild West imagery was easily transferred onto America's overseas "frontiers." This transfer was facilitated by the fact that American imperialists understood overseas expansion to continue American westward expansion. In his Wild West show, in 1899 Buffalo Bill Cody thus replaced the reenactment of "Custer's Last Stand" with the "Battle of San Juan Hill," honoring the valor of Theodore Roosevelt and his "Rough Riders" against Spanish troops in Cuba. In turn, Cody claimed that Roosevelt and his regiment had adopted the term "Rough Riders" from his show, which contained a segment called "Congress of Rough Riders of the World," with Cody representing the "King of All the Rough Riders of the World." Cody was a "hero" of the American West, who had participated in the Plains wars against the Cheyenne in South Dakota during the 1870s. During the 1890s Cody became an avid proponent of American overseas expansion. He shared this passion, as he well knew, with Theodore Roosevelt, who in turn used frontier imagery to describe both his own imperialist exploits and imperialism in general. Entirely in keeping with his anti-Indian sentiments, Roosevelt thus equated the native population in the newly acquired American overseas territories with American Indians, explicitly stating that "the Filipinos were 'savages' like the 'Apache.'"[29]

Nineteenth-century Germany's most notorious proponent of overseas expansion, Carl Peters, was in complete agreement with both Theodore Roosevelt and William Cody and with his compatriot Friedrich Ratzel. Not only did he share the German geographer's veneration for the United States in general and the American West in particular but, like Ratzel, Peters also espoused a strong bourgeois liberalism, despite his at times extreme nationalism. Although Peters' post-1945 image has been traditionally defined by his chauvinism, attempts to explain Peters and his imperialist aspirations by merely pointing to his links to nationalist circles in late nineteenth-century Germany take too narrow a view. Peters celebrated independent entrepreneurship and frequently criticized Imperial Germany's slow-working and incompetent administration and its aristocratic representatives. Like Ratzel, he displayed genuine admiration for Anglo-American political institutions and the independent spirit of American frontiersmen. Again like Ratzel, he was active on behalf of the NLP, and in 1895 he ran unsuccessfully for parliament as a national-liberal candidate (he lost against a völkisch-nationalist candidate of the Anti-Semitic Party). In addition, Peters self-consciously defined his colonialist visions as "liberal": In his words, "liberale Kolonialpolitik" [liberal colonial politics] was indispensable for successful overseas expansion.[30]

[29] Frederick Jackson Turner, "American Colonization," in *The Eloquence of Frederick Jackson Turner*, 190; Albrecht Wirth, *Das Wachstum der Vereinigten Staaten von Nordamerika und ihre auswärtige Politik* (Bonn: Universitäts-Buchdruckerei von Carl Georgi, 1899), 25; Peters, *Schriften*, vol. 1; Richard Slotkin, "Buffalo Bill's 'Wild West' and the Mythologization of the American Empire," in *Cultures of United States Imperialism*, ed. Amy Kaplan and Donald E. Pease (Durham: Duke University Press, 1993), 177–78; Wrobel, *The End of American Exceptionalism*, 1, 2, 21, 37, 57–61. On other German-American academic connections see Chapter 4.

[30] Peters, *Schriften*, vol. 1, 321–22; Siegfried von Kardorff, *Wilhelm von Kardorff. Ein nationaler Parlamentarier im Zeitalter Bismarcks und Wilhelms*

Peters hailed from the small town of Neuhaus, situated along the Elbe River a bit to the southeast of Hamburg. The town had been part of the Kingdom of Hannover since 1815 and became part of the state of Prussia in 1866 when Peters was ten years old. His father was the local Lutheran minister, yet the family was globally connected: Peters' uncles lived in England and the United States. In his memoirs, Peters noted again and again that his youth was shaped by his longings for personal achievement and that his father was a keen follower of the exploration of Africa by the British: "Yet I definitely remember from my early childhood that my father followed Livingston's travels with passionate interest. The open map of Africa was always on his sofa table, and frequently...he pointed to the lake region in East Africa and said: 'There lies Africa's future'." Peters went on to study at the universities of Göttingen, Tübingen, and Berlin. In Berlin he "was lucky," in his own words, to be able to take classes with the historian Georg Waitz, a liberal and former representative of the revolutionary parliament in Frankfurt in 1848–49. Peters remained in Berlin until 1880, when he passed his teacher examination, after which he returned to Hannover. Shortly after he left Berlin, his English uncle asked him to live with him in London. Peters did not miss out on this opportunity

II (Berlin: E. S. Mittler & Sohn, 1936), 361; Sheehan, *German Liberalism in the Nineteenth Century*, 276–78; Richard Parry, "'In a Sense Citizens, but Not Altogether Citizens...'": Rhodes, Race, and the Ideology of Segregation at the Cape in the Late Nineteenth Century," *Canadian Journal of African Studies* 17, no. 3 (1983): 380–81; Langewiesche, *Liberalismus in Deutschland*, 219–20; Walter LaFeber, *The American Search for Opportunity, 1865–1913* (Cambridge: Cambridge University Press, 1993), 57–59; Christian Geulen, "'The Final Frontier...'": Heimat, Nation und Kolonie um 1900: Carl Peters," in *Phantasiereiche. Zur Kulturgeschichte des deutschen Kolonialismus*, ed. Birthe Kundrus (Frankfurt/New York: Campus Verlag, 2003) 41–42; Birthe Kundrus, "Die Kolonien – "Kinder des Gefühls und der Phantasie," in *Phantasiereiche. Zur Kulturgeschichte des deutschen Kolonialismus*, ed. Birthe Kundrus (Frankfurt/New York: Campus Verlag, 2003), 10; Arne Perras, *Carl Peters and German Imperialism, 1856–1918* (Oxford: Clarendon Press, 2004), 10; Jennifer Pitts, *A Turn to Empire: The Rise of Imperial Liberalism in Britain and France* (Princeton: Princeton University Press, 2005), 20–21.

and moved to England in late 1880. At least in retrospect, Peters believed that it was this first stay in England that inflamed his passion for imperialism. What interested and fascinated Peters about British colonialism and imperialism was not so much the chance to gain esteem and fame through colonialist activities. Instead, it was imperialism's domestic ramifications for English society that caught his eye:

> Yet when I thought about it, then I already realized back then that . . . it was also primarily this nation's enormous colonial activities that provided every Englishman with the opportunity to establish his own economic independence somewhere in this world free from both foreign and domestic interference of his own government. When I compared my friends in Germany to my friends and relatives in England, I saw that the former . . . lived on their knees . . . , while the latter walked the earth independent of favors from up high, while being respectful toward their equals and those below them.

Of course, Peters knew nothing about the life of ordinary Britons or the English working class; he only knew London's high society to which his uncle had introduced him. Nevertheless, in Peters' view colonialism played a prominent role in this milieu: It provided the foundation on which politically liberal and "respectful" gentlemen, such as Peters' acquaintance Joseph Chamberlain, a left-liberal politician and ardent colonialist, could operate. (Chamberlain, the father of Neville Chamberlain, would become colonial secretary in 1895.)[31]

In the spring of 1882 Peters returned to Germany to continue his academic career, but the unexpected death of his uncle forced him to return to England in late 1882 to settle his family's affairs. At this time, Peters published a Schopenhauer-inspired philosophical work, *The World of the Will and the Will of the World*, expecting to build an academic career on this publication.

---

[31] Peters, *Schriften*, vol. 1, 49, 55, 56, 121, 126; Guido Wölky, *Roscher, Waitz, Bluntschli und Treitschke als Politikwissenschaftler. Spätblüte und Untergang eines klassischen Universitätsfaches in der zweiten Hälfte des 19. Jahrhunderts* (Ruhr Universität Bochum, 2006), 219. Peters complained about the German "Untertanenmanier" multiple times in his writings. See for example also Peters, *Schriften*, vol. 1, 67–69.

However, the book was not well received. As a result, Peters toyed with the idea of emigrating to the United States and working for his other uncle in Chicago. However, inspired by the blossoming colonialist movement in Germany he decided to return to Berlin in October 1883, and in March of the following year Peters founded the Society for German Colonization. This society soon began to sell share certificates and eventually raised enough funds to finance a "land grab expedition" to East Africa. The expedition "signed" a number of assignment contracts with local tribal leaders that enabled Peters to claim possession of the territories described in these treaties. In February 1885, after Peters returned to Germany, he obtained an imperial charter of protection from Chancellor Bismarck for his newly acquired African possessions. Afterward, although Peters had been neither the sole organizer nor the only participant in the East Africa expedition, he made himself out to have been the true "founder" of German East Africa. In 1887, Peters obtained more coastal territory for German East Africa, and in 1889–90, he became the leader of the German Emin Pasha relief expedition, which competed with an English expedition led by Henry Morton Stanley. Both expeditions were interested in Emin Pasha's ability, as "governor" of Equatoria (today Southern Sudan), to rubber-stamp an annexation of the territory nominally under his control by either the British or the German Empire. Peters lost the race to find Emin, but the German government had already decided that Equatoria was not worth a crisis in German-English relations and informed London that Berlin was not interested in this territory. This diplomatic move made Peters' efforts useless from the beginning. Yet the race between Stanley and Peters into the heart of the "Dark Continent" fueled the public imagination and excitement about Africa in both Germany and England and therefore contributed further to Peters' now global fame and popularity.

Partly because of his efforts to further his public image as a colonial conqueror, and partly because of his frantic and manifold colonial activities between 1885 and 1890, Peters fame grew exponentially, until, by the mid-1890s, he had become the German Empire's best known and only "colonial hero." However, he was not well liked by a number of high-ranking German officials and other influential figures in the German Empire, most importantly Otto von Bismarck's son, Herbert von Bismarck. Peters was too brazen, too independent, too arrogant, and too full of himself to climb smoothly through the ranks of the foreign affairs department, which nominally oversaw the administration of the German colonies until 1907. Peters thus never became governor of the colony he had helped found. Instead, in 1891, he accepted a position as Imperial High Commissioner for the Kilimanjaro area and attempted to establish German control in this region while displaying haughtiness and brutality toward the African population. This strategy only exacerbated the tension between the local tribes and their titular German rulers. In the winter of 1891 and spring of 1892, Peters hanged two Africans, a man and a woman. It appears likely that he had taken the woman as his concubine and eventually killed her and her suspected partner out of jealousy.

It is fairly obvious that, during his time at Mount Kilimanjaro, Peters attempted to "perform" colonialism: He was not merely a white conqueror but also a colonial hero. Peters thus had a double image to uphold and to confirm. As a result, Peters literally and figuratively acted out his colonialist fantasies and tried to turn them into a brutal, murderous, and sexualized reality. One could also argue that at the foothills of Mount Kilimanjaro Peters attempted to act in a "Wild West manner." Certainly, in 1891–92 Peters consciously or unconsciously blurred the lines between being a colonizer, a colonial hero, and a symbol of German imperialism. Peters was in good company: In 1876, while participating in the Plains wars in South Dakota, Buffalo Bill Cody had his image as Wild West hero to uphold and therefore at times exchanged his military uniform for one of his stage costumes. When wearing his stage outfit, he was especially brutal toward Indians and also made doubly sure that his fellow scouts knew when he had taken a Cheyenne scalp.[32]

[32] Peters, *Schriften*, Vol. 1, 63, 64, 65, 378; Slotkin, "Buffalo Bill's 'Wild West' and the Mythologization of the American Empire," 167–68; Perras, *Carl*

Unlike the Plains wars in 1876, the German expedition to
the foothills of Mount Kilimanjaro did not end with success
for the white conquerors. The Germans' foothold in this region
was weak, and Peters' dreams of conquest turned into night-
mares of defeat and retreat. Because of his brutal conduct, Peters
added fuel to a fire that would eventually consume his successor Albrecht von Bülow in June 1892, when Bülow's contingent was attacked and killed by local tribes. By the time of the
"Bülow disaster," as it came to be known in Berlin, Peters had
already returned to Germany's capital. Paul Kayser, the director of the colonial office, initially did not know what to do
with Peters, but eventually commissioned him to write a book
about the development of German East Africa. In 1893, Peters
traveled to the United States for a number of months. At the
same time, a dispute broke out within the colonial office over
whether Peters should be decorated for his work on Kilimanjaro. This debate made information about Peters' conduct in
1891–92 available to administrative circles in Berlin, and from
there it spread. In 1896 August Bebel, the leader of the Social
Democratic Party (SPD), sharply attacked Peters in the Reichstag, thereby making all of Germany aware of Peters' brutality.
One year later, Peters fell hard. He was convicted of malfeasance
in office and dismissed from the colonial service. This sentence
fueled Peters' disgust with the stifling workings of the German
administrative system, which in turn resulted in his increased
promotion of "American-style" laissez-faire colonialism. In an
1897 article he compared the failure of French colonialism in
North America with the successes of the British and Americans. He chided the French for having attempted to control
the American settlers too much, whereas their Anglo-American
counterparts had been left alone: "[A] system of bureaucratic
regimentation... does not lead to the creation of healthy and
viable colonial startups. Instead, in order to achieve this goal,

Peters and German Imperialism, 1856–1918, 211–13, 227–28; Michael Perraudin and Jürgen Zimmerer, eds., *German Colonialism and National Identity*
(Milton Park: Routledge, 2011), 169–70.

free and unfettered individual activities of the colonists are necessary."[33]

The paradoxical end result of Peters' laissez-faire and entrepreneurial attitude toward colonialism was abandonment of the colonial project: "Where the citizenry of a country does not possess the strength to take root in such independent manner in a foreign country, the state should renounce colonial politics altogether.... A seedling of colonial politics that can only vegetate in the constant shade of the state and because of state-sanctioned irrigation should better not be planted at all." Peters, maybe even more than Ratzel, had a strong streak of liberal self-confidence, and he expected colonial expansion to allow him to freely express these individualist urges. For both men, German colonialism was never solely a state-sanctioned process geared only toward aggrandizing the German nation: Ultimately these expansionists believed colonialism to be a liberal and individualist venture. During the first half of the nineteenth century, for German liberals the United States provided guidelines on how to organize the Germany of the future, at home and abroad. In addition they also held illusionary hopes for actual German colonies on American soil. During the second half of the nineteenth century German liberals moved the American colonial model out of the purely intellectual realm into real-life politics, scrutinizing it for concrete examples for Germany's own colonial empire.[34]

---

[33] Peters, *Schriften*, vol. 1, 63, 64, 65, 378; Perras, *Carl Peters and German Imperialism, 1856–1918*, 211–13, 27–28; Perraudin and Zimmerer, eds., *German Colonialism and National Identity*, 169–70.

[34] Peters, *Schriften*, vol. 1, 378; Horst Dippel, "Die Wirkung der amerikanischen Revolution auf Deutschland und Frankreich," *200 Jahre amerikanische Revolution und moderne Revolutionsforschung. Geschichte und Gesellschaft* Sonderheft, no. II (1976); Horst Dippel, *Germany and the American Revolution* (Wiesbaden: Steiner, 1978); Horst Gründer, *Geschichte der deutschen Kolonien* (Paderborn: Schöningh, 1985), 58–59, 63–77; Willi Paul Adams, *Deutschland und Amerika* (Berlin: Colloquium Verag, 1985); Alexander Schmidt, *Reisen in die Moderne* (Berlin: Akademie Verlag, 1997); Volker Depkat, *Amerikabilder in politischen Diskursen* (Stuttgart: Klett-Cotta, 1998); Egbert Klautke, *Unbegrenzte Möglichkeiten. "Amerikanisierung" in Deutschland und Frankreich (1900–1933)* (Stuttgart: Franz Steiner Verlag, 2003).

Because colonialism depended on an individualist entrepreneurial spirit, Peters believed that all successful colonies displayed similarly liberal characteristics regardless of their geographic location. He used the examples of North America, Africa,
and Australia to prove his point. Unsurprisingly, Peters also
argued that the treatment of native populations in the world's
successful colonies was similar. Answering an indictment of his
cruel actions in Africa by Eugen Richter, one of the few anticolo-
nialists in the liberal camp in late nineteenth-century Germany,
Peters reasoned that natives were handled in comparable fashion
worldwide, regardless of whether their lands were colonized by
a monarchy like Germany or by a republic like the United States.
Peters thus counseled Richter to consider the treatment of Native
Americans at the hands of American settlers: "How the conquer-
ing nation is organized politically has nothing to do with how
it manages subdued peoples; whether despotism, aristocracy, or
democracy: it does not make a difference."[35]

Peters felt that the United States provided the best possible illustration of his pro-colonialist argument and, based on
his analysis of the liberal colonization methods of the Anglo-
Americans, proclaimed that there existed no alternative to "liberale Kolonialpolitik" [liberal colonialism]. Conveniently, the
well-documented American cruelty against Native Americans –
in his view an inevitable consequence of a laissez-faire administration that allowed settlers to deal with problems as they saw
fit – also permitted him to put his own brutality against black
Africans in perspective, thereby foreshadowing how some apologists of the brutal war in GSWA would use similar American
examples ten years later. For Peters, America's triumphant rise
to world power status was simultaneously a triumph for liberal
colonialism. In consequence, he argued that the kind of colonization policy that had led to the establishment of the United States
as the most successful of all European colonial settlements should

---

[35] Peters, *Schriften*, vol. 1, 393, 406–07; Perras, *Carl Peters and German Imperialism, 1856–1918*, 10, 44–45; Wehler, *Bismarck und der Imperialismus*,
338.

be used to "deduce the program for practical colonial policies for all times."[36]

In some ways Peters was an exception among German colonialists. He was neither a bureaucrat nor a member of the military, yet he was one of Germany's few colonial heroes with genuine and broad public appeal. As a result, Peters' fall in 1897 was problematic for the German colonial project as a whole. Despite his popularity, Peters had prominent political enemies in Germany, among them August Bebel, the chairman of the anticolonialist Social Democratic Party, and Eugen Richter, the leader of the small, left-liberal Freisinnige Volkspartei [Liberal People's Party]. Richter's towering personality and political views kept the FSVP out of the liberal colonialist mainstream, but only months after his death in 1906 the party became ardently procolonialist. In addition, Peters had opponents in the German colonial administration, and despite being a fervent nationalist and expansionist, he also had problems with the Pan-German League. For the extreme right, which began to take increasing control of the Pan-German League in the early years of the twentieth century, Peters was too liberal, uncomfortably critical of some features of German cultural and political life, and, perhaps most problematically, had nothing against Jewish Germans. On the contrary, he was worried that anti-Semitic sentiments would drive Jews away from German politics and therefore away from contributing to the German national project – a development that would weaken Germany.[37]

Although Peters' dishonorable dismissal from colonial service in 1897 ruined his prospects of becoming governor of East Africa, he remained popular even after the indictment. Peters' 1904 book *England and the English* sold around 20,000 copies, much more than any of his pre-scandal publications. Moreover in 1905 – during the war in GSWA – fifty-one Reichstag deputies (among them Peters' friend Wilhelm von Kardorff of the Reichspartei

[36] Peters, *Schriften*, vol. 1, 378, 386, 393, 408–09.
[37] Perras, *Carl Peters and German Imperialism, 1856–1918*, 222.

[National Party] and Franz von Arenberg from the moderate
Center Party) tendered a request for Peters' exoneration. At the
same time, only two Reichstag representatives openly criticized
the brutal way Germany was fighting the rebels in Southwest
Africa: the Social Democrats August Bebel and Georg Ledebour.
Emperor William II was only too happy to oblige those peti-
tioning for Peters' exculpation. The rehabilitation of "Hangman
Peters" (a nickname given to Peters by SPD newspapers) thus
occurred while far worse atrocities than he had ever committed
were being perpetrated.[38]

Native Americans, American Expansion, and German Southwest Africa

Warfare in Southwest Africa followed a sequential pattern similar to genocides perpetrated along the American frontier and in
other areas of European colonial expansion. After the war's conclusion, the *Deutsche Kolonialzeitung* [German Colonial Times]
drew parallels between the conflict in "Southwest" and measures taken against Indians along the American frontier. The
Kolonialzeitung was the official paper of the Deutsche Kolonialgesellschaft [German Colonial Association], an expansionist lobbying organization in close alliance with the Pan-German
League and the Naval League. Summarizing a speech given by
Josef Lettenbaur, at the time German consul in Cincinnati, the
Kolonialzeitung argued that the appeal of Lettenbaur's talk was
grounded in his references to "American colonial history" and
"America's experience with Indians." The American example
showed that "the submission of native peoples" was the precondition of colonization; only afterward could "the dove with the
palm branch . . . appear and bring the blessings of civilization."[39]

[38] Ibid., 214–15; Kardorff, *Wilhelm von Kardorff. Ein nationaler Parlamentarier
     im Zeitalter Bismarcks und Wilhelms II*, 362.
[39] *Jahresbericht der Deutschen Kolonialgesellschaft 1888* (Berlin: Carl Hey-
     manns Verlag, 1889), 1; "Kolonialer Vortrag vor Deutschamerikanern,"

During the Herero and Nama uprisings, images of the American West became staple metaphors in public debates about German colonialism. At the same time however, German colonialists attempted to go beyond using the American West only metaphorically: They actively sought knowledge on how white Americans had conquered and settled the West. When German proponents of settler colonialism, whether in Berlin or in the colonies, made reference to the United States and its expansionist history, they did so from a perspective of transnational respect and genuine interest. As we later see, this vantage point set them apart from post-1918 and especially from Nazi mentions of the American West.

Among the reasons for the Herero rebellion were the ruthless behavior of German settlers and the exploitative practices of white merchants that increasingly resulted in the Herero's loss of their cattle on which their livelihood depended. After a German lieutenant had made death threats against the Herero chief Samuel Maharero, the Herero, who were eventually joined by the Nama, began in January 1904 to wage a costly war against Germany that lasted until 1907. Initially, the small German protection force was surprised by the course of events. Within weeks, Herero fighters had surrounded settlements in the colony's central-west region. They ransacked farms and police stations, cut the telegraph and railway links to Southwest Africa's capital Windhoek, and killed 123 German soldiers and settlers. The colony's governor, Theodor Gotthilf von Leutwein, who was not able to control the rebellion with the small militia contingent at his disposal (around 800 men), asked that Berlin send military support. The support sent from Berlin eventually totaled 14,000 troops, initially under the command of Lieutenant-General Lothar von Trotha, who had served overseas before. Leutwein and Trotha soon began to disagree over how to deal with the uprising: Whereas the goal of the colony's civilian

Deutsche Kolonialzeitung (1909), 565; *Jahresbericht der Deutschen Kolonialgesellschaft 1914/1915* (Berlin: 1916), 29; Madley, "Patterns of Frontier Genocide 1803–1910," 167–68.

governor was a negotiated surrender that envisioned targeting those Herero factions that were most determined to fight against German rule, in August 1904 Trotha attempted to encircle the mass of Herero fighters at the Waterberg in central Southwest Africa. This battle resulted in thousands of casualties. After the battle, Trotha implemented a policy of genocide to eliminate not only the rebel factions of the Herero but also the people as a whole. He ordered that all routes back to the Herero tribal lands be cut off, so that the Herero were driven toward the waterless Omaheke Desert where most perished. On October 2, 1904, Trotha made his extermination strategy public by issuing an order that threatened the Herero with total annihilation. This order was posted throughout the colony and read to the German troops. Emperor Wilhelm II (strongly influenced by Chancellor Bülow) compelled Trotha to rescind this order, but the end result of the war was genocide nevertheless. In 1911, only 15,000 Herero were still alive from prewar estimates as high as 80,000. The Nama also did not fare well: Their numbers were reduced by around 50 percent, from an estimated 20,000 to less than 10,000.[40]

In all, the German government spent more than 585 million Marks in colonial bonds on these genocidal ventures. Next to the atrocities committed, it was therefore financial concerns that forced Germans to discuss both the necessity and the political nature of their colonial empire. This debate shaped the results of the so-called Hottentot elections of 1907 – an alliance of Chancellor Bülow's government with the election winners in a coalition that consisted of Germany's liberal and conservative parties, all of which supported colonialism and unequivocally backed the

---

[40] Horst Drechsler, *Aufstände in Südwestafrika* (Berlin (East): Dietz, 1984), 51; Gründer, *Geschichte der deutschen Kolonien*, 120–22, 163; Hendrik Lorenzen, "Stereotypen des kolonialen Diskurses in Deutschland und ihre innenpolitische Funktionalisierung bei den 'Hottentottenwahlen' 1907" (Master's thesis, Universität Hamburg, 1991), 55–59; Jürgen Zimmerer, *Deutsche Herrschaft über Afrikaner* (Münster: Lit, 2001); Madley, "Patterns of Frontier Genocide 1803–1910," 181; Christopher Clark, *The Iron Kingdom: The Rise and Downfall of Prussia, 1600–1947* (Penguin Books, 2006), 604–06.

war in Southwest Africa. Compared to the 1903 elections, the turnout increased by almost 9 percent, as one million more Germans went to the polls. In 1907, liberals used the issue of colonialism to fire up their base and attract voters from segments of the population that before 1907 had refrained from voting in national elections. In fact, of all the parties it was the left-liberal FSVP, not the more right-wing National-Liberal Party, that gained the most seats: eight. The other left-liberal party and the more right-wing NLP each won four additional seats. The two main conservative parties, the Deutsche Reichspartei (German National Party) and the German Conservative Party, gained three and seven seats, respectively.[41]

The success of the pro-colonialist parties in January 1907 did not mean that the sentiments they embraced and promoted remained uncontested. Compared to 1903, the SPD actually gained about 250,000 votes in 1907. However, because of the first-past-the-post system and widespread gerrymandering, especially in Prussia's eastern provinces, the SPD lost almost half of its parliamentary seats. Whereas in the 1903 elections (as they would again in the 1912 elections), many left-liberal voters had cast their second ballot (in districts where there were runoffs between the first- and second-place candidates) for the SPD candidate, in 1907, the SPD's clear anticolonial stance deterred liberal voters from doing the same. Gerrymandering also had a large impact on the SPD's representation in the Reichstag. The party won an impressive 29 percent of all ballots cast, but received only 43 seats in the Reichstag. In comparison, the moderate Catholic Center Party got only 19.4 percent of the public vote and received 105 seats. The disparity between popular vote totals and Reichstag representation was even more glaring for the conservative parties. In other words, although greatly disadvantaged in the Reichstag, the voices of SPD parliamentarians represented

---

[41] George Crothers, *The German Elections of 1907* (London: 1941); Gründer, *Geschichte der deutschen Kolonien*, 58, 121–22; Lorenzen, "'Hottentotten-wahlen'", 87–88; Conrad, *Globalisierung und Nation im Deutschen Kaiserreich*, 85–86.

the anticolonialist views embraced by the most popular political party in Wilhelmine Germany. Social-democratic criticism of the German troops' actions was direct and acerbic. August Bebel called the German military strategy "beastly" and warned of the "complete extermination" of the Herero as early as March 1904. However, references to America were notably absent from the speeches of Bebel and Georg Ledebour (the SPD's other prominent speaker on colonial matters). Clearly, American examples were more suited to supporting the cause of those who defended German practices in GSWA. Yet in the end the SPD's relentless censure had little impact on German colonial policies, despite giving voice to strong anticolonial tendencies in German society. Members of the nonsocialist factions (including more than once Center Party representative Matthias Erzberger) often defended General von Trotha and agreed that, as long as hostilities in GSWA were ongoing, criticism of either the German troops or their commanders was unpatriotic.[42]

On December 6, 1904, Hermann Müller, who hailed from the Silesian town of Sagan and represented the left-liberal FSVP, was expressly critical of the administrative measures undertaken in GWSA, but not for the same reasons as the Social Democrats: He demanded to know why German colonial administrators had so far failed to build American-style reservations. He argued,

Just think back to the battles with the Indians, which the United States of America had to endure in the Wild West! At this point, the report about the Herero uprising already addresses the question of reservations, yet only reservations protecting the land of the natives, not reservations also having autonomous native administrations . . . where blacks can live and

[42] Lorenzen, "'Hottentottenwahlen'," 87–89; *Reichstagsdebatte (January-19-1904)*, 365; *Reichstagsdebatte (March-07-1913)*, 1893, 1897, 1900; *Reichstagsdebatte (March-17-1904)* 1892, 1893; *Reichstagsdebatte (December-06-1904)*, 3384; *Reichstagsdebatte (December-02-1905)*, 111. Reichstag deputies addressed warfare in GSWA in January, March, May, and December 1904; in May and December 1905, and in December 1906. Lorenzen, "'Hottentottenwahlen'," 63–65. In all of these debates, Trotha was criticized only once by a left-liberal deputy, Karl Schrader, a member of the Freisinnige Vereinigung. *Reichstagsdebatte (December-05-1905)*, 103.

love according to their preferences, for all I care even work and slack off however they like.

Müller "urgently" proposed the compilation of a report detailing how other nations and "the United States of America have proceeded and are proceeding in those of their lands that house foreign cultures." Müller was obviously intrigued by the fact that reservations in America created areas of de facto racial segregation of natives and whites.[43]

Müller was only one person in a long line of influential German liberals, both on the right and the left, who advocated that Germany's colonial ventures should emulate American examples: Ratzel, Bernhard Dernburg, Gustav Schmoller (a progressive social reformer, well-known economist, and co-founder of the Action Committee for Colonial Politics, a nonpartisan association promoting the cause of German colonialism), Wilhelm Solf (the Reichskolonialamt's third state secretary from 1911 to 1918), and the very racist left-liberal Paul Rohrbach came before and after him. Ratzel, Müller, and Rohrbach were especially taken with the exemplary potential of the American frontier, American westward expansion, and American Indian policies.[44]

Yet not all of these liberals drew the same lessons from American examples. Referring to Nazi imperialists during World War II, historian David Blackbourn notes, "To speak of Indians was to contemplate extermination." Did the liberal and progressive proponents of German colonialism before 1914 – in other words those who referenced America the most – share this sentiment?

43 Rheinische Missions-Gesellschaft, *Berichte der Rheinischen Missionsgesellschaft*, vol. 52 (Barmen: 1896); *Reichstagsdebatte (December-06–1904)*, 3391; Drechsler, *Aufstände in Südwestafrika*, 48; Gründer, *Geschichte der deutschen Kolonien*, 118.
44 Helmut Walser Smith, "The Logic of Colonial Violence: Germany in Southwest Africa (1904–1907); the United States in the Philippines (1899–1902)," in *German and American Nationalism: A Comparative Perspective*, ed. Hartmut Lehmann and Hermann Wellenreuther (New York: Berg, 1999), 211. On Rohrbach's liberalism see also Dirk van Laak, *Imperiale Infrastruktur: Deutsche Planungen für eine Erschließung Afrikas 1880 bis 1960* (Paderborn: Schöningh, 2004), 184–85.

Over the past ten years, a number of historians have revisited the positions on colonialism taken by German liberals during the early years of the twentieth century, among them Helmut Walser Smith, Erik Grimmer-Solem, and Andrew Zimmerman. All agree that German liberals, both right and left leaning, were deeply committed to German colonialism and were also quite tolerant of violent and near genocidal treatment of native peoples in German Southwest Africa. However, not all of those, liberal or otherwise, who referenced the American frontier and American Indian policies advocated exterminatory practices in Germany's colonies. Instead, Germans applied U.S. frontier lessons in the Southwest African context much as American frontier enthusiasts used the myth of the "vanishing native" to explain the disappearance of Indians as a natural, automatic, and inevitable process without (white) human culprits.[45]

Oscar Wilhelm Stübel, the RKA-B's director from 1900–05, thus compared the Herero uprising to a natural disaster, implying that neither his office nor GSWA's administration was responsible for its occurrence. Dernburg followed his predecessor's lead. In his January 1907 speech on behalf of Schmoller's Action Committee, Dernburg referred to the United States as "the biggest colonial endeavor the world has ever known," at the beginning of which stood "the complete annihilation of its native peoples." According to Dernburg, the natives' "disappearance" could not have been avoided, because extinction is an inescapable fact of nature: "[S]ome native tribes have to vanish, just as some animals perish because of the impact of civilization." He did express regret over these developments and was elated that the German

45 Helmut Walser Smith, "The Talk of Genocide, the Rhetoric of Miscegenation: Notes on the Debates in the German Reichstag Concerning Southwest Africa, 1904–14," in *The Imperialist Imagination: German Colonialism and its Legacy*, ed. Sara Friedrichsmeyer, Sara Lennox, and Susanne Zantop (Ann Arbor: University of Michigan Press, 1998), 113; Smith, "The Logic of Colonial Violence," 209–11; Conrad, *Globalisierung und Nation im Deutschen Kaiserreich*, 85; Grimmer-Solem, "The Professors' Africa," 313–15; Andrew Zimmerman, *Alabama in Africa: Booker T. Washington, the German Empire, and the Globalization of the New South* (Princeton: Princeton University Press, 2010).

colonies "were not too heavily burdened with such tribes," meaning ethnic groups fated to become extinct. Yet from the way
Dernburg portrayed the native peoples in Germany's colonies in
January 1907, his listeners could only deduce that at least some
of these tribes were in fact destined "to vanish," just as had
happened along the American frontier.[46]

Dernburg gave this speech only several days after conditions
in the Shark Island concentration camp for interned Nama and
Herero near the city of Lüderitz in GSWA had reached their
lowest point: In December 1906 alone, 276 of 1,464 incarcer-
ated Nama died, a mortality rate of 18.9 percent. These deaths
were clearly the result of the way both German military and
civil authorities handled the internees, and Dernburg knew it. To
explain these terrible facts, he nevertheless used the premise of
the "vanishing native," which, in Dernburg's own words, was
proven by the "complete annihilation" of America's Indians.
That many Herero and Nama on Shark Island had died was
"deeply regrettable," but these deaths had occurred "because
of the climate there, . . . because of exhaustion, . . . because of the
war and its stresses and strains, . . . because of a different and
unfamiliar mode of life." Dernburg never openly acknowledged
any wrongdoing on the part of the German military and stated to
the Reichstag that "it is impossible to criticize the commander's
action."[47]

Despite these statements, Dernburg was not at all supportive
of the brutal warfare practiced by German troops in GSWA. After
being named director of the RKA-B, he immediately inquired into
the conditions on Shark Island, and by April 1907 his actions had
resulted in a dramatic improvement in the camp's living conditions. Dernburg also questioned local authorities about why they
had made no earlier efforts to better the situation. So why in

[46] Dernburg, "Speech in Front of the Kolonialpolitisches Aktionskomité," 8.
[47] *Reichstagsdebatte (May-08–1907),* 1501–02; Isabel V. Hull, *Absolute Destruction: Military Culture and the Practices of War in Imperial Germany* (Ithaca, NY: Cornell University Press, 2004), 86.

January 1907 did he resort to using the "vanishing Indian" premise in his speeches to audiences in Germany? There is one likely answer. Dernburg was confronted with the atrocities German troops had committed (and were still committing) the moment he assumed office. He abhorred mindless brutality, but was an ardent believer in the German colonial project. To restore domestic faith in the viability of Germany's only settler colony, he therefore wanted to quiet domestic criticism and most importantly the SPD's frequent attacks on the way the Herero and Nama were treated.[48]

Acknowledging inhumane military practices in GSWA would have weakened the tenuous pro-colonialist, liberal-conservative alliance that had won the elections in 1907. In addition, it would have negatively affected Dernburg's own position within the administration, diminishing his chances to earn the advance praise heaped on him by the emperor and the German and international press. After all, Dernburg's appointment was supposed to symbolize a departure from Germany's so far largely unsuccessful "Kolonialpolitik," especially in GSWA. To deflect public criticism, Dernburg thus used one of the most powerful rhetorical tools available to him: the "scientific fact" that America's Indians had "vanished" as a "natural" consequence of both the continent's initial colonization and subsequent U.S. westward expansion. In all likelihood, Dernburg had his doubts about whether this premise applied to the Shark Island concentration camp. Yet because American westward expansion was appealing and because of the need to build support for a new kind of colonial politics – efficient, scientific, and ultimately more humane – he nonetheless used American examples of "disappearing" natives. This interpretation of Dernburg's refusal to explicitly criticize the German military's actions in GSWA at least during his first months in office is supported by his frank exchange with Trotha two years later. By 1909, Dernburg felt secure enough to denounce the Social Darwinist ideas underwriting

[48] Hull, *Absolute Destruction*, 86–88.

Trotha's extermination strategy and even engaged in a debate with the general that was covered in the *Berliner Neueste Nachrichten*, a Berlin daily.[49]

It would be a mistake, however, to conclude that all liberal colonial enthusiasts shared Dernburg's concerns. A case in point is Rohrbach, a trained theologian and one of the most popular colonial publicists of the left-liberal milieu in Germany before World War I. Rohrbach, who had occupied the post of settlement commissar for Southwest Africa between 1903 and 1906, was willing to take comparisons of GSWA to the settlement of America in a different direction than did Dernburg: Rohrbach accepted the mass murder committed in this colony, at least after it had occurred. In his most popular book, *The German Idea in the World*, Rohrbach explained that circumstances in GSWA were unique within the German Empire. In most German colonies, "the native element will maintain its place next to the white one... because the African natives are adaptable to the European economy and similarly necessary." In comparison, in America or Australia, "the economic integration of both Indians and Australians failed," which necessitated exterminatory measures: "[S]ettler administrations in New England offered official bounties for Indian scalps, regardless of whether they came from men, women, or children." In consequence, America "became entirely 'white man's land'." In Rohrbach's view, such exterminatory actions were impractical in all German colonies except for GSWA. There, very few "Bushmen" remained who "still give us troubles." As a result, in Southwest Africa the otherwise impractical Anglo-American examples of "expulsion and extinction," as Rohrbach phrased it in 1912, applied.[50]

[49] *Berliner Neueste Nachrichten*: "Zur Dernburgschen Eingeborenenpolitik" (March-6-1909), "Eingeborenenfragen" (March-8-1909), "Die Erwiderung des Staatssekretärs Dernburg am 2. März" (March-13-1909), *Reichstagsdebatte (March-02-1909)*, 7270.
[50] Smith, "The Logic of Colonial Violence," 211; Frank Becker, "Kolonialherrschaft und Rassenpolitik," in *Rassenmischehen*, ed. Frank Becker (Franz Steiner Verlag, 2004), 20; Horst Gründer, "Zum Stellenwert des Rassismus im Spektrum der deutschen Kolonialideologie," in *Rassenmischehen* –

Thus referencing the United States could have a wide array of intentions, ranging, in Rohrbach's case, from implicit postfactum justifications of genocide to paternalistic concerns over the well-being of native populations. The Christian-Social representative Reinhard Mumm argued for American-style reservations to protect and educate the colony's native tribes: "I am thinking of the natives in Southwest... Wouldn't it be possible... just as we have Indian reservations in North America to create native reservations in the interest of those aboriginals who initially have a hard time with our culture? After all, these people are also human!"[51]

The American frontier was thus seen as especially relevant for GSWA. During the war years between 1904 and 1907, the German Colonial Association even financed a study trip to the American West for the civil engineer Alexander Kuhn. Kuhn was supposed to explore how German endeavors in GSWA could benefit from applying "civilizing" techniques used by Americans in the West, especially in Arizona. Once he had arrived, Kuhn felt that a comparison between "the situations of the natives here [in the United States] and there [in Southwest Africa] naturally presented itself. Not only that of the imported [sic] Negroes but especially that of the Indians, whose final prostration took a long series of bloody wars." Kuhn argued that "the rearrangement of the situation of the Natives [in GSWA] will have to be

---

Mischlinge – Rassentrennung, 39; Josef Anker, "Paul Rohrbach," in *Allgemeine Deutsche Biographie* (Berlin: Rohmer–Schinkel, 2005), 5–6; Benjamin Madley, "From Africa to Auschwitz: How German Southwest Africa Incubated Ideas and Methods Adopted and Developed by the Nazis in Eastern Europe," *European History Quarterly* 35, no. 3 (2005); Paul Rohrbach, *Der deutsche Gedanke in der Welt* (Königstein: Langewiesche, 1915), 124–25; Gründer, *Geschichte der deutschen Kolonien*, 124.

[51] *Reichstagsdebatte (March-17–1904)*, 1896; *Reichstagsdebatte (March-07–1913)*, 4364; Helmut Busch, "Reinhard Mumm," in *Allgemeine deutsche Biographie & Neue deutsche Biographie* (Berlin: Rohmer–Schinkel, 1997), 582–83. Helmut Walser Smith wrongly attributes Mumm's quote to the left-liberal Ernst Müller. Smith, "The Talk of Genocide," 114–15; Helmut Walser Smith, *The Continuities of German History: Nation, Religion, and Race across the Long Nineteenth Century* (Cambridge: Cambridge University Press, 2007), 201.

tackled very soon." In his view, American Indian reservations were exemplary and should be emulated in GSWA: "Even those of us who feel completely liberated from the German original sin of adoring everything foreign just because it is foreign neverthe-less have much to learn from the measures the Americans have taken to solve the Native problem."[52]

Likewise, the pro-colonialist (and anti-SPD) publications of Schmoller's Action Committee, most prominently the *Guide to Colonial Politics* (henceforth *KF*), argued that GSWA displayed the same initial growing pains as the young American colonies: "Virginia... after 20 years had a population base of only 1,000 inhabitants.... The other European settlements in today's United States developed along similar lines... [T]wenty years after the first settlement of North America an English Social Democrat could have justifiably disputed North America's suitability for colonization because of the fact that only 1,000 to 2,000 English-men lived there."[53]

Theodor Leutwein, GSWA's governor from 1898 to 1905, who rose from a conservative army background to one of Impe-rial Germany's top colonial offices, also used frontier imagery. For him, America's westward expansion provided effective illus-trations demonstrating the suitability of Southwest Africa for German settlement (Leutwein compared the colony to Nevada,

---

[52] Kuhn, *Zum Eingeborenenproblem in Deutsch-Südwestafrika*, 3. See also *Deutsche Kolonialzeitung*, no. 15 (1903): 145–46; ibid., no. 16: 156–57; *Deutsche Kolonialzeitung*, no. 20 (1905): 198; ibid., no. 39: 411–13; ibid., no. 46: 472; and these references in *Beiträge zur Kolonialpolitik und Kolonial-wirtschaft* (1900–01): M. Hans Klössel, "Grund und Boden in Nordamerika," 576–78; Carl Stroever, "Treibende Kräfte amerikanischer Kolonialpolitik," 129–32; Eduard Wirth, "Die jüngste Entwicklung Nordamerikas," 609–11; Rudolf A. Hermann, "Von der Kolonialpolitik der nordamerikanischen Union," *Beiträge zur Kolonialpolitik und Kolonialwirtschaft* 4 (1902/1903): 1–5; G. K. Anton, "Zur Landfrage in den Kolonien," *Beiträge zur Kolo-nialpolitik und Kolonialwirtschaft* 5 (1903): 2–5; Ferdinand Gessert, "Das Wasserrecht des amerikanischen Westen mit Bezug auf Deutsch-Süd-West-Afrika," *Zeitschrift für Kolonialpolitik, Kolonialrecht und Kolonialwirtschaft* 8, no. 7 (1906): 441–46.

[53] Kolonialpolitisches Aktionskomité, ed., *Kolonialpolitischer Führer* (Berlin: Wedekind, 1907), 12, 13, 16.

Wyoming, and Colorado and, like the *KF*, made references to colonial Virginia). In his memoirs, published in 1906, he argued that the war in GSWA had been caused by conditions that had also existed in the American West: "[I]t is the same battle that once was fought by North-American settlers." Leutwein reinterpreted the origins of the war in Southwest Africa against the backdrop of the American frontier, thus exonerating his administration. In his memoirs, he recalled the bloody conflict not as the result of German failures, but rather as the inevitable result of (white) European expansion, which occurred similarly whether in North America or elsewhere around the globe.[54]

Before 1914, one of the most attractive features of using the United States as a model for colonization was its appeal to various pro-colonialist groups. Left- and right leaning liberals as well as conservatives and nationalists recognized the exemplary character of America, especially regarding Southwest Africa. This observation neither implies that America signified one and the same thing for everybody referencing it, nor that the United States was the only point of orientation used in discussions of the war in GSWA. Yet before, during, and immediately after the national elections of 1907, bringing up America helped create and maintain a discursive framework that, although determined by liberal political tenets, nevertheless remained attractive for colonialists of different political persuasions as well.

By 1914, German perceptions of the United States, shaped by liberal imperialists and scholars, had established powerful images of the American frontier that were used to bolster both pro-colonialist arguments and specific colonial policies, for example the (ultimately unsuccessful) establishment of reservations for indigenous peoples in GSWA. During the 1890s men like Carl Peters had exploited and further developed these metaphors to rationalize their agitation for colonies, whereas a decade later

---

[54] Theodor Leutwein, *Deutsch-Süd-West-Afrika* (Berlin: Dietrich Reimer, 1898), 36–37, 42–43; Theodor Leutwein, *Elf Jahre Gouverneur in Deutsch-Südwestafrika*, 3rd ed. (Berlin: E. S. Mittler & Sohn, 1908), 289–90; Gustav Warneck, *Die gegenwärtige Lage der deutschen evangelischen Mission* (Berlin: Martin Warneck, 1905), 8.

colonial administrators like Leutwein or Rohrbach used them to justify their actions in GSWA. In all of these instances, the allegedly peculiarly German "identificatory enthusiasm for things Indian," as Susanne Zantop put it, played little or no role. Naturally, Germans used imagery of American expansion and American Indians for expedient national ends. Yet the importance of Friedrich Ratzel's pro-expansionist thought for the American scientific community reveals that Germans also returned the favor. In consequence, late nineteenth- and early twentieth-century visions of American westward expansion and the treatment of Native Americans had two complementary dimensions: On the one hand, these images were products of transnational processes of intellectual exchange. On the other, they were used to justify similar practices of expansion within two different national contexts. In the United States tropes about "empty lands" and "Indian savages" bolstered notions of a benign American exceptionalism, which posited that settling the American West contributed both to the spread of civilization and the stabilizing of the exceptional American republic. In Germany, understanding the American frontier in unexceptional and global terms helped generate excitement for overseas expansion and sometimes even acceptance for the violent measures presumably necessitated by imperialist policies.

Viewed from the perspective of German liberals, the United States demonstrated that successful colonialism rested on racialized notions of individual freedom: American westward expansion and Indian policies appeared to be almost exclusively driven by the pioneer spirit of white frontiersmen, who were in turn protected and supported by the liberal political system of the United States. The importance of American examples for the debates surrounding Germany's only settler colony, Southwest Africa, also demonstrates that German liberals, both left- and right-leaning, viewed colonialism as "their" political project. Already during the late nineteenth century, Carl Peters perceived America as a liberal colonial empire and argued forcefully for American-style settler colonialism. Friedrich Ratzel agreed. Independent white settlers knew best "how to till the soil" on foreign land and how to "deal" with native populations. Liberals thus accepted violence against conquered ethnic groups and, in some cases, sanctioned forms of what is now called ethnic cleansing with the aim of opening "living space" to whites. As a result, politicians like Dernburg or Rohrbach could invoke images of the American West as "white man's land" to justify the situation in Southwest Africa during and after the Herero and Nama uprising.

Throughout the second half of the nineteenth and even more during the early years of the twentieth century, German liberal colonialists perceived America as an unexceptional colonial empire; this view made the transplantation of measures taken along the American frontier to Southwest Africa both feasible and justifiable. Influential German imperialists argued for the emulation of American methods, thereby countering notions that promoted nationalist or "German-centric" approaches to overseas expansion. To be sure, chauvinist ideas of Germans as being better at colonizing than other Europeans existed. However, similar sentiments could frequently be found in other nations, including the United States. German imperialists sometimes rather sulkily commented on the fact that other powers appeared to condemn the German inability to spread civilization around the globe. In 1902, a writer for a monthly publication of the German Colonial Association thus bitterly complained that American imperialists treated the German contribution to "world politics" as completely "negligible."[55]

This author's prickly response to American comments on the achievements of German imperialism illustrates that during the late nineteenth and early twentieth centuries the domestic debate about overseas expansion was remarkably open to outside input. International criticism was read and commented on; examples set by other imperial powers were analyzed and, as in the case of American westward expansion and Indian policies, recommended for imitation in GSWA. In consequence, despite being

---

[55] Poultney Bigelow, *The Children of the Nations* (London: W. Heinemann, 1901); Hermann, "Von der Kolonialpolitik der nordamerikanischen Union," 4–5; Zantop, *Colonial Fantasies*, 7.

widespread, feelings of sympathy toward Indians had little influence on colonial politics during the fin-de-siècle and the early years of the twentieth century in Germany. In contrast, sentiments of liberal colonialism and racial superiority certainly did.[56]

[56] Zantop, *Colonial Fantasies*, 7.

3

The American South and Racial
Segregation in the German Colonies

In his classic *The Origins of the New South* (1951), historian C.
Vann Woodward argued that, after the removal of federal troops
in 1877, the American South became economically dependent on
the northern "Yankee Empire." As the term "empire" suggests, in
Woodward's view this dependency was in essence a colonial one,
displaying similarities to the relationship of Europe's colonies to
their motherlands. So far, this book has focused on the connections between German colonialism and America's westward
expansion. This chapter looks at a different region of the United
States. In the early years of the twentieth century, German colonialists too believed that the American South exhibited colonial characteristics, yet their evaluation of these qualities was
diametrically opposed to Woodward's. In their view, instead of
resembling a colonial dependency, the "New South" was exemplary for colonizers all over the world, particularly for settlers
in Germany's African colonies and for colonial administrators in
Berlin.[1]

Before World War I, Europeans experimented with various
forms of racial control in their colonies, a development that
was noticed in the United States. According to historian Glenda

---

[1] C. Vann Woodward, *Origins of the New South, 1877–1913* (Louisiana State
University Press, 1951), 291–320 (esp. 297, 311).

Gilmore, "white Southerners imagined they heard a long-awaited
distress signal that summoned them to rescue a white race drown-
ing in a rising tide of color." This chapter traces the story of the
early twentieth-century Germans who sent out such distress sig-
nals. Like white Southerners, German colonialists believed that
"Southern experience counted for something": Through newspapers, books, and official correspondence between German diplomats in the United States and their superiors in Berlin, Germans
received and actively sought information about the so-called
"Negro problem" in the United States. Before the First World
War, German colonialists found the American South's solutions
to this assumed predicament inspiring and worthy of imitation
in Germany's colonies; these solutions were so stimulating and
praiseworthy, in fact, that the attractiveness of Southern Jim
Crow provisions, from the perspective of colonial administrators
in Africa, far surpassed that of geographically closer examples
of racial segregation; for example, in South Africa's Transvaal
province.[2]

Recently, scholars have begun to examine the role of
German-American exchanges within the economic framework
of nineteenth- and early twentieth-century colonialism. The most
important work in this respect is Andrew Zimmerman's *Alabama
in Africa*. Zimmerman shows how questions and methods of
labor organization and control connected sugar beet fields in the
German East with both cotton sharecropping in the "redeemed"
post–Civil War American South and attempts to introduce these
"New South" agricultural schemes and forms of racialized labor
control in the German colony of Togo. Yet because German
colonialists were so eager to learn how to successfully implement racial segregation measures from American examples, links
between America and German colonialism were by no means
limited to the question of how to turn the German colonies'
African inhabitants into a productive workforce according to
"New South" models. Although some scholars have analyzed

[2] Glenda E. Gilmore, *Defying Dixie: The Radical Roots of Civil Rights, 1919–
1950* (Norton, 2008), 15–18.

connections between Nazi race policies and Jim Crow provisions in the American South (these links are considered in the following chapter), the ties between American race codes and racial segregation measures in the German colonies before 1914 have gone largely unnoticed and are therefore explored in the following pages.[3]

The focus of German colonialists and colonial administrators in Berlin on American examples of racial segregation was tied to the fact that the presence of America within expansionist debates had a long tradition in Germany. Moreover, during the early years of the twentieth century German relations with the other European great powers were on a seemingly steady downhill slope, whereas the United States appeared to be less entangled in the complicated web of European international affairs. America therefore attracted the gaze of German colonialists. With respect to questions of race control and to the issue of settler colonialism, for nineteenth- and early twentieth-century German colonizers the United States remained both exemplary and unexceptional. Germans looked toward the United States because American race codes appeared to be quite typical when viewed against the backdrop of European imperialism. This regularity made such measures attractive because it lent them an

---

[3] Johnpeter Grill and Robert L. Jenkins, "The Nazis and the American South in the 1930s: A Mirror Image?," *Journal of Southern History* 58, no. 4 (1992); Fatima El-Tayeb, *Schwarze Deutsche: Der Diskurs um 'Rasse' und Nationalität 1890–1933* (Campus Fachbuch, 2001); Birthe Kundrus, "Von Windhoek nach Nuernberg? Koloniale 'Mischehenverbote' und die nationalsozialistische Rassengesetzgebung," in *Phantasiereiche. Zur Kulturgeschichte des deutschen Kolonialismus*, ed. Birthe Kundrus (Frankfurt a. M.: Campus Verlag, 2003); Sebastian Conrad and Jürgen Osterhammel, *Das Kaiserreich transnational. Deutschland in der Welt 1871–1914* (Vandenhoeck & Ruprecht, 2004); Andrew Zimmerman, "A German Alabama in Africa: The Tuskegee Expedition to German Togo and the Transnational Origins of West African Cotton Growers," *American Historical Review* 110 (2005); Sven Beckert, "From Tuskegee to Togo: The Problem of Freedom in the Empire of Cotton," *Journal of American History* 92, no. 2 (2005); Sebastian Conrad, *Globalisierung und Nation im Deutschen Kaiserreich* (Munich: C. H. Beck, 2006); Gilmore, *Defying Dixie*; Andrew Zimmerman, *Alabama in Africa: Booker T. Washington, the German Empire, and the Globalization of the New South* (Princeton: Princeton University Press, 2010).

aura of real possibility and appeared to make them reproducible elsewhere. Moreover, Germans who admired American racial segregation policies did not necessarily subscribe to ideas of a positive German exceptionalism. Instead, they wanted the German Empire to be typical too. To achieve this goal, Germany, like the United States and its big European neighbors, needed to expand globally, and it needed to heed the examples provided by others, especially the United States. Neither the proponents of racial segregation in the United States (Woodrow Wilson being the most obvious example) nor their counterparts in Imperial Germany were limited to backward-looking or chauvinist circles. It was precisely because of America's importance for liberal-colonialist views that before World War I the United States became an important historical and sociopolitical backdrop against which colonial administrators, settlers, and proponents of overseas expansion formulated their solutions to the perceived problem of racial mixing in the German colonies.

Racial Segregation in German Colonial Practice and Metropolitan Discourse, 1905–1914

In 1905, Hans Tecklenburg, vice governor of German Southwest Africa, issued the first mixed-race marriage ban in Germany's colonies. Others were to follow: German East Africa's governor instituted a similar measure in 1906, and Wilhelm Solf, governor of German Samoa and after September 1911 state secretary of the Reichskolonialamt in Berlin, enacted a segregationist ban for Samoa in January 1912. Solf's decree unwisely originated from the metropole and provoked the Reichstag – which had previously turned a blind eye to colonial miscegenation orders (which violated German citizenship law) – to take note of this issue. Unfortunately for German pro-colonialists and proponents of racial segregation, liberal and conservative alike, after the January 1912 elections the Reichstag had a left-center majority. SPD deputies formed the strongest faction with

110 seats, followed by the Center Party with eighty-eight. The 1912 elections reversed the outcome of the 1907 elections, which had resulted in a pro-government and pro-colonialist Reichstag majority composed of conservative, nationalist, and right- and left-leaning liberal parties. The right-liberal majority produced by the 1907 elections had deprived the moderate Center Party of its role as a government-supporting party. As a result, it became more critical of government measures. Consequently, whereas before 1907 some Center Party representatives, in particular Matthias Erzberger, had expressed quite racist viewpoints in support of the brutal war against the Herero and Nama in GSWA, during the 1912 miscegenation debates the party joined forces with the Social Democrats in vehemently contesting the scientific racism that underwrote the pro-race-code arguments made by Solf, the liberal parties, and conservative and nationalist Reichstag deputies.

Unlike the RKA's first state secretary Bernhard Dernburg, Solf could thus not rely on a well-disposed Reichstag. But like Dernburg, he was a political liberal. After World War I, his political convictions led him to become one of the left-liberal Deutsche Demokratische Partei (DDP) candidates for the Weimar Republic's first parliament, the national assembly of 1919. Before he became state secretary of the RKA in 1911, he had made a name for himself as the skilled and capable governor of German Samoa, who, unlike the governors of Germany's African colonies, held his colony's native population in high esteem and, as a result, managed to avoid large-scale uprisings or conflict during his tenure. Yet he did not draw on his "noble savage" image of native Samoans when promoting colonial miscegenation bans in Berlin. Solf believed instead that the tenets of scientific racism and the example of the American South had more persuasive potential for his audience of metropolitan lawmakers.[4]

---

[4] George Steinmetz has argued that Solf's attempts to stop racial mixing between Germans and Samoans were "motivated in part by his commitment to the survival of the Samoan 'race' and culture." Yet whatever Solf's reasons for decreeing this ban in January 1912, when defending it in the Reichstag some months

Solf's metropolitan-issued segregation decree for Samoa put the question of colonial race ordinances on the Reichstag deputies' agenda in Berlin, and on May 8, 1912, the Reichstag passed two resolutions with SPD and Center votes: The first strongly censured the existing racial segregation decrees in the German colonies and called for the unconditional recognition of mixed-race marriages. The second, even more worrisome for Solf, asked for a national law to regulate and strengthen the parliament's influence in the colonies. If the SPD-Center majority were to put such a piece of legislation before the Reichstag (in fact, each individual deputy had a so-called Initiativrecht [i.e., the right to propose legislation]) the law could, if passed, quash locally decreed race bans in Germany's colonies and weaken the power of Solf's own office, and that of colonial administrators on the ground to boot. This was an unlikely development given that, to become law, such legislation would have to be approved not only by the Reichstag but also by the deputies of the German states, who were represented in the Federal Council (Bundesrat), which in turn was dominated by Prussian delegates. However, because of the results of the 1912 election both the government and Solf's RKA needed at least to take the wishes of the Center Party seriously (cooperation with the SPD was out of the question). This scenario had clearly been far from Solf's intentions in January 1912. What to do? The colonial secretary and the RKA found answers to this question by closely studying state and local race codes in the United States. Turning to America was a way of dealing with this clash of interests in Germany's center and along the German Empire's colonial periphery.[5]

later, he only invoked negative racial stereotypes. Compare George Steinmetz, *The Devil's Handwriting: Precoloniality and the German Colonial State in Qingdao, Samoa, and Southwest Africa* (Chicago: University of Chicago Press, 2007), 14–15, 346–48.

[5] Marcus Kreuzer, "Parliamentarization and the Question of German Exceptionalism: 1867–1918," *Central European History* 36 (2003): 339; *Reichstagsdebatte (May-07–1912)*, 1730; *Reichstagsdebatte (May-08–1912)*, 1744. For the FVP's voting, see *Reichstagsdebatte (May-08–1912)*, 1747, 1773–76; *Reichstagshandbuch: 13. Legislaturperiode (1912)*, 419. On the legislative process and the Reichstag's constitutional powers in the German Empire, see Ernst

"So that he doesn't become slothful": The United States, Racial Control, and German Colonialism

On March 27, 1906, Ernst zu Hohenlohe-Langenburg, the head of the RKA-B, sent out a letter to the German embassies in Paris, the Hague, and London. In respect to the issue of mixed-race marriages in the German colonies, Hohenlohe-Langenburg was interested in learning "how this question...has been legally or practically solved in a) the French, b) the Dutch, c) the British colonies." On April 6, the first reply arrived from London. It stated that "in the English colonies...no ordinances exist that prohibit or limit marriages between natives and non-natives."[6]

The replies from all three embassies affirmed that no miscegenation laws existed in any European colony (although this information was in fact inaccurate). In 1908, however, one year after the colonial section of the Foreign Office had become the Imperial Colonial Office (RKA), a paper addressed to Hohenlohe's successor, the liberal and reformist ex-banker Bernhard Dernburg, was added to the RKA's "miscegenation file." This commentary, authored by the German consul in New Orleans, Ferdinand von Nordenflycht, openly linked the "race question" in the United States to the situation in the German colonies: "Incidentally, the Negro question is relevant only to United States domestic policy, and its development would be of only historical interest for us, if the areas of protection did not exist, which

Rudolf Huber, *Deutsche Verfassungsgeschichte seit 1789*, 3 vols., vol. III (Stuttgart: W. Kohlhammer Verlag, 1963), 920–21.

[6] BArch. R 1001/5420, pp. 2–3, 6; Gerhard A. Ritter, "Bernhard Dernburg," in *Allgemeine deutsche Biographie & Neue deutsche Biographie* (Berlin: Bürklein–Ditmar, 1957), 607–08. Dernburg succeeded Hohenlohe-Langenburg as director of the Colonial Office in December 1906 and became the newly formed RKA's state secretary in May 1907. It should be noted that, although the Transvaal was already part of the British Empire in 1906, the race codes that existed in this British colony were not mentioned in Schnee's response to Hohenlohe-Langenburg. As this chapter shows, even after metropolitan officials had been made aware of these laws, the Transvaal nevertheless only played a minor role (compared to the United States) in the arguments made by those who supported miscegenation provisions in the German colonies.

could draw lessons for their native populations from the experience Americans have gained with Negroes."[7]

Nordenflycht's paper was thirty-one typewritten pages long (by far the longest and most detailed report in the RKA's dossier on mixed-race marriages), and the RKA's officers made multiple copies to be kept on file, "because of its fundamental importance for the question of the legal status of the natives." Eventually Nordenflycht's analysis sparked a burst of activity among the RKA staff. Dernburg drew heavily on American examples when justifying or explaining his policies. But beginning in early 1912 it was the third and last Reichskolonialamt state secretary, Wilhelm Solf (1911–18), who focused his attention on the information on race codes in the American South available in his office's files. Surprisingly, he continued to do so up until the outbreak of World War I, although the interest of the German public and the Reichstag in this matter quickly waned after the parliamentary debates on the "miscegenation question" ended in May 1912. The following analysis offers an explanation for this sequence of events.[8]

America's liberal and decentralized political system made the United States a very attractive example for liberal German proponents of miscegenation bans, because the U.S. government allowed great freedom of action to its southern states (and some others) – the American periphery from the RKA's perspective. The liberal Solf therefore took an especially keen interest in local U.S. race codes after it became clear that it would be very hard to achieve a solution of this issue at the national level in Germany. Solf's approach rested on a long tradition. During the nineteenth

[7] BArch. R 1001/5420, p. 74.
[8] BArch. R 1001/5420, pp. 74–104, 105, 119–20. Information on the U.S. South collected by the RKA included newspaper clippings and consulate reports on lynching (BArch. R 1001/5420, pp. 3, 8, 9, 131), Nordenflycht's earlier mentioned report, correspondence with American newspaper journalists (BArch. R 1001/5420, pp. 116–17), Solf's detailed handwritten notes (BArch. R 1001/5420, pp. 119–24), and requests for academic papers on "the Negro problem" in the United States (BArch. R 1001/5420, p. 134).

century, German colonialists and expansionists had looked westward to the United States for inspiration. At the end of the nineteenth century, expansionist perspectives that persistently linked America's emergence as a new world power to the country's successful application of various forms of racialized social and economic control were popular among representatives of different political groups, and most importantly many liberals. In the late 1890s, the national-liberal Carl Peters argued that the kind of colonization policy that had made the United States the most successful of all European colonial settlements should be used to "develop the program for practical colonial policies for all times." For Peters, America's triumphant rise to world power status was simultaneously a triumph for liberal colonialism. He proclaimed that there existed no alternative to an American-style "liberal colonialism."[9]

Peters' statements echoed arguments made repeatedly by Friedrich Ratzel. As we have seen, Ratzel's many geopolitical writings about the United States praised the "American character," the U.S. Constitution, and, most importantly, minimally regulated Anglo-American settlement policies in North America. These methods harnessed the motivations and energies of individual settlers instead of forcing them under a rigid system of state control. A multitude of decentralized pioneering efforts

---

[9] El-Tayeb, *Schwarze*, 48, 101; Kundrus, "Von Windhoek nach Nuernberg?," 119–20; Carl Peters, *Carl Peters gesammelte Schriften*, ed. Walter Frank, 3 vols., vol. 1 (Munich: C. H. Beck'sche Verlagsbuchhandlung, 1943), 378, 386, 393, 409. On imperialism and the left-liberal milieu in early twentieth-century Germany, see Erik Grimmer-Solem, "The Professors' Africa: Economists, the Elections of 1907, and the Legitimation of German Imperialism," *German History* 25, no. 3 (2007); Helmut Walser Smith, "The Talk of Genocide, the Rhetoric of Miscegenation: Notes on the Debates in the German Reichstag Concerning Southwest Africa, 1904–14," in *The Imperialist Imagination: German Colonialism and its Legacy*, ed. Sara Friedrichsmeyer, Sara Lennox, and Susanne Zantop (Ann Arbor: University of Michigan Press, 1998); Helmut Walser Smith, "The Logic of Colonial Violence: Germany in Southwest Africa (1904–1907); the United States in the Philippines (1899–1902)," in *German and American Nationalism: A Comparative Perspective*, ed. Hartmut Lehmann and Hermann Wellenreuther (New York: Berg, 1999).

organized independently by numerous white Anglo-Americans and European immigrants had resulted in the permanent settlement of most of North America.[10]

Ratzel admired how laissez-faire attitudes permeated and governed American society, at local, state, and federal levels. Of course, it was also a given for Ratzel that those who enjoyed and effectively used the liberality and freedom of the American political system were white. Short of reinstituting slavery, white Americans were thus free to tackle the "problem" of racial difference as they saw fit. According to Ratzel, since the abolition of slavery a broad range of evidence had accumulated to suggest "that an interest in his work has to be instilled in the colored worker so that he does not become slothful." This 1880 remark from Ratzel signaled a new and very concrete sense of urgency regarding matters of racial difference and the controlling of race, a sentiment that at the time was quickly becoming commonplace among German proponents of colonial expansion: Without slavery, how could native populations in the European colonies (and African Americans in the U.S. South) be persuaded to work for their white masters?[11]

However, this "colonial workers' question" [koloniale Arbeiterfrage], an issue that Germans began to discuss in earnest during the first years of the twentieth century, was only one of the many consequences of Germany's acquisition of colonies, and only one of the topics that created congruent interests in Imperial Germany and the southern United States. In his 1893 *Politische Geographie der Vereinigten Staaten von Nord-Amerika* [Political Geography of the United States], Ratzel demonstrated that in the United States the problem of how to "manage the Negro" was not limited to controlling and overseeing black economic productivity

[10] Friedrich Ratzel, *Politische Geographie der Vereinigten Staaten von Amerika*, 2. Aufl. ed., 2 vols. (Munich: R. Oldenbourg, 1893), 95; Friedrich Ratzel, *Der Staat und sein Boden geographisch betrachtet* (Leipzig: S. Hirzel, 1896), 86, 97, 98. For literature on Ratzel, see Chapter 2, note 21.
[11] Friedrich Ratzel, *Culturgeographie der Vereinigten Staaten von Nordamerika unter besonderer Berücksichtigung der wirtschaftlichen Verhältnisse*, 2 vols. (Munich: 1880), 214.

through the sharecropping system. The equally important question of how to restrain blacks socially was solved through racial segregation. Ratzel thus noted that mixed-race marriages were "prohibited in more than just the Southern States." When he traveled the United States in 1874–75, Ratzel witnessed the dawn of what historian George M. Frederickson termed "the era of laissez-faire segregation," which was shaped by "a strong reliance on custom and an avoidance of overtly discriminatory legislation." Later, when Ratzel incorporated his impressions into his *Politische Geographie*, he not only referred to the race codes that had been instituted after he left the United States but also admiringly pointed out that these laws were not imposed from above. Instead, they had grown out of long-standing local traditions that proscribed "interaction between the races." During and after the wars in GSWA and GEA between 1904 and 1908, German colonial administrators and settlers also developed segregationist practices – practices they justified with explicit references to the United States.[12]

In 1906, even Emperor Wilhelm II took note of the United States' attractiveness as a model colonial empire, when he echoed Ratzel's and Peters' visions of America's commendable "liberale Kolonialpolitik." On the occasion of his appointment of the left-liberal Bernhard Dernburg as secretary of the newly created Reichskolonialamt, Wilhelm exclaimed, "I need Americans!" Dernburg came from a liberal and business-oriented family, and he had worked in a New York bank as a young man. Both German and American newspapers believed that his appointment was the result of his liberal convictions and his American business background. The liberal *Nationalzeitung* [National Times] even interpreted it as a "triumph of Americanism."[13]

A couple of months before he became the first state secretary of the new RKA, Dernburg delivered a forceful speech in Berlin

---

[12] George M. Fredrickson, *White Supremacy: A Comparative Study in American and South African History* (New York: Oxford University Press, 1980), 259–60; Ratzel, *Politische Geographie der Vereinigten Staaten von Amerika*, 282.
[13] Wilhelm II quoted in Zimmerman, *Alabama*, 374, 375.

in which he advocated modern and "scientific" colonial policies. Even Americans picked up on this speech's frequent references to America's history as a colonizing power and to the country's "Negro problem." On January 9, 1907, the *New York Times* reported, "Throughout the evening long references were made to the colonization experiences of the United States. Herr Dernburg, speaking of the treatment of natives in the German colonies, and tracing the evolution of the American Negro, declared that Americans admitted that the Negro question was the most serious problem of the greatest Republic in the world." The day before this synopsis of his speech was printed in the *New York Times*, Dernburg had indeed argued that "this mass of 9 million quarter- and half-educated negroes" was "a danger to the existence of the North American republic." The only way to solve this "problem" not only in the United States but especially in the German colonies was a laissez-faire approach to colonial politics: "Here, only deliberate and rational actions by especially trained and educated people, whose room to maneuver must not be overly restricted, will help. Not too many regulations, no bureaucracy, but men with common sense and free opinions."[14]

Dernburg's views carried weight – and during the 1907 parliamentary elections helped Chancellor Bülow renew the old cooperation between liberals and conservatives in the Reichstag, which had supported so many of the policies of Otto von Bismarck, Bülow's famous predecessor. This "Bülow Bloc," an alliance of all liberal and conservative and nationalist parties that backed the war against the Herero and Nama in Southwest Africa, won the elections. As a result, the Bülow government gained in strength, and Dernburg and his policies gained prestige and support. Some left-wing liberals, unlike members of Ratzel's National Liberal Party, had not supported German colonialism from the beginning. Eugen Richter, one of Carl Peters' sharpest

---

[14] "Germans Cite Our Colonies," *New York Times* (New York: January 9, 1907); Kolonialpolitisches Aktionskomité, *Offizieller stenographischer Bericht über die Versammlung in der Berliner Hochschule für Musik am 8. Januar 1907*, 7–8.

critics during the 1890s, is the primary example of this faction of
German political liberalism. However, (left-) liberals did eventually come around to enthusiastically sponsoring Germany's "cultural mission" abroad, especially after Richter's death in 1906.
Imperial Germany's most influential and famous colonial administrators Bernhard Dernburg and Wilhelm Solf certainly did.[15]

Both state secretaries gravitated toward the progressive wing
of German political liberalism while simultaneously sharing
Ratzel's and Peters' enthusiasm for American-style methods. In
addition, Dernburg and Solf worked closely with conservatives in
the Reichstag and, like Ratzel and Peters, embraced "quite racist"
attitudes toward Germany's colonial subjects, despite their association with a more humane and "modern" colonialism. Solf's
left-liberal reputation thus did not keep him from vigorously
defending (and expanding) the existing miscegenation bans in
the German colonies, although his progressive repute was often
the subject of criticism and ridicule by right-wing and conservative newspapers. According to these papers' editorialists, Solf's
only saving grace as colonial secretary was his clear stance on and
leadership role in the miscegenation question, which, in the eyes
of the conservative *Die Post*, turned him from "Saul to Paul."[16]

By the spring of 1912, the parliamentary representatives of
German conservatism and liberalism were in a minority position
in the Reichstag, but because of the empire's autocratic structure,
they nevertheless wielded quite a substantial amount of power
when it came to colonial matters, especially vis-à-vis their political opponents (particularly Social Democrats and Center Party
politicians). Following the "Dernburg turn" in 1906–07, liberal
tenets had gained a firm grip on the organization of German

[15] Zimmerman, *Alabama*, 377, 378; Conrad, *Globalisierung und Nation im Deutschen Kaiserreich*, 84–85; Grimmer-Solem, "Professors' Africa"; Smith, "The Talk of Genocide," 113–14.
[16] For commentaries on Solf's liberalism by conservative papers, see an edi-torial by Johannes W. Harnisch in *Deutsch-Übersee* (no date), titled "Fuer die Rassenvermanschung," a feature in the *Deutsche Kolonialzeitung*, no. 13 (March 30, 1912), and an article in *Die Post*, no. 138 (March 20, 1912). Clippings in BArch R 1001/5417 pp. 95–96, 102, 103.

colonialism. The liberalization of the German colonial administration both in Berlin and on the ground was exemplified by the
policies of Georg Albrecht von Rechenberg, who in 1906 became
GEA's first civilian governor. He attempted to reboot the German colonial enterprise in East Africa through a brokering of
white and black interests that would turn the colony into an economically viable center for international colonial trade. Albert
Hahl, governor of New Guinea from 1902–14, pursued similar
objectives. In addition to an interest in the scientific exploration
of New Guinea, Hahl implemented policies that were primarily aimed at the colony's financial development. During Hahl's
tenure, New Guinea's economic output increased sixfold. In
addition, both the conception and completion of many colonial
infrastructure projects during the Dernburg era embodied a new,
liberal, and economically minded approach toward colonialism.
Although German liberals had supported and in fact clamored
for colonialist activities all through the nineteenth century, their
actual influence on practical colonial politics thus expanded significantly during the last decade before the Great War.[17]

Jim Crow and Mixed-Race Marriage Bans in the German Colonies from 1905 to 1912

To carry out his new approach to colonial policy, Dernburg
traveled not only to the German colonies but also to the United
States, where he visited Alabama, Mississippi, Louisiana, Texas,

[17] On the prevalence of "America" in liberal colonialist debates during the mid-
nineteenth century, see Matthew P. Fitzpatrick, *Liberal Imperialism in Germany: Expansionism and Nationalism, 1848–1884* (New York: Berghahn
Books, 2008), 41, 87, 166–67, 182–83. For liberal policies in the German
colonies, see Fritz Fischer, *Griff nach der Weltmacht: Die Kriegszielpolitik
des kaiserlichen Deutschlands 1914/18* (Düsseldorf: Droste Verlag, 1961),
495; Ulrich van der Heyden, "Georg Albrecht von Rechenberg," in *Allgemeine deutsche Biographie & Neue deutsche Biographie* (Berlin: Pütter-
Rohlfs, 2003), 231–32. On metropolitan (left-) liberal takes on colonialism
and the increasing appeal of liberal political tenets for German colonial settlers during the first decade of the twentieth century, see Lora Wildenthal,
German Women for Empire, 1884–1945 (Durham: Duke University Press,
2001), 98–100.

and Oklahoma. He admired and commended the sharecropping system, because it combined free labor with methods of social and racial control. Back in Europe, Dernburg stated that while in the United States he had realized "that cotton growing was essentially a Negro's job." In his view "an ideal system would be one in which the White man would act as director of Negro labor, subjecting his workers to discipline, so that they could be relied upon to work regularly." Naturally Dernburg's ideas about an unfettered, liberal, and of course economically viable colonial self-government applied only to white settlers.[18]

Dernburg believed that in the United States only "state-administered hygienic measures" prevented a decline of the "Negro population," arguing that these unreliable and "inherent" characteristics of African Americans could also be found among natives in the German colonies. In consequence, they had to be controlled and educated, just as were African Americans in the American South. However, these measures could not be decided on centrally in the metropole, but had to be administered by local colonial officers and settlers, the "men with common sense and free opinions" he had called on in 1907. During his tenure at the Reichskolonialamt, Dernburg was largely concerned with improving the financial situation of the German colonies so they could eventually become self-reliant and economically viable without subsidies from the metropole. In his mind the control of race was inseparably connected to this task.[19]

Dernburg traveled to the United States for inspiration in 1909, yet in regard to racial segregation, German colonial administrators and settlers had picked up on the exemplary potential of the American South much earlier. In newspapers, settlers thus likened their cause to that of the American Confederacy, and only one year into the genocidal campaign against the Herero and Nama in German Southwest Africa, the colony's vice governor Hans Tecklenburg wrote to Berlin that he had come to the

---

[18] Quoted in Wildenthal, *German Women for Empire*, 98–102.
[19] Bernhard Dernburg, "Baumwollproduktion und Negerfrage in den Vereinigten Staaten," *Zeitschrift für Socialwissenschaft*, no. 5 (1911): 349–50.

conclusion that mixed-race marriages were "impermissible," although they were in fact permitted by existing legislation. In addition, he stated that the "result of the judicial examination of this matter corresponds completely with what the colony's administration has to consider necessary for social and political reasons." On the next page of his letter, Tecklenburg referred to "the experience of other nations in this important matter." He argued that miscegenation had led to the "degradation of the European race in the former Spanish colonies in Central and South America." In contrast, "the United States and England's African colonies" had instituted "a strict separation between Caucasians and colored Africans." Concluding this description, Tecklenburg reiterated, "In the United States, marriages between whites and blacks are prohibited."[20]

Of course, Tecklenburg's accounts of racial separation policies in South Africa and the United States were not entirely accurate. Although segregationist legislation existed in the Transvaal province of the British Union of South Africa, other South African provinces had no official race codes. There also existed no federal prohibition (only state regulations) against mixed-race marriages in the United States. Yet over time, German colonial administrators began to refine their arguments for racial segregation, and the more they learned about Jim Crow regulations, the more attractive they found the example of the American South. Not only were Southern legal codes more thorough than the provisions in the Transvaal but they were also a perfect match for the liberal and American trajectory of German colonial policies after 1906: They showed that there were ways in which the colonial periphery could make sociopolitical decisions fairly independently from metropolitan politics and regulations. In 1905, Tecklenburg's references to America already prefigured how German colonial administrators would eventually frame and contextualize their case for marriage bans and other segregationist measures.[21]

---

[20] BArch. R 1001/5423, pp. 68, 69.
[21] Jonathan Hyslop, "White Working-Class Women and the Invention of Apartheid: 'Purified' Afrikaner Nationalist Agitation for Legislation against

Hans Tecklenburg's original 1905 prohibition was supported by many settlers and, most importantly, upheld by the court system in Southwest Africa. Because of the way this regulation was interpreted by colonial judges, it flew in the face of German citizenship law, which stated that the children of women married to German men automatically obtained their father's citizenship. In Southwest Africa, however, Tecklenburg's decree even rendered mixed-race marriages contracted before 1905 invalid. In addition, local administrators treated mixed-race children not as Germans but as "natives." Tecklenburg and other colonial officials, like the governor of GEA, took advantage of a legal gray zone. They argued that while legislation for regulating marriages of "non-natives" among each other and "natives" among each other existed, marriages across racial lines (i.e., between colonizers and natives) were not explicitly addressed in the applicable laws and were therefore prohibited. This opaque argumentation was repeated by a number of imperialist legal scholars in Germany.[22]

When the Reichskolonialabteilung under Hohenlohe began to collect information on miscegenation regulations worldwide, it was first and foremost responding to pressure from the colonies, not to groups in the metropole. In Southwest Africa, actions taken by individuals and associations informed Tecklenburg's initial prohibition and subsequent handling of this issue: In Windhoek, Protestant pastors refused to allow mixed-race children

'Mixed' Marriages, 1934–9," *Journal of African History* 36, no. 1 (1995): 65.

[22] *Reichstagshandbuch: 13. Legislaturperiode (1912)*, 1725; Dieter Gosewinkel, *Einbürgern und Ausschließen: Die Nationalisierung der Staatsangehörigkeit vom Deutschen Bund bis zur Bundesrepublik Deutschland* (Göttingen: Vandenhoek und Ruprecht, 2001), 303–09 (esp. 305–06); Harald Sippel, "Rechtspolitische Ansätze zur Vermeidung einer Mischlingsbevölkerung," in *Rassenmischehen – Mischlinge – Rassentrennung*, ed. Frank Becker (Stuttgart: Franz Steiner Verlag, 2004), 154–55. On settlers pressuring for legislation concerning miscegenation, see Tecklenburg to Reichskolonialabteilung, October 23, 1905 (BArch. R 1001/5423, p. 68), article in *Koloniale Rundschau 1909* (clipping in Dernburg's collection of materials on 'Mischrasseehen', BArch. R 1001/5417, p. 57).

into their kindergartens, schools did not accept them either, and sports and farmers' associations turned down membership applications on the grounds of the applicants' relationships to black women. In the metropole, the Reichskolonialamt was sensitive to pressure from the colonies as the RKA's detailed 1912–13 collection of colonial opinions on the matter of miscegenation regulations demonstrates.[23]

The "miscegenation problem," as Solf put it in 1912, was thus never primarily a metropolitan issue. It had been a pressing topic for settlers and local colonial administrators long before it was discussed by parliamentarians in the Reichstag. As early as 1897 the governor of GSWA, Theodor Leutwein, wanted to see miscegenation prohibited, yet the Reichskolonialabteilung was not willing to accept his request. Six years later, Tecklenburg, Leutwein's deputy governor, again called for "a strong legislative barrier between non-natives and natives." From the viewpoint of colonial administrators, Berlin was not responding to demands from the colonies the way it should. In 1897 Berlin had actually confirmed that race was not to be considered when it came to marriages in the colonies and the citizenship of biracial children. However, once German colonial rule was threatened by massive uprisings in both GSWA (1904–07) and GEA (1905–07), pressure from settlers and local administrators increased, and so did the metropolitan willingness to take their demands seriously.[24]

Hohenlohe's letter described in the beginning of the chapter was the first sign of this mood change in Berlin. During Dernburg's subsequent tenure as state secretary, it was both politically expedient and very much in line with the state secretary's political philosophy to grant local colonial administrators a relatively free

---

[23] BArch. R 1001/5421, pp. 24, 29, 30, 31, 33, 35; BArch. R1001/5423, p. 79; Smith, "The Talk of Genocide," 116–17.

[24] Jürgen Zimmerer, "Von Windhuk nach Warschau. Die rassische Privilegiengesellschaft in Deutsch-Südwestafrika, ein Modell mit Zukunft?," in *Rassenmischehen – Mischlinge – Rassentrennung. Zur Politik der Rasse im deutschen Kolonialreich*, ed. Frank Becker (Stuttgart: Franz Steiner Verlag, 2004), 98–99, 101.

hand in this matter. Moreover, the report Dernburg had received from the German consulate in New Orleans showed that, even if national legislation decreed racial equality, the decentralized American federal system granted more than enough political power to individual states to enable them to establish racialized law codes within their state lines: "Experience has shown that within the framework of federal laws, legislation in individual states has retained enough leeway to secure the political primacy of the white population within these states under all circumstances." Nordenflycht's report therefore indicated a potential solution in case diverging interests in the matter of mixed-race marriages should arise between Germany's colonies and Berlin.[25]

Jim Crow in Berlin: Parliamentary Miscegenation Debates, the RKA, and the American South

In GSWA (September 23, 1905) and GEA (March 17, 1906) mixed-race marriage bans were prompted by bloody wars of rebellion. In German Samoa, a similar restriction was decreed on January 12, 1912. Because the German Samoan decree's sociopolitical context (no state of war existed in Samoa in 1912) and its place of issue (Berlin) were different from the ones in Southwest and East Africa, it was this prohibition and not the much more stringent one in GSWA that resulted in the most acrimonious debates about the "miscegenation question" in the German parliament. Before 1912, parliamentary references to the already existing regulations in GSWA and GEA had been few and far between. Although the Reichstag had limited influence on the German Empire's executive institutions, by the early years of the twentieth century it had nevertheless become the center of German political life and political legitimacy, and parliamentarians took their role seriously. Solf's decree challenged the implicit laissez-faire attitude toward colonial miscegenation regulations that most Reichstag deputies had displayed so far. After all, this

[25] BArch. R 1001/5420, p. 77; Sippel, "Rechtspolitische Ansätze," 153.

provision had not been decreed by a far-away colonial governor, but had originated in Berlin.[26]

Speaking on May 2, 1912, Solf asked the parliamentarians, "[G]entlemen, what is the 'Negro question' in the United States if not a miscegenation question?" Then, he argued that Lincoln's Emancipation Proclamation and the Thirteenth Amendment were "bad omens for all colonizing nations" and concluded with the prediction that "the brutality of lynching . . . will persist until state laws and the general public sentiment [Volksempfinden] have become consistent." When Solf used the term "state laws," he was referring to those states in the Union without Jim Crow laws. As he knew from the RKA's files, southerners viewed reports of lynchings in the North as validation of their own handling of the "Negro problem," and Solf certainly approved of southern race codes. He praised them in his May 1912 Reichstag speeches, thereby setting the parameters for his own department's use of Jim Crow legislation between 1912 and 1914: Whereas the Reconstruction Amendments to the federal constitution were "bad omens" and highlighted the dangers of race mixing (a global and colonial problem not limited to America), race codes in the American South (and elsewhere in the United States) provided impressive counterexamples worthy of imitation in the German colonies, if settlers and local administrators chose to implement them.[27]

During the Reichstag debates, Solf's references to lynching in the northern United States were taken directly from the RKA's files: A commentary compiled by a staff member of the German consulate in Chicago quoted southerners who in reference to a

[26] "Wilson und die letzten Mohikaner," *Simplicissimus*, May 1, 1917, 1648; Kreuzer, "Parliamentarization," 339–45; Dieter Langewiesche, *Liberalismus in Deutschland, in Neue historische Bibliothek* (Frankfurt am Main: Suhrkamp, 1988), 637–40; Manfred Rauh, *Die Parlamentarisierung des Deutschen Reiches* (Düsseldorf: Droste, 1977); Jonathan Sperber, "Comments on Marcus Kreuzer's Article," *Central European History* 36, no. 3 (2003). Compare Steinmetz, *Devil's Handwriting*, 346–47.

[27] BArch. R 1001/5420, p. 73; *Reichstagsdebatte (May-02-1912)*, 1648; *Reichstagsdebatte (May-07-1912)*, 1226–27.

lynching in Springfield, Illinois, argued that this "gruesome case was merely proof of the correctness of the way the South treated its Negroes." Based on these sources, the RKA state secretary believed that in those American states without segregationist laws lynching would continue until "state law and public opinion" had been harmonized. Moreover, the situation in the United States strongly indicated that there existed the need for race-based legislation in the German colonies.[28]

Although this assessment was correct when it came to Solf's own sphere of responsibility (i.e., the German colonies and their administrators and settlers), it could not be further from the truth regarding the parties that had won the majority of votes in the 1912 Reichstag election: the Social Democrats and the Catholic Center Party. The SPD and Center Party together had received 51.2 percent of the vote (SPD, 34.8%; Center Party, 16.4%). Simultaneously, the conservative parties and the National Liberal Party had lost votes. The SPD and the Center Party were undeniably at odds on many issues. Moreover, the SPD's success in these elections was partly the result of an alliance with the left-liberal Fortschrittliche Volkspartei (FVP), and not the consequence of any kind of collaboration with the Center Party. Nevertheless, the miscegenation debates resulted in a temporary cooling of SPD-FVP relations: During the plenum discussions, the two most prominent specialists for colonial questions of both parties, Georg Ledebour (SPD) and Carl Braband (FVP), went verbally for each other's throats and questioned not only each other's political beliefs but also the ideological foundations of the other party. At the same time Center Party and Social Democrats agreed on a rejection of Solf's decrees and called for a resolution sanctioning the legality of mixed-race marriages in all German colonies. The Social Democrat Alfred Henke justified the SPD's call for this resolution by proclaiming that the Reichstag was "obligated to guarantee" the protection of natives, although this demand did not imply that he accepted German colonialism: "[I]f

---

[28] BArch. R 1001/5420, p. 72; *Reichstagsdebatte (May-02–1912)*, 1648.

nobody else does it, we Social Democrats will do so with pride. We are convinced that this too is our task, and we will therefore continue to criticize German colonialism [deutsche Kolonialpolitik] for which, as already stated, we cannot feel any enthusiasm." In turn, the Center Party deputy Adolf Gröber explicitly criticized the use of scientific racism to justify colonial race codes, remarking that

whoever reads the literature on these questions is taking on quite an arduous task. Reading thoughts that are only meant to achieve one single goal does not belong to the nice things in life: All arguments are geared towards the permanent rule of the white race, and to this end natives are not even to be allowed to receive an adequate school education.... These are views that betray a brutality which one does not want to see in German literary work.[29]

In 1912, because of the strong opposition of the SPD and the Center Party, those who argued for racialized marriage provisions were in a tough spot and had to choose their words well to be at least potentially convincing. The United States was a fellow "world power" and therefore provided attractive and compelling examples. The National-Liberal Party representative Hartmann Freiherr von Richthofen thus began his contribution to the debate by explicitly comparing (and equating) the situation in the German colonies with that of the South after 1865:[30]

---

[29] The RKA's files contained numerous references to lynchings in Illinois (BArch. R 1001/5420, pp. 72, 74). Election statistics taken from the German Historical Museum's website, www.dhm.de/lemo/objekte/statistik/wa1912/index.html (accessed July 3, 2009). See also David E. Kaiser, "Germany and the Origins of the First World War," *Journal of Modern History* 55, no. 3 (1983): 458; Kreuzer, "Parliamentarization," 356–57. On the relationship between government and parliament after the January 1912 elections, see Gosewinkel, *Einbürgern*, 306–07; Mark Hewitson, "The Kaiserreich in Question: Constitutional Crisis in Germany before the First World War," *Journal of Modern History* 73, no. 4 (2001): 727; Smith, "The Talk of Genocide," 118; Ledebour's and Braband's exchanges in *Reichstagsdebatte (May-07-1912)*, 1734; *Reichstagsdebatte (May-08-1907)*, 1743. For the SPD's and the Center Party's criticism of miscegenation provisions, see *Reichstagsdebatte (April-29-1912)*, 1521; *Reichstagsdebatte (May-07-1912)*, 1725.
[30] *Reichstagsdebatte (May-07-1912)*, 1729.

[W]hen the institution of slavery still existed . . . whites felt so superior to the local Negro population that they were not afraid of messing around with Negro women when they felt like it. Yet after slavery was abolished, the impending danger was recognized. Then the realization set in that, since Negroes had now been given the same rights, whites risked no longer being recognized as superior. In consequence, the white population's ability to spread culture could be lost. This is the real reason why today there are still marriage bans in America, and why in the United States a situation has developed that . . . makes racial mixing between whites and blacks nearly impossible. . . . In our colonies – and the state secretary will confirm this, I believe – things have developed along similar lines; a development that I think is a healthy one. Formerly, when there were only a handful of Germans in our colonies, one took pretty much the same viewpoint as in America before abolition. Anyone who fancied it amused himself with Negro women and did not worry about any cultural danger connected with this behavior. Things have changed now. . . . This very correct development would undoubtedly be interrupted by again allowing mixed-race marriages.

Liberal parliamentarians like von Richthofen were not the only ones defending miscegenation provisions. Reinhard Mumm, a member of the Christian-Social Party and the Pan-German League, steered the debate into even more racialized waters, arguing that "because of racial self interest" in the United States neither whites nor blacks accepted mixed-race marriages. Moreover, in an attempt to counter egalitarian arguments by SPD and religious arguments by Center Party representatives, Mumm introduced racial purity as an asset that needed to be defended: "There exist very different theories about race; one cannot simply slur over this question. Culturally important reflections like the teachings of Count Gobineau and those of the Bayreuth circle . . . cannot be easily overlooked." Mumm made racial purity a matter of personal ethics and recognized the obstacles to nationally decreed miscegenation provisions, both in parliament, because they ran counter to German citizenship law, and in the colonies, because of their impracticability.[31]

Once the notion of racial purity had been introduced, the liberal von Richthofen thankfully adopted it and accused Center

[31] Ibid., 1733.

Party representative Matthias Erzberger, one of the sharpest critics of mixed-marriage bans, of lacking "Rassegefühl!" [race consciousness]. Then von Richthofen returned to using American examples by arguing that miscegenation codes in the American South had strengthened southern "race consciousness" to such a degree that "intercourse between whites and blacks has pretty much ceased to occur." The RKA's materials on the United States did indeed contain references to the "bitter sentiment against the black race" among white Southerners that in their eyes justified the cruelest measures necessary to maintain "order and progress." The fact that this information was both in the RKA's files and became part of the Reichstag's deliberations about the "miscegenation question" testifies to its ubiquity within pro-colonialist circles.[32]

Von Richthofen's elaborations on the beneficial consequences of southern Jim Crow institutions for American "race consciousness" were meant to have a powerful impact on the debate, an intention revealed by his use of this notion for ad hominem attacks against Center Party representatives. Yet he closed his speech with a differently slanted reference to the United States, which highlighted the international dimension of German colonial policies in general and of mixed-marriage bans in particular. Social Democratic deputies had argued that racialized legislation would be a stain on the German Empire's reputation. Von Richthofen could not disagree more: "This fear is without foundation, I believe. America has long occupied the same vantage point and I have never heard that the United States' reputation has suffered even the slightest bit because of it." For von Richthofen, the American republic's status as a world power was not tainted by the existence of racial inequality in some of its member states; on the contrary: America's exemplary "race consciousness" made the United States an even more commendable model for German policies.[33]

---

[32] BArch. R 1001/5420, p. 72; *Reichstagsdebatte (May-08–1907)*, 1742.
[33] *Reichstagsdebatte (May-08–1907)*, 1743.

Von Richthofen's attitude toward the United States explains why administrators both in Berlin and in the colonies paid more attention to the American South than to South Africa's Transvaal province, another region in the world where racial segregation measures were in effect. The attractiveness of the Transvaal's race code as a model for legislation in the German colonies was limited for several reasons. Although mixed-race unions were prohibited in the Transvaal, the province was forced to recognize marriages contracted in other South African provinces. Most importantly, however, the existence of race codes within the borders of a single province of one of the British Empire's dominions was simply much less remarkable than American Jim Crow provisions. The persuasiveness of von Richthofen's arguments rested on the fact that southern race codes were authoritative because they were American (the RKA possessed exact information on both the number of American states that had instituted such codes and what these laws actually decreed). After all, the United States, like the German Empire, was in the process of challenging Britain's status as world power.[34]

A Liberal American Solution?

Given the political make-up of the Reichstag after the January 1912 elections, it was unlikely that Solf and the RKA's parliamentary allies would be able to convince a majority of deputies to work on national legislation prohibiting mixed-race marriages in all colonies or even to support Solf's ban for Samoa. Before the "miscegenation problem" was even discussed in front of the general plenum, it was debated among a smaller group of deputies in the budget commission, where SPD and Center Party representatives had made their opposition very clear. In April and May 1912, the RKA and conservative and liberal parliamentarians

---

[34] BArch. R 1001/5420, pp. 126–27; *Reichstagsdebatte (May-02–1912)*, 1648–49; *Reichstagsdebatte (May-07–1912)*, 1727, 1729, 1733, 1734; *Reichstagsdebatte (May-08–1912)*, 1742, 1743, 1746.

knew where they stood. Although they gave their best during the general deliberations over the miscegenation question, on May 8, 1912, the Reichstag majority passed a resolution demanding exactly the opposite of what the settlers in the colonies, the RKA, and those deputies sympathetic to this cause had wanted: It called for legislation that would recognize mixed-race marriages everywhere in the German Empire.[35]

Between 1912 and August 1914 two developments took place. On the one hand, the Reichstag's resolution of May 8, 1912, was never translated into German law. On the other, and despite the fact that it had become clear that it would be impossible to achieve a nationally legislated solution to the "miscegenation problem," the RKA's files show that Solf and other administrators increased their study of American examples. Solf thus compiled his lengthy notes on Jim Crow provisions only after the Reichstag had passed its resolutions. The same was true for Solf's subordinates' efforts to borrow copies of American legal directories or to contact American scholars, among them William Benjamin Smith, a professor of mathematics at Tulane University, who in 1905 had written a racist tract titled *The Color Line: A Brief on Behalf of the Unborn*. This work justified southern race codes by attempting to demonstrate the racial inferiority of blacks and the dangers of racial mixing. Smith also had connections to Germany, earning his PhD in Göttingen in 1879. Throughout his life, Smith was interested in Protestant theology (he published a number of books on this subject, some only in German and in Germany). His passion for religion had influenced his decision to study at Göttingen, where Anton Paul de Lagarde, a specialist in oriental languages and a famous (albeit disputatious) theologian, was professor at the time. Lagarde, who aimed at establishing a "national Christianity," was one of Imperial Germany's most aggressive anti-Semites (acquainted, among others, with Adolf Stoecker, the anti-Semitic founder of the Christian-Social Party), and advocated the deportation of Jewish Germans to Palestine. Lagarde's radical anti-Semitism

---

[35] *Reichstagsdebatte (May-08-1912)*, 1747.

went hand in hand with his expansionist advocacy of a Central Europe dominated and colonized by Germany.[36] In *The Color Line*, Smith proposed to make blacks permanently subservient to white Americans. Smith's proposal thus resembled his teacher Lagarde's vision for a comparable exploitative caste system for Germans vis-à-vis Eastern Europeans. Although Smith, in all likelihood, came to Germany already well equipped with negative notions about African Americans, his encounter with Lagarde at Göttingen may have shaped these beliefs. Through the RKA's activities, Smith's justification of racial exploitation was thus (re-) imported to Germany and bolstered Solf's overall defense of the miscegenation decrees.[37]

The RKA also sought advice from the American historian Archibald Cary Coolidge. Coolidge received his PhD from the University of Freiburg in 1892 and became professor at Harvard in 1908. During the academic year 1913–14 he returned to Germany, holding a visiting position at the Friedrich-Wilhelm University in Berlin (today's Humboldt University). In February 1914, the RKA asked the Association for Continuing Education in the Political Sciences [Gesellschaft für Staatswissenschaftliche Fortbildung] for a copy of a talk Coolidge had given to this association. Coolidge's lecture described the "growing race consciousness" in the United States and other nations as a "remarkable phenomenon," explaining that "mixed-race marriages are partially prohibited, and that both the people and the best minds of America do not wish racial mixing with colored races." The RKA had already filed very positive reviews of this speech, yet

---

[36] BArch. R 1001/5420, pp. 98–99, 123; William Benjamin Smith, *The Color Line: A Brief on Behalf of the Unborn* (1905); Jürgen Schriewer, "Paul de Lagarde," in *Allgemeine deutsche Biographie & Neue deutsche Biographie* (Berlin: Krell–Laven, 1982), 412.

[37] Smith, *Color Line*, 174; Walter P. Weaver, *The Historical Jesus in the Twentieth Century* (Harrisburg, PA: Trinity Press, 1999), 54–55; Schriewer, "Paul de Lagarde," 412. On Paul de Lagarde, see also Helmut Walser Smith, *The Continuities of German History: Nation, Religion, and Race across the Long Nineteenth Century* (New York: Cambridge University Press, 2008), 177; Ulrich Sieg, *Deutschlands Prophet: Paul de Lagarde und die Ursprünge des modernen Antisemitismus* (Munich: Hanser, 2007).

was keen to obtain the complete script, because "the talk must contain valuable material concerning the mixed-race question." Coolidge returned to America before the outbreak of the Great War. There, he continued the forays into scientific racism that had so endeared him to the RKA. Although his official area of expertise at Harvard was European history, during the 1914–15 academic year Coolidge prepared a lecture series titled "Race Relations in the United States." Inspired by the enthusiastic reception of his treatment of this topic in Germany, Coolidge thus carried his interest in questions of scientific racism and the social segregation of races back home across the Atlantic.[38]

The RKA's inquiries into the American legal system and its attempts to contact American scholars were undertaken for the purpose of gaining more information on how precisely in the United States local race codes coexisted with federal guarantees of racial equality. The RKA files show that the department was quite aware of this paradox, and during the parliamentary debates Center Party deputy Gröber had even termed the coexistence of nominal constitutional equality with de facto inequality in many states an "injustice." Even after the Reichstag resolution had been passed, the RKA thus did not give up the search for a satisfactory solution to the miscegenation question, and given the department's consistent (even heightened) interest in Jim Crow provisions between 1912 and 1914, the United States clearly played a major role in its considerations.[39]

In the end, only a decentralized and laissez-faire handling of the issue was viable. In light of the SPD's and the Center

---

[38] BArch. R 1001/5420, p. 131.
[39] BArch. R 1001/5420, pp. 116–17 (letter by a correspondent of the *Chicago Daily News* that explains the coexistence of race codes with the U.S. Constitution and that mentions *Hubbell's Legal Directory* as further resource), 119–24; (Solf's personal notes), 127; (handwritten notes of RKA officer referencing specific American law cases), 131; (contact request for Coolidge). Between 1913 and September 1914, Solf and his subordinates created more than twenty pages concerning Jim Crow provisions in the United States. For the same period, the RKA's files only contain about five pages on South Africa, and other colonies worldwide, in none of which "provisions concerning marriages between natives and non-natives" existed (pp. 120, 121).

Party's rejection of mixed-race marriage bans and the majority status of these parties in the Reichstag the RKA deemed further discussions about miscegenation provisions in parliament too problematic. The Reichskolonialamt's America-focused activities between 1912 and the fall of 1914 therefore reflected the department's perceived need to forestall any additional "metropolitanization" of the mixed-race marriage question. After all, the Reichstag in Berlin had ignored local race-based marriage ordinances in the colonies, even when they violated German law, as long as these decrees did not originate in Berlin. Maintaining the status quo that until 1912 had allowed both the colonial periphery and the RKA great freedom of action was therefore much more promising than a push for a national law addressing the mixed-race marriage question. As the Reichstag debates had shown, such an attempt could result in a worsening of the situation. The American double standard of federal racial equality provisions that tolerated local race codes was therefore very appealing for Solf and the RKA.[40]

Solf's focus on the United States picked up Bernhard Dernburg's liberal and "American" approach to colonialism after the brief interlude of the conservative Friedrich von Lindequist as the RKA's second state secretary (1910–11). Solf's even-handed take on colonial politics allowed him to see the advantages in a tactical retreat after the mixed-race marriage debates in the Reichstag. Between 1912 and 1914, he thus increased his knowledge of the way individual American states circumvented the Fourteenth and Fifteenth Amendments. On August 11, 1913, several days before he was scheduled to travel to Cameroon, Solf handwrote an analysis of how Jim Crow provisions in individual American states operated within the U.S. federal framework: "The Emancipation Proclamation of September 22, 1862 put Negroes completely on par with whites." Then Solf listed all Reconstruction Amendments to the Federal Constitution, only to conclude that, despite these provisions, "especially in the Southern states racial mixing is not tolerated and social interaction is banned.... The South

---

[40] *Reichstagsdebatte (May-08–1912)*, 1747.

quickly repressed the Negro politically and socially through legislation." This was an important realization because the miscegenation debates in the Reichstag had demonstrated that only
locally decreed provisions could maintain racial segregation in
the German colonies. Clearly, no acceptable national solution
was forthcoming, and RKA decrees did not work either because
they attracted too much attention in the metropole.[41]

However, what Solf could do was to maintain the status quo
and in laissez-faire fashion let the settlers and administrators
in the colonies run things as they saw fit. After all, the RKA's
files appeared to demonstrate that the United States operated
according to exactly the same principles. Wherever in the United
States the local population's "race consciousness" or "social cus-
toms" demanded, segregationist decrees existed. To maintain a
similar situation in the German protection areas, local colonial
miscegenation provisions needed to be kept out of the metropolitan political limelight. Solf's department followed this tenet dili-
gently and successfully between 1912 and 1914. The RKA asked
the colonies for their opinions on the miscegenation question,
adding statements from governors and settler councils (affirmative throughout) to its files. It also did not change any of the
existing miscegenation provisions in, for example, GSWA or
GEA. However, whenever specific individual cases threatened
to disturb metropolitan lawmakers, the RKA forced exceptions
on colonial authorities to avoid national and international problems. These actions helped keep the miscegenation question out
of future Reichstag debates. In turn, this strategy increased the
chance of preserving the freedom of action of the RKA and the
colonial governors.[42]

The way Solf and the RKA in Berlin handled the "miscegenation problem" between the end of the Reichstag debates and the

---

[41] BArch. R 1001/5420, p. 121; Ludwig Brandl, "Wilhelm Solf," in *Biographisch-Bibliographisches Kirchenlexikon* (Traugott Bautz, 1995), 758–
63.

[42] BArch. R 1001/5421, pp. 24–35; Gosewinkel, *Einbürgern*, 309; Sippel,
"Rechtspolitische Ansätze," 153.

beginning of World War I suggests that at least in Berlin German colonial officers could not simply translate their views into action, in any case not on the national political level. True, in the end the resolution passed by the SPD and the Center Party had no consequences for the German colonies, because local ordinances regarding mixed-race marriage bans remained in effect. However, it did influence how the highest colonial authorities in Berlin carefully and defensively negotiated and safeguarded these practices by keeping them out of the national glare of publicity. Moreover, the resolution also showed that, regarding colonial questions in general and the issue of miscegenation bans in particular (including this question's many connections to the United States), left- and right-wing liberals were in complete agreement with the RKA's policies and actively defended them. On May 8, 1912, only four out of a total of forty-two left-liberal deputies joined the Social Democrats and the Center Party in their rejection of race-based marriage bans in the German colonies, whereas the rest voted against this resolution, together with the National-Liberal Party and the conservative and nationalist parties.[43]

Partly as a result of Solf's strategy and partly as a result of backroom dealings between Chancellor Bethmann-Hollweg and the Center Party, parliamentary interest in the miscegenation question quickly subsided after May 8, 1912. On the one hand, the government decided not to give in to pressure from various colonialist lobby organizations and the Pan-German League to make racialized considerations part of the new German citizenship law, something the Center Party strongly opposed. On the other, the Center Party refrained from following up on the demands formulated in the "pro-mixed-race marriage" resolution its deputies had voted for together with the SPD – and without Center Party support, there was no parliamentary majority

---

[43] *Reichstagsdebatte (May-07–1912)*, 1730; *Reichstagsdebatte (May-08–1907)*, 1744, 1773–76; *Reichstagshandbuch: 13. Legislaturperiode (1912)*, 419; Gosewinkel, *Einbürgern*, 309.

for passing a law aimed at specifically protecting mixed-race marriages in the German colonies. Sustained cooperation between the SPD and the Center Party could have resulted in such a piece of legislation being put before the Reichstag. Yet at least for the Center Party, decisively shaping the new German citizenship law, which the Reichstag began debating in February 1912 (and which would eventually go into effect on July 22, 1913), easily trumped the quite literally peripheral colonial problem of protecting mixed-race marriages in Germany's overseas territories.[44]

This solution was not at all what German colonial settlers, administrators in the colonies, and colonial lobby organizations had wanted. Although the RKA was able to protect their racialized interests in the colonies, on the national level the new German citizenship law reaffirmed that natives living in the German colonies could potentially obtain German citizenship and thereby full legal equality under German law. To be sure, this was not meant to be an automatic process. Instead of solving the mixed-race marriage question one way or the other, the 1913 citizenship law implicitly allowed an intrinsic tension between race and citizenship in the colonies and in the German mainland to persist, which fueled Solf's interest in the relationship between individual U.S. states and the federal government regarding race codes.[45]

The United States loomed large in both German colonial discourse and practice. When it came to creating societies based on racial privilege in the German colonies, a number of powerful

[44] Gosewinkel, *Einbürgern*, 309. In March 1914, George Ledebour, when raising the issue of mixed-race marriages again during a general debate over the German colonies, thus wondered aloud why nothing had come of the "pro-mixed-race marriage" resolution passed by the Center and the SPD in 1912. Little did he know that the Center Party had no more interest in the issue after having played a decisive role in shaping the new citizenship law. See *Reichstagsdebatte (March-11-1914)*, 8015.

[45] Compare Gosewinkel, *Einbürgern*, 308–09; Zimmerer, "Von Windhuk nach Warschau. Die rassische Privilegiengesellschaft in Deutsch-Südwestafrika, ein Modell mit Zukunft?," 117.

German administrators in the metropole and in the colonies, as well as most liberal and some conservative politicians, perceived the United States as a viable, concrete, and impressive model. The American republic had interested German reformist liberals throughout the nineteenth century, not only for reasons of general political and ideological kinship but also because certain political and structural features of the United States appeared to be more directly relevant to Germans than those of Germany's big European neighbors France and Great Britain. Before 1848, German liberal nationalists were thus particularly drawn to the American constitution's federalism. However, after unification and the founding of the German Empire, other characteristics of the American system were seen as increasingly important, especially perceptions of the United States as a liberal colonial empire.

Perhaps one of the most significant qualities of reading both America's westward expansion and the United States' handling of racial minorities – for the most part in the American South – as evidence of the viability of rational, decentralized, and laissez-faire organizational principles was the fact that such views could transcend party lines. Twice before 1914 colonial questions generated a political environment in Berlin that enabled the liberal parties to dominate Reichstag debates and arguably situate the colonial policies of the German government in a distinctly liberal political framework that was also accepted by nationalist and conservative parties: once during and after the "Hottentot elections" in 1907 and again during the 1912 Reichstag debates over mixed-race marriage prohibitions in the German colonies. In 1912, the United States and southern Jim Crow provisions provided the central intellectual and sociopolitical backdrop against which liberal positions were formulated. Two years later, Solf could thus boast that since 1907, the year of the "Dernburg turn," the German colonies' productivity had been increasing at an impressive rate. The newly applied liberal, progressive, and "American" methods had therefore clearly, at least from the RKA's perspective, been successful in the field of colonial economics. As a result, Solf saw no reason not to apply them (even if he had to keep quiet about it) to the pressing question of racial segregation, especially if local settlers demanded it. Before 1914, it was the SPD and the Center Party's opposition that defined the limits of attempts to justify racial segregation in the German colonies by using American examples.[46]

[46] Ratzel, *Der Staat und sein Boden*, 3391; Zimmerman, "German Alabama," 1387–88; Grimmer-Solem, "Professors' Africa," 325; Jens-Uwe Guettel, "The Myth of the Pro-Colonialist SPD: German Social Democracy and Imperialism before the First World War," *Central European History* 45, no. 3 (2012). For a British perspective of successes of the "Dernburg turn" see, "Editorial Notes and Comments," *United Empire* 5, no. 4 (1914): 305.

4

America, Race, and German Expansionism from the Great War to 1945

On May 1, 1917, the German satirical magazine *Simplicissimus* published a cartoon that showed a group of Native Americans looking somewhat aghast as President Woodrow Wilson yells at them: "You cowards! If you hadn't let us exterminate you, you could be fighting for America's freedom now!" The United States' entry into World War I on the side of Great Britain and France altered German perceptions of America. Before the war, German colonialists had viewed American race policies, westward expansion, and Indian policies as exemplary, even with respect to measures directed against Native Americans. After the United States officially joined Germany's enemies in 1917, and even more so when, as many Germans saw it, America "betrayed" President Wilson's January 1918 fourteen-point peace resolution by giving in to British and French demands at the Paris peace talks in the spring of 1919, America ceased to be seen as exemplary, even by those who had felt a kinship with the United States before 1914. In May 1917, *Simplicissimus*, a magazine known before the war for its caustic criticism of German politics, therefore became one of the most scathing critics of the United States. The magazine's contributors, like many liberal politicians and academics, felt let down by America when they realized that their affection for the United States was not reciprocated.[1]

Before World War I, the German frontier was neither exclusively nor primarily an Eastern European phenomenon. As we have seen, during the nineteenth century the German frontier was in North America – for example, in the minds of 1848 revolutionaries. After 1884, it was in Germany's colonies, especially in Southwest Africa. German expansionism changed irreversibly during and after the Great War, however. Between 1914 and 1918, radical nationalists increasingly located the German frontier in the vast conquered territories to the east of Germany's 1914 border with Russia. In part, the Nazis' later frenzied focus on Eastern Europe as the exclusive target region for German settler colonies was a result of this development. Moreover, Nazi ideologues also used their post-1918 "living space in the East" fantasies to criticize Germany's acquisition of overseas colonies before World War I: In their view, these possessions had been the result of the German Empire's wrong-headed "liberalist" imperialism. Ultimately, the Third Reich's attempts to gain living space in Eastern Europe during World War II were conscious efforts to reverse Imperial Germany's liberal and often America-focused global expansionism. For the Nazis, the German frontier in the East therefore had little in common with the American one that German liberal colonialists had considered exemplary before the Great War. For ideological reasons, Nazi officials often chose not to reference the United States as an expansionist or racist prototype, sometimes even when this approach obviously suggested itself.[2]

[1] "Wilson und die letzten Mohikaner," *Simplicissimus*, May 1 1917, Ann Taylor Allen, *Satire and Society in Wilhelmine Germany: Kladderadatsch and Simplicissimus 1890–1914* (Lexington: The University Press of Kentucky, 1984), 43.
[2] Isabel V. Hull, "Military Culture and the Production of 'Final Solutions' in the Colonies," in *The Specter of Genocide*, ed. Robert Gellately and Ben Kiernan (Cambridge: Cambridge University Press, 2003); Birthe Kundrus, "Von Windhoek nach Nuernberg? Koloniale 'Mischehenverbote' und die nationalsozialistische Rassengesetzgebung," in *Phantasiereiche. Zur Kulturgeschichte des deutschen Kolonialismus*, ed. Birthe Kundrus (Frankfurt a. M.: Campus Verlag, 2003); David Furber, "Near as Far in the Colonies: The Nazi Occupation

World War I was cataclysmic, bringing about major political and structural transformations that reshaped German expansionism. Although the war demarcated the end of Germany's overseas empire, colonialism as an idea and as a positive subject of political debates continued. In fact, after the colonies were lost, colonialism began to acquire a changed relevance for German discussions of expansion. Yet as a matter of practical politics, it became a thing of the past. After 1918 memories, fantasies, and myths of the German colonial empire were propagated within a framework quite different from the sociocultural backdrop of German colonialism before 1914. Liberal colonialists like

of Poland," *The International History Review* 26, no. 3 (2004); Horst Gründer, "Zum Stellenwert des Rassismus im Spektrum der deutschen Kolonialideologie," in *Rassenmischehen - Mischlinge - Rassentrennung. Zur Polik der Rasse im deutschen Kolonialreich*, ed. Frank Becker (Stuttgart: Franz Steiner, 2004); Isabel V. Hull, *Absolute Destruction: Military Culture and the Practices of War in Imperial Germany* (Ithaca, N.Y.: Cornell University Press, 2004), 1; Jürgen Zimmerer, "Von Windhuk nach Warschau. Die rassische Privilegiengesellschaft in Deutsch–Südwestafrika, ein Modell mit Zukunft?," in *Rassenmischehen - Mischlinge - Rassentrennung. Zur Polik der Rasse im deutschen Kolonialreich*, ed. Frank Becker (Stuttgart: Franz Steiner Verlag, 2004); Pascal Grosse, "What Does German Colonialism Have To Do With National Socialism? A Conceptual Framework," in *Germany's Colonial Pasts*, ed. Eric Ames (Lincoln: University of Nebraska Press, 2005); Benjamin Madley, "From Africa to Auschwitz: How German Southwest Africa Incubated Ideas and Methods Adopted and Developed by the Nazis in Eastern Europe," *European History Quarterly* 35, no. 3 (2005); Jürgen Zimmerer, "The Birth of the Ostland out of the Spirit of Colonialism: A Postcolonial Perspective on the Nazi Policy of Conquest and Extermination," *Patterns of Prejudice* 39, no. 2 (2005); David Blackbourn, *The Conquest of Nature: Water, Landscape and the Making of Modern Germany* (London: Jonathan Cape, 2006), 280–96 (esp. 82); Matthew P. Fitzpatrick, "The Pre-History of the Holocaust? The Sonderweg and Historikerstreit Debates and the Abject Colonial Past," *Central European History* 41 (2008); Matthew P. Fitzpatrick, "The Threat of 'Woolly-haired Grandchildren': Race, the Colonial Family and German Nationalism," *The History of the Family* 14 (2009); Robert Gerwarth and Stephan Malinowski, "Hannah Arendt's Ghosts: Reflections on the Disputable Path from Windhoek to Auschwitz," *Central European History* 42, no. 02 (2009): 299. On the importance of overseas colonialism (especially in Africa) for German culture and politics in general, see especially Dirk van Laak, *Imperiale Infrastruktur: Deutsche Planungen für eine Erschließung Afrikas 1880 bis 1960* (Paderborn: Schöningh, 2004).

Dernburg and Solf lost their importance and influence, while shrill calls for continental expansion were heard more loudly than ever before. Moreover, the war gave German expansionism a powerfully attractive focus: Eastern Europe. By late 1917, the German army occupied vast territories in the East. This development provided nationalists with the ephemeral hope that the conflict's sacrifices had not been in vain. Simultaneously, it inspired radically new expansionist fantasies, for example in the mind of the young Heinrich Himmler, who in the last years of the Great War became a believer in Germany's mission to settle the East. In 1917–18, the Pan-German League, the quickly growing ultra-nationalist German Fatherland Party, and the leadership of the German military demanded large-scale annexations in Eastern Europe. The Treaty of Brest-Litovsk realized these expansionist visions for several months in 1918. If there ever was a German equivalent to the American West, where else could it be found than in these territories that reached from the Baltic to the Black Sea, the vast "Wild East"? And were these expansionist activities in Eastern Europe therefore merely attempts to put into practice prewar ideas about the importance of the German East and its colonization and thus belong to the realm of Germany's pathological continuities?[3]

The answer is a clear no. To be sure, before 1914 liberals and progressive thinkers like Max Weber, as well as more conservative economists like Max Sering, were concerned with how to make the East attractive for ethnic Germans and to stem this region's "Polonization" – sentiments infamously expressed in Weber's 1895 inaugural address at the University of Freiburg, and shared (though only to a certain degree) by the Pan-German League of which Weber was a member at one time. However, in contrast to post-1918 Nazi living space visions, prewar concerns about colonizing the East were, with few exceptions, limited to the eastern provinces of Prussia (i.e., regions that were already part of the German Empire). During the 1880s and 1890s, anti-Semitic right-wingers thus approved of the Prussian

---

[3] Blackbourn, *The Conquest of Nature*, 284.

government's mass expulsions of Polish and Russian (and frequently Jewish) noncitizens, who often were seasonal labor migrants, from these parts of Prussia: Maybe these measures would make the East more attractive for German settlers. Yet overseas expansionists like Carl Peters made fun of such contiguously Eastern European colonial fantasies, with good reason: "'We should rather Germanize the East instead of reaching across the oceans.' But 200,000 people emigrate annually and unstoppably across the ocean! So, even if we begin to 'Germanize the east' (a truly exquisite little phrase), these 200,000 fellow citizens are still lost to us." Peters overestimated the attractiveness of African colonies for German settlers (although Africa loomed large in the German colonial imaginary), but he was correct about the large exodus of ethnic Germans from Prussia's eastern provinces and the overall unattractiveness of the German East for Germans.[4]

Despite his strong Prussophile sentiments, Peters promoted colonialism in Africa as an alternative to what he believed to be completely unrealistic fantasies of, for example, the full Germanization of the Prussian province of Posen, a mostly Polish region. During World War I, he even argued that if only the German Empire had been more committed to overseas colonialism when it was still possible (during the 1880s), the war could have been prevented: "Economic and truly liberal colonialism! Building train tracks and cities; constructing transit routes

[4] Carl Peters, *Carl Peters gesammelte Schriften*, ed. Walter Frank, 3 vols., vol. 1 (München/Berlin: C. H. Beck'sche Verlagsbuchhandlung, 1943), 338. Paul de Lagarde voiced ideas about further eastern expansion and the Pan-German League did so as well, yet only during the years of its lowest popularity between 1905 and 1909. On Pan–German and Fatherland Party ideas about Eastern Europe, see Heinz Hagenlücke, *Deutsche Vaterlandspartei: Die nationale Rechte am Ende des Kaiserreiches* (Düsseldorf: Droste Verlag, 1997), 202–03; Vejas Gabriel Liulevicius, *The German Myth of the East* (Oxford: Oxford University Press, 2009), 105, 17. See also Wolfgang J. Mommsen, *Max Weber and German Politics: 1890–1920* (Chicago: University of Chicago Press, 1984 [1959]), 71, 79, 206, 207, 210, 211; Andrew Zimmerman, "Decolonizing Weber," *Postcolonial Studies* 9, no. 1 (2006): 57, 64–66, 73–74; Laak, *Imperiale Infrastruktur*, 53.

on land and on water! Tilling the soil and mining the earth's treasures! Welcoming every member of a foreign nation who wants to partake in such worthy endeavors! Such is the spirit that defines humanity's active peoples and gives them their position in the community of nations."[5]

There can be no question that Peters' brand of liberalism was permeated by racism and intense feelings of nationalism. Yet unlike the extreme right, which during the war embraced increasingly radical and Eastern-Europe-focused ideas, Peters maintained his "classic" liberal-imperialist sentiments and was quite willing to respect the interests of other nations, provided they were white. In 1917, therefore, Peters saw the dissolution of Imperial Russia as a chance for a lasting structural change within Europe, which would result in a peace without greedy German annexations in the East: "The place of an enemy bloc [the Russian Empire] will be taken over by a group of related peoples and nations. Their relationship to us will be friendly." For Peters, Germany's ultimate war aim was to "maintain our overseas trade and our position within the global market," a goal that in his view necessitated British defeat. Yet he was willing to posit that "whether our European borders are slightly enlarged or slightly narrowed... plays only a subordinate role" in maintaining Germany's position, although of course military requirements in respect to Germany's borders had to be taken into account. In a postwar world without a hostile Triple Entente, this goal could be reached both without annexations and without the German Empire's prewar fixation on the maintenance of a large and overly costly army. As a result, in classically liberal fashion he argued that "the 15 per cent tax 'handicap,' with which our economy is burdened because of the military, especially compared to America's industry, could be largely abolished." For Peters, a strong army was not a means in itself. As long as it was necessary and served German interests it needed

---

[5] Peters, *Schriften (Vol. 1)*, 362–63, 476; Carl Peters, *Carl Peters gesammelte Schriften*, ed. Walter Frank, 3 vols., vol. 3 (München & Berlin: C. H. Beck'sche Verlagsbuchhandlung, 1944), 498–99.

to be maintained, yet ideally he favored lean and inexpensive administrative structures both at home and in the colonies; he also wanted citizens at home and settlers in the colonies to pay as little taxes and have as much political power and self-government as possible, although his promotion of these political tenets did not mean that Peters wanted Germany to become a democracy.[6]

These liberal views did not make Peters an affable person. During World War I, he was prone to choleric outbursts, especially against Great Britain, because he could neither forget nor forgive English mob violence against Germans in 1914 and the way in which he was forced to leave England after war had broken out. Still reeling from his expulsion (Peters had mostly lived in Great Britain since the late 1890s) and reacting to news of the internment of German citizens in France, in 1915 he thus wondered sardonically why the German authorities should not do the same to the population in the German-occupied parts of France. In a short, one-page piece written during the Battle of the Somme in 1916 on the spur of the moment, Peters ranted that, to prepare for a long defensive struggle, the occupied lands in the West and the East should be cleared of the native population. Statements like these have defined Peters' image after 1945. However, such radical outbursts were rare for him during the war. In fact, especially in 1917 and 1918, when the extreme right began to organize itself into the short-lived German Fatherland Party, which embraced radically expansionist demands, Peters began to publish almost exclusively moderate pieces. Yet even his earlier outbursts should not surprise us: Peters was an obnoxious, racist, and at times brutal egomaniac; he was also a nationalist and colonial expansionist. But these qualities did not prevent him from being a liberal; on the contrary, they were part and parcel of imperial liberalism. Nineteenth- and early twentieth-century liberalism, whether in Germany or elsewhere, was home to deeply rooted and long-standing expansionist, racist, and ethnically exclusionist sentiments. Although there were of course

---

[6] Peters, *Schriften (Vol. 3)*, 498-99; Peters, *Schriften (Vol. 1)*, 476.

anti-imperialist liberals (within the German context Eugen Richter and Ludwig Bamberger need to be mentioned), Peters, Max Weber, and many non-German figureheads of nineteenth-century imperial liberalism – among them Alexis de Tocqueville and J. S. Mill – held racist and exclusionist beliefs. Contrary to long-standing perceptions of Peters as a radically national-ist, illiberal bully and Weber as a nuanced, liberal-democratic critic of the German Empire's autocratic structure, it was Peters who in 1917–18 sounded conciliatory and even normatively "lib-eral," especially in respect to his visions of the peacetime situation in Eastern Europe, whereas Weber's anti-Polish sentiments ran rampant. Espousing attitudes that were also embraced by hyper-nationalist Free Corps fighters, in 1918 Weber even proposed to lead any student who had "decided not to make any grand speeches but silently to see to it that the first Polish official who dares to enter Danzig is hit by a bullet." The traditional separa-tion of "bad" radical nationalists and good democratic liberals thus simply does not hold up: Peters could be nationalist and liberal, and so could Weber.[7]

Unlike Weber, however, who helped write the Weimar consti-tution before his death in 1920, Peters was of course eventually appropriated by Nazi propaganda. This occurred largely because of his popularity during the early 1890s, memories of which still lingered after his death in 1918. Yet even though Peters' liberal colonialism was diametrically opposed to the Nazis' Eastern-Europe-focused expansionism, his personal story (despite Peters'

---

[7] Richard Parry, "'In a Sense Citizens, but Not Altogether Citizens . . .': Rhodes, Race, and the Ideology of Segregation at the Cape in the Late Nineteenth Century," *Canadian Journal of African Studies* 17, no. 3 (1983): 380-81; Walter LaFeber, *The American Search for Opportunity, 1865–1913* (Cam-bridge: Cambridge University Press, 1993), 57–59; Cornelius Torp, *Max Weber und die preußischen Junker* (Tübingen Mohr Siebeck, 1998), 86; Zimmerman, "Decolonizing Weber," 64. For Peters' radical wartime statements, see Peters, *Schriften (Vol. 3)*, 480, 482. On the French internment of Germans and Ger-man speakers, see Jean-Claude Farcy, *Les camps de concentration Français de la première guerre mondiale 1914–1920* (Paris: Antropos-Economica, 1995); Camille Maire, *Des Alsaciens-Lorrains otages en France: 1914–1918* (Stras-bourg: Universitaires de Strasbourg, 1998).

rejection of anti-Semitism) could be spun in such a way as to blame the Jewish Paul Kayser, Imperial Germany's colonial director during the heyday of Peters' colonialist activities, for Peters' failure to "conquer" more territory and, most important, his fall from grace. Kayser had supported Peters as long as he could, however. Moreover, if Peters bore any grudge against him, it was not because of Kayser's religion. In fact, in his memoirs Peters partially exculpated Kayser from blame in respect to the "Peters' scandal": "I firmly believe that Kayser, for example, much resented playing the role he was forced to play." Nazi propaganda, ironically, even turned Peters into a pioneer of racial hygiene and segregation, although this interpretation ignores Peters' eagerness to have sexual relations with African women. It is in fact rather obvious that the Kilimanjaro killings were the consequence of Peters' jealousy of the suspected other partner of his African concubine. Carl Peters as portrayed by the popular actor Hans Albers in the 1941 Nazi propaganda movie was thus an ideological construct.[8]

Although Peters, Ratzel, and later Dernburg and Solf used their fascination with and knowledge of the United States to promote and administer overseas colonialism, the agricultural economist and more conservative Max Sering, with whom Max Weber maintained friendly but disputatious relations, attempted to apply his firsthand observations of the American West to the task of promoting "inner colonization" in the German East. Yet early on, Sering had to cope with the realization that lessons learned from America only possessed limited applicability within Germany. Based on his research on American agricultural techniques he had to admit that a direct "transfer of [American] institutions and economic methods to other countries is rarely possible." In *The Colonization in Eastern Germany* (1893), a 330-page study on internal colonization attempts in the German East (i.e., the settling of ethnic Germans in regions inhabited

---

[8] Peters, *Schriften (Vol. 1)*, 87; Michael Perraudin and Jürgen Zimmerer, eds., *German Colonialism and National Identity* (Milton Park: Routledge, 2011), 169–70.

mostly by ethnic Poles), Sering therefore made only a handful
of terse and cursory references to the United States. In fact, Sering's most detailed comparisons between the German East and
the American West demonstrated that the American frontier was
quite different from Prussia's eastern provinces. He argued that
colonizers in "old cultural lands" like the German East "could
not proceed in the same way as colonizers on the vast and relatively poor soils made available for settlement by the North-
American government." Furthermore, Sering pointed out that
one of the main goals of German settlements in the East was
for colonists to maintain their German identity vis-à-vis the Polish majority population. As a result, the American West could
not serve as a model: "In North America nothing has more contributed to the quick Anglicization of foreign colonists than legal
provisions that effected their settlement in individual farms and
their spatial dispersal among a majority of native farmers. In
Posen-Western Prussia it is our goal to create nationally cohesive
colonies. Especially because of this reason the establishment of a
system of individual farms has been continuously avoided."[9]

Sering therefore did not transplant settlement schemes from
the North American frontier to the German East. He knew far
too much about the American West to propose it as a model for
the German East, despite being impressed by the American frontier. Most important, at least before 1914 he respected that, in
those areas targeted for German settlements, the majority of the
population was not ethnically German, but Polish. Sering was
clearly unwilling to consider measures of ethnic cleansing and
therefore had to concede that the American single-farm model

---

[9] Compare Peters' polemics against radical visions of German expansion in
Europe: Peters, *Schriften (Vol. 1)*, 146–47; Max Sering, *Die landwirthschaftliche Konkurrenz Nordamerikas in Gegenwart und Zukunft* (Leipzig:
Duncker & Humblot, 1887), 710. For Sering's extremely brief positive comparisons of the German East with the American West, see Max Sering, *Die
innere Kolonisation im östlichen Deutschland* (Leipzig: Duncker & Humblot,
1893), 160, 172, 180, 205. For his longer elaborations on why the German
East could *not* be modeled after the American West, see Sering, *Die innere
Kolonisation im östlichen Deutschland*, 166–67, 213, 230.

did not work in the German East, because this system would have made it too hard for German settlers to maintain their "German-ness." Before World War I, the East was thus merely one target of colonialist sentiments, and a problematic and highly contested one at that. Yet while German overseas expansionists looked to the United States in general and in particular to the American West and the "New South" for colonization or race-control models, the East presented a very different situation. For Sering, ultimately, the East was not and could never be Germany's equivalent to the American West.[10]

Even the Pan-German League, many members of which were much more radically expansionist than Sering, was not narrowly focused on the East. It even advocated expansionist goals in Western Europe. Ideas of "living space in the East" as Germany's "true destiny" began to make increasing sense only between 1915 and 1917 when Germany's advances along the Eastern Front appeared to make Germany's boundaries in Eastern Europe expandable. Yet this eastern frontier enthusiasm inspired by the successes of German troops was not shared by those who had decisively shaped German colonial

[10] For evaluations of Sering as a "direct transporter" of the American West to Eastern Germany and Sering's attitudes toward Poles, see David Blackbourn, "The Conquest of Nature and the Mystique of the Eastern Frontier in Germany," in *Germans, Poland, and Colonial Expansion to the East*, ed. Robert L. Nelson (New York: Palgrave Macmillan, 2009), 151 (note 40); Robert L. Nelson, "The 'Archive for Inner Colonization,' the German East and World War I," in *Germans, Poland, and Colonial Expansion to the East*, ed. Robert L. Nelson (New York: Palgrave MacMillan, 2009), 66; Robert L. Nelson, "From Manitoba to the Memel: Max Sering, Inner Colonization and the German East," *Social History* 35, no. 4 (2010): 447–48. Other German social scientists, among them most importantly Georg Friedrich Knapp, did in fact draw on the United States as a potential model for Eastern Prussia. Yet Knapp was not interested in the American West, but exclusively in the coercive labor relations between black sharecroppers and white landowners in the "redeemed" so-called New South. Knapp saw this tightly controlled and coercive relationship between blacks and whites in the American South as potentially applicable in the German East vis-à-vis the region's Polish population. Andrew Zimmerman, "A German Alabama in Africa: The Tuskegee Expedition to German Togo and the Transnational Origins of West African Cotton Growers," *American Historical Review* 110 (2005): 1373.

discourse and German colonial policies before 1914. Bound to older imperialist traditions, during the war many liberals were extremely worried about right-wing expansionist fantasies aimed at large-scale eastern annexations. The United States, American westward expansion, and American race provisions had provided an important context for policies in the German colonies before 1914, but did not inspire radical hopes for sweeping eastward expansion during the war. Although liberal imperialists had never been opposed to more informal economic-imperialist aspirations of the German Empire in the eastern regions, aspirations for an actual German frontier in Eastern Europe gained mass support only around the time the United States had entered the conflict on the side of the Entente (1917), an event that irreparably damaged America's attractiveness as an expansionist model.[11]

By the end of World War I, radical right-wing organizations had succeeded in mobilizing more than 1.2 million Germans for their goals, who mostly joined the short-lived Deutsche Vaterlandspartei. Although the Pan-German League had existed since 1891, it was the crisis of the war years that enabled it and other associations, among them the Deutsche Vaterlandspartei, to gain increased public support. In 1901, the Pan-German League had around 22,000 members, and by 1914, its membership was reduced to only 17,000. In 1918, however, it had more than doubled in size, to more than 36,000 members. Yet the Pan-German League of 1918 was not the League of 1891. During the 1890s, the League was home not only to radical right-wingers but also right- and left-liberals like Friedrich Ratzel, Max Weber, and Carl Peters. Most moderates had either left the League by 1903 or, like Peters, had problems with its programmatic development. Weber left in 1899, Ratzel died, and Peters criticized the League's anti-Semitism.[12]

[11] Blackbourn, *The Conquest of Nature*, 284; Mark Mazower, *Hitler's Empire. Nazi Rule in Occupied Europe* (London: Penguin Books, 2008), 26–27.
[12] Roger Chickering, *We Men Who Feel Most German: A Cultural Study of the Pan-German League, 1886–1914* (Boston: George Allen & Unwin, 1984), 227, 323; Hagenlücke, *Deutsche Vaterlandspartei: Die nationale Rechte am Ende des Kaiserreiches*, 27, 39, 204–12; Arne Perras, *Carl Peters and German*

For Weber, the League was, ironically, not anti-Polish enough. Although Weber supported Germany's overseas expansion and "world politics," he was never as enthusiastic about settler colonies as many of his long-time associates, among them most prominently Friedrich Naumann. Over the course of the twentieth century, Weber and his political thought have been variously classified as liberal, progressive, or nationalist. He clearly did not always share the views embraced by other left-liberal and progressive imperialists such as his friend Naumann, or Paul Rohrbach and Bernhard Dernburg, all of whom moved in and out of the sphere of Naumann's Nationalsozialer Verein [National-Social Association]; nor did he completely share the views of Gustav Schmoller's Verein für Sozialpolitik [Association for Social Policy] and the Kolonialpolitisches Aktionskomité [Action Committee for Colonialism]. Yet Weber nevertheless associated almost exclusively with these men and their organizations, and it was within these left-liberal and progressive circles that he was highly respected.

In fact, the intense cooperation between German progressives before the Great War and their often close personal relationships resulted in one of the most direct liberal continuities of twentieth-century German political history: After 1949, the most prominent liberal politician of the newly founded Federal Republic of Germany, its first president Theodor Heuss, proudly and repeatedly mentioned his many deep political conversations with Max Weber before and during World War I. Heuss maintained that Weber had had a profound influence on him and had shaped his liberal political creed. Among the many things that set Weber apart from the radical right during World War I was the fact that, at least for much of the war, the conflict did not radicalize his thought. He even attempted (although unsuccessfully in the end) to temper his anti-Polish tendencies: He learned the language and advocated conceptions for a moderate peace that would entail the

Imperialism, 1856–1918 (Oxford: Clarendon Press, 2004), 183, 222. For Peters' personal attitudes toward Jews see also his essay "Der Zionismus" in Peters, *Schriften (Vol. 3)*, 321–25.

creation of a newly independent Poland. Nevertheless, ultimately, Weber was greatly affected by Germany's defeat, especially the growing certainty even before the terms of the Versailles Treaty were announced that Germany would lose territory in the East, so in late 1918 he became radically anti-Polish again.[13]

The Pan-German League recovered from its loss of prominent members like Weber and Ratzel only during World War I (between 1903 and 1908, the League's membership plummeted to an all-time low of around 14,000). After 1910 it was a relatively small political pressure group that attacked the German government from the right. The creation of the so-called Cartel of Productive Estates in 1913 allied the League with more traditional conservative forces and thus broadened its operating range and influence. Nevertheless, as historian Margaret Lavinia Anderson points out, before the outbreak of World War I, the radical right was becoming marginalized in the German Empire's public sphere – a development that was only reversed beginning in August 1914. The Fatherland Party, which received support from the League, organized itself outside of the Reichstag in September 1917 and explicitly rejected the "Peace Resolution" of the majority parties in the German parliament (Center Party, SPD, Progressives). Although both the Pan-Germans and the Fatherland Party were expansionist, their goals were not at all identical to those of the German colonialist movement. Influential liberal imperialists like Dernburg, Solf, Hermann Oncken, Friedrich Naumann, Max Weber, and especially Paul Rohrbach were in fact scared of both the Pan-Germans and the Fatherland Party and repeatedly attacked both organizations and their annexationist war aims between 1915 and 1918.[14]

[13] Mommsen, *Max Weber and German Politics: 1890–1920*, 71, 79, 206, 207, 210–12; Zimmerman, "Decolonizing Weber," 57, 64–66, 73–74; Laak, *Imperiale Infrastruktur*, 184–85. On Weber and Heuss, see also Marianne Weber, *Max Weber: A Biography* (New Brunswick: Transaction Publishers, 1988), liii; Theodor Heuss, *Max Weber in seiner Gegenwart* (Mohr, 1958).

[14] Walter Mogk, *Paul Rohrbach und das 'Größere Deutschland:' Ethischer Imperialismus im Wilhelminischen Zeitalter* (München: Wilhelm Goldmann Verlag, 1972); Chickering, *We Men Who Feel Most German: A Cultural Study*

German Liberals and the United States during the 1920s

Germany's defeat turned questions that so far had only existed along the colonial periphery of the Germany Empire into explicitly metropolitan concerns. Germany had lost not only its overseas possessions but also 20 percent of its contiguous European territory. Centuries of European growth (from a Prussian perspective) and decades of global expansion (from the perspective of the united Germany after 1871) were reversed. In turn, colonialist concepts and anxieties – for example, Friedrich Ratzel's "living space" notion (and its many echoes in both scientific and popular literature) – also shifted from their previous association with Germany's colonial empire and became linked to continental concerns.

In addition, questions of miscegenation and race control moved from the colonial periphery to metropolitan Germany: After the official end of combat operations on November 11, 1918, Allied troops occupied the Rhineland region in western Germany. There the French army deployed a number of colonial regiments, thereby also stationing West African troops on German soil. Whereas the general German population in the occupied areas had few problems with the black French troops, from the vantage point of German colonialists and radicalized nationalists this situation was doubly insulting: Not only had Germany lost its African possessions but also a role reversal had taken place within Germany, in which black Africans had authority over white Germans. Given the concerns over the miscegenation problem in the German colonies even before the beginning of the Great War, it is not surprising that the Rhineland occupation served as a lightning rod for those outraged by Germany's forced transformation from colonizer to colonized. Especially

of the Pan-German League, 1886–1914, 227, 323; Hagenlücke, *Deutsche Vaterlandspartei: Die nationale Rechte am Ende des Kaiserreiches*, 27, 39, 204–12; Martin Llanque, *Demokratisches Denken im Krieg: Die deutsche Debatte im Ersten Weltkrieg* (Berlin: Akademie–Verlag, 2000); Margaret Lavinia Anderson, *Practicing Democracy: Elections and Political Culture in Imperial Germany* (Princeton: Princeton University Press, 2000), 428.

for conservatives, nationalists, and liberals, the "horror on the Rhine" and "black shame" (terms for the French occupation regime) thus became political rallying cries.[15]

Before 1914, German colonialists could at least claim that Germany and the United States were equals and could accept American examples as coming from a fellow world power. During the 1920s, this claim became impossible for many reasons, including Germany's territorial losses and the presence of foreign (and nonwhite) soldiers on German soil. Germany had lost its status as world power, while the United States was on the rise. As a result, the admiring tone that characterized so much writing about American expansionism and racial policies toward both Native and African Americans before 1914 became bitter and jealous after 1918. Simultaneously, those left-liberal politicians who before 1914 had established themselves as the most potent and successful actors in colonial matters quickly began to lose their influence after 1918. At least indirectly, Germany's forced decolonization thus contributed to the demise of German political liberalism during the 1920s. After all, before 1914, some of the biggest political successes of German liberals since the 1880s had been linked to German colonialism, best signified by the strong showing of liberal parties in the "Hottentot elections" of 1907 and by Dernburg's and Solf's tenure at the RKA. With colonialism as a matter of practical politics out of the picture, after 1918 liberal politicians lost one of their key spheres of political activity.[16]

---

[15] Lora Wildenthal, *German Women for Empire, 1884–1945* (Durham: Duke University Press, 2001), 179; Iris Wigger, *Die "Schwarze Schmach am Rhein:" Rassistische Diskriminierung zwischen Geschlecht, Klasse, Nation und Rasse* (Münster: Westfälisches Dampfboot, 2007), 11; Richard S. Fogarty, *Race & War in France: Colonial Subjects in the French Army, 1914–1918* (Baltimore: The Johns Hopkins University Press, 2008), 278.

[16] In 1912, the successes of the left–liberal FVP were almost exclusively the result of Social Democratic voters giving FVP candidates the votes in districts in which the SPD candidate did not have a chance in the run-off elections. The popularity of the successor parties (DDP, DVP) of both the left–liberal Progressive People's Party and the right-liberal National–Liberal Party spiked during the early Weimar years, in 1919 and 1920, respectively. Moreover, according to Lora Wildenthal, the DVP became "the" colonial-revisionist party

Moreover, after 1918 the issue of colonialism and the United States' function within the framework of colonialist debates also lost its potentially nonpartisan character. Before 1914, colonialist sentiment in general and American expansionist examples in particular created intersections between liberals and rightist parties. In addition to the fact that the United States served as the primary intellectual backdrop for both the war in GSWA and the mixed-race marriage debates in 1912, German liberal colonialists also established ties between American institutions and the German colonies. Booker T. Washington's Tuskegee Institute thus played an important role in German plans to turn Togo into a cotton-exporting colony. American sharecropping methods were to be transplanted to Africa, a venture that was overseen by Tuskegee graduates. Before 1914, American ideas and methods as well as tangible cooperation with Americans were indispensable tools for those in charge of the German colonial empire.[17]

After 1918, rational and practical debate among German conservatives, nationalists, and liberals was often hindered by feelings of humiliation, evoked by Germany's losses and America's alleged gains. Yet these feelings were not shared across the board by all segments of German society. The United States retained its model function for some Germans, especially for labor activists, and some economists and industrialists. The U.S. model did fall from favor when it came to questions of colonialism, empire, and expansion, however. For example, after 1918 even liberal academics began to analyze America's expansionism from a different angle than before the war. The United States was now viewed as "sneaky" as it had "silently" constructed an empire precisely

during the 1920s. However, this tactical move did not help the party. Both the DVP and the DDP lost more and more votes until they were relegated to political insignificance after the 1930 elections. Wildenthal, *German Women for Empire*, 182; Dieter Langewiesche, *Liberalismus in Deutschland*, 1. Aufl. ed., *Neue historische Bibliothek* (Frankfurt am Main: Suhrkamp, 1988), 243.

[17] Sven Beckert, "From Tuskegee to Togo: The Problem of Freedom in the Empire of Cotton," *The Journal of American History* 92, no. 2 (2005); Andrew Zimmerman, *Alabama in Africa: Booker T. Washington, the German Empire, and the Globalization of the New South* (Princeton: Princeton University Press, 2010).

during the years when Germany was losing its ability to be Central Europe's hegemonic power. Moreover, America's "modern imperialism" after 1893 was believed to be clearly linked to its earlier, more "primitive" expansion westward, which had resulted in "the extermination of whole peoples." The United States could therefore not be trusted. After having successfully established dominance over a whole continent and then over adjacent regions, the United States was next targeting Europe and Germany.[18]

The changed attitude toward the United States and American expansionism among liberal academics in Germany after World War I was exemplified by Hermann Oncken, a famous and influential historian at the University of Göttingen. Before 1914, Oncken had been an open admirer of the United States and American politicians, especially of outspoken imperialists like Theodore Roosevelt and Alfred Thayer Mahan. Oncken had also lived and taught in the United States. Following Frederick Jackson Turner, Oncken argued that both American continental expansion and postfrontier imperialism had had a profound and positive influence on the development of the United States. In Oncken's prewar works, especially in an article titled "America and the Great Powers" (1910), the liberal German fascination with American expansionism is pervasive. After 1918, like so many other liberals Oncken could not forgive the United States for joining Great Britain and France. His changed attitude was even noticed by American officials. The U.S. ambassador in Germany between 1933 and 1937, William E. Dodd (himself a historian), thus noted in his diary that even the "best of the Germans," among them "friends like Oncken," could not look past America's participation in the Great War on the side of Great Britain and France.[19]

---

[18] Mary Nolan, *Visions of Modernity* (New York: Oxford University Press, 1994), 17; Arthur Salz, "Der Imperialismus der Vereinigten Staaten," *Archiv für Sozialwissenschaft und Sozialpolitik* 50, no. 3 (1923): 565, 569, 616.

[19] Oncken and Dodd cited in Fritz T. Epstein, "Germany and the United States: Basic Patterns of Conflict and Understanding," in *Issues and Conflicts: Studies in Twentieth Century American Diplomacy*, ed. George L. Anderson (Lawrence: University of Kansas Press, 1959), 292, 293, 298.

Between 1914 and 1918, a similar distancing took place in the United States, at least to a degree. Before the war, Germany's liberal professorial elite had been in close contact with American academics and progressive reformers, many of whom had come to Germany to receive at least portions of their academic training. In addition, before 1914 many American progressives and social reformers had perceived the German "big state" system with its welfare provisions and social legislation as exemplary. The outbreak of war threw many American progressives into deep inner turmoil, especially those who had been to Germany and had been trained by academic and liberal luminaries such as Gustav Schmoller and Lujo Brentano, or had admired the sociopolitical concepts of Friedrich Naumann and Max Weber. Among these Americans were the progressive reformer Frederick C. Howe; the economist Richard T. Eley; the writer Randolph Bourne; and the African American sociologist, historian, and civil-rights activist W. E. B. DuBois. Even during the war, American admiration and respect for German progressive "social engineering" achievements ran deep, although by 1917 these feelings began to be buried under an increasingly thick layer of anti-German sentiment. Yet in 1916, Theodore Roosevelt, true to his own progressive beliefs, could still admit that "this country has more to learn from Germany than from any other nation – and this as regards fealty to non-utilitarian ideals, no less than as regards the essentials of social and industrial efficiency, of that species of socialized governmental action which is absolutely necessary for individual protection and general well-being under the conditions of modern industrialism." Yet by 1918, the "good" and progressive Germany these Americans had admired before 1914 (maybe even until 1916) had disappeared. From their perspective, it had been drowned out by a "bad," reactionary Germany whose feudal, medieval, and warlord-like Junker-elites had driven the country into war, which in turn had driven all previously "good" Germans insane.[20]

[20] Roosevelt quoted in Daniel T. Rodgers, *Atlantic Crossings: Social Politics in a Progressive Age* (Cambridge: Harvard University Press, 1998), 272–77.

Germans returned the favor, so to speak. After 1918 they stopped uttering approving evaluations of the United States, and the American empire ceased to look like a model. Instead, it appeared "Janus-faced" and threatening. In 1923, the influential left-liberal economist and political scientist Lujo Brentano (who before the war had himself been a member of the large circle of liberal imperialists) reevaluated America's constant expansion during the nineteenth century that culminated in the United States' acquisition of overseas colonies in the 1890s. Adolf Hasenclever, a historian at the University of Göttingen, came to analogous conclusions. Clearly taking aim at prewar expressions of sympathy and admiration for the United States, he asked why even "experts of [American] history... have let themselves be so thoroughly misled about this nation's aggressive character?... How can it be that during a single century the United States has expanded like no other big power of the old European continent... and has never been criticized for this behavior?"[21]

World War I created such deep intellectual chasms and so effectively interrupted many prewar German-American affinities that after 1918 the United States lost much of its former appeal in questions of race and (reverse-) colonialism. Whereas in 1912 Jim Crow laws provided the key backdrop for arguments for racial segregation in the German colonies, American racial segregation measures were completely ignored by the many outraged German critics of the French deployment of colonial troops for the occupation of the Rhineland. Even Wilhelm Solf refrained from using American examples when attacking this "Horror on the Rhine," although he probably knew more about American segregation measures than any other German politician of the time.

---

[21] James Sheehan, *The Career of Lujo Brentano: A Study of Liberalism and Social Reform in Imperial Germany* (Chicago: The University of Chicago Press, 1966), 180–85, 201–03; Lujo Brentano, "Die Entwicklung der Vereinigten Staaten zum Imperialismus" *Archiv für Politik und Geschichte* (1923): 224–43 (esp. 40); Adolf Hasenclever, "Der amerikanische Imperialismus," *Vergangenheit und Gegenwart*, no. 5 (1928): 267, 268, 269; Salz, "Der Imperialismus der Vereinigten Staaten," 565.

It was thus left to an American, the actress and right-wing activist Ray Beveridge, to point out that the conditions that existed in the occupied Rhineland would not be tolerated in the American South. Before the Great War, Beveridge had had acting engagements in the United States and Germany. She also spent time in South Africa and in 1901 was hosted by Cecil Rhodes. During the war, she toured the United States "propagandizing for the German cause;" she continued this activity after 1918, although from within Germany, where she became one of the most vocal and racist opponents of what she termed "die schwarze Schmach" [the black shame] – the presence of French colonial troops in Germany. In 1922, Beveridge even went so far as to call on Germans to adopt the American practice of lynching, although nobody acted on it.[22]

The differences between the careful analysis of Jim Crow regulations by liberals such as Hermann von Richthofen or Wilhelm Solf before the war and Beveridge's shrill promotion of racially motivated violence after 1918 were obvious. During the 1920s, liberals abstained from referencing the United States even in such a convenient case as the Rhineland occupation. Though outraged by the deployment of African soldiers, liberals like Count Max von Montgelas criticized Beveridge as "over the top," and others refused to take note of her. The tone of Beveridge's talk nevertheless fit the times. Although her racism had both American and colonial origins, through her panicked promotion of racial hatred and her shrill portrayal of Germany as victim of a corrupt France, Beveridge was channeling the emotional and psychological fallout of World War I, the subsequent defeat, and the multiple crises of the early 1920s, as did the Nazis' Eastern-Europe-focused expansionism.[23]

[22] Ray Beveridge, *Die schwarze Schmach - Die weisse Schande* (Hamburg: Verlag F. W. Rademacher, 1922), 20; Jared Poley, *Decolonization in Germany: Weimar Narratives of Colonial Loss and Foreign Occupation* (Bern: Peter Lang, 2005), 188.

[23] Wigger, *Die "Schwarze Schmach am Rhein:" Rassistische Diskriminierung zwischen Geschlecht, Klasse, Nation und Rasse*, 63.

"Yes, Yes, America, you're better off. But, please, keep your benevolence to yourself": Nazi Expansionism and America[24]

After 1918, German colonial revisionism developed along increasingly radical lines, as indicated, among other things, by Beveridge's frenzied and racialized diatribes. In Weimar Germany, female colonialist activists began to embrace ideas of a race-based ("völkisch") morality, which quickly became commonplace in colonialist circles. In turn, embrace of these ideas moved many colonialists, who clamored for the return of Germany's lost overseas possessions, much further to the right than they had been before the war. Ultimately, concepts of race and racial purity were also supposed to provide an ethical yardstick for Germans at home. Those who argued for new German expansionism attempted to find solace in ideas of a racialized inner strength and renewal, which would have to precede any attempts to enlarge the country's territory.[25]

Racism and feelings of white German superiority were of course nothing new within the framework of expansionist debates. Yet before 1914, these sentiments were integrated into discussions that were often led by colonial administrators and academics who exchanged ideas through a transatlantic network: German scholars like Hermann Oncken lived and taught in the United States, whereas Americans such as William Benjamin Smith or Archibald Cary Coolidge studied and lectured in Germany. Germany's defeat weakened this expansionist-minded transatlantic community, which affected the role the

[24] "Amerika, du hast es besser," *Völkischer Beobachter*, July 15 1938. This article was about the abduction of Charles Lindbergh's baby and argued that the "aggressor nation" Germany would offer a better and safer home for "the children of America's capitalists" than the United States.

[25] Grosse, "What Does German Colonialism Have To Do With National Socialism? A Conceptual Framework," 118–19; Wildenthal, *German Women for Empire*, 173, 176. On Rohrbach, see Josef Anker, "Paul Rohrbach," in *Allgemeine Deutsche Biographie* (Berlin: Rohmer - Schinkel, 2005), 5–6. Rohrbach had already attacked the Pan-German League and its ideas of wide-ranging annexations in Eastern Europe during World War I.

United States played in German expansionist debates. To be sure, German intellectuals had never unanimously viewed America in a positive light. Oswald Spengler's popular tome *The Decline of the West* (finished in 1914 and published in 1918) highlighted the antiliberal, nationalist-conservative, and anti-American tendencies among some German intellectuals even before the war. The various "intellectuals' addresses" – among them most famously the appeal *To the Cultured World* [An die Kulturwelt] and the *Declaration of University Professors of the German Empire* [Erklärung der Hochschullehrer des Deutschen Reiches] – that rejected accusations of war crimes and denied charges of German war guilt also show that at least in 1914 and 1915 most German academics and intellectuals, liberal and conservative alike, were willing to support both the German war effort and simultaneously mute their demands for domestic reform, at least for the time being. Yet this informal coalition of various political groups and individuals did not last long. In 1916 the National-Liberal Party in particular began to show signs of inner strife: Whereas some National Liberals began to clamor for large-scale, radically nationalist, and Pan-German-inspired war aims, others counseled moderation and moved closer to the concepts promoted by the left-liberal FVP.[26]

Yet it took the multiple social, cultural, political, and economic crises of the war, defeat, and the interwar years to shape the expansionist demands and goals that burgeoned in the minds of Nazi ideologues such as Alfred Rosenberg, Richard Walther Darré, Adolf Hitler, and Heinrich Himmler and (especially in Rosenberg's and Himmler's cases) from there to shape the directives of those in charge of the occupied eastern territories after 1939. Simultaneously, the men who had administered

[26] Langewiesche, *Liberalismus in Deutschland*, 227–32, 250–51; Philipp Gassert, *Amerika im Dritten Reich. Ideologie, Propaganda und Volksmeinung, 1933–1945* (Stuttgart: Franz Steiner Verlag, 1997), 84; Hagenlücke, *Deutsche Vaterlandspartei: Die nationale Rechte am Ende des Kaiserreiches*, 68–69. See also Konrad Jarausch, *Students, Society, and Politics in Imperial Germany. The Rise of Academic Illiberalism* (Princeton: Princeton University Press, 1982), 417.

the German colonial regime before 1918 underwent a process of marginalization. The postwar fate of one of the most racist proponents of prewar colonialism, Paul Rohrbach, illustrates this development. Rohrbach, like other liberal German colonialists, had visited the United States before World War I. He had been interested in obtaining personal impressions of "the filling of the empty space" of the American West. Rohrbach's interest in studying American westward expansion was reflected in his comparisons of GSWA's natives to Indians and the colony to the "empty space" of the American West.[27]

During the war, Rohrbach consistently criticized demands for aggressive eastward expansion, believing that Eastern Europe was not and never could be Germany's equivalent to the American West. For the avid colonialist Rohrbach, European and German settler colonies could be established only where no native population existed or where the native population was, in his view, racially and culturally inferior. This had been the case in the Americas and still was in Africa, but not in Eastern Europe. In 1916, Rohrbach thus met with Chancellor Bethmann-Hollweg and argued that repressive measures should be taken against the Pan-German League, because translations of Pan-German pamphlets misled Britons, Frenchmen, and Americans into believing that "Pan-German equals German." Between 1915 and 1918, Rohrbach (together with other liberal publicists, academics, and avid liberal colonialists – including Martin Hobohm, and Friedrich Naumann) engaged in sustained journalistic criticism of the Pan-Germans' radical nationalism and also attacked the Fatherland Party because of its shrill expansionist demands. On September 8, 1918, a little more than two months before the end of the war, Rohrbach argued that Germany's future role in Eastern Europe could not be approached "from a Pan-German vantage point of violence.... If we become oppressors ourselves... we will hardly be capable of maintaining our position in Eastern Europe in sustainable fashion."[28]

[27] See Chapter 2.
[28] Paul Rohrbach, *Die alldeutsche Gefahr*, ed. Martin Hobohm (Berlin: Verlag von Hans Robert Engelmann, 1918), 5, 6, 10, 24, 41, 42. Compare

After the war, Rohrbach supported the new German republic and called on his compatriots "to follow the democratic path." As it did for fellow colonialists Solf and Dernburg, the DDP – the FVP's successor organization – became Rohrbach's party of choice. During the 1920s, Rohrbach traveled extensively and visited the United States for a second time. Rohrbach lamented that Germans did not engage with the American people more directly and more intensely. He inveighed against German politicians for focusing too narrowly on domestic problems instead of actively trying to learn from the world's biggest republic. He also tried to interest Americans in Germany's troubles. However, Rohrbach eventually came to the conclusion that the close contacts between Germans and Americans that had existed before 1914 could not be revived, a fact that he regretted.[29]

During the early 1930s, in view of the successes of the National Socialist German Workers Party (NSDAP), Rohrbach became increasingly concerned with the fragmentation of political allegiances in Germany. He thus tried to bridge the sociocultural gaps between the few remaining moderate middle-class ("bürgerliche") parties. Before the national elections of July 1932, he published an editorial in which he called on German Protestants to vote for the Catholic Center Party. Rohrbach wanted the Center Party to become an inter-confessional, liberal to moderately conservative parliamentary counterweight to the

---

also Llanque, *Demokratisches Denken im Krieg: Die deutsche Debatte im Ersten Weltkrieg*, 142; Mogk, *Paul Rohrbach und das 'Größere Deutschland:' Ethischer Imperialismus im Wilhelminischen Zeitalter*, 34; Zimmerer, "The Birth of the Ostland," 212, 217, 218. In his famous but contentious *Griff nach der Weltmacht*, Fritz Fischer lumped Rohrbach together with the Pan-German League, arguing that "practically" Rohrbach's war aims and those of other liberals were identical with the ones voiced by the Fatherland Party and the Pan-German League. Fritz Fischer, *Griff nach der Weltmacht: Die Kriegszielpolitik des kaiserlichen Deutschlands 1914/18* (Düsseldorf: Droste Verlag, 1961), 190.

[29] Paul Rohrbach, *Monarchie, Republik und politische Parteien in Deutschland* (Stuttgart: J. Engelhorns Nachf., 1920), 5–6; Paul Rohrbach, *Amerika und wir. Reisebetrachtungen von Paul Rohrbach* (Berlin: Buchenau & Reichert Verlag, 1926), 129. See also his positive references to the American political system in Paul Rohrbach, *Deutschland! Tod oder Leben?* (München: F. Bruckmann A.G., 1930), 236–37.

Nazis: "I believe it is the right thing to cast one's vote so it results in a direct strengthening of the one party that is the actual opponent of the National Socialists on a middle-class [bürgerliche] basis. And that is the Center Party." Rohrbach also appealed directly to Chancellor Franz von Papen to openly commit the German government to fight against the NSDAP's "moral anarchy." In his open letter to Papen, Rohrbach called the fight against Hitler and his party "a battle for our [Germany's] reputation" and "our Christian morals." After Hitler became chancellor on January 30, 1933, Rohrbach abandoned his resistance to the Nazis. Instead, he concentrated exclusively on his pro-colonial activities, activities that the new regime tolerated. However, virtually no high-ranking Nazi was interested in overseas colonies as settlement areas for Germans. Between 1933 and the first years of World War II, Rohrbach published books and pamphlets that called for a return of Germany's former colonies; however, he never shared the obsession of Hitler, Rosenberg, or Himmler with "living space in the East."[30]

Whereas Rohrbach ceased his resistance to the Nazis once they were in power, fellow liberal colonialist Wilhelm Solf did not. Like Bernhard Dernburg and Rohrbach, Solf became a "common sense" republican after November 1918 and even served as the young republic's first foreign minister. He also ran as a parliamentary candidate for the DDP and after the Nazi takeover founded the "Solf Circle," a group of opponents to Hitler's regime. Dernburg also became involved in the affairs of the

---

[30] Paul Rohrbach, "Protestanten, Nichtkatholiken, wählt Zentrum!," *Kölnische Volkszeitung*, 06–26–1932; Paul Rohrbach, *Herr Reichskanzler von Papen – Lösen Sie auf!* (München: Im Selbstverlag, 1932), 14; Anker, "Paul Rohrbach," 6. Rohrbach's last publication before the end of the war was another book about colonialism in Africa, titled *Contributions to a Practical Approach to the Colonial Sciences in Africa*. Ironically, this work was published in 1943, the year when the NSDAP's colonial office was dissolved. Paul Rohrbach, *Osteuropa historisch-politisch gesehen* (Potsdam: Rütten & Loening Verlag, 1942), 244; Peter Zimmermann, "Kampf um den 'Lebensraum'. Ein Mythos der Kolonial- und der Blut-und-Boden-Literatur," in *Die deutsche Literatur im Dritten Reich*, ed. Horst Prumm and Karl Denkler (Stuttgart: Philipp Reclam jun., 1976), 170–71.

Weimar Republic and served as vice chancellor and finance minister under the republic's second chancellor Philipp Scheidemann. In addition, Dernburg served as a Reichstag deputy for the DDP from 1920 until 1930. He then retired and died in 1937.[31]

Continuities between German colonialism, German liberalism, and the Nazi regime existed as well. Franz Ritter von Epp (who participated in both the suppression of the Boxer Rebellion and the war in GSWA) and Heinrich Schnee (who could look back on a long and distinguished career as a high-ranking administrator in the RKA and who was the last governor of German East Africa) were active in the German colonialist movement during the 1920s. Both men eventually decided to join forces with the Nazis. Epp became a party member in 1928, and Schnee, who during the 1920s had been a Reichstag deputy for the DVP, one of the successor parties of the National Liberals, joined the Nazi Party in 1933. The NSDAP welcomed any support it could get from "respectable" national-conservative (Epp) and bourgeois (Schnee, Hjalmar Schacht) circles. Colonial revisionists were allowed to continue their activities during the 1930s, their efforts became especially relevant during the summer of 1940, when out of the blue, African colonies appeared to be falling into Germany's hands like "ripe fruit." In June, July, and August 1940, Hitler was convinced that after France's defeat Great Britain would make peace with Germany. Germany could then reclaim its former colonies from the French and add the Belgian Congo and other territories to the mix to gain a "German Central Africa." As long as Germany and England were at war, however, reclaiming Germany's colonies from the French was too risky, because it might prompt the French fleet to join the Free French or the British Navy. Great Britain held firm and these hopes never materialized. By the fall of 1940, Hitler had (again) banished the idea of German colonies in Africa from his mind,

[31] Ludwig Brandl, "Wilhelm Solf," in *Biographisch-Bibliographisches Kirchenlexikon* (Traugott Bautz, 1995), 758–63; Gerhard A. Ritter, "Bernhard Dernburg," in *Allgemeine deutsche Biographie & Neue deutsche Biographie* (Berlin: Bürklein - Ditmar, 1957), 607–08.

and Epp's and Schnee's activities became increasingly atavistic. In 1943 they had to witness the dissolution of the German Colonial League. It was deemed "insignificant for the war."[32]

These hopes in the summer months of 1940 notwithstanding, ultimately the upper ranks of the NSDAP never shared Schnee's and Epp's colonial revisionism. To be sure, Hermann Schnee's activities during the 1920s show that some colonialists made the journey from German liberalism to outspoken support of the Nazis (and party membership): They hoped that the Nazis would back their brand of colonial revisionism. The career of Hjalmar Schacht developed along similar lines. Schacht strongly supported the effort to regain German colonies and moved from being a member of the DDP to becoming minister of economics and maintaining his position as president of the Reichsbank under the Nazis (until 1937 and 1939, respectively). Yet Hitler, Himmler, Rosenberg, and Darré were not at all interested in the kind of colonial revisionism championed by men like Schnee and Schacht (and, ultimately, Epp as well) for one simple reason: In their view, overseas possessions could never be German settler colonies. Hitler's frequent tirades against colonial revisionism before and after the summer months of 1940 leave no doubt that unless African territories fell into German hands without much effort he had no sympathy for traditional concepts of colonialism. To solve the "space emergency" of the German people, a "greater living space" had to be gained – but only in Europe and not "based on liberal-capitalist notions through the exploitation of colonies."[33]

After the 1930 Reichstag elections, Schnee and Schacht hoped to enlist the increasingly popular Nazis in their causes. Schacht was initially successful and, until about 1936, had a significant amount of influence within the Nazi regime, which while still in the process of establishing itself welcomed the support of respectable politicians and economists like Schacht. During

---

[32] Wildenthal, *German Women for Empire*, 182.
[33] Hitler quoted in Ian Kershaw, *Hitler, 1936–45: Nemesis* (W. W. Norton, 2001), 47; Klaus Hildebrand, *Vom Reich zum Weltreich. Hitler, NSDAP und koloniale Frage 1919–1945* (München: Wilhelm Fink Verlag, 1969), 66–70, 525 (Hitler), 652–73. See also Mazower, *Hitler's Empire*, 116–17.

the early 1930s, increased backing from reputable echelons of German society helped the NSDAP conceal its radicalism and attenuate its "rabble-rouser" image, thereby providing the party a fake aura of bourgeois respectability, which, in turn, helped make possible the takeover of power in 1933. Yet the Nazis gladly accepted support from bourgeois and national-conservative circles only for as long as they believed they needed it. Historian Klaus Hildebrand thus argues in *Vom Reich zum Weltreich* that "the National Socialists . . . were in no way advocates for colonial revisionism," and recent research has confirmed this classic 1969 evaluation. All three men – Schacht first, in 1936–37, then Schnee, and, finally, in 1943, Epp, who had never been a liberal to begin with and who, because of the anti-aristocratic sentiment embraced by many leading Nazis, was ridiculed as "Baron Douchebag" [Baron Depp] – came to realize that their colonial goals were not at all identical with those of high-ranking Nazi expansionists. Schacht increasingly disagreed with the regime in respect to other economic questions as well. After 1937, he was in contact with Carl Goerdeler and later became a fringe member of the resistance.[34]

Against "Liberalist" Imperialism: Nazi Lebensraum Visions as Antiliberalism and Anticolonialism

Defeat in war, territorial losses both in Europe and overseas, and the short-lived conquest of vast eastern territories in 1917–18 became intellectual departure points for Nazi ideologues.

---

[34] Hildebrand, *Vom Reich zum Weltreich*, 66–70. Hildebrand's analysis has been confirmed very recently by Karsten Linne, *Deutschland jenseits des Äquators? Die NS-Kolonialplanungen für Afrika* (Berlin: Christoph Links Verlag, 2009), 165–66. See also Fitzpatrick, "The Pre-History of the Holocaust? The Sonderweg and Historikerstreit Debates and the Abject Colonial Past"; Robert Gerwarth and Stephan Malinowski, "Der Holocaust als 'kolonialer Genozid'? Europäische Kolonialgewalt und nationalsozialistischer Vernichtungskrieg," *Geschichte und Gesellschaft* 33 (2007); Gerwarth and Malinowski, "Hannah Arendt's Ghosts." On Schacht after 1933, see Kershaw, *Hitler, 1936–45: Nemesis* 18–20, 47–49; Gerhard Schulz, "Nationalpatriotismus im Widerstand," *Vierteljahreshefte für Zeitgeschichte* 32, no. 3 (1984): 332–33.

In demanding complete abandonment of the Versailles Treaty, ostensibly the Nazis also demanded the return of Germany's former colonial possessions. Yet compared to liberal colonial revisionists like Rohrbach, the leading national-socialist figures took a much more radical approach when reevaluating Germany's expansionist past, a phenomenon highlighted by the minor role the United States played in their considerations. Hitler's analysis of America and American expansionism, although positive during the late 1920s, was superficial and frequently factually incorrect. However, overall his views showcased a general tendency during the 1920s and 1930s: The United States changed from a concrete example for German expansionism to a mere intellectual construct, a foil that solely reflected German domestic concerns.[35]

Within the framework of expansionist discourse three developments took place during the Weimar years. Liberal academics like Hasenclever, Brentano, and Oncken reversed the positions that they had taken vis-à-vis American expansionism during the prewar years, thus transforming the United States from hero to villain. In addition, the contacts and fruitful (at least from the perspective of administrators like Dernburg, Solf, and Rohrbach) German-American exchanges on colonial matters ended. At the same time, Nazi propagandists began to draw their own lessons from Germany's defeat. Although scholars have recognized that Nazi proponents of eastward expansion defined themselves in contrast to the German Empire's overseas imperialism, their explicit association of Imperial Germany's colonialism with German political liberalism has so far escaped historians' attention. Viewed from a Nazi perspective, pre-1914 German colonialism had been a "liberalist" project. In fact, before the Great War German expansionism had failed because it had been pushed and supported by liberals. In his infamous *The Myth of the 20th Century* (the title referred to Houston Stewart Chamberlain's racist

[35] Adolf Hitler, *Hitlers zweites Buch*, ed. Gerhard L. Weinberg, *Quellen und Darstellungen zur Zeitgeschichte* (Stuttgart: Deutsche Verlags-Anstalt, 1961), 34–35, 99–100.

The Foundations of the 19th Century), Alfred Rosenberg – who
participated in Hitler's so-called Beer-Hall Putsch in 1923, and
during World War II became Minister for the Occupied Eastern Territories – accused the German Empire of "liberalist cow-
ardice" because it had not drawn the proper conclusions from
Germany's "territorial emergency" [Raumnot]: "During the past
decades, attempts to control even the most remote corners of
the earth with cannons, in order to maintain 'quiet and order'
among the exploited peoples, were a sign not of strength but of
weakness, just as an overt and massive police force within a state
does not indicate its vigor but its rottenness."[36]

National-socialist expansionism consciously set itself apart
from the colonialism of the prewar years. The goal was not to
acquire far-away "protection areas," but contiguous territories
in Eastern Europe. Rosenberg thus mused that "the spirit of
history has not at all moved from East to West." Instead, its
direction was "from West to East," especially after Germany's
defeat. For him, the term "Western" denoted corrupt democracies and "French-Jewish systems of thought." Although the East
had played a role in German expansionism before and after 1871,
Eastern Europe had never been the main focus of the expansionist
designs of the driving personalities behind Germany's colonialist

[36] Alfred Rosenberg, *Der Mythus des 20. Jahrhunderts* (Munich: Hoheneichen-
Verlag, 1933), 637, 674. Compare most importantly Woodruff D. Smith,
The Ideological Origins of Nazi Imperialism (New York: Oxford University Press, 1986), 81, 82, 238–55. In his classic *Ideological Origins*, Smith
dedicates barely two pages to the phenomenon of "liberal imperialism." Yet
Rosenberg and Hitler clearly deemed "liberal imperialism" to have been very
influential before 1918. Both men considered the German Empire's imperial-
ist and colonialist policies to have been "liberal." In her synthesis of recent
studies on German and Nazi imperialism, Shelley Baranowski mentions the
Nazis' specific antiliberal bias in passing. Shelley Baranowski, *Nazi Empire:
German Colonialism and Imperialism from Bismarck to Hitler.* (New York:
Cambridge University Press, 2011), 7. To this day, the most careful study of
the Nazis' attitudes toward the German Empire's colonial activities remains
Klaus Hildebrand's 1969 *Vom Reich zum Weltreich*. Although Hildebrand
points out Hitler's and Rosenberg's explicit rejection of German imperialism
before 1914, he does not pick up on their evaluation of Imperial colonial policies as quintessentially liberal. Hildebrand, *Vom Reich zum Weltreich*, 70–89
(esp. 84–85).

ventures between 1884 and 1914. Liberal colonialists like Peters or Ratzel looked westward, preferably to the North American continent, because the American frontier inspired them in concrete ways. After it had become too obvious that America was not "available" anymore (as some liberal expansionists still dreamt in 1848), Ratzel and others directed their gaze to Africa, because their intellectual and political peers in other powerful countries were doing exactly the same. Despite their strong nationalist leanings, liberal colonialists participated constantly in transnational debates about expansion.[37]

Hitler and Rosenberg rejected liberal colonialism for this very reason. Racism and nationalism had been part and parcel of liberal German expansionist policies before 1914. Yet from a Nazi vantage point, these sentiments had merely been fig leaves for a "liberalist" system that ultimately denied the existence of racial differences and wanted to create a "world republic" without distinct nations and peoples. No doubt, the Nazis' counter-conception of "living space in the East" was not entirely new, because Hitler, Rosenberg, and Richard Walther Darré freely used terms taken from the writings of liberal colonialists like Friedrich Ratzel, who, ironically, had put his academic prestige behind the National-Liberal Party's demands for colonies in Africa. However, the Nazi ideologues' use of one of Ratzel's key terms and reference to some of his concepts did not mean that they accepted the premises of prewar liberal colonialism. Although their unwavering dedication to settler colonialism in Eastern Europe had close intellectual ties to the annexationist frenzy of the Fatherland Party during the late war years, it was also a deliberate renunciation of the main prewar colonialist trajectories. Why care about Africa or about America's settlers? In Rosenberg's view, it was Germany's "destiny" to create a "Nordic Europe," and American examples were largely irrelevant to this goal. The same held true for Hitler. Although some scholars have maintained that the "Führer" was fascinated with the American West, his allusions to the American frontier were

37 Rosenberg, *Mythus des 20. Jahrhunderts*, 640, 641, 642, 675–76.

in fact infrequent. In respect to Hitler's *Mein Kampf*, historian Günter Schubert has therefore noted that "the astounding narrowness of his horizon is also evidenced by the fact that Hitler hardly noticed a world power like the United States of America." In fact, the almost 800-page tome makes only one explicit reference to the American frontier and in such a cursory fashion (barely more than two sentences) that it is simply impossible to read any kind of fascination with it into Hitler's only published work. Throughout his life, Hitler's mentions of the American West would remain infrequent and superficial.[38]

Since the eighteenth century Germans had espoused imperialist designs in Central and Eastern Europe; for example Max Sering tried to promote German settlements in the predominantly Polish regions of West Prussia and Posen, which had been Prussian (and after 1871 also German) since 1772 and 1793, respectively. Yet Nazi plans for "Germanic" settler colonialism in the regions further east were much more radical. As a result, Hitler and Rosenberg described them as a departure from Germany's pre-1914 colonial enterprises. In Hitler's so-called *Second Book* (1928) he thus described Germany's prewar colonialism as "nonsensical" and argued that the German Empire's goal should have been "the incorporation of those German regions in Europe that because of their history alone should be a natural part not only of the German nation, but of a German Empire." In Hitler's view, the German colonial ventures had been motivated by

---

[38] Ibid. Scholars have pointed to four passages in *Mein Kampf* that supposedly reference the American West. Compare Caroll P. Kakel, *The American West and the Nazi East. A Comparative and Interpretive Perspective* (Basingstoke: Palgrave Macmillan, 2011), 1, 27, 35; Alan E. Steinweis, "Eastern Europe and the Notion of the 'Frontier' in Germany to 1945," *Yearbook of European Studies* 13 (1999), 56–57. However, a look at these passages reveals that only the one referenced earlier (*Mein Kampf*, p. 333) actually refers to life along the frontier, although merely as a metaphor for the need to separate "higher" from "lower" races. See Adolf Hitler, *Mein Kampf* (München: Zentralverlag der N.S.d.A.P., 1936), 24–25, 153, 313, 333. See also Gerhard L. Weinberg, "Hitler's Image of the United States," *The American Historical Review* 69, no. 4 (1964): 1007–08. Günter Schubert's quote in this paragraph is taken from Weinberg, "Hitler's Image of the United States," 1007.

economic interests and were "bourgeois" rather than "völkisch" (i.e., focused on the biologically determined interests of racially pure Germans). If the German Empire had followed the only true political maxim – namely to protect the racially superior Germanic elements in Central Europe – instead of the "liberalist" acquisition of overseas colonies, prewar politicians would have engaged in "bounteous living-space policies [Raumpolitik] in Europe itself" and not wasted German resources and manpower in Africa and elsewhere.[39]

In the *Second Book* Hitler addresses the United States in more detail than in *Mein Kampf*. On five of around 180 typescript pages, he refers to the United States as "Großraum" [great space], although even on those pages he jumps from subject to subject and does not exclusively concentrate on North America. Barely mentioning any verifiable facts (references to the country's actual size or population statistics were left blank because Hitler did not know these facts when he was dictating the text), he depicts the United States as a state dominated by superior Nordic races; Hitler's jealousy of the United States because of its advantageous "space to population" ratio is clear. Historian Adam Tooze therefore argues that beginning in 1928 the United States became quite important for Hitler, although not as a positive example for a future, eastward-expanding Greater Germany, but as bogey, as a nation that because of the large landmass it controlled was more advantageously situated than any European nation and was therefore a threat. This interpretation builds on historian Andreas Hillgruber's influential "intentionalist" (i.e., based on Hitler's intentions) explanation of Nazi foreign policy objectives. In the 1960s, Hillgruber posited that Nazi foreign policy goals rested on a stage-by-stage plan [Stufenplan] that envisioned a showdown between the newly created "world power" Germany with its vast eastern Lebensraum and the United States. Fear of being dominated by the United States was widespread during the 1920s, in Germany and elsewhere in Europe, and contributed to visions of a peacefully united "Pan Europe." Hitler detested these ideas, and his references to the United States in the *Second*

[39] Hitler, *Hitlers zweites Buch*, 87, 101.

Book were meant to sharpen the profile of his arguments: "[I]n the future, North America can only be challenged and checked by a state that understands... [how] to improve its people's racial qualities." Americans were thus not depicted as exemplary, but as "the real threat to German predominance in the world."[40] At the height of the Roaring Twenties and the expansion of the economic bubble that would burst just one year later, America with its booming industry, high number of privately owned cars (a phenomenon that fascinated Hitler), and seductive popular culture appeared indeed to be destined to become a hegemonic power. Yet the United States had played no role for Hitler when he had first formulated his Lebensraum obsessions in *Mein Kampf*. Instead, his Lebensraum ideology had been conceived as the complete opposite of the German Empire's failed colonial and foreign policy activities. Most important, in 1924 this expansionist vision did not require even a passing reference to the United States: "In this way, we National Socialists consciously draw a line through prewar foreign policy objectives. We return to where one left off six-hundred years ago. We will end the Germanic peoples' continuous trek to Southern and Western Europe and direct our gaze to the lands in the east. We will once and for all end all prewar colonial and economic policies and move toward the soil policies of the future." Hitler's disregard of the United States in 1924 made sense: Admitting that this country was an important power would have also meant conceding that America's entry into the war in 1917 had dashed any chance of a German victory. This realization also would have made obsolete the "stab-in-the-back" myth, which held that Germany had not been vanquished by enemies "in the battlefield," but by internal Jewish-socialist conspirators.[41]

---

[40] Ibid., 128–32; Weinberg, "Hitler's Image of the United States," 1009; Andreas Hillgruber, *Hitlers Strategie: Politik und Kriegführung 1940–1941* (Frankfurt a. M.: Bernard & Graefe, 1965); Andreas Hillgruber, *Kontinuität und Diskontinuität in der deutschen Außenpolitik von Bismarck bis Hitler* (Düsseldorf: Droste, 1969); Adam Tooze, *The Wages of Destruction: The Making and Breaking of the Nazi Economy* (Viking, 2007), xxiv, 10–11.

[41] Hitler, *Mein Kampf*, 742; Adolf Hitler, *Adolf Hitler: Monologe im Führerhauptquartier 1941–1944*, ed. Werner Jochmann (Hamburg: Albrecht

Reflecting economic developments since 1924, in his *Second Book* Hitler loosely grafted the United States onto his Lebensraum ideas and incorporated it into his strategic vision, only to again remove it from this position during the Great Depression. In fact, once the Nazis were in power, the image of the United States spat out by Nazi propaganda publications quickly diverged from the tone of Hitler's 1928 remarks. During the 1930s and 1940s, Hitler often described the United States as a rotten structure, not as a future hegemon, because he believed it to be severely and long lastingly (maybe even permanently) weakened by the Great Depression. Hitler might have made these remarks, especially after 1939, to alleviate fears among army generals that a U.S. intervention in the war would have the same consequences as in 1917, namely Germany's defeat. Yet it is clear that painting the United States as a "Jew-infested" and "rotten" edifice served the regime and Hitler himself much better than the brief racialized positive interpretations of "the American Union" in the *Second Book*: If it was true that "international Jewry" controlled the United States, then the outrage expressed by both the American public and government circles vis-à-vis Germany's anti-Semitic measures after 1933 and especially after the pogrom of November 9–10, 1938, could be easily explained. During the late 1930s (as in 1924) the United States became again largely irrelevant for Hitler, at least from a strategic perspective: In both the 1936 Four-Year-Plan Memorandum and the so-called Hossbach Protocol from 1937, the United States played basically no role in Hitler's considerations of the global situation.[42]

In *Mein Kampf* and the *Second Book* Hitler made abundantly clear that he was not interested in reestablishing Germany's

Knaus Verlag, 1980), 24; *Der Prozess gegen die Hauptkriegsverbrecher vor dem Internationalen Militärgerichtshof. Nürnberg 14. November 1945 – 1. Oktober 1946*, vol. XXV (Nuremberg: 1947), 402–13 (Document 386–PS); Weinberg, "Hitler's Image of the United States," 1010–13; Tooze, *The Wages of Destruction*, 282–83; Harold James, "The Wages of Destruction: The Making and Breaking of the Nazi Economy. Review by Harold James," *Central European History* 40, no. 2 (2007): 369.
[42] Hitler, *Mein Kampf*, 742; Hitler, *Monologe im Führerhauptquartier*, 24; *Der Prozess gegen die Hauptkriegsverbrecher vor dem Internationalen*

pre-Versailles borders, and he also ranted against pre-1914 German colonialism and imperialism. The Nazis' negative attitude toward colonial revisionism became even more apparent in the *Guidelines for Colonial Propaganda* issued by Joseph Goebbels' ministry in late 1933. Although pro-colonial agitation was tolerated and regaining Germany's colonies was part of the Nazis' overarching goal of nullifying the Versailles Treaty, Goebbels' *Guidelines* stated that future German overseas possessions should "not serve as settlement areas for German peasants." Moreover, Goebbels' personal feelings regarding colonial questions were obvious: "It should also be noted that colonial propaganda is a low-priority, non-essential question for our people." As long as pro-colonialists appeared to support or at least not hamper the regime's ideology and goals, they were allowed to continue their agitation. Hitler's and the regime's take on traditional colonialism was therefore entirely functional. The same can be said about America's position within Nazi debates about expansionism and race. The Nazis' and Hitler's views of America therefore almost never reflected "the realities of German-American ties and relations and of life in the United States," as historian Philipp Gassert has argued. Instead, propagandistic references to America merely echoed specific and often evolving National-Socialist perspectives on domestic problems.[43]

"The United States under a Jewish Dictatorship" – Nazi Anti-Americanism after 1933[44]

After January 30, 1933, the Nazis began to systematically dismantle Weimar Germany's democratic structures, a process that

Militärgerichtshof. Nürnberg 14. November 1945 - 1. Oktober 1946, 402–13 (Document 386-PS); Weinberg, "Hitler's Image of the United States," 1010–13; Tooze, *The Wages of Destruction*, 282–83; James, "The Wages of Destruction: The Making and Breaking of the Nazi Economy. Review by Harold James," 369.

[43] *Guidelines* quoted in Zimmermann, "Kampf um den 'Lebensraum'," 170; Gassert, *Amerika im Dritten Reich*, 87. See also Fitzpatrick, "The Pre-History of the Holocaust? The Sonderweg and Historikerstreit Debates and the Abject Colonial Past."

[44] Headline in the *Völkischer Beobachter* (January 6, 1939)

did not remain hidden from Western observers. The rapidly increasing antidemocratic and anti-Semitic tendencies of the Hitler regime evoked strongly negative coverage in the American press, and the American Jewish Congress called for a boycott of German products. In response, positive takes on America and U.S. policies became rare in Germany. This development was by no means a reversal of Hitler's 1928 positions. Anti-Americanism had always been part of the Nazi worldview, especially in Rosenberg's case. After 1933 when anti-American sentiments were played up and pro-American views disappeared, this was "a shift in emphasis, but not in substance." In October 1937, President Roosevelt gave his "quarantine speech," an address clearly directed against Germany (and Italy and Japan). Nazi Germany's propaganda machine reacted fiercely, which led to a significant worsening of German-U.S. relations. After the "Pogrom Night" of November 1938 relations deteriorated even further. They reached their pre–World War II nadir in the spring of 1939 after Germany annexed all of Czechoslovakia and Hitler made public verbal attacks on the American president.[45]

Most apparent Nazi continuities with the pre-1914 German reception of America thus turn out to be superficial at best. In fact, even when American examples could have been useful for the regime, they were not used to the extent one would expect because other political and ideological considerations outweighed their utility. Moreover, when U.S. references did appear, they did not convey the traditional (liberal) German considerations of the United States as a model empire. For clear-cut ideological and political reasons, there was no Nazi equivalent to Imperial Germany's contacts with American institutions regarding the economic development of Germany's colonies, or the colonial department's efforts to study American race codes as models for colonial segregation policies, or the sustained discussion and justification of the war in GSWA against an American backdrop. Once the Nazis were in power, American examples were hardly ever used to openly justify expansionist or racial

[45] Gassert, *Amerika im Dritten Reich*, 98, 247.

designs, plans, or policies. Before 1937, positive mentions of the United States occurred here and there, but even during this period they were drowned out by the regime's sustained negative propaganda campaign against the United States. Even in an area that touched the core of Hitler's belief system – his obsession with racial purity – affirmative reviews of American examples dwindled after 1933.[46]

One of the most significant examples of this development is the astonishing insignificance of American segregation laws in justifications of the Nuremberg race laws of 1935. In 1912, when the German Reichstag discussed the racial segregation measures in the German colonies, the main proponents of such provisions were neither ultranationalist nor narrow-minded chauvinists. Instead, they were liberals and progressives whose political visions often transcended national borders and rested on notions of respect for other Western (and white) nations, among them very prominently the United States. Yet for Nazi jurists like Roland Freisler or other advocates of race laws after 1933, including Reinhard Heydrich and the Reichsärzteführer [National Leader of Medical Doctors] Gerhard Wagner, racial segregation measures enacted by republics like the United States proved to be highly problematic. Although one would expect the authors of disquisitions aimed at justifying the 1935 Nuremberg race laws to draw on Jim Crow provisions often and approvingly, their writings do not display the admiration for the United States so prevalent in the 1912 mixed-race marriage debates. Instead, national-socialist authors criticized and slighted Jim Crow measures. In addition, the NSDAP's main daily, the *Völkische Beobachter*, and Alfred Rosenberg's more high-brow *Nationalsozialistische Monatshefte* completely ignored American racial segregation provisions. Immediately before and after the institution of the Nuremberg Laws in September 1935, the *Beobachter* criticized lynchings in the United States and the growing influence of communism in America, yet was entirely

---

[46] Ibid., 96. German and American eugenicists maintained their contacts after 1933. They only ceased between 1937 and 1939. See note 48.

silent on the topic of racial segregation: Unlike in 1912, in 1935 America was not allowed to be exemplary. Instead, in an editorial on Abraham Lincoln, the *Beobachter* sardonically remarked that the "humanitarian-liberalist principles of the Declaration of Independence... forced Lincoln against his better judgment to advocate the emancipation of the Negroes." Less than a half-year before the Nuremberg race laws were instituted, the *Beobachter* used America as a negative example in respect to racial segregation measures.[47]

The writings of Heinrich Krieger, an engineer and trained jurist who from 1933 until the end of World War II authored numerous publications on topics of race, racial hygiene, race laws, and colonialism, best illustrate this phenomenon. In 1936, he published a lengthy book titled *Das Rasserecht in den Vereinigten Staaten* [Race Law in the United States]. The title of this volume and its publication date (one year after the Nuremberg Laws had been instituted) might lead present-day readers to expect a laudatory account of segregation in the United States intended to justify Nazi race laws. Even the 1936 announcement of Krieger's book in the *Großdeutscher Pressedienst* appeared to indicate that this was the case. Clearly the author of this notice had not read Krieger's book. In fact, *Race Law in the United States* was highly critical of American racial segregation measures. Krieger was most disapproving of the complete lack of a central guiding force behind the many and very different state laws:

The almost complete absence of an ideological battle fought over these race laws lets one suspect the existence of a core perspective and continuously search for it.... Yet such a higher vantage point does not exist. In liberalist co-existence, i.e. separated from any kind of higher principle, two forces face each other: One represents an ideological system, the other only immediate and individual demands.... In fact, the term "race law" or "law of the races"... in respect to the United States is completely unknown.

---

[47] "Neger sollte gelyncht werden," *Völkische Beobachter* 12-21-1934; "Abraham Lincoln und das Rasseproblem Amerikas," *Völkische Beobachter* 04–16-1935.

Krieger condemned America's "liberalist" and "individual demands"-focused democratic ideology for hampering the development of "actual" race laws – a term that for him could only denote provisions not instituted in a piecemeal and decentralized fashion. Like the Nuremberg Laws, "true" race laws had to be guided by a clearly formulated racial ideology. American segregation provisions had been instituted "too late" and were "too weak" to serve as a model for Germany. American race law was "casuistic" (i.e., it consisted of too many contradictory and uncoordinated provisions). German National Socialism should not imitate such a system, but should move beyond incomplete and individualized approaches to both race and law. From the perspective of official Nazi propaganda, it was therefore not the United States that was exemplary for Germany. Instead, German eugenicist and race decrees should be a model for America: According to the *Völkischer Beobachter* "scientists in the United States were increasingly convinced that the laws of the Third Reich were exemplary."[48]

The core message of the many commentaries and texts published in support of the Nuremberg Laws and further segregation measures was clear: Only under the self-consciously nonliberal and nondemocratic leadership of the National Socialists could "true" race and racial hygiene laws be instituted. A 1939 article published in the journal, *Advances in Inheritance Pathology, Racial Hygiene and Related Fields*, confirmed this view. Quoting the racial hygienist Otmar Freiherr von Verschuer, the piece sharply criticized the "individualist mind-set" of the United States and other Western nations, arguing that "under the banner of unfettered individualism racial hygiene can never reach

[48] Heinrich Krieger, *Das Rasserecht in den Vereinigten Staaten* (Berlin: Junker und Dünnhaupt Verlag, 1936), 145, 342–43; Kundrus, "Von Windhoek nach Nuernberg? Koloniale 'Mischehenverbote' und die nationalsozialistische Rassengesetzgebung," 119. *Großdeutscher Pressedienst* cited and *Völkischer Beobachter* paraphrased in Stefan Kühl, *The Nazi Connection: Eugenics, American Racism, and German National Socialism* (New York: Oxford University Press, 1994), 90, 99. Only after the German race laws had been criticized by American sources did some commentators point out the American "double standard" by referencing U.S. race codes. Ibid., 98–99.

its healing potential. Instead, it demands an attitude towards life which accepts personal sacrifice, which subjects personal goals to the well-being of the whole." Verschuer's importance in German academia after 1933 was largely due to the fact that he had been a member of a radically nationalist Freicorps unit during the early years of the Weimar Republic, had participated in the Kapp Putsch, and probably helped carry out a number of political murders. Verschuer was also among the world's leading "racial hygienists" and the academic mentor of the concentration camp "medic" Josef Mengele at the University of Frankfurt during the 1930s. His political background and scientific interests and work naturally endeared him to the Nazi regime.[49]

Given Germany's isolated situation shortly before the beginning of World War II, in 1939 such direct criticism of the United States in a German eugenicist journal was hardly surprising. However, the original year of publication for this article was 1928. Even before 1933, as Verschuer's acerbic condemnation of the United States and other Western democracies shows, key Nazi scientists roundly rejected America because of the country's democratic system. When it came to questions of racial segregation and the social control of racial differences Verschuer, a die-hard antidemocrat and a towering presence among Nazi academics, was unwilling to acknowledge American examples because he did not accept the validity of the U.S. political system. Although there existed significant connections between German and American eugenicists during the 1920s and 1930s (the Rockefeller Foundation supported Verschuer's work, for example), after 1933 these ties posed an ideological dilemma because of the increasingly anti-American Nazi propaganda. Publications like the *Völkischer Beobachter* therefore tried to make sure that their readers did not get the impression that Nazi Germany was on the receiving end in respect to eugenics and race laws, merely

---

[49] Bruno Steinwallner, "Rassenhygienische Gesetzgebung und Maßnahmen im Ausland. 2. Teil. Rassenhygienische Gesetzgebung und Maßnahmen förderlicher Art," *Fortschritte der Erbpathologie, Rassenhygiene und ihrer Grenzgebiete* III (1939): 56 (note 1); Kühl, *The Nazi Connection*, 21; Franz Menges, "Josef Mengele," in *Allgemeine deutsche Biographie & Neue deutsche Biographie* (Berlin: 1994), 70.

implementing measures already practiced in liberal-democratic republics like the United States. Reporting on the 1936 conference of the International Federation of Eugenics Organizations the *Beobachter* tried to create the exact opposite impression, stating that the conference recognized the "absolutely leading position of Germany in genetic research and in practical measures in the arena of racial welfare."[50]

Yet even after 1933 German eugenicists acknowledged their indebtedness to measures enacted in various U.S. states. The European and North American eugenics movements had been closely linked across national borders and oceans since their beginnings in the last years of the nineteenth century. After coming to power, the Nazis were neither willing to nor capable of openly severing all international ties and instantly doing away with all elements of traditional respectability domestically. In the regime's effort to create a "racially pure" national community, it was therefore initially convenient for it to use and build on existing eugenicist concepts and ideas. Before 1933, the German eugenicist movement, although it had international connections, had been relatively weak and had had no impact on legislation, either in the German Empire or the Weimar Republic. In contrast, in the United States, several states, most prominently Indiana (1907) and California (1909), had sterilization laws, which, in California alone, resulted in more than 65,000 sterilizations. In fact, the 1933 Decree on Preventing Hereditarily Ill Progeny, passed a mere six months after the Nazis seized power, was able to be drawn up so quickly because it incorporated various international precedents, including the California sterilization law. Because of the regime's initial insecurity, the law also was promoted not as a uniquely German measure but as a decree that tied Nazi Germany to values and, more important, scientific findings shared and agreed on internationally. As a result, this decree was positively received by American eugenicists.[51]

---

[50] *Völkischer Beobachter* quoted in Kühl, *The Nazi Connection*, 21, 31.
[51] Ibid., 37–39; Helmut Walser Smith, "Jenseits der Sonderweg-Debatte," in *Das Deutsche Kaiserreich in der Kontroverse*, ed. Sven Oliver Müller and Cornelius Torp (Göttingen: Vandenhoeck & Ruprecht, 2009), 45, 46.

The 1935 Nuremberg race laws were a different matter, however, because the international eugenics movements could not be easily enlisted to support racial segregation measures against Jews. The 1935 decrees therefore had to be justified against an ideological and not a scientific backdrop. As a result, as Heinrich Krieger made quite clear, state legislation in the United States could not be referenced as a model for Nazi Germany, because even U.S. race laws embodied (white) democratic principles. Because it was left to individual white Americans to decide whether they wanted race provisions in their state or not, U.S. race decrees were a "casuistic" offspring of "liberalist" political principles and thus of little value to the proudly antiliberal and antidemocratic Third Reich.[52]

For Nazi scientists, jurists, and other academics such as Johann von Leers, a historian and one of the most prolific anti-Semitic authors for the Nazi cause both before and after 1933, as well as Günther Hecht and Bruno Steinwallner, the verdict was clear: Because of America's rampant liberalism and its democratic constitution, its Jim Crow provisions were not "true race laws" in the national-socialist sense. Steinwallner thus argued that ultimately it was the "ideological mind-set" of a nation that determined whether segregation or racial hygiene provisions were consequential or not. Hecht posited that the tenets of Nazi ideology, with their focus on racial hygiene and racial biology as embraced by the "new" Germany after 1933, stood in sharp contrast to nations "with a liberalist mishmash-of-humanity ideology" [Menschheitsbrei-Ideologie] such as the United States. Most important, segregation laws in other countries never focused on the Nazis' main target: the Jews. For that reason, Jim Crow provisions simply could not possess exemplary qualities. In fact, because of the perceived "strong influence of Jews on American

---

[52] Lothar Gruchmann, "'Blutschutzgesetz' und Justiz. Zur Entstehung und Auswirkung des Nürnberger Gesetzes vom 15. September 1935," *Vierteljahrshefte für Zeitgeschichte* 31, no. 3 (1983): 418; Otto Dov Kulka, "Die Nürnberger Rassengesetze und die deutsche Bevölkerung im Lichte geheimer NS-Lage-und Stimmungsberichte," *Vierteljahreshefte für Zeitgeschichte* 32, no. 4 (1984): 601–02.

politics," after 1933 Nazi commentators and authors could not refer to American examples without disparaging references to the United States' supposed "Jew problem."[53]

Hecht's publications also show that the Nazis' expansionist visions were consciously antitraditional and connected to a "new" approach to racial hygiene and purity. In his 1938 *The Colonial Question and Racialized Thinking* [Kolonialfrage und Rassegedanke], a short book published by the NSDAP's Department of Race Politics, Hecht outlined the party's ideas for a new German colonialism, which he carefully distinguished from Germany's old "liberalist" expansionism. Although he frequently referred to French and British failures in Africa, Hecht nevertheless refrained from making demands for the return of Germany's African colonies. Instead, he argued that Germany's future colonialism had to be completely determined by ideas of racial purity and hygiene, not by liberalist concerns with capitalist exploitation. Hecht's book, while praising individual "German colonial pioneers" and specific colonial segregationist measures, nevertheless rejected older colonialist traditions, both German and European, and especially attacked the Reichstag's 1912 resolution demanding the acceptance of mixed-race marriages in the German colonies. Back then, "as is still done by the parliaments of other nations today," the German Reichstag and colonial administrators in Berlin were mistakenly guided by "solely humanitarian, Jewish-liberalist, and Christian ideas." In Hecht's view, Nazi expansionists should and would do things differently. What Hecht did not mention, of course, was that liberal colonial administrators like Wilhelm Solf had in fact defended the race codes that existed in German colonies like Southwest Africa. Yet it was impossible for Hecht to admit that there existed important links between German colonial race codes and liberal colonialists

---

[53] Johann von Leers, *Blut und Rasse in der Gesetzgebung: Ein Gang durch die Völkergeschichte* (München: J. F. Lehmanns Verlag, 1936), 102–03; Günther Hecht, *Kolonialfrage und Rassegedanke, Schriftenreihe des Rassenpolitischen Amtes der NSDAP und des Reichsbundes der Kinderreichen* (Berlin: Verlag Neues Volk, 1938), 2; Steinwallner, "Rassenhygienische Gesetzgebung," 60–61; Gassert, *Amerika im Dritten Reich*, 204.

like Solf or Dernburg. Nazi academics like Hecht were thus unwilling to tie their presumably ideologically sound and national-socialist expansionism and racism to "Jewish-liberalist" pre-1914 colonialism.[54]

Unlike for liberal or even Christian-Social admirers of American racial segregation measures, such as Reinhard Mumm in 1912, for the Nazis political ideology easily outweighed the potential usefulness and exemplary character of race-based measures taken by other nations. As a result, Nazi administrators never attempted to take political advantage of an approach to race shared by white southerners. Instead, they fruitlessly tried to win over ethnic German Americans, in the southern United States and elsewhere by appealing to their ties to Germany. In 1936, Hans Grimm, the author of the best-selling novel *Volk ohne Raum* [A People without Space, 1926], toured the United States and spoke to German American audiences to promote Nazi Germany's unilateral renouncement of the Versailles Treaty. Nazis believed that German Americans would be susceptible to this message because of "völkisch" bonds, which easily trumped the obvious parallels regarding racial segregation in the South and Nazi Germany. From this vantage point, even Americans from the South were too deeply steeped in republican and democratic ideals to be able to appreciate national-socialist ideas.[55]

---

[54] Hecht, *Kolonialfrage*, 24–25. Stefan Kühl's excellent *The Nazi Connection*, an analysis of the links between German and American eugenicists during the 1930s, is sometimes wrongly assumed to provide evidence for the claim that "Nazi Germany formulated its racial laws of 1935 using the example of the South in the United States." See for example Richard H. King and Dan Stone, *Hannah Arendt and the Uses of History: Imperialism, Nation, Race, and Genocide* (New York: Berghahn Books, 2007), 3. Instead, Kühl explicitly argues that, unlike the activities of German colonialists before 1914, the "cultivation of non-German eugenicists, geneticists, and anthropologists by the Nazi regime was not based primarily on a desire to acquire scientific information." Kühl, *The Nazi Connection*, 88.

[55] Johnpeter Grill and Robert L. Jenkins, "The Nazis and the American South in the 1930s: A Mirror Image?," *The Journal of Southern History* 58, no. 4 (1992): 668.

From the American West to the German East?

The discontinuities between the use of American models by German imperial administrators and settlers before 1914 and racialized Nazi precepts after 1933 did not stop with the explicit rejection of the exemplary potential of American segregation statutes. Before 1914, using the United States as a model always meant emphasizing the attractiveness and popularity of the American frontier, which had supposedly been pushed westward by rugged and independent pioneers. The idea of independence and individualism was at the core not only of Friedrich Ratzel's and Carl Peters' admiration of America but also was the foundation of Dernburg's and Solf's "American" approach to colonial policies. Dernburg envisioned financially profitable colonies, run by self-reliant and independent settlers, with no need for financial subsidies from the metropole. In addition, Solf strongly believed that if the settlers wished to institute miscegenation bans, they should be able to do so and not be stifled by metropolitan regulations. After 1933, official propaganda publications were mostly silent about the "free" American West. For ideological reasons the independent, individualist spirit of settlers and pioneers could not be easily used for national-socialist propaganda purposes. As a result, official publications such as the *Völkische Beobachter*, if they referred to "the West" at all, attempted to dampen the traditional appeal of frontier individualism. In April 1935, the *Beobachter* published a short article titled "The Wild West Lives On," written in its usual hyper-sardonic style. Of course, the article did not present the appealing sides of "Wild West romanticism," but instead focused on "brutal" and deadly feuds between the owners of cattle herds; these feuds, despite "the spread of modern, civilizing influences" still persisted in America's western states, a phenomenon the *Beobachter* portrayed as shocking.[56]

---

[56] Erik Grimmer-Solem, "The Professors' Africa: Economists, the Elections of 1907, and the Legitimation of German Imperialism," *German History* 25, no. 3 (2007): 325; "Der 'Wilde Westen' lebt noch! 'Weidelandgesetz' in den USA. Fehden mit Revolvern und Lasso zwischen Herdenbesitzern," *Völkische Beobachter* 04-20–1935.

The disparaging attitude of the *Völkische Beobachter* toward frontier individualism foreshadowed the insignificance of what Carl Peters had once termed American-style "liberal colonialism" for Hitler's and Himmler's colonization plans for the vast conquered Eastern European territories. For a brief moment, the initial success of the Wehrmacht's invasion of the Soviet Union in late 1941 appeared to make the realization of these plans possible, yet liberal colonialist tenets had no influence on the unsuccessful attempts to execute these settlement designs. In fact, in the German-occupied territories between 1941 and 1943 the future settlers' standing was "far removed from the rhetoric of vigorous pioneers." The price they would pay for the allocation of land in these areas was "complete lack of autonomy . . . the Third Reich was the 'giver' to whom they owed everything." Himmler's and Hitler's visions of settling Eastern Europe with racially superior Germanic peoples thus had hardly anything in common with the sentiments that underpinned the tenets of liberal colonialism in early twentieth-century Germany.[57]

Official publications like the *Völkische Beobachter* printed fewer and fewer positive references to the United States or the American West after 1933 and hardly any after 1937–38. Pamphlets or books by ideologues like Hecht or Krieger followed this lead. However, America did not disappear completely from Nazi discourse. Given the breadth and depth of the pre-1914 use of the American frontier by German colonialists; the pervasiveness of imagery of the American West, of Indian battles, and pioneer life along the American frontier in American, European, and German popular literature both before and after 1918; and Hitler's own penchant for Karl May's western novels, it is hardly surprising that Nazi ideologues, including Hitler and Himmler, occasionally referenced these topics. It would be astonishing if they had not done so. However, the problem with assuming that

---

57 Blackbourn, *The Conquest of Nature*, 287. Compare Madley, "From Africa to Auschwitz: How German Southwest Africa Incubated Ideas and Methods Adopted and Developed by the Nazis in Eastern Europe"; Zimmerer, "Von Windhuk nach Warschau. Die rassische Privilegiengesellschaft in Deutsch-Südwestafrika, ein Modell mit Zukunft?" See also Furber, "Near as Far."

Hitler was "obsessed" with the American West is the fact that these allusions occurred so rarely and intermittently. After the invasion of the Soviet Union in 1941 had begun (yet before its failure became obvious after Stalingrad), a Himmler-controlled SS publication envisioned turning Russia's black earth zone into a "European California" and Hans Frank called Jews "flat-foot Indians" (1942). In his table monologues (his talk during meals, recorded in more than 400 pages), Hitler termed the Volga "our Mississippi" (1941); he equated partisan fighters with Indians in the fall of 1941 and summer of 1942 (apparently, reading Karl May had not made Hitler sympathetic toward the fate of Native Americans); and he once stated that "Americans were in touch with the emptiness of the vast, open spaces" (June 1943).[58]

These scattered and hurried remarks – always made in passing, as add-ons or subclauses to other statements – have been interpreted to indicate the Nazis' or, more specifically, Hitler's fixation on the American West. At first glance, these mentions bear some resemblance to statements made by German colonial officials and proponents of German imperialism during the last years of the nineteenth and early years of the twentieth centuries. These similarities are superficial, however. Before 1914, the cooperation between German authorities and American institutions such as the Tuskegee Institute regarding the development of the German colonies, the study of Indian reservations by German engineers, and the scrutiny of Jim Crow provisions by metropolitan officials grew out of genuine (albeit sometimes grudging) feelings of respect for the United States. In contrast, a deep hatred of "liberalist" and democratic structures permeated Nazi images of America. For Nazi officials, and most important for men like Hitler and Himmler, references to America were nothing but a utilitarian foil that could be twisted, distorted, and disregarded completely depending on the occasion and circumstance. In the

[58] Hitler, *Monologe im Führerhauptquartier*, 78, 90, 91, 168, 398; Wendy Lower, *Nazi Empire-Building and the Holocaust in the Ukraine* (Chapel Hill: University of North Carolina Press, 2005), 3, 19; Blackbourn, "The Conquest of Nature and the Mystique of the Eastern Frontier in Germany," 305.

early fall of 1941, before the German offensive became bogged down in the mud of the Russian autumn rain, Hitler looked for metaphors to help him describe the settlement opportunities that appeared to be opening up in Eastern Europe. The European settlement of North America was one source of such metaphors, but in his excited rants in September and October 1941 Hitler used other comparisons as well (and in more detail); most were to British India, but he also made some less obvious associations: "[T]o us, the new eastern territories appear to be an empty waste land. But: Flanders too is a completely flat region and nevertheless beautiful." The newly acquired territories "had to lose their Asiatic-steppe outlook and become Europeanized!" These lands were therefore not supposed to become a German version of the American West, but were to be turned into an anti-America – a sentiment entirely consistent with Nazi propaganda since 1937 at the very latest: "Europe is becoming interesting in itself, Europe – and not America – will become the land of boundless opportunity."[59]

Yet when Hitler used the expression "land of boundless opportunity" he was of course only thinking about the opportunities that these eastern lands would offer to the Greater German Empire, not to rugged, individualist, and independent settlers. In Hitler's expansionist schemes there was little opportunity even for private entrepreneurs in the envisioned "Eastern Empire" [Ostreich]: "In fact, there only exists a barter currency here in the east. We will have a separate Eastmark currency. If the exchange rate is 1:5, a traveler who comes here with 100 Reichsmark will get 100 Eastmark in exchange while the German Reich gets the balance." In the late nineteenth century, the liberal imperialist Friedrich Ratzel could admiringly and in lengthy fashion comment on the mutually reinforcing relationship between the stability of America's republican character and

[59] Hitler, *Monologe im Führerhauptquartier*, 78, 90, 91, 168, 398; Hildebrand, *Vom Reich zum Weltreich*, 715–16; Steinweis, "Eastern Europe and the Notion of the 'Frontier'."; Lower, *Nazi Empire-Building and the Holocaust in the Ukraine*, 3, 19; Blackbourn, *The Conquest of Nature*, 280, 288, 292; Tooze, *The Wages of Destruction*, 469–70; Kakel, *The American West*, 35.

the westward-moving frontier. Although Hitler, Himmler, and Rosenberg adopted Ratzel's "living space" phrase, they certainly did not agree with the geographer's positive evaluation of American republicanism. The Ostreich was not supposed to benefit individuals, but solely the Nazi state. For Nazi purposes the allure of open spaces thus had to be divested of any links to the American West and the concepts of freedom and individualism. The scarcity of positive references to the United States in official Nazi publications after 1933 and their almost complete disappearance after 1937 reflect the efforts to this end undertaken by Joseph Goebbels' propaganda ministry. As the short list of remarks by Hitler and Himmler indicates, references to the American frontier by Nazi leaders were in fact quite rare.[60]

---

[60] Historians who assume that the Nazis were fascinated by the American frontier often reference a short piece published by historian Alan Steinweis in 1999, titled "Eastern Europe and the Notion of the 'Frontier'." Yet much of Steinweis's article is dedicated to general, not specifically America-focused frontier notions embraced by Nazi planners and the prominence of the American West in Ratzel's works. Steinweis himself calls Hitler's references to the American West "anecdotal" and "crude." In addition to two quotes from Hitler's *Mein Kampf* (in one of which Hitler does not even mention the American West but merely the "New World" in general), Steinweis's main source published between 1933 and 1945 that focuses on the territory of the United States as a "great space" is Otto Maull's *Die Vereinigten Staaten von Nordamerika als Großreich*. This book, however, does not recommend the United States as an example for Nazi Germany's settlement policies in Eastern Europe. Instead, Maull's main intention was to assure the Nazi leadership that it did not have to fear an American intervention. Maull therefore stressed repeatedly that because of its position as a "gigantic great empire" [gewaltiges Großreich] the United States' "natural inclination" was to refrain from interference in European affairs. He closed the book with a warning to Americans: The United States had to deal with "a plethora of severest problems." America should therefore follow its "true interests," and not, as any reader could clearly read between the lines, oppose Nazi Germany's actions in Europe. Hitler, *Monologe im Führerhauptquartier*, 337; Blackbourn, *The Conquest of Nature*, 280; Tooze, *The Wages of Destruction*, 469–70; Mark Mazower, *Hitler's Empire. Nazi Rule in Occupied Europe* (London: Penguin Books, 2009), 584; Kakel, *The American West*, 35. Compare Otto Maull, *Die Vereinigten Staaten von Nordamerika als Großreich* (Berlin: 1940), 152–53; Steinweis, "Eastern Europe and the Notion of the 'Frontier'," 56–57, 61–62, 65. Compare Gassert, *Amerika im Dritten Reich*, 241.

After 1933, German depictions of the United States increasingly became propagandistic make-believe efforts stripped of any concrete links to American realities. Official publications depicted America as corrupt, violent, and "infested" with Jews in an attempt to convince the German public that after the Nazi seizure of power their country offered better opportunities than the "land of opportunity." Later random and non-public references to the American West and the frontier made by Nazi officials after 1939–41 were a different form of make-believe. After all, the Americans had conquered most of North America; why should not the Germans conquer all of Europe? Joseph Goebbels and Hermann Göring remained somewhat skeptical of this comparison, and after 1937 Goebbels' propaganda machine spat out exclusively negative references to America. It seems that these two men recognized better than other high-ranking Nazi officials, including Hitler and Himmler, that these allusions had little to do with American realities (or the realities of the Eastern Front). Because of the regime's overall rejection of America's democratic structures, infrequent references to the American West made by members of the Nazi leadership were nothing more than distorted and skeletal caricatures of the attitudes displayed by men like Dernburg, Solf, Ratzel and Carl Peters at the beginning of the twentieth century.[61]

Dissociated from a liberal acceptance or at the very least respect for American democracy and republicanism, the exemplary qualities of the American model empire became hollow shells after 1933. Carl Schmitt, a highly venerated jurist, political philosopher, and ardent supporter of the Nazis, unintentionally demonstrated this development in his last academic publication before 1945, *Völkerrechtliche Grossraumordnung* (Ordering Great Spaces under International Law, 1940). Schmitt was in a delicate position in the late 1930s, because in 1936 an SS publication had attacked his national-socialist credentials, specifically the depth of his anti-Semitism. After these attacks, Schmitt lost his party responsibilities and retained "merely" his academic

[61] Blackbourn, *The Conquest of Nature*, 284.

titles and professorial status. In 1939, given the general trajectory of German propaganda against the United States, he knew full well that he could not risk painting too positive a picture of the history of the United States, not even of the country's expansionism. His book thus mainly aimed to justify Nazi Germany's war of aggression and German annexations, and it was probably intended to (re-) endear Schmitt to the upper echelons of the regime.[62]

In his book, Schmitt labeled the Monroe Doctrine "extraordinary" and "noteworthy." He argued that it had introduced a new principle into world politics – claims to hegemony in certain geographical areas. In other words, it was a "great space" concept based on political ideas – the democratic-liberal principles of the U.S. Constitution. Yet Schmitt made sure to clearly disassociate himself from those political principles: "To repeat: Not the Monroe Doctrine itself but rather its core, the idea of an order of great territories under international law, can be applied to other historical situations and other friend-foe groupings." Only after removing American politics and American political history from the Monroe Doctrine could Schmitt dare talk about its potentially exemplary character. Several weeks after Schmitt had first put forth these ideas, Hitler also referenced the Monroe Doctrine in an April 1939 Reichstag speech, although there is no evidence that he knew of Schmitt's concept. In this speech, Hitler juxtaposed Franklin D. Roosevelt's peace demands with America's expansionist history and the Monroe Doctrine. As usual, his references to the United States were brief, and his overall (and very obvious) intention was to embarrass President Roosevelt, not to present America as an example for Nazi Germany, although

---

[62] Carl Schmitt, *Völkerrechtliche Grossraumordnung* (Berlin: Deutscher Rechtsverlag, 1941), 19–20; Lothar Gruchmann, *Nationalsozialistische Großraumordnung. Die Konstruktion einer 'deutschen Monroe-Doktrin'* (Stuttgart: 1962); Gassert, *Amerika im Dritten Reich*, 296–97; Reinhard Mehring, "Schmitt, Carl," *Neue Deutsche Biographie [Onlinefassung]* 23 (2007); Reinhard Mehring, *Carl Schmitt: Aufstieg und Fall* (München: C. H. Beck, 2009), 393–94. Compare Tooze, *The Wages of Destruction*, 282–83; Mazower, *Hitler's Empire*, 557–58.

he did admit that Germany supported "a similar doctrine for Europe."[63]

Less than five months before the invasion of Poland these allusions had important tactical significance: In his cables to Berlin, Hans Thomsen, the chargé d'affaires at the German Embassy in Washington, DC, had suggested that, to counter interventionist sentiments among American politicians, official German statements should repeat that, just as Germany respected the Monroe Doctrine, it expected respect for its spheres of interest in Europe. Hitler's mention of the Monroe Doctrine therefore neither signified a deeper engagement with American history and American political thought nor indicated any long-lasting impact of this concept on Nazi foreign policy and the regime's expansionist plans.[64]

Moreover, the brevity of Hitler's references to the United States is telling: Hitler was prone to speak at length about subjects that interested or fascinated him. In *Mein Kampf* Hitler takes more than thirty pages to describe his eastern Lebensraum visions and more than one hundred pages to explain race, racial purity, and these topics' importance for Germany's defeat in World War I (without a single meaningful reference to America). In the *Second Book*, race, race war, and the need for an eastward (and military) reorientation of Germany's foreign policy goals occupy more than sixty pages, only five of which mention the United States somewhat consistently. Finally, in Hitler's *Table Talk*, musings about museums in Austrian, German, and French cities, or on the benefits of unprocessed food, for example, take up more room than all of his remarks on the United States "as greater space" and the American West combined. Hitler thus had clear and obvious interests, fascinations, and obsessions, but

---

[63] Schmitt, *Völkerrechtliche Grossraumordnung*, 19–20; Wolfgang Domarus, *Hitler: Speeches and Proclamations 1932–1945* (Würzburg: Domarus Verlag, 1996), 1586; Mehring, *Carl Schmitt: Aufstieg und Fall*, 393–94.

[64] Domarus, *Hitler: Speeches and Proclamations 1932–1945*, 1586; Gassert, *Amerika im Dritten Reich*, 296–97, 301. Hitler had mentioned the Monroe Doctrine once before 1939. Ibid., 100. Compare Mazower, *Hitler's Empire*, 577–78.

views of the United States as an exemplary colonial model were not among them.[65]

As a result, Carl Schmitt was well advised to refrain from appearing too infatuated with American history. America was dangerous, not only as a potential opponent of Nazi Germany but also intellectually. The United States was too closely paired with liberal and democratic ideology and with an individualistic "can do" spirit not to be seen as a constant challenge to the Nazi idea of a state based on the dictatorial "leader principle" [Führerprinzip]. Although Schmitt intended to use the "core" of the Monroe Doctrine to legitimize Germany's aggressive war aims and territorial conquests in Eastern Europe, the upper echelon of Nazi leaders was not convinced. With the exception of Hermann Göring, who was cynical about Hitler's and Himmler's grandiose settlement designs in the East and held his protective hand over Schmitt, the legal scholar did not manage to reengage with the Nazi leadership after 1936, despite his attempts to sycophantically justify their aims. Using the history of American expansion in the nineteenth century as the basis for a defense of Hitler's attempted conquest of all of Eastern Europe was not a good idea, given the attacks on things American by Nazi propaganda organs.

Ultimately, there existed a profound divide between Hitler's cursory references to the American West and the intense scrutiny of the United States by German colonialists before 1914. This divide was not primarily based on the deeper level of understanding of the United States shared by Solf, Dernburg, and many other German imperialists: Although they knew much more about America than did Hitler, pre-1914 German colonialists misunderstood the United States as well. Influenced by their own racialized preconceptions, they, for example, did not understand that African American sharecroppers in the "redeemed" South had nothing in common with the people of German-Togo

---

[65] Hitler, *Mein Kampf*, 245–363; Hitler, *Monologe im Führerhauptquartier*, 399–400; Hitler, *Hitlers zweites Buch*, 43–117; Weinberg, "Hitler's Image of the United States," 1006–21.

216 *German Expansionism, Imperial Liberalism*

and that therefore their efforts to model cotton growing in Togo after American examples were destined to fail. Most important perhaps, they severely underestimated the importance of the U.S. federal government for the colonization of the American West. Of course, their quasi-mythical overestimation of the significance of the settlers' individualistic ("liberal") pioneer spirit for American westward expansion was itself a transatlantic phenomenon and even more widespread in the United States. Ratzel, Schmoller, Weber, Sering, Dernburg, Solf, the engineer Alexander Kuhn, the left-liberal representative Hermann Müller, and even Carl Peters thus all tried to comprehend and seriously engage with American realities and, from a present-day perspective, myths in a framework of transnational and transatlantic respect that rested on the assumption that Europeans and white North Americans shared a common culture. Hitler's references to the American West and the United States in general lacked all of these qualities. His mentions of the American frontier had nothing to do with the United States or American history, but only reflected Germany's problems as he perceived them. The settlement of the American West therefore never served as a concrete model for Nazi imperialism in Eastern Europe.[66]

---

[66] Gassert, *Amerika im Dritten Reich*, 87; Frevert, "Europeanizing Germany's Twentieth Century," 90; Zimmerman, "German Alabama," 1368.

Conclusion

Imperial Liberalism, Nazi Expansionism, and the Continuities of German History

By trying to separate the Monroe Doctrine from American politics, Carl Schmitt wanted to sell his argument that Nazi Germany's claims to hegemony in Europe could be justified against the backdrop of the United States' traditional assertion of supremacy in the Western hemisphere. Yet because of the regime's propaganda warfare against the United States and American liberal political ideals, Schmitt's reasoning did not convince the upper echelons of the regime. In the eyes of Joseph Goebbels, the main orchestrator of Nazi Germany's public display of anti-Americanism, the United States was too obviously a "liberal-ist" and "Jew-infested" republic to be exemplary for the Third Reich.

With few exceptions, between 1776 and 1914 admiring and observant attitudes toward America's westward-moving frontier and perceptions of the United States as a model empire were voiced by German reformers and progressives, and were situated within the extensive intellectual range of German liberalism. German appreciation of American westward expansion and American race policies was by and large liberal because liberals from all over the broad spectrum of German political liberalism recognized a kinship between their own ideology and the political system of the United States. This was true for Carl

Peters, Ratzel, von Richthofen, Solf, Dernburg, Rohrbach, and many more. Their political convictions did not make these liberals "nice" people from a present-day perspective, and today's meaning of the term "liberal" (especially in the United States, where the term is often used to denote left-wing and even, when used by the political right, "socialist" politics) barely applies to them. Many if not most German liberals (just like their non-German counterparts) were racists and die-hard expansionists, and often added a dose of uncompromising nationalism to their politics. However, these elements do not necessarily indicate that liberal German expansionists were direct precursors of the Nazis.

Nevertheless it cannot be denied that German and European colonialist traditions were stepping stones for the Nazis' expansionist policies and that, as Mark Mazower has argued, the Nazis were "heirs" to the European imperialist tradition. In addition, Nazi ideologues occasionally referenced the American frontier. Why, then, should we bother to differentiate Nazi expansionism from pre-1914 liberal colonialism? Why should we care that perceptions of the United States and contacts with Americans played an important role with respect to concepts of race control and overseas expansion in German colonial discourse and practice before World War I, while they became increasingly irrelevant after 1918? We should care because a careful analysis of the ruptures and links between "classic" (i.e., pre-1914) imperialism and Nazi expansionism might help prevent us – present-day Americans, Germans, and "Westerners" in general – from embracing a complacent presentism in respect to issues of race and the global, potentially oppressive reach of Western, liberal-democratic states. A longue durée perspective that links the second half of the twentieth century and even our own time to the eighteenth, nineteenth, and early twentieth centuries might help prevent that complacency, as it reveals some unexpected and uncomfortable historical continuities, and not exclusively German ones, originating long before 1945 and extending into the present. These continuities may not be those we expect, but this does not mean we should ignore the potential repercussions of allowing certain trends in thought, even if they are in fact "liberal," to endure over time.[1]

Among the great number of high-quality scholarly works that have approached German history from a longue durée outlook, three methodologies stand out. The first and maybe most famous one can be found in Theodor Adorno and Max Horkheimer's *The Dialectics of the Enlightenment*. Writing in 1943–44, Adorno and Horkheimer argued that it was not liberalism's failure that made the Nazis possible; rather, the success of liberalism's increasingly reified rationalist and scientific dimensions during the nineteenth and early twentieth centuries created the conditions necessary for the regime's murderous excesses. Indeed, according to these two cultural pessimists, the Nazis' violence, racism, and anti-Semitism were the dark and inseparable undersides of the Enlightenment and modern liberalism. For Horkheimer and Adorno "the liberal thesis serves as an apology for the existing order ... which in reality cannot exist without disfiguring human beings.... Its essence, however it may hide itself at times, is the violence which today is openly revealed." The second approach, diametrically opposed to Adorno and Horkheimer's analysis, was put forth only six years later by Hannah Arendt in *The Origins of Totalitarianism*. For Arendt, totalitarian ideologies like Nazism (and Stalinism) could be traced to European colonialism and to the encounters of white settlers in South Africa with the vast African landscape and the continent's native inhabitants. These settlers' new, borderless way of life led them to abandon notions characteristic of stable nation-states. Instead, over time settlers embraced sweeping imperialist visions of creating states organized according to racial hierarchies and concepts of continuous expansion. Yet Arendt also made clear that Pan-Germanism and Pan-Slavism were much more important for the development of German and Soviet

---

[1] See also Helmut Walser Smith, *The Continuities of German History: Nation, Religion, and Race Across the Long Nineteenth Century* (New York: Cambridge University Press, 2008), 38.

totalitarianism than European imperialism. The third approach is, of course, the thesis of Wehler, Dahrendorf, and Fritz Fischer (et al.) of the German Sonderweg. According to this model, it was the failure of liberal ideas, which had their origins in Enlightenment thought, and of their social class of origin, the bourgeoisie, to assert themselves in Germany during the nineteenth century that made the Nazi seizure of power possible.[2]

Historian Eric Kurlander has recently presented an innovative new version of the Sonderweg approach's focus on the failures of German liberalism. For him, the "fall" of German liberalism did not occur in 1848 or during the 1860s. Rather, he draws a straight line from increasingly völkisch/racist liberal milieus in specific regions of Imperial Germany during the 1890s to these locales voting for the National Socialists in the early 1930s. Political developments within the framework of German political liberalism, which had no equivalent among either French or British liberals, thus contributed directly to the Nazis' electoral successes in 1930, 1932, and 1933. Helmut Walser Smith has also revisited the question of German historical continuities, although he focuses not on sociopolitical but on cultural and intellectual continuities – among them concepts such as racism, including increasingly racialized forms of anti-Semitism, and the growing willingness in the late nineteenth and early twentieth centuries among liberal imperialists such as Paul Rohrbach to consider race-based policies of expansion, expulsion, and extinction. For Smith, these continuities did not connect to the Holocaust directly, but made it possible "to think, support and enact" this genocide.[3]

[2] Max Horkheimer and Theodor Adorno, *Dialectic of Enlightenment: Philosophical Fragments*, ed. Gunzelin Schmid Noerr (Stanford: Stanford University Press, 2002), 138–39; Hannah Arendt, *The Origins of Totalitarianism* (San Diego: Harcourt, 1968).

[3] Eric Kurlander, *The Price of Exclusion: Ethnicity, National Identity, and the Decline of German Liberalism, 1898–1933* (New York: Berghahn Books, 2006), 2–3; Smith, *The Continuities of German History*, 233.Woodruff D. Smith's classic study *The Ideological Origins of Nazi Imperialism* also argues for a straight developmental line from some aspects of pre-1914 imperialism (specifically ideas of settler colonialism and living space) to Nazi expansionism:

Yet although the German Empire's pre-1914 colonialism served as a stepping stone for Nazi expansionism, it nevertheless cannot be reduced to this role. Moreover, pre-1914 German expansionism should not be evaluated merely against a German backdrop. On the contrary, it was specifically those elements of German prewar imperialism that after World War I functioned as jumping-off points for Nazi ideologues to formulate their own positions – in particular the German Empire's acquisition of overseas colonies – that connected Imperial Germany globally and moved its colonial policies out of the domestic sphere of, for example, the Pan-German League's racialized nationalism. Both domestic and international observers recognized the 1907 "Dernburg turn," which ushered in an explicitly liberal and progressive era of colonial politics, as a turning point for German colonialism. Yet this perception was misleading insofar as it seemed to indicate that liberal colonialism became important only after 1907. Instead, liberal sentiments played a fundamental role in the debates that led up to Germany's acquisition of colonies in 1884 and determined thereafter how colonialism was framed, understood, publicly defended, put into practice, and translated into electoral victories for liberal parties (as in 1907). In addition, liberal, entrepreneurial, and individualist ideas motivated colonizers such as Carl Peters and their associates on a personal level, providing them with intellectual justification and enthusiasm for their colonizing enterprises. Ultimately, liberal colonial sentiments were products of debates and processes, both intellectual and material, in which other nations, in particular the United States, played decisive roles. There can be no doubt

Woodruff D. Smith, *The Ideological Origins of Nazi Imperialism* (New York: Oxford University Press, 1986), 256. Oded Heilbronner too has made the argument that there existed liberal continuities between the German Empire and the emergence of the Nazis during the 1920s. However, he explicitly excludes "classic" bourgeois liberals from these trajectories and focuses exclusively on radical-bourgeois liberalism: Oded Heilbronner, "'Long Live Liberty, Equality, Fraternity and Dynamite': The German Bourgeoisie and the Constructing of Popular Liberal and National-Socialist Subcultures in Marginal Germany," *Journal of Social History* 39, no. 1 (2005): 182–83. For other recent contributors to this debate see Introduction, note xiii.

that racist viewpoints were important elements of this transatlantic imperialist network and that German liberal colonialists eagerly embraced them. Yet the significance of racism within liberal circles did not appear out of nowhere in the late 1890s and by no means denoted a national peculiarity of German liberalism. For example, the left-liberal Reichstag deputy Hermann Müller clearly justified and explained his views on the necessity of racial segregation and the establishment of native reservations in GSWA not against a local or even German backdrop, but against both American and global-imperialist ones. During the early years of the twentieth century, in liberal German circles racism was a transnational and often America-focused regularity, firmly situated in the comprehensive context of European and American expansionism. It was never exclusively determined by domestic or national considerations.[4]

Highlighting the tensions between Nazi ideology and pre-1914 liberal colonialism and the concepts of race linked to it, the previous chapters thus suggest an alternative to approaching the relationship between Nazi expansionism and imperialism as a search for either historical continuities or ruptures. Hitler and Nazi ideologues like Rosenberg needed colonialism and imperialism as a thesis against which they could formulate their ideas – their antithesis of continental expansion, expulsion, and, eventually, extermination. For them, ironically, even outright racism could be antithetical to their beliefs, at least when practiced within the framework of a liberal democracy such as the United States. Instead of admiring Jim Crow decrees and accepting them as exemplary for their racial segregation measures, Nazi ideologues at times juxtaposed "true" race laws, which by necessity

---

[4] Compare Kurlander, *The Price of Exclusion*, 5. For the English reception of the "Dernburg turn" see for example "Editorial Notes and Comments," *United Empire* 5, no. 4 (1914). See also Chapter 2. For Franco-German transnational exchanges in respect to colonialism see Alain Chatriot and Dieter Gosewinkel, eds., *Koloniale Politik und Praktiken Deutschlands und Frankreichs 1880–1962. Politiques et pratiques coloniales dans les empires allemands et français*, vol. 6, *Schriftenreihe des Deutsch-Französischen Historikerkomitees* (Stuttgart: Franz Steiner Verlag, 2010).

were national-socialist, antiliberal, and antidemocratic, with the "weak," casuistic, and "liberalist" provisions that existed in the American South. The Nazis rejected the United States as "liberalist" and "Jew-infested." By doing so they also consciously distanced themselves from the admiration that pre-1914 German colonialists had expressed for American liberal expansionism and measures of race control.

Given the obvious tensions between Nazi ideology and pre-1914 liberal imperialist traditions, a dialectical interpretation of the correlation between these two phenomena suggests itself. Such an approach neither indicates a naïve application of Karl Marx's dialectical materialism nor an uncritical adherence to Adorno and Horkheimer's pessimistic version of history's dialectical progression. Instead, it reveals that the pre-1914 imperialism and post-1918 visions of living space in the East existed as perceived opposites within a framework of dialectical tension, and not as a straight line of gradual historical development. From the Nazis' point of view, Germany's defeat in 1918 demonstrated the rottenness of the German Empire's expansionism, which had been not so much German or Aryan as it had been liberal. Yet by rejecting German prewar imperialism, the Nazis also reified it. Carl Peters had employed the label "liberal colonialism" before the Nazis picked it up, but their assessment of the German Empire's imperialism as "bourgeois" and "liberalist" and, as a result, misguided and unsuccessful provided this classification with its ultimate and, contrary to the way Peters meant it, negative validity. Nazi expansionism was thus tied to the German Empire's liberal colonialism: It needed the latter as an Other, as a vilified but necessary point of departure.[5]

<hr>

[5] Marx's dialectical materialism is most famously and succinctly defined in the preface to *A Contribution to the Critique of Political Economy* (http://www.marxists.org/archive/marx/works/1859/critique-pol-economy/preface.htm). The image of a "dialectical framework of friction" used here is based on Marx's critique of Hegel's idealistic dialectics in Marx's *Economic and Philosophic Manuscripts of 1844*, yet owes at least as much to Bruno Bauer's definition of dialectics (harshly attacked by Marx in his *Critique of the Hegelian Dialectic*

In turn, the perspective outlined in this book can and should inform the search for remnants and echoes of liberal imperialism after 1945. Although Nazi expansionism, the consciously constructed antithesis to pre-1914 colonialism, ceased to exist with Germany's defeat, the liberal traditions of European and German colonialism did not disappear. After 1945, they reemerged, often (but not always) purged of their expansionist and violent dimensions, in new and at times surprising contexts. Mark Mazower has pointed out that German colonialist ideas had reverberations well outside the German-speaking regions of Europe, namely in the first Israeli national plans for population distribution. This book shows that it is possible to trace the legacies of pre-1914 liberal colonialism and its proponents to post-1945 German history as well. Although most European colonial powers (including, although often ignored, Great Britain in Kenya) attempted, often in brutal and bloody ways, to hold onto at least some of their colonies after 1945, Nazi expansionism forever tainted ideas of direct European or North American rule over colonial territories. The francophone poet and anti-imperialist politician Aimé Césaire thus argued that the Nazis' effort to dominate all of Europe should open Europeans' eyes to the terrible injustices inherent in their own imperialism abroad. To some degree, this "eye opening" did occur. Yet the Cold War brought altered versions of (formerly imperialist) liberalism, purged of concepts of territorial expansion, to the postwar political fore as well, especially the belief that liberal regimes almost by definition embraced notions of human equality and were incapable of the murderous excesses of the Nazi regime.[6]

Unlike Adorno and Horkheimer's pessimistic interpretation of modern European history, the classic Sonderweg notion had a happy ending. The catastrophe of World War II, the Holocaust, and, perhaps most important, the loss of the "German East"

and *Philosophy as a Whole*) (http://www.marxists.org/archive/marx/works/download/pdf/Economic-Philosophic-Manuscripts-1844.pdf, pp. 63–67).
[6] Mark Mazower, *Hitler's Empire: Nazi Rule in Occupied Europe* (London: Penguin Books, 2008), 585, 593.

(i.e., the loss of those European regions on which Nazi expansionism had focused), finally made possible the success of a liberal democratic system, at least in West Germany. Yet David Blackbourn and Geoff Eley's criticism of this ultimately triumphant history of Western liberalism laid bare its many problems, including most prominently that it ignored Germany's "silent bourgeoisification" and liberalization in the late nineteenth century. In addition, this book demonstrates that German liberalism was especially powerful in both creating and shaping German overseas expansionism before 1914. From a current-day perspective, liberal-imperialist sentiments do not look particularly pretty, nor are they easy to accept as the precursors to modern-day liberal-democratic Germany. Yet Dernburg, Solf, Ratzel, Peters, Rohrbach, Naumann, Weber, and many others saw themselves as liberal and progressive reformers. Their construction of pseudoscientific frameworks that connected expansion and racism with progress, white domestic equality, national unity, and notions of social and economic necessity sprang from convictions that retained at least some attractiveness after 1945 – although during the postwar decades these liberal-democratic and progressive tenets lost their association with political liberalism and permeated almost the entire West German political landscape.

During the imperialist era, liberals projected racial and cultural hierarchies across the globe, in which whites were supposed to exert social and economic control over allegedly inferior colonial natives. During the era of decolonization after 1945, migrants, often from the former European colonies, moved to the formerly colonizing nations of Western Europe to take over jobs for which no local workers could be found. Whereas before 1914 Germans subjugated overseas territories populated by supposedly racially inferior others, beginning in the late 1950s and early 1960s individuals of apparently incompatible cultures immigrated to former colonial metropoles. In West Germany, unlike in France or Great Britain, these migrants did not come from the country's former colonies but from southern and southeastern Europe and from Turkey. Because their cultures were nevertheless perceived as incompatible with German culture, it was felt that these labor migrants needed to be controlled as well. Moreover, until the late 1970s at the very earliest, both German politicians and the German public refused to recognize the inevitability of their permanent presence in Germany and therefore the need to accept them as actual immigrants and to integrate them into German society: This sentiment was expressed in the slogan, "Germany is no immigration country."[7]

As a result, these immigrants were labeled "guest workers" and thus became clearly denoted internal minorities. The frequent use of this ill-defined term created the comforting impression that their status in Germany was provisional and that they would be sent home when no longer needed. Because of the initial refusal of West Germany's economic and political elites to see them as actual immigrants, debates about how to assimilate, control, or expel migrant populations (which by now have become a permanent fixture of life in Germany) continue to this day and move within a framework akin to that of liberal colonialist discourse before 1914. A recent example of this phenomenon is the "leading culture" debate, which between 2000 and 2006 revolved around concepts of a presumably superior German "leading culture" that immigrants needed to accept and embrace if they wanted to remain in Germany; another one is the massive popularity of Thilo Sarrazin's racist anti-immigration book *Germany Abolishes Itself* (2010). This book, which was cautiously praised by Hans-Ulrich Wehler, warns of the dangers of a growing culturally and genetically inferior (mostly Muslim and Turkish) immigrant population – one that because of its high birth rate compared to that of "native" Germans threatens German culture and productivity. Sarrazin's sentiments pick up

---

[7] Andrew Zimmerman, "Decolonizing Weber," *Postcolonial Studies* 9, no. 1 (2006): 53–54; Heike Knortz, *Diplomatische Tauschgeschäfte. "Gastarbeiter" in der westdeutschen Diplomatie und Beschäftigungspolitik 1953–1973* (Köln: Böhlau Verlag, 2008), 22–23; Karin Hunn, *"Nächstes Jahr kehren wir zurück …" Die Geschichte der türkischen "Gastarbeiter" in der Bundesrepublik* (Göttingen: Wallstein Verlag, 2005), 9.

where Weber's anti-Polish attitude left off: Recall that Weber
noted fearfully that, in those Prussian regions "permeated" by
Poles, Catholic Germans in particular tended to sink down to
their lower "cultural and physical level" and were thus "lost
to the [German] national community." It is therefore problematic to link Sarrazin's racism to the Nazis. Instead, it is much
more closely related to early twentieth-century liberal imperialist
tenets.[8]

After 1949, West Germany tried to reconnect to the presumably "good" traditions and legacies of German political liberalism, among them the 1848 revolution and the concepts of
Max Weber. The latter quickly became a kind of "founding
father" of the Federal Republic. Yet of course, Weber belonged
to the large and influential circle of late nineteenth- and early
twentieth-century liberal imperialists and also had been, together
with Friedrich Ratzel and Carl Peters, a founding member of the
Pan-German League. In 1959, historian Wolfgang J. Mommsen pointed out the strong expansionist tendencies, which he
traced exclusively to Weber's nationalism, in Weber's thought.
As Mommsen recalled in 1984, his book "received a rather
stormy reception." Mommsen's revelations did not prevent the
first generations of West German historians, especially Hans-
Ulrich Wehler, from defending the new and tenuous liberal order
of the Bundesrepublik by drawing on concepts, ideas, and personalities linked to the framework of late nineteenth- and early
twentieth-century imperial liberalism, in particular Weber. To
be sure, Weber's reflections remain potentially relevant to this
day, but using them without an explicit awareness that they are
inseparably tied to late nineteenth- and early twentieth-century

---

[8] Max Weber, *Der Nationalstaat und die Volkswirtschaftspolitik: Akademische
Antrittsrede* (Freiburg: Akademische Verlagsbuchhandlung von J. C. B. Mohr,
1895), 3–5; Hartwig Pautz, "The Politics of Identity in Germany: The Leitkultur Debate," *Race & Class* 46, no. 4 (2005): 39–52; Zimmerman, "Decolonizing Weber," 53–54; Thilo Sarrazin, *Deutschland schafft sich ab. Wie wir
unser Land aufs Spiel setzen.* (Munich: Deutsche Verlags-Anstalt, 2010), 214–
15, 259–65; Hans-Ulrich Wehler, "Ein Buch trifft ins Schwarze," *Die Zeit*,
October 9, 2010.

imperial liberalism is problematic. In Andrew Zimmerman's view, Weber's "subtle mixing of race, culture, and class" thus had and, because of the sociologist's continuing popularity especially among right-wing intellectuals, still has a "decisive impact on the racialized political economy of most of the world."[9]

Weber's new lease on intellectual life within West German academia (and elsewhere) after 1949 is not the only example of the resurfacing of pre-1914 imperial liberalism during the 1950s and 1960s. Hannah Arendt's *The Origins of Totalitarianism*, one of the founding texts of postcolonial studies according to Pascal Grosse, is one of the earliest perspectives on the connections between nineteenth-century European imperialism and Nazism, although such a reading of Arendt has recently evoked criticism. I suggest a different interpretation of *The Origins of Totalitarianism*. Scrutiny of its passages that deal with European imperialism reveals that Arendt in fact separates the race-based and expansionist sentiments that white European settlers developed on the South African plains from life and culture in nineteenth-century Europe and North America: "The Boers were the first European group to become completely alienated from the pride Western man felt in living in a world created and fabricated by himself. They treated the Natives as raw material and lived on them as one might live on the fruits of wild trees. Lazy and unproductive, they agreed to vegetate on essentially the same level as the black tribes had vegetated for thousands of years." The European colonies therefore became "laboratories of modernity" insofar as within them new, race-based organizational structures

---

[9] On the importance of Weber for Hans-Ulrich Wehler, see his remarks on the occasion of becoming an honorary member of the American Historical Association in January 2000 (http://www.ghi-dc.org/publications/ghipubs/bu/026/b26wehler.html); Hans-Ulrich Wehler, *The German Empire, 1871–1918* (Dover, NH: Berg Publishers, [1973] 1985), 1; Christopher Clark, *The Iron Kingdom: The Rise and Downfall of Prussia, 1600–1947* (London: Penguin Books, 2006), 708 (note 35). On Max Weber see Chapters 2 and 4. See especially Zimmerman, "Decolonizing Weber," 54–57, 63; Wolfgang J. Mommsen, *Max Weber and German Politics: 1890–1920* (Chicago: University of Chicago Press, [1959] 1984), vii, 68–69, 81–82.

developed, which were completely alien to the political frame-work of liberal nationalism that had been cultivated in Europe.[10] Arendt therefore juxtaposes the ultimately emancipatory world of nineteenth-century liberal nation-states with new racial-ized and expansionist sentiments that developed within the frameworks of Pan-Germanism and Pan-Slavism and in the colonies: "To the salutary restraint of national institutions and politicians we owe whatever benefits the non-European peoples have been able . . . to derive from Western domination." Ironi-cally, the language she uses in her description of colonial devel-opments echoes liberal imperialist attitudes. Carl Peters would have agreed with Arendt's description – highly problematic from a present-day perspective – of the life and culture of the African nations that the white settlers encountered, and so would Ratzel, Rohrbach, and Weber. In fact in her application of "classic" (Enlightenment, liberal) eighteenth- and nineteenth-century char-acterizations of "savage natives," Arendt goes so far as to trace the origins of both the corrosion of the liberal nation-state by "imported" totalitarian regimes and the genocidal massacres undertaken by them not merely back to the views and behav-ioral patterns developed by white settlers in Africa, but specifi-cally to the Africans these Europeans encountered, murdered, and enslaved. Arendt appears to suggest that the European settlers in Africa were in fact infected by the strange and alien manners of the "Dark Continent" and therefore adopted the brutality of its native population for their own purposes. During the 1912 miscegenation debates in the Reichstag, right-wing supporters of racial segregation drew on fears of "contamination" by native

---

[10] Arendt, *The Origins of Totalitarianism*, 194; Pascal Grosse, "From Colonial-ism to National Socialism to Postcolonialism: Hannah Arendt's Origins of Totalitarianism," *Postcolonial Studies* 9, no. 1 (2006): 37, 38, 42. Compare Dirk A. Moses, "Hannah Arendt, Imperialisms, and the Holocaust," in *Ger-man Colonialism: Race, the Holocaust, and Postwar Germany*, ed. Volker Langbehn and Mohammad Salama (New York: Columbia University Press, 2011), 72–93; Robert Gerwarth and Stephan Malinowski, "Hannah Arendt's Ghosts: Reflections on the Disputable Path from Windhoek to Auschwitz," *Central European History* 42, no. 2 (2009).

character traits, arguing that a métis population in the colonies would consist of "uncomfortable and dangerous consorts." Arendt's statement that the whites' "senseless massacre of native tribes on the Dark Continent was quite in keeping with the traditions of these tribes themselves" bears an eerie resemblance to these sentiments.[11]

On the other hand, Arendt posits that European liberalism and the presumably sustainable nationalism linked to it in countries such as France, Great Britain, and, to a large degree, also the German Empire stood, literally, a world apart from both the radical expansionist sentiments that developed in the colonies and, more important from her perspective, from the continental expansionism of Pan-Slavism and Pan-Germanism. In Arendt's view, overseas imperialism had indeed, though inadvertently and unintended by liberal imperialists at home, given rise to new and radically racialized sentiments. Nevertheless, ultimately European overseas expansionism was tied to the emancipatory structures of the liberal European nation-state in Great Britain, as well as in France and in Imperial Germany. Continental expansionism was not, however: "While overseas imperialism, its antinational tendencies notwithstanding, succeeded in giving a new lease on life to the antiquated institutions of the nation-state, continental imperialism was and remained unequivocally hostile to all existing political bodies." *The Origins of Totalitarianism* thus indicates that liberal nationalism and imperialism did not in fact construct the historical foundation for Nazism and Stalinism. Unsurprisingly, this conclusion made Arendt's arguments a good fit for the ideological needs of the West during the 1950s, particularly for the young Federal Republic. Over time, Arendt has

---

[11]   Arendt, *The Origins of Totalitarianism*, 131, 134, 185, 189, 192, 206. In my view it is unconvincing to argue that the sections of Arendt's work that are quoted and referenced here were meant to literally "voice" the viewpoints of European settlers and therefore do not represent Arendt's own views. The relevant passages in Arendt's work simply do not corroborate this interpretation. Compare Richard H. King and Dan Stone, *Hannah Arendt and the Uses of History: Imperialism, Nation, Race, and Genocide* (New York: Berghahn Books, 2007), 9–10.

therefore at least symbolically been appropriated by the Federal Republic of Germany and can now be encountered directly in the center of Germany's capital, with one of the streets bordering the Holocaust Memorial, located just south of Berlin's Brandenburg Gate, bearing her name.[12]

Arendt could not see what was so obvious to Aimé Césaire after 1945 perhaps because her focus was directed more toward Europe than to the colonies. The magnitude of the crimes committed by the Nazis made it impossible for her to link the Nazi regime to the Europe of seemingly stable and "civilized" nation-states before 1914. As a result, she focused on developments at both the intellectual and colonial margins of this "good" Europe; among those developments were corrosive conceptions of race and the state that had emerged not only in the colonies but also, and more important, in the Pan-German and Pan-Slavic movements in Europe itself. These associations and the ideas they promoted pointed toward a dark future and cleared paths that would eventually lead to the Nazis' seizure of power. This interpretation, unlike that of Césaire, at the very least partially exculpated American, European, and German liberal nationalism and imperialism, shielding them from closer scrutiny regarding their own potential for expansion, oppression, violence, and the justification of genocidal measures. Therefore, during the 1950s Arendt's views became a welcome ideological antidote to the perceived threat emanating from the "totalitarian" Soviet Union. Driven by the same ideological needs, after 1945 a similar process of reshaping and partially reinventing the past fortified the myth that the United States had never been, unlike most European states, an imperialist nation.[13]

[12] Arendt, *The Origins of Totalitarianism*, 134, 225; Grosse, "From Colonialism to National Socialism to Postcolonialism," 35, 42–43. For Arendt's conviction of the inseparable connection between political liberalism and pre-1914 imperialism, see Arendt, *The Origins of Totalitarianism*, 151–53.

[13] Compare King and Stone, *Hannah Arendt and the Uses of History*, 250; R. W. Van Alstyne, *The Rising American Empire* (Oxford: Basil Blackwell, 1960), 6–7.

The intent here is neither to vilify Max Weber and certainly not Hannah Arendt nor to criticize those post-1945 historians who at times structured their methodologies around these intellectuals. Nevertheless, after World War II, pre-1914 liberal-imperialist sentiments, perhaps because they were consciously rejected by the Nazis, were seamlessly integrated into the postwar order in West Germany. This integration may also explain why so few West German historians took German imperialism seriously and why the first scholarly work that focused not only on pre-1914 German colonialism but also on the darkest chapter of German colonial history – the genocidal war against the Herero and Nama in Namibia – was not written by a West German scholar. Instead, it was the East German historian Horst Drechsler who brought the genocide of the Herero and Nama back into the realm of public debate in 1966.[14]

The connections between German colonialism and American westward expansion and racial policies are part of the history of German liberalism during the nineteenth and early twentieth centuries. Yet even though liberal imperialism and its legacies reach far into the twentieth century (certainly beyond the year 1945), they should not be confused with Nazi expansionism. The main trajectories of German imperialism did not point toward a future Nazi "Eastern Empire." In part they faced back to the late eighteenth century, to the revolution of 1848, and to liberal colonialist discourse and practices before 1914. More important, as the previous chapters show, German imperialism was shaped as much by transatlantic connections as it was driven by domestic dynamics. Because of these lateral transnational links, the United States' westward expansion, slavery, and racial segregation measures in the "redeemed" U.S. South became part and parcel of German colonialist discourse and practice during the nineteenth and early twentieth centuries.

---

[14] Horst Drechsler, *Südwestafrika unter deutscher Kolonialherrschaft: Der Kampf der Herero und Nama gegen den deutschen Imperialismus (1884–1915)* (Berlin (East): Akademie-Verlag, 1966).

Bibliography

Periodicals

Allgemeine Deutsche Bibliothek. Berlin/Stettin/Kiel: F. Nicolai & C. E. Bohn, 1765–93.
Allgemeine Literatur-Zeitung. Halle: C. A. Schwetschke, 1785–1849.
Allgemeine Welt- und Völkerkunde. Naumburg, 1833–36.
Annalen der Gesetzgebung und Rechtsgelehrsamkeit. Berlin/Stettin: E. F. Klein, 1791.
Beiträge zur Kolonialpolitik und Kolonialwirtschaft. Berlin: 1899–1903.
Berliner Neueste Nachrichten. Berlin: Wolff, 1881–1919
Berlinisches Journal für Aufklärung. Berlin, 1788–90.
Berlinische Monatsschrift. Berlin: Haude und Spener, 1783–96.
Bibliothek der neuesten Weltkunde: Geschichtliche Übersicht der denkwürdigsten Erscheinungen bei allen Völkern der Erde, ihrem literarischen, politischen und sittlichen Lebens. Aarau: Sauerländer, 1828–42.
Das Ausland. Stuttgart: J. F. Cotta'schen Buchhandlung., 1828–93.
Deutsche Chronik. 1774–77.
Deutsche Kolonialzeitung: Organ der Deutschen Kolonialgesellschaft. München: 1884-1943.
Deutsche Monatsschrift. Berlin, 1790–1800.
Didaskalia. Heidelberg/Frankfurt a. M.: J. L. Heller, 1831–82.
Die Gartenlaube: Illustriertes Familienblatt. Leipzig/Berlin: Scherl, 1853–1937
Die Neue Zeit: Wochenschrift der deutschen Sozialdemokratie. 1883–1923.

Globus: Illustrierte Zeitschrift für Länder- und Völkerkunde. 1862–
    1910.
Göttingisches historisches Magazin. Hannover: Helwing, 1787–91.
Göttingisches Magazin der Wissenschaften und Litteratur. Göttingen,
    1780–85.
*Hamburgisches Magazin, oder gesammelte Schriften, zum Unterricht
    und Vergnügen, aus der Naturforschung und den angenehmen Wis-
    senschaften überhaupt.* Hamburg: G. C. Grund, 1747–63.
Historisches Journal. Berlin, 1799–1800.
Jahresbericht der Deutschen Kolonialgesellschaft. Berlin: Carl Hey-
    manns Verlag, 1889–1929.
Journal von und für Deutschland. 1784–92.
Magazin für das Neueste aus der Physik und Naturgeschichte. Gotha,
    1781–91.
Minerva. Ein Journal historischen und politischen Inhalts. Hamburg,
    1792–1810; Leipzig, 1811–58.
Miszellen für die neueste Weltkunde. Aarau: Sauerländer, 1807–13.
Monatsschrift für Deutsche. Leipzig, 1800–02.
Morgenblatt für gebildete Stände. Stuttgart; Tübingen: Cotta, 1807–37.
*Nationalsozialistische Monatshefte: Zentrale politische u. kulturelle
    Zeitschrift d. NSDAP.* München: Zentralverlag d. NSDAP, 1930–44.
Neue Deutsche Monatsschrift. Berlin, 1795.
Neues Göttingisches Historisches Magazin. Hannover: Helwing, 1791–
    94.
Neues Hannoversches Magazin. Hannover, 1791–1813.
North American Review. Boston: 1815–.
Politisches Journal nebst Anzeigen von gelehrten und anderen Sachen.
    Hamburg, 1781–1839.
Sozialistische Monatshefte. 1895/6–1933.
The United States Magazine and Democratic Review. 1837–59.
Überlieferungen zur Geschichte unserer Zeit. Aarau: Sauerländer, 1817–
    23.
Vaterlandschronik. Stuttgart, 1788–89.
Vaterländische Chronik. 1787.
*Völkischer Beobachter (Berliner Ausgabe): Kampfblatt der national-
    sozialistischen Bewegung Großdeutschlands.* München/Berlin: Eher,
    1930–45.
Vorwärts. Berlin: 1891–.
Zeitschrift für Kolonialpolitik, Kolonialrecht und Kolonialwirtschaft.
    Berlin: 1904–12.

Books and Journal Articles

Adam, Uwe D. Judenpolitik im Dritten Reich. Düsseldorf: Droste, 2003.

Adams, David Keith, and Cornelis A. van Minnen. *Reflections on American Exceptionalism, European Papers in American History 1.* Staffordshire: Keele University Press, 1994.

Adams, Willi Paul. "The Declaration of Independence in Germany." *Journal of American History* (1999): 62–75.

———. *Deutschland und Amerika.* Berlin: Colloquium Verag, 1985.

Allen, Ann Taylor. *Satire and Society in Wilhelmine Germany: Kladderadatsch and Simplicissimus 1890–1914.* Lexington: University Press of Kentucky, 1984.

Alter, Manfred. *Die deutsche Kinder-und Jugendliteratur zwischen Gründerzeit und Novemberrevolution.* Berlin (East): Der Kinderbuchverlag, 1981.

Aly, Götz. *Warum die Deutschen? Warum die Juden? Gleichheit, Neid und Rassenhass, 1800–1933.* Frankfurt am Main: S. Fischer, 2011.

Ames, Eric, Marcia Klotz, and Lora Wildenthal. *Germany's Colonial Pasts.* Lincoln: University of Nebraska Press, 2005.

Anderson, Margaret Lavinia. *Practicing Democracy: Elections and Political Culture in Imperial Germany.* Princeton: Princeton University Press, 2000.

Anderson, Margaret Lavinia, and Kenneth Barkin. "The Myth of the Puttkamer Purge and the Reality of the Kulturkampf: Some Reflections on the Historiography of Imperial Germany." *Journal of Modern History* 54, no. 4 (1982): 647–86.

Andrée, Karl. "Unsere schwarzen Brüder." *Globus* 1 (1862).

Angermann, Erich. "Der deutsche Frühkonstitutionalismus und das amerikanische Vorbild." *Historische Zeitschrift* 219 (1974): 1–33.

Anker, Josef. "Paul Rohrbach." In *Allgemeine Deutsche Biographie.* Berlin: Rohmer–Schinkel, 2005.

Anton, G. K. "Zur Landfrage in den Kolonien." *Beiträge zur Kolonialpolitik und Kolonialwirtschaft* 5 (1903).

Arendt, Hannah. *The Origins of Totalitarianism.* San Diego: Harcourt, 1968.

Askew, John B. "Praktische Kolonialpolitik." *Die Neue Zeit: Wochenschrift der deutschen Sozialdemokratie* 29, no. 1 (1911): 552–59.

Augstein, Karl. "Weiter Weg zu Winnetou." *Der Spiegel*, May 1, 1995, 130–44.

Bade, Klaus J. *Fabri und der Imperialismus in der Bismarckzeit.* Freiburg: Atlantis-Verlag, 1975.

Ballantyne, Tony. *Orientalism and Race: Aryanism in the British Empire.* New York: Palgrave, 2002.

Baranowski, Shelley. *Nazi Empire: German Colonialism and Imperialism from Bismarck to Hitler.* New York: Cambridge University Press, 2011.

Bassin, Mark. "Turner, Solov'ev, and the 'Frontier Hypothesis.'" *Journal of Modern History* 65, no. 3 (1993): 473–511.

Bauman, Zygmunt. *Modernity and the Holocaust*. Ithaca: Cornell University Press, 1989.

Becker, Frank. "Kolonialherrschaft und Rassenpolitik." In *Rassenmischehen – Mischlinge – Rassentrennung: Zur Politik der Rasse im deutschen Kolonialreich*, edited by Frank Becker. Stuttgart: Franz Steiner Verlag, 2004.

———, ed. *Rassenmischehen – Mischlinge – Rassentrennung: Zur Politik der Rasse im deutschen Kolonialreich*. Stuttgart: Franz Steiner Verlag, 2004.

Beckert, Sven. "From Tuskegee to Togo: The Problem of Freedom in the Empire of Cotton." *Journal of American History* 92, no. 2 (2005): 498–526.

Behnen, Michael. *Quellen zur deutschen Aussenpolitik im Zeitalter des Imperialismus 1890–1911*. Darmstadt: Wissenschaftliche Buchgemeinschaft, 1977.

Bergmann, Peter. "American Exceptionalism and the German 'Sonderweg' in Tandem." *International History Review* 23, no. 3 (2001).

Bernasconi, Robert. "Kant as an Unfamiliar Source of Racism." In *Philosophers on Race: Critical Essays*, edited by Julie K. Ward and Tommy Lee Lott. Oxford: Blackwell, 2002.

Betts, Raymond F. "Immense Dimensions: The Impact of the American West on Late Nineteenth-Century European Thought about Expansion." *Western Historical Quarterly* 10, no. 2 (1979): 149–66.

Beveridge, Ray. *Die schwarze Schmach – Die weisse Schande*. Hamburg: Verlag F. W. Rademacher, 1922.

Bigelow, Poultney. *The Children of the Nations*. London: W. Heinemann, 1901.

Billington, Ray Allen. *The Genesis of the Frontier Thesis*. San Marino: Huntington Library, 1971.

———. *Land of Savagery / Land of Promise*. New York: Norton, 1981.

———. "The Plains and Deserts through European Eyes." *Western Historical Quarterly* 10, no. 4 (1979): 467–87.

Blackbourn, David. "The Conquest of Nature and the Mystique of the Eastern Frontier in Germany." In *Germans, Poland, and Colonial Expansion to the East*, edited by Robert L. Nelson. New York: Palgrave Macmillan, 2009.

———. *The Conquest of Nature: Water, Landscape and the Making of Modern Germany*. London: Jonathan Cape, 2006.

———. *History of Germany, 1780–1918*. Oxford: Blackwell Publishing, 1997.

_____. *The Long Nineteenth Century*. New York: Oxford University Press, 1998.

Blackbourn, David, and Geoff Eley. *Mythen deutscher Geschichtsschreibung. Die gescheiterte bürgerliche Revolution von 1848*: Ullstein Taschenbuchverlag, 1986.

_____. *The Peculiarities of German History*. New York: Oxford University Press, 1984.

Bley, Helmut. *Namibia under German Rule*. Münster: LIT Verlag, 1996.

Blinkhorn, Martin, ed. *Fascists and Conservatives: The Radical Right and the Establishment in Twentieth-Century Europe* London: Unwin Hyman, 1990.

Bloch, Max. "Die Sozialistischen Monatshefte und die Akademikerdebatte in der deutschen Sozialdemokratie vor 1914." *Mitteilungsblatt des Instituts für soziale Bewegungen*, no. 40 (2008).

Block, Robert H. "Fredrick Jackson Turner and American Geography." *Annals of the Association of American Geographers* 70, no. 1 (1980): 31–42.

Blumenau, Hermann. *Deutsche Auswanderung und Colonisation*. Leipzig: J. E. Wappäus, 1846.

Bodek, Richard. "The Not-So-Golden Twenties: Everyday Life and Communist Agitprop in Weimar-Era Berlin." *Journal of Social History* 30, no. 1 (1996): 55–78.

Bönker, Dirk. "Ein *German Way of War*? Deutscher Militarismus und maritime Kriegsführung im Ersten Weltkrieg." In *Das Deutsche Kaiserreich in der Kontroverse*, edited by Sven Oliver Müller and Cornelius Torp. Göttingen: Vandenhoeck & Ruprecht, 2009.

Bonnell, Andrew G. "Was German Social Democracy before 1914 Antisemitic?" *German History* 27, no. 2 (2009): 259–69.

Bowler, Peter J. *Evolution: The History of an Idea*. Berkeley: University of California Press, 1989.

Brandl, Ludwig. "Wilhelm Solf." In *Biographisch-Bibliographisches Kirchenlexikon*. Nordhausen: Traugott Bautz, 1995.

Braun, Adolf. "Die Wahlen in Bayern." *Die Neue Zeit: Wochenschrift der deutschen Sozialdemokratie* 25, no. 1 (1907).

Braun, Otto. "Der 25. Januar in Ostpreußen." *Die Neue Zeit: Wochenschrift der deutschen Sozialdemokratie* 25, no. 1 (1907).

Brenner, Peter J. *Reisen in die Neue Welt*. Tübingen: Niemeyer, 1991.

Brentano, Lujo. "Die Entwicklung der Vereinigten Staaten zum Imperialismus" *Archiv für Politik und Geschichte* (1923): 224–43.

Bright, Charles, and Michael Geyer. "World History in a Global Age." *American Historical Review* 100, no. 4 (1995): 1034–60.

Burleigh, Michael. *Germany Turns Eastwards: A Study of Ostforschung in the Third Reich*. Cambridge: Cambridge University Press, 1988.

Busch, Helmut. "Reinhard Mumm." In *Allgemeine deutsche Biographie & Neue deutsche Biographie*. Berlin: Pütter–Rohlfs, 1997.

Callahan, Kevin. "'Performing Inter-Nationalism' in Stuttgart in 1907: French and German Socialist Nationalism and the Political Culture of an International Socialist Congress." *International Review of Social History* 45 (2000).

Calloway, Colin G. "'We Have Always Been the Frontier:' The American Revolution in Shawnee Country." *American Indian Quarterly* 16, no. 1 (1992).

———. *The World Turned Upside Down*. Boston: Bedford Books, 1994.

Calloway, Colin G., Gerd Gemünden, and Susanne Zantop, eds. *Germans and Indians: Fantasies, Encounters, Projections*. Lincoln: University of Nebraska Press, 2002.

———. "Historical Encounters across Five Centuries." In *Germans and Indians: Fantasies, Encounters, Projections*, edited by Colin G. Calloway, Gerd Gemünden, and Susanne Zantop. Lincoln: University of Nebraska Press, 2002.

Camman, Alexander. "Porträt Hans-Ulrich Wehler." *Frankfurter Allgemeine Zeitung*, October 9, 2011.

Carpenter, Ronald H. *The Eloquence of Frederick Jackson Turner*. San Marino: Huntington Library, 1983.

Cass, Lewis. "Removal of the Indians." *North American Review* (1830): 62–121.

Chatriot, Alain, and Dieter Gosewinkel, eds. *Koloniale Politik und Praktiken Deutschlands und Frankreichs 1880–1962. Politiques et pratiques coloniales dans les empires allemands et français. Vol. 6, Schriftenreihe des Deutsch-Französischen Historikerkomitees*. Stuttgart: Franz Steiner Verlag, 2010.

Chickering, Roger. *The Great War and Urban Life in Germany: Freiburg, 1914–1918*. Cambridge: Cambridge University Press, 2007.

———. *We Men Who Feel Most German: A Cultural Study of the Pan-German League, 1886–1914*. Boston: George Allen & Unwin, 1984.

Clark, Christopher. *The Iron Kingdom: The Rise and Downfall of Prussia, 1600–1947*. London: Penguin Books, 2006.

Class, Heinrich. *Wenn ich der Kaiser wär': Politische Wahrheiten und Notwendigkeiten*. Leipzig: Dieterich, 1912.

Coleman, William. "Science and Symbol in the Turner Frontier Hypothesis." *American Historical Review* 72, no. 1 (1966): 22–49.

Conklin, Alice L. "Colonialism and Human Rights, A Contradiction in Terms? The Case of France and West Africa, 1895–1914." *American Historical Review* 103, no. 2 (1998): 419–42.

————. *European Imperialism, 1830–1930: Climax and Contradiction.* Boston: Houghton Mifflin, 1999.

Conrad, Sebastian. *Globalisation and the Nation.* New York: Cambridge University Press, 2010.

————. *Globalisierung und Nation im Deutschen Kaiserreich.* Munich: C. H. Beck, 2006.

Conrad, Sebastian, and Jürgen Osterhammel. *Das Kaiserreich transnational. Deutschland in der Welt 1871–1914.* Göttingen: Vandenhoeck & Ruprecht, 2004.

Conze, Werner, and Wolfgang Zorn. *Die Protokolle des Volkswirtschaftlichen Ausschusses der deutschen Nationalversammlung 1848/49.* Boppard am Rhein: Harald Boldt Verlag, 1992.

Crothers, George. *The German Elections of 1907.* London: P. S. King & Son, 1941.

Dahrendorf, Ralf. *Society and Democracy in Germany.* New York: Anchor Books, 1969.

Depkat, Volker. *Amerikabilder in politischen Diskursen.* Stuttgart: Klett-Cotta, 1998.

Dernburg, Bernhard. "Baumwollproduktion und Negerfrage in den Vereinigten Staaten." *Zeitschrift für Socialwissenschaft*, no. 5 (1911): 349–50.

————. "Speech in Front of the Kolonialpolitisches Aktionskomité." In *Reichstagsauflösung und Kolonialpolitik*, edited by Gustav Schmoller. Berlin: Wedekind, 1907.

Dippel, Horst. *Die Amerikanische Verfassung in Deutschland im 19. Jahrhundert.* Goldbach: Keip Verlag, 1994.

————. "Die Wirkung der amerikanischen Revolution auf Deutschland und Frankreich." *200 Jahre amerikanische Revolution und moderne Revolutionsforschung. Geschichte und Gesellschaft Sonderheft*, no. II (1976): 101–21.

————. *Germany and the American Revolution.* Wiesbaden: Steiner, 1978.

————. "Gustav Körner." In *Neue deutsche Biographie.* Berlin: Bayerische Akademie der Wissenschaften, 1980.

Domarus, Wolfgang. *Hitler: Speeches and Proclamations 1932–1945.* Würzburg: Domarus Verlag, 1996.

Drechsler, Horst. *Aufstände in Südwestafrika.* Berlin (East): Dietz, 1984.

————. *Let Us Die Fighting: The Struggle of the Herero and Nama against German Imperialism (1884–1915).* London: Zed Press, 1980.

————. *Südwestafrika unter deutscher Kolonialherrschaft: Der Kampf der Herero und Nama gegen den deutschen Imperialismus (1884–1915).* Berlin (East): Akademie-Verlag, 1966.

Duden, Gottfried. *Bericht über eine Reise nach den westlichen Staaten Nord-Amerikas und einen mehrjährigen Aufenthalt am Missouri.* Elberfeld: Lucas, 1829.

Eckert, Andreas. "Namibia – ein deutscher Sonderweg in Afrika?" In *Völkermord in Deutsch-Südwestafrika. Der Kolonialkrieg (1904–08) in Namibia und seine Folgen,* edited by Jürgen Zimmerer and Joachim Zeller, 226–38. Berlin: Links, 2003.

El-Tayeb, Fatima. *Schwarze Deutsche: Der Diskurs um 'Rasse' und Nationalität 1890–1933.* Frankfurt am Main: Campus Fachbuch, 2001.

Eley, Geoff. *Forging Democracy: The History of the Left in Europe, 1850–2000.* Oxford: Oxford University Press, 2002.

––––––. *Reshaping the German Right: Radical Nationalism and Political Change after Bismarck.* New Haven: Yale University Press, 1980.

––––––. "Review: James Sheehan and the German Liberals: A Critical Appreciation." *Central European History* 14, no. 3 (1981): 273–88.

Eley, Geoff, and James Retallack. *Wilheminism and Its Legacies: German Modernities, Imperialism, and the Meaning of Reform, 1890–1930.* New York: Berghahn, 2003.

Engelsing, Rolf. *Analphabetentum und Lektüre.* Stuttgart: J. B. Metzlersche Verlagsbuchhandlung, 1973.

Epstein, Fritz T. "Germany and the United States: Basic Patterns of Conflict and Understanding." In *Issues and Conflicts: Studies in Twentieth Century American Diplomacy,* edited by George L. Anderson. Lawrence: University of Kansas Press, 1959.

Essner, Cornelia. *Die "Nürnberger Gesetze" oder die Verwaltung des Rassenwahns 1933–1945.* Paderborn: Ferdinand Schöningh Verlag, 2002.

Estwick, Samuel. *Considerations on the Negroe Cause Commonly So Called, Addressed to the Right Honourable Lord Mansfield, Lord Chief Justice of the Court Of King's Bench.* London: J. Dodsley, 1773.

Farcy, Jean-Claude. *Les camps de concentration Français de la première guerre mondiale 1914–1920.* Paris: Antropos-Economica, 1995.

Feest, Christian F. "Europe's Indians." In *The Invented Indian,* edited by James A. Clifton. New Brunswick: Transaction Publishers, 1996.

––––––. "Germany's Indians in a European Perspective." In *Germans and Indians: Fantasies, Encounters, Projections* Edited by Colin G. Calloway, Gerd Gemünden, and Susanne Zantop. Lincoln: University of Nebraska Press, 2002.

––––––. "The Indian in Non-English Literature." In *History of Indian-White Relations,* edited by Wilcomb E. Washburn. Washington, DC: Smithsonian Institution, 1988.

Fenske, Hans. "Imperialisitische Tendenzen in Deutschland vor 1866: Auswanderung, überseeische Bestrebungen, Weltmachtsträume." *Historisches Jahrbuch* 97/98 (1978).

―――. "Ungeduldige Zuschauer: Die Deutschen und die europäische Expansion, 1815–1880." In *Imperialistische Kontinuität und nationale Ungeduld im 19. Jahrhundert*, edited by Wolfgang Reinhard. Frankfurt am Main: Fischer, 1991.

Feuchtwanger, Edgar. *Imperial Germany, 1850–1870*. Florence: Routledge, 2001.

Fischer, Fritz. *Griff nach der Weltmacht: Die Kriegszielpolitik des kaiserlichen Deutschlands 1914/18*. Düsseldorf: Droste Verlag, 1961.

Fischer, Lars. *The Socialist Response to Antisemitism in Imperial Germany*. Cambridge: Cambridge University Press, 2007.

Fitzpatrick, Matthew P. *Liberal Imperialism in Germany: Expansionism and Nationalism, 1848–1884*. New York: Berghahn Books, 2008.

―――. "The Pre-History of the Holocaust? The Sonderweg and Historikerstreit Debates and the Abject Colonial Past." *Central European History* 41 (2008).

―――. "The Threat of 'Woolly-Haired Grandchildren': Race, the Colonial Family and German Nationalism." *History of the Family* 14 (2009): 356–68.

Fletcher, Roger. *Revisionism and Empire: Socialist Imperialism in Germany 1897–1914*. London: George Allen & Unwin, 1984.

―――. "Revisionism and Wilhelmine Imperialism." *Journal of Contemporary History* 23, no. 3 (1988): 347–66.

Flint, Kate. *The Transatlantic Indian*. Princeton: Princeton University Press, 2009.

Fogarty, Richard. *Race and War in France: Colonial Subjects in the French Army, 1914–1918*. Baltimore: The Johns Hopkins University Press, 2008.

Frech, Stefan. *Wegbereiter Hitlers? Theodor Reismann-Grone. Ein völkischer Nationalist (1863–1949)*. Paderborn: Ferdinand Schöningh, 2009.

Fredrickson, George M. *White Supremacy: A Comparative Study in American and South African History*. New York: Oxford University Press, 1980.

Frevert, Ute. "Europeanizing Germany's Twentieth Century." *History and Memory* 17, no. 1–2 (2005).

Furber, David. "Near as Far in the Colonies: The Nazi Occupation of Poland." *International History Review* 26, no. 3 (2004): 541–79.

Gall, Lothar. *Europa auf dem Weg in die Moderne, 1850–1890*. Munich: Oldenbourg Verlag, 1997.

Games, Allison. "AHR Forum: Atlantic History: Definitions, Challenges, and Opportunities." *American Historical Review* 111, no. 3 (2006).

Gassert, Philipp. *Amerika im Dritten Reich. Ideologie, Propaganda und Volksmeinung, 1933–1945.* Stuttgart: Franz Steiner Verlag, 1997.

————. "'Without Concession to Marxist or Communist Thought': Fordism in Germany, 1923–1939." In *Transatlantic Images and Perceptions: Germany and America since 1776*, edited by David E. Barclay and Elisabeth Gläser-Schmidt. Cambridge: Cambridge University Press, 1997.

Gerstäcker, Friedrich. *California Gold Mines.* Oakland: Biobooks, 1946.

————. *Die Frauen in den Backwoods oder Wäldern des Westens von Amerika.* Wien, 1846.

————. *Neue Reisen.* 3 vols. Jena: Hermann Costenoble, 1876.

————. *Reisen.* 4 vols. Stuttgart: J. G. Cotta'scher Verlag, 1853.

————. *Streif- und Jagdzüge.* 2 vols. Dresden & Leipzig: in der Arnoldschen Buchhandlung, 1844.

Gerwarth, Robert, and Stephan Malinowski. "Der Holocaust als 'kolonialer Genozid'? Europäische Kolonialgewalt und nationalsozialistischer Vernichtungskrieg." *Geschichte und Gesellschaft* 33 (2007): 439–66.

————. "Hannah Arendt's Ghosts: Reflections on the Disputable Path from Windhoek to Auschwitz." *Central European History* 42, no. 2 (2009): 279–300.

Gessert, Ferdinand. "Das Wasserrecht des amerikanischen Westen mit Bezug auf Deutsch-Süd-West-Afrika." *Zeitschrift für Kolonialpolitik, Kolonialrecht und Kolonialwirtschaft* 8, no. 7 (1906).

Geulen, Christian. "'The Final Frontier...' Heimat, Nation und Kolonie um 1900: Carl Peters." In *Phantasiereiche. Zur Kulturgeschichte des deutschen Kolonialismus*, edited by Birthe Kundrus. Frankfurt: Campus Verlag, 2003.

Geyer, Michael, and Charles Bright. "World History in a Global Age." *American Historical Review* 100, no. 4 (1995): 1034–60.

Gilmore, Glenda E. *Defying Dixie: The Radical Roots of Civil Rights, 1919–1950.* New York: Norton, 2008.

Gläser, Elisabeth, and Hermann Wellenreuther. *Bridging the Atlantic, Publications of the German Historical Institute.* New York: Cambridge University Press, 2000.

Gollwitzer, Heinz. *Geschichte des weltpolitischen Denkens.* Vol. II. Göttingen: Vandenhoeck & Ruprecht, 1982.

Gosewinkel, Dieter. *Einbürgern und Ausschließen: Die Nationalisierung der Staatsangehörigkeit vom Deutschen Bund bis zur Bundesrepublik Deutschland.* Göttingen: Vandenhoek und Ruprecht, 2001.

Gosewinkel, Dieter, and Alain Chatriot, eds. *Koloniale Politik und Praktiken Deutschlands und Frankreichs 1880–1962. Politiques et pratiques coloniales dans les empires allemands et français.* Vol. 6, *Schriftenreihe des Deutsch-Französischen Historikerkomitees.* Stuttgart: Franz Steiner Verlag, 2010.

Gould, Stephen Jay. "Morton's Ranking of Races by Cranial Capacity." *Science* 200, no. 4341 (1978).

Graichen, Gisela, and Horst Gründer. *Deutsche Kolonien. Traum und Trauma.* Munich: Ullstein, 2005.

Greene, Jack P. *The Intellectual Construction of America.* Chapel Hill: University of North Carolina Press, 1993.

Grill, Johnpeter, and Robert L. Jenkins. "The Nazis and the American South in the 1930s: A Mirror Image?" *Journal of Southern History* 58, no. 4 (1992): 667–94.

Grimmer-Solem, Erik. "Imperialist Socialism of the Chair: Gustav Schmoller and German Weltpolitik, 1897–1905." In *Wilhelminism and Its Legacies: German Modernities, Imperialism, and the Meaning of Reform, 1890–1930*, edited by Geoff Eley and James Retallack. New York: Berghahn Books, 2003.

————. "The Professors' Africa: Economists, the Elections of 1907, and the Legitimation of German Imperialism." *German History* 25, no. 3 (2007): 313–47.

Grosse, Pascal. "From Colonialism to National Socialism to Postcolonialism: Hannah Arendt's Origins of Totalitarianism." *Postcolonial Studies* 9, no. 1 (2006): 35–52.

————. "What Does German Colonialism Have to Do with National Socialism? A Conceptual Framework." In *Germany's Colonial Pasts*, edited by Eric Ames. Lincoln: University of Nebraska Press, 2005.

Gruchmann, Lothar. "'Blutschutzgesetz' und Justiz. Zu Entsehung und Auswirkung des Nürnberger Gesetzes vom 15. September 1935." *Vierteljahrshefte für Zeitgeschichte* 31, no. 3 (1983): 418–42.

————. *Nationalsozialistische Großraumordnung. Die Konstruktion einer 'deutschen Monroe-Doktrin'.* Stuttgart: Deutsche Verlags-Anstalt, 1962.

Gründer, Horst. *Geschichte der deutschen Kolonien.* Paderborn: Schöningh, 1985.

————. "Zum Stellenwert des Rassismus im Spektrum der deutschen Kolonialideologie." In *Rassenmischehen – Mischlinge – Rassentrennung. Zur Politik der Rasse im deutschen Kolonialreich*, edited by Frank Becker, 27–42. Stuttgart: Franz Steiner, 2004.

Gründer, Horst, and Gisela Graichen. *Deutsche Kolonien. Traum und Trauma.* Munich: Ullstein, 2005.

Guettel, Jens-Uwe. "From the Frontier to German South-West Africa: German Colonialism, Indians, and American Westward

Expansion." *Modern Intellectual History* 7, no. 3 (2010): 523–52.

_____. "Liberal Colonialism, German Colonial Miscegenation Bans, and the American South, *1905–1914.*" Presented at the GSA Annual Conference, Washington, DC, 2009.

_____. "The Myth of the Pro-Colonialist SPD: German Social Democracy and Imperialism before the First World War." *Central European History* 45, no. 3 (2012).

_____. "Reading America, Studying Empire: German Perceptions of Indians, Slavery, and the American West, 1789–1900." Ph.D. Dissertation, Yale University, 2007.

Haeckel, Ernst. *Natürlich Schöpfungsgeschichte*, Vol. 1. Berlin: Georg Reimer, [1868] 1902.

Hagedorn, Hermann. *Roosevelt in the Badlands*. Boston: Houghton Mifflin, 1921.

Hagenlücke, Heinz. *Deutsche Vaterlandspartei: Die nationale Rechte am Ende des Kaiserreiches*. Düsseldorf: Droste Verlag, 1997.

Hartz, Louis. *The Liberal Tradition in America: An Interpretation of American Political Thought since the Revolution*. New York: Harcourt Brace, 1955.

Hasenclever, Adolf. "Der amerikanische Imperialismus." *Vergangenheit und Gegenwart*, no. 5 (1928): 265–81.

Hasse, Ernst. *Deutsche Politik*. Munich: J. F. Lehmann's Verlag, 1908.

Hecht, Günther. *Kolonialfrage und Rassegedanke, Schriftenreihe des Rassenpolitischen Amtes der NSDAP und des Reichsbundes der Kinderreichen*. Berlin: Verlag Neues Volk, 1938.

Heckart, Beverly. *From Bassermann to Bebel*. New Haven: Yale University Press, 1974.

Hegel, Georg Friedrich Wilhelm. *Vorlesungen über die Philosophie der Geschichte*. Stuttgart: Reclam, 1961.

_____. *Lectures on the Philosophy of World History*. Cambridge: Cambridge University Press, 1975.

Heidegger, Hermann. *Die Deutsche Sozialdemokratie und der nationale Staat, 1870–1920*. Göttingen: Musterschmidt-Verlag, 1956.

Heilbronner, Oded. "'Long Live Liberty, Equality, Fraternity and Dynamite': The German Bourgeoisie and the Constructing of Popular Liberal and National-Socialist Subcultures in Marginal Germany." *Journal of Social History* 39, no. 1 (2005).

Hellwald, Friedrich von. *Amerika in Wort und Bild. Eine Schilderung der Vereinigten Staaten*, Vol. 1. Leipzig: Heinrich Schmidt & Carl Günther, 1883.

_____. *Amerika in Wort und Bild. Eine Schilderung der Vereinigten Staaten*, Vol. 2. Leipzig: Heinrich Schmidt & Carl Günther 1885.

_____. *Kulturgeschichte in ihrer natürlichen Entwicklung bis zur Gegenwart*, Vol. IV. Leipzig: Friesenhahn, 1898.

_____. *Naturgeschichte des Menschen*, Vol. 1. Stuttgart: W. Spemann, 1882.

Hering, Rainer. *Konstruierte Nation: Der Alldeutsche Verband 1890–1939*. Hamburg: Hans Christians Verlag, 2003.

Hermann, Rudolf A. "Von der Kolonialpolitik der nordamerikanischen Union." *Beiträge zur Kolonialpolitik und Kolonialwirtschaft* 4 (1902/1903).

Heske, Henning. "Karl Haushofer: His Role in German Politics and in Nazi Politics." *Political Geography* 6, no. 2 (1987): 135–44.

Heuss, Theodor. *Max Weber in seiner Gegenwart*. Tübingen: Mohr, 1958.

Hewitson, Mark. "The Kaiserreich in Question: Constitutional Crisis in Germany before the First World War." *Journal of Modern History* 73, no. 4 (2001).

Heyden, Ulrich van der. "Georg Albrecht von Rechenberg." In *Allgemeine deutsche Biographie & Neue deutsche Biographie*. Berlin: Pütter–Rohlfs, 2003.

Hiedeking, Jürgen, and James A. Henretta, eds. *Republicanism and Liberalism in America and the German State, 1750–1850*. New York: Cambridge University Press, 2002.

Hildebrand, Klaus. *Das Vergangene Reich: Deutsche Außenpolitik von Bismarck bis Hitler 1871–1945*. Stuttgart: Deutsche Verlags-Anstalt, 1995.

_____. *Deutsche Außenpolitik 1871–1918*. Vol. II, *Enzyklopädie Deutscher Geschichte*. Munich: R. Oldenbourg Verlag, 1989.

_____. *Vom Reich zum Weltreich. Hitler, NSDAP und koloniale Frage 1919–1945*. Munich: Wilhelm Fink Verlag, 1969.

Hilferding, Rudolf. "Parvus, Die Kolonialpolitik und der Zusammenbruch. Leipziger Buchdruckerei, A-G. 155 Seiten. Preis 1 Mark: [Rezension]." *Die Neue Zeit: Wochenschrift der deutschen Sozialdemokratie* 25, no. 2 (1907): 687–88.

Hillgruber, Andreas. "Der Faktor Amerika in Hitlers Strategie." *Aus Politik und Zeitgeschichte* 19 (1966): 3–21.

_____. *Hitler's Strategie: Politik und Kriegführung 1940–1941*. Frankfurt a. M.: Bernard & Graefe, 1965.

_____. *Kontinuität und Diskontinuität in der deutschen Außenpolitik von Bismarck bis Hitler*. Düsseldorf: Droste, 1969.

Hipler, Bruno. *Hitlers Lehrmeister – Karl Haushofer als Vater der NS-Ideologie*. St. Ottilien: EOS-Verlag, 1996.

Hitler, Adolf. *Adolf Hitler: Monologe im Führerhauptquartier 1941–1944*, edited by Werner Jochmann. Hamburg: Albrecht Knaus Verlag, 1980.

————. *Hitlers zweites Buch*, edited by Gerhard L. Weinberg. Stuttgart: Deutsche Verlags-Anstalt, 1961.

————. *Mein Kampf*. Munich: Zentralverlag der N.S.d.A.P., 1936.

Hoffmann, Adolph. "Ursachen und Wirkungen. Betrachtungen zum 25. Januar 1907." *Die Neue Zeit: Wochenschrift der deutschen Sozialdemokratie* 25, no. 1 (1907): 639–41.

Hofstadter, Richard. *The American Political Tradition and the Men Who Made It*. New York: Vintage Books, 1948.

Horkheimer, Max, and Theodor Adorno. *Dialectic of Enlightenment: Philosophical Fragments*, edited by Gunzelin Schmid Noerr. Stanford: Stanford University Press, 2002.

Huber, Ernst Rudolf. *Deutsche Verfassungsgeschichte seit 1789*, Vol. III. Stuttgart: W. Kohlhammer Verlag, 1963.

Hull, Isabel V. *Absolute Destruction: Military Culture and the Practices of War in Imperial Germany*. Ithaca, NY: Cornell University Press, 2004.

————. "Military Culture and the Production of 'Final Solutions' in the Colonies." In *The Specter of Genocide*, edited by Robert Gellately and Ben Kiernan. Cambridge: Cambridge University Press, 2003.

Humboldt, Alexander von. "Über die zukünftigen Beziehungen von Europe und Amerika." *Morgenblatt für gebildete Stände*, no. 33–34 (1826).

Humboldt, Alexander von, and Ingo Schwarz. *Alexander von Humboldt und die Vereinigten Staaten von Amerika: Briefwechsel, Beiträge zur Alexander-von-Humboldt-Forschung*, 19. Berlin: Akademie Verlag, 2004.

Hunn, Karin. *"Nächstes Jahr kehren wir zurück . . ." Die Geschichte der türkischen "Gastarbeiter" in der Bundesrepublik*. Göttingen: Wallstein Verlag, 2005.

Hyrkkänen, Markku. *Sozialistische Kolonialpolitik: Eduard Bernsteins Stellung zur Kolonialpolitik und zum Imperialismus 1882–1914. Ein Beitrag zur Geschichte des Revisionismus*. Helsinki: SHS, 1986.

Hyslop, Jonathan. "White Working-Class Women and the Invention of Apartheid: 'Purified' Afrikaner Nationalist Agitation for Legislation against 'Mixed' Marriages, 1934–9." *Journal of African History* 36, no. 1 (1995): 57–81.

Jacobsen, Hans-Adolf. "'Kampf um Lebensraum': Zur Rolle des Geopolitikers Karl Haushofer im Dritten Reich." *German Studies Review* 4, no. 1 (1981): 79–104.

Jacoby, Karl. "'The Broad Platform of Extermination': Nature and Violence in the Nineteenth-Century North American Borderlands." *Journal of Genocide Research* 10, no. 2 (2008): 249–67.

James, Harold. "The Wages of Destruction: The Making and Breaking of the Nazi Economy. Review by Harold James." *Central European History* 40, no. 2 (2007).

Janeck, Undine. *Zwischen Gartenlaube und Karl May. Deutsche Amerikarezeption in den Jahren 1871–1913.* Aachen: Shaker Verlag, 2003.

Jarausch, Konrad. *Students, Society, and Politics in Imperial Germany: The Rise of Academic Illiberalism.* Princeton: Princeton University Press, 1982.

Jelavich, Peter. "Anti-Semitism in Imperial Germany: Cultural Code or Pervasive Prejudice." *Jewish Quarterly Review* 99, no. 4 (2009).

Jenkins, Robert L., and Johnpeter Grill. "The Nazis and the American South in the 1930s: A Mirror Image?" *Journal of Southern History* 58, no. 4 (1992): 667–94.

Jones, David S. "Virgin Soils Revisited." *William and Mary Quarterly* 60, no. 4 (2003).

Junker, Detlef. "The Continuity of Ambivalence: German Views of America, 1933–1945." In *Transatlantic Images and Perceptions. Germany and America since 1776,* edited by David Barclay and Elisabeth Glaser-Schmidt. Cambridge: Cambridge University Press, 1997.

———. *Kampf um die Weltmacht. Die USA und das Dritte Reich 1933–1945.* Düsseldorf: Schwann 1988.

Kaiser, David E. "Germany and the Origins of the First World War." *Journal of Modern History* 55, no. 3 (1983): 442–74.

Kakel, Caroll P. *The American West and the Nazi East: A Comparative and Interpretive Perspective.* Basingstoke: Palgrave Macmillan, 2011.

Kane, Murray. "Some Considerations on the Frontier Concept of Frederick Jackson Turner." *Mississippi Valley Historical Review* 27, no. 3 (1940): 379–400.

Kant, Immanuel. "Über den Gebrauch teleologischer Prinzipien in der Philosophie." *Der Teutsche Merkur* 1 (1788).

Kaplan, Amy. "'Left Alone with America': The Absence of Empire in the Study of American Culture." In *Cultures of United States Imperialism,* edited by Amy Kaplan and Donald E. Pease. Durham: Duke University Press, 1993.

Kaplan, Amy, and Donald E. Pease, eds. *Cultures of United States Imperialism.* Durham: Duke University Press, 1993.

Kardorff, Siegfried von. *Wilhelm von Kardorff. Ein nationaler Parlamentarier im Zeitalter Bismarcks und Wilhelms II.* Berlin: E. S. Mittler & Sohn, 1936.

Kautsky, Karl. "Der 25. Januar." *Die Neue Zeit: Wochenschrift der deutschen Sozialdemokratie* 25, no. 1 (1907): 589–95.

———. *Sozialismus und Kolonialpolitik: Eine Auseinandersetzung.* Berlin: Vorwärts, 1907.

Kershaw, Ian. *Hitler, 1889–1936: Hubris.* New York: Norton, 1999.

———. *Hitler, 1936–45: Nemesis.* New York: Norton, 2001.

Kiernan, Ben. *Blood and Soil: A World History of Genocide and Extermination from Sparta to Darfur.* New Haven: Yale University Press, 2007.

King, Richard H., and Dan Stone. *Hannah Arendt and the Uses of History: Imperialism, Nation, Race, and Genocide.* New York: Berghahn Books, 2007.

Klautke, Egbert. *Unbegrenzte Möglichkeiten. "Amerikanisierung" in Deutschland und Frankreich (1900–1933).* Stuttgart: Franz Steiner Verlag, 2003.

Klössel, M. Hans. "Grund und Boden in Nordamerika." *Beiträge zur Kolonialpolitik und Kolonialwirtschaft* (1901–02): 576–78.

Knortz, Heike. *Diplomatische Tauschgeschäfte. "Gastarbeiter" in der westdeutschen Diplomatie und Beschäftigungspolitik 1953–1973.* Köln: Böhlau Verlag, 2008.

Kocka, Jürgen. "Asymmetrical Historical Comparison: The Case of the German Sonderweg." *History and Theory* 38, no. 1 (1999): 40–50.

———. "German History before Hitler: The Debate about the German Sonderweg." *Journal of Contemporary History* 23, no. 1 (1988): 3–16.

Koebner, Richard. "The Concept of Economic Imperialism." *Economic History Review* 2, no. 1 (1949).

Koehl, Robert L. *RKFDV: German Resettlement and Population Policy 1939–1945.* Cambridge, MA: Harvard University Press, 1957.

Koller, Christian. "Eine Zivilisierungsmission der Arbeiterklasse? Die Diskussion über einer "sozialistische Kolonialpolitk" vor dem Ersten Weltkrieg." In *Zivilisierungsmissionen*, edited by Jürgen Osterhammel and Boris Barth. Konstanz: UVK Verlagsgesellschaft mbH, 2005.

Kort, Pamela. "'The Unmastered Past of the Indians' Murder.'" In *I like America: Fictions of the Wild West*, edited by Pamela Kort and Max Hollein. Munich: Prestel, 2006.

Kramer, Paul. "Empires, Exceptions, and Anglo-Saxons: Race and Rule between the British and United States Empires, 1880–1910." *Journal of American History* 88, no. 4 (2002): 1315–53.

Krätschell, Hermann. *Carl Peters, 1856–1918: Ein Beitrag zur Publizistik des imperialistischen Nationalismus in Deutschland.* Berlin: Freie Universität Berlin, 1959.

Kreuzer, Marcus. "Parliamentarization and the Question of German Exceptionalism: 1867–1918." *Central European History* 36 (2003): 327–57.

Krieger, Heinrich. *Das Rasserecht in den Vereinigten Staaten*. Berlin: Junker und Dünnhaupt Verlag, 1936.

Kühl, Stefan. *The Nazi Connection: Eugenics, American Racism, and German National Socialism*. New York: Oxford University Press, 1994.

Kuhn, Alexander. *Zum Eingeborenenproblem in Deutsch-Südwestafrika*. Berlin: Dietrich Reimer (Ernst Vohsen), 1905.

Kulka, Otto Dov. "Die Nürnberger Rassengesetze und die deutsche Bevölkerung im Lichte geheimer NS-Lage-und Stimmungsberichte." *Vierteljahreshefte für Zeitgeschichte* 32, no. 4 (1984).

Kundrus, Birthe. "Die Kolonien – "Kinder des Gefühls und der Phantasie." In *Phantasiereiche. Zur Kulturgeschichte des deutschen Kolonialismus*, edited by Birthe Kundrus. Frankfurt a. M.: Campus Verlag, 2003.

————. "Von Windhoek nach Nuernberg? Koloniale 'Mischehenverbote' und die nationalsozialistische Rassengesetzgebung." In *Phantasiereiche. Zur Kulturgeschichte des deutschen Kolonialismus*, edited by Birthe Kundrus, 110–31. Frankfurt a. M.: Campus Verlag, 2003.

Kurlander, Eric. *The Price of Exclusion: Ethnicity, National Identity, and the Decline of German Liberalism, 1898–1933*. New York: Berghahn Books, 2006.

Laak, Dirk van. *Imperiale Infrastruktur: Deutsche Planungen für eine Erschließung Afrikas 1880 bis 1960*. Paderborn: Schöningh, 2004.

LaFeber, Walter. *The American Search for Opportunity, 1865–1913*. Cambridge: Cambridge University Press, 1993.

Langbehn, Volker, and Mohammad Salama. *German Colonialism: Race, the Holocaust, and Postwar Germany*. New York: Columbia University Press, 2011.

Langewiesche, Dieter. *Liberalismus in Deutschland*. Frankfurt a. M.: Suhrkamp, 1988.

Leers, Johann von. *Blut und Rasse in der Gesetzgebung: Ein Gang durch die Völkergeschichte*. Munich: J. F. Lehmanns Verlag, 1936.

Leutwein, Theodor. *Deutsch-Süd-West-Afrika*. Berlin: Dietrich Reimer, 1898.

————. *Elf Jahre Gouverneur in Deutsch-Südwestafrika*, 3rd ed. Berlin: E. S. Mittler & Sohn, 1908.

Liebersohn, Harry. *Aristocratic Encounters: European Travelers and North-American Indians*. Cambridge: Cambridge University Press, 1998.

Liebert, Eduard von, and Theodor Reismann-Grone. "Überseepolitik oder Festlandspolitik?" Paper presented at the Alldeutscher Verbandstag, Worms 1905.

Linne, Karsten. *Deutschland jenseits des Äquators? Die NS-Kolonialplanungen für Afrika*. Berlin: Christoph Links Verlag, 2009.

Lipset, Seymour Martin. *American Exceptionalism: A Double-Edged Sword*. New York: Norton, 1996.

List, Friedrich. *The National System of Political Economy*. New York: Kelley, 1966.

Liulevicius, Vejas Gabriel. *The German Myth of the East*. Oxford: Oxford University Press, 2009.

———. "The Languages of Occupation: Vocabularies of German Rule in Eastern Europe in the World Wars." In *Germans, Poland, and Colonial Expansion to the East*, edited by Robert L. Nelson. New York: Palgrave Macmillan, 2009.

———. *War Land on the Eastern Front*. Cambridge: Cambridge University Press, 2000.

Livingstone, David N. "Science and Society: Nathaniel S. Shaler and Racial Ideology." *Transactions of the Institute of British Geographers, New Series* 9, no. 2 (1984): 181–210.

Llanque, Martin. *Demokratisches Denken im Krieg: Die deutsche Debatte im Ersten Weltkrieg*. Berlin: Akademie-Verlag, 2000.

Lorenzen, Hendrik. "Stereotypen des kolonialen Diskurses in Deutschland und ihre innenpolitische Funktionalisierung bei den 'Hottentottenwahlen' 1907." Master's thesis, Universität Hamburg, 1991.

Lower, Wendy. *Nazi Empire-Building and the Holocaust in the Ukraine*. Chapel Hill: University of North Carolina Press, 2005.

Lutz, Hartmut. "German Indianthusiasm: A Socially Constructed German National(ist) Myth." In *Germans and Indians. Fantasies, Encounters, Projections*, edited by Colin G Calloway, Gerd Gemünden, and Susanne Zantop. Lincoln: University of Nebraska Press, 2002.

Madley, Benjamin. "California's Yuki Indians: Defining Genocide in Native American History." *Western Historical Quarterly* 39, no. 3 (2008).

———. "From Africa to Auschwitz: How German Southwest Africa Incubated Ideas and Methods Adopted and Developed by the Nazis in Eastern Europe." *European History Quarterly* 35, no. 3 (2005).

———. "Patterns of Frontier Genocide 1803–1910." *Journal of Genocide Research* 6, no. 2 (2004): 167–92.

Madsen, Deborah L. *American Exceptionalism*. Edinburgh: Edinburgh University Press, 1998.

Maire, Camille. *Des Alsaciens-Lorrains otages en France: 1914–1918*. Strasbourg: Universitaires de Strasbourg, 1998.

Malinowski, Stephan, and Robert Gerwarth. "Der Holocaust als "kolonialer Genozid"? Europäische Kolonialgewalt und nationalsozialistischer Vernichtungskrieg." *Geschichte und Gesellschaft* 33 (2007): 439–66.

———. "Hannah Arendt's Ghosts: Reflections on the Disputable Path from Windhoek to Auschwitz." *Central European History* 42, no. 2 (2009): 279–300.

Mann, Gunter, and Franz Dumont. *Die Natur des Menschen, Soemmerring-Forschungen, Bd. 6.* Stuttgart: G. Fischer, 1990.

Marx, Karl. *A Contribution to the Critique of Political Economy,* 1859.

———. "Critique of the Hegelian Dialectic and Philosophy as a Whole." 1844.

Mauch, Christof. "Indianer und Schwarze aus deutscher Perspektive: Sichtweisen des 19. Jahrhunderts." *Amerikastudien* 40, no. 4 (1995).

Maull, Otto. *Die Vereinigten Staaten von Nordamerika als Großreich.* Berlin: De Gruyter, 1940.

May, Karl. *Winnetou I.* Bamberg: Bayerische Verlagsanstalt, [1892] 1950.

Mazower, Mark. *Hitler's Empire: Nazi Rule in Occupied Europe.* London: Penguin Books, 2009.

Mehring, Franz. "Nach den Wahlen." *Die Neue Zeit: Wochenschrift der deutschen Sozialdemokratie* 25, no. 1 (1907): 649–52.

Mehring, Reinhard. *Carl Schmitt: Aufstieg und Fall.* Munich: C. H. Beck, 2009.

———. "Schmitt, Carl." *Neue Deutsche Biographie [Onlinefassung]* 23 (2007): 236–38.

Meiners, Christoph. *Geschichte der Ungleichheit der Stände unter den vornehmsten europäischen Völkern.* 2 vols. Hannover: Im Verlage der Helwingischen Buchhandlung, 1792.

———. "Über die Bevölkerung von America." *Göttingisches Historisches Magazin* 3 (1788).

———. "Über die Natur der Americaner." *Göttingisches Historisches Magazin* 2 (1790).

———. "Über die Rechtmässigkeit des Negern-Handels." *Göttingisches Historisches Magazin* 2 (1788): 398–416.

———. "Ueber die Ursachen des Despotismus." *Göttingisches Historisches Magazin* 2 (1788): 193–229.

———. "Zweyte Abhandlung über die Natur der Americaner." *Göttingisches Historisches Magazin* 2 (1790).

Menges, Franz. "Josef Mengele." In *Allgemeine deutsche Biographie & Neue deutsche Biographie.* Berlin: Pütter–Rohlfs, 1994.

Michael, John S., and Stephen Jay Gould. "A New Look at Morton's Craniological Research." *Current Anthropology* 29, no. 2 (1988): 349–54.

Missions-Gesellschaft, Rheinische. *Berichte der Rheinischen Missionsgesellschaft.*, Vol. 52. Barmen: 1896.

Mogk, Walter. *Paul Rohrbach und das 'Größere Deutschland': Ethischer Imperialismus im Wilhelminischen Zeitalter.* Munich: Wilhelm Goldmann Verlag, 1972.

Mommsen, Wolfgang J. *Das Ringen um den nationalen Staat. Die Gründung und der innere Ausbau des Deutschen Reiches unter Otto von Bismarck 1850 bis 1890.* Berlin: Propyläen Verlag, 1993.

———. *Max Weber and German Politics: 1890–1920.* Chicago: University of Chicago Press, [1959] 1984.

———. "Wandlung der Liberalen Idee im Zeitalter des Imperialismus." In *Liberalismus und imperialistischer Staat. Der Imperialismus als Problem liberaler Parteien in Deutschland*, edited by K. Holl and G. List. Göttingen: Vandenhoeck & Ruprecht, 1975.

Moses, Dirk A. "Hannah Arendt, Imperialisms, and the Holocaust." In *German Colonialism: Race, the Holocaust, and Postwar Germany*, edited by Volker Langbehn and Mohammad Salama. New York: Columbia University Press, 2011.

Müller, Frank Lorenz. "Imperialist Ambitions in Vormärz and Revolutionary Germany: The Agitation for German Settlement Colonies Overseas, 1840–1849." *German History* 17, no. 3 (1999): 346–68.

Müller, Thomas. *Imaginierter Westen: Das Konzept des "deutschen Westraums" im völkischen Diskurs zwischen politischer Romantik und Nationalsozialismus.* Bielefeld: Transcript, 2009.

Naranch, Bradley. *"Global Proletarians, Uncle Toms, and Native Savages: The Antinomies of Black Identity in Nineteenth-Century* Germany." Paper presented at the Black Diaspora and Germany across the Centuries Conference, German Historical Institute, Washington, DC, 2009.

———. "Made in China: Austro-Prussian Overseas Rivalry and the Global Unification of the German Nation." *Australian Journal of Politics and History* 56, no. 3 (2010).

Nelson, Robert L. "The 'Archive for Inner Colonization,' the German East and World War I." In *Germans, Poland, and Colonial Expansion to the East*, edited by Robert L. Nelson. New York: Palgrave MacMillan, 2009.

———. "From Manitoba to the Memel: Max Sering, Inner Colonization and the German East." *Social History* 35, no. 4 (2010).

Nichols, Roger L. "Western Attractions: Europeans and America." *Pacific Historical Review* 74, no. 1 (2005): 1–17.

Nipperdey, Thomas. *Deutsche Geschichte 1866–1918. Vol. II – Macht-staat und Demokratie.* Munich: C. H. Beck, 1992.

Nolan, Mary. *Visions of Modernity.* New York: Oxford University Press, 1994.

Noske, Gustav. *Kolonialpolitik und Sozialdemokratie.* Stuttgart: J. H. W. Dietz, 1914.

Noyes, John K. "Commerce, Colonialism, and the Globalization of Action in Late Enlightenment Germany." *Postcolonial Studies* 9, no. 1 (2006): 81–98.

Osterhammel, Jürgen. *Europe, the "West" and the Civilizing Mission.* London: German Historical Institute, 2005.

———. *Liberalismus als kulturelle Revolution: Die widersprüchliche Weltwirkung einer euroäischen Idee.* Stuttgart: Stiftung Bundespräsident-Theodor-Heuss-Haus, 2003.

Otto, Viktor. *Deutsche Amerika-Bilder. Zu den Intellektuellen-Diskursen um die Moderne 1900–1950.* Munich: Wilhelm Fink, 2006.

Painter, Nell Irvin. "Why White People Are Called 'Caucasian?'" Paper presented at the Fifth Annual Gilder Lehrman Center International Conference: Collective Degradation: Slavery and the Construction of Race, Yale University, November 7–8 2003.

Parry, Richard. "'In a Sense Citizens, but Not Altogether Citizens . . . ': Rhodes, Race, and the Ideology of Segregation at the Cape in the Late Nineteenth Century." *Canadian Journal of African Studies* 17, no. 3 (1983).

Pautz, Hartwig. "The Politics of Identity in Germany: The Leitkultur Debate." *Race & Class* 46, no. 4 (2005): 39–52.

Penny, H. Glenn. "Elusive Authenticity: The Quest for the Authentic Indian in German Public Culture." *Comparative Studies in Society and History* 48, no. 4 (2006): 798–818.

———. "Illustrating America. Images of the North American Wild West in German Periodicals, 1825–1890." In *I like America: Fictions of the Wild West,* edited by Pamela Kort and Max Hollein. Munich: Prestel, 2006.

Perras, Arne. *Carl Peters and German Imperialism, 1856–1918.* Oxford: Clarendon Press, 2004.

Perraudin, Michael, and Jürgen Zimmerer, eds. *German Colonialism and National Identity.* Milton Park: Routledge, 2011.

Peters, Carl. *Carl Peters gesammelte Schriften.* Edited by Walter Frank. 3 vols. München/Berlin: C. H. Beck'sche Verlagsbuchhandlung, 1943–44.

Peukert, Detlev. *The Weimar Republic: The Crisis of Classical Modernity.* New York: Hill and Wang, 1992.

Pfeiffer, Ida. *A Lady's Second Journey Round the World*. New York: Harper, 1856.

_____. *A Lady's Visit to California, Biobooks no. 23*. Oakland: Biobooks, 1950.

_____. *Reise in die Neue Welt: Amerika im Jahre 1853*. Wien: Promedia, 1994.

_____. *A Lady's Travels around the World*. London: George Routledge & Co, 1852.

Pitts, Jennifer. *A Turn to Empire: The Rise of Imperial Liberalism in Britain and France*. Princeton: Princeton University Press, 2005.

Pitts, Jennifer, and Alexis de Tocqueville. *Writings on Empire and Slavery*. Baltimore: Johns Hopkins University Press, 2001.

Poley, Jared. *Decolonization in Germany: Weimar Narratives of Colonial Loss and Foreign Occupation*. Bern: Peter Lang, 2005.

Ratzel, Friedrich. *Dr. A Petermanns Mitteilungen aus Justus Perthes Geographischer. Anstalt* 41 (1895).

_____. *Anthropogeographie*, 2nd ed. Stuttgart: J. Engelhorn, 1899.

_____. *Culturgeographie der Vereinigten Staaten von Nordamerika unter besonderer Berücksichtigung der wirtschaftlichen Verhältnisse*, 2 vols. Munich, 1880.

_____. *Der Lebensraum: Eine biogeographische Studie*. Darmstadt: Wissenschaftliche Buchgemeinschaft, [1901] 1966.

_____. *Der Staat und sein Boden geographisch betrachtet*. Leipzig: S. Hirzel, 1896.

_____. *Die Vereinigten Staaten von Amerika*, 2nd ed., vol. 2. Munich: R. Oldenbourg, 1893.

_____. *Die Vereinigten Staaten von Nord-Amerika*. 2 vols. Munich: R. Oldenbourg, 1878.

_____. *Physikalische Geographie und Naturcharakter der Vereinigten Staaten von Nord-Amerika*. Munich, 1878.

_____. *Politische Geographie*. Munich: R. Oldenbourg, 1897.

_____. *Politische Geographie der Vereinigten Staaten von Amerika*. 2. Aufl. ed. 2 vols. Munich: R. Oldenbourg, 1893.

_____. *Sketches of Urban and Cultural Life in North America*. Edited by Stewart A. Stehlin. New Brunswick: Rutgers University Press, [1876] 1988.

_____. *Städte und Culturbilder aus Nordamerika*. 2 vols. Leipzig: F. A. Brockhaus, 1876.

_____. "Über allgemeine Eigenschaften der geographischen Grenzen und über die politischen Grenzen." *Berichte über die Verhandlungen der Königlich Sächsischen Gesellschaft der Wissenschaften zu Leizpig, Philologisch-Historische Klasse* 44 (1892): 53–105.

————. *Wider die Reichsnörgler: Ein Wort zur Kolonialfrage aus Wählerkreisen.* Munich, 1884.

Ratzel, Friedrich, and Karl Haushofer. *Erdenmacht und Völkerschicksal; eine Auswahl aus seinen Werken.* Stuttgart: A. Kröner, 1940.

Rauh, Manfred. *Die Parlamentarisierung des Deutschen Reiches.* Düsseldorf: Droste, 1977.

————. *Föderalismus und Parlamentarismus im Wilhelminischen Reich.* Düsseldorf: Droste, 1973.

Raumer, Friedrich et al. *Reisen durch die Vereinigten Staaten von Nordamerika.* Leipzig: Verlag von August Weichardt, 1848.

Reismann-Grone, Theodor, and Eduard von Liebert. "Überseepolitik oder Festlandspolitik?" Paper presented at the Alldeutscher Verbandstag, Worms 1905.

Repp, Kevin. *Reformers, Critics, and the Paths of German Modernity: Anti-Politics and the Search for Alternatives, 1890–1914.* Cambridge, MA: Harvard University Press, 2000.

Ritter, Gerhard A. "Bernhard Dernburg." In *Allgemeine deutsche Biographie & Neue deutsche Biographie* Berlin: Bürklein–Ditmar, 1957.

Rodgers, Daniel T. *Atlantic Crossings: Social Politics in a Progressive Age.* Cambridge, MA: Harvard University Press, 1998.

Rohrbach, Paul. *Amerika und wir. Reisebetrachtungen von Paul Rohrbach.* Berlin: Buchenau & Reichert Verlag, 1926.

————. *Der deutsche Gedanke in der Welt.* Königstein: Langewiesche, 1915.

————. *Deutschland! Tod oder Leben?* Munich: F. Bruckmann A.G., 1930.

————. *Die alldeutsche Gefahr.* Edited by Martin Hobohm. Berlin: Verlag von Hans Robert Engelmann, 1918.

————. *Herr Reichskanzler von Papen – Lösen Sie auf!* Munich: Im Selbstverlag, 1932.

————. *Monarchie, Republik und politische Parteien in Deutschland.* Stuttgart: J. Engelhorns Nachf, 1920.

————. *Osteuropa historisch-politisch gesehen.* Potsdam: Rütten & Loening Verlag, 1942.

————. "Protestanten, Nichtkatholiken, wählt Zentrum!" *Kölnische Volkszeitung*, June 26, 1932.

Rosenberg, Alfred. *Der Mythus des 20. Jahrhunderts.* Munich: Hoheneichen-Verlag, 1933.

Rössler, Mechthild, and Sabine Schleiermacher. *Der "Generalplan Ost": Hauptlinien der nationalsozialistischen Planungs- und Vernichtungspolitik.* Berlin: Akademie-Verlag, 1993.

Rupp-Eisenreich, Britta. "Choses occultes en histoire des sciences humaines: le destin de la 'science nouvelle' de Christoph Meiners." *Ethnographie* 90–91 (1983): 131–83.

Salz, Arthur. "Der Imperialismus der Vereinigten Staaten." *Archiv für Sozialwissenschaft und Sozialpolitik* 50, no. 3 (1923): 565–616.

Sammons, Jeffrey L. *Ideology, Mimesis, Fantasy: Charles Sealsfield, Friedrich Gerstäcker, Karl May, and Other German Novelists of America*. Chapel Hill: University of North Carolina Press, 1998.

———. "Nineteenth-Century German Representations of Indians from Experience." In *Germans and Indians: Fantasies, Encounters, Projections*, edited by Colin G. Calloway, Gerd Gemünden, and Susanne Zantop Lincoln: University of Nebraska Press, 2002.

Sarrazin, Thilo. *Deutschland schafft sich ab. Wie wir unser Land aufs Spiel setzen*. Munich: Deutsche Verlags-Anstalt, 2010.

Schaller, Dominik J. "From Conquest to Genocide: Colonial Rule in German Southwest Africa and German East Africa." In *Empire, Colony, Genocide. Conquest, Occupation, and Subaltern Resistance in World History*, edited by A. Dirk Moses. New York: Berghahn Books, 2008.

Schiebinger, Londa L. "The Anatomy of Difference." *Eighteenth-Century Studies* 23, no. 4 (1990).

———.*The Mind Has No Sex? Women in the Origins of Modern Science*. Cambridge, MA: Harvard University Press, 1989.

Schippel, Max. "Die Schicksalsstunde der deutschen Kolonien." *Sozialistische Monatshefte* 25, no. 3 (1919).

Schmidt, Alexander. *Reisen in die Moderne*. Berlin: Akademie Verlag, 1997.

Schmitt, Carl. *Völkerrechtliche Grossraumordnung*. Berlin: Deutscher Rechtsverlag, 1941.

Schmoller, Gustav et al., eds. *Kolonialpolitischer Führer*. Berlin: Wedekind, 1907.

Schorske, Carl. *German Social Democracy, 1905–1917: The Development of the Great Schism*. Cambridge, MA: Harvard University Press, 1955.

Schriewer, Jürgen "Paul de Lagarde." In *Allgemeine deutsche Biographie & Neue deutsche Biographie*. Berlin: Krell–Laven, 1982.

Schröder, Hans-Christoph. *Gustav Noske und die Kolonialpolitik des Deutschen Kaiserreichs*. Berlin: Dietz, 1979.

———. *Sozialismus und Imperialismus*. Hannover: Verlag für Literatur und Zeitgeschehen, 1968.

Schubert, Günter. *Anfänge nationalsozialistischer Aussenpolitik*. Cologne: Verlag Wissenschaft und Politik, 1963.

Schulz, Gerhard. "Nationalpatriotismus im Widerstand." *Vierteljahreshefte für Zeitgeschichte* 32, no. 3 (1984).

Sering, Max. *Die innere Kolonisation im östlichen Deutschland.* Leipzig: Duncker & Humblot, 1893.

———. *Die landwirthschaftliche Konkurrenz Nordamerikas in Gegenwart und Zukunft.* Leipzig: Duncker & Humblot, 1887.

Shafer, Byron E. *Is America Different?: A New Look at American Exceptionalism.* Oxford: Oxford University Press, 1991.

Sheehan, James J. *The Career of Lujo Brentano: A Study of Liberalism and Social Reform in Imperial Germany.* Chicago: University of Chicago Press, 1966.

———. *German Liberalism in the Nineteenth Century.* Chicago: University of Chicago Press, 1978.

Sieg, Ulrich. *Deutschlands Prophet: Paul de Lagarde und die Ursprünge des modernen Antisemitismus.* München: Hanser, 2007.

Simo, David. "Colonization and Modernization: The Legal Foundation of the Colonial Enterprise; A Case Study of German Colonization in Cameroon." In *Germany's Colonial Past*, edited by Eric Ames, Marcia Klotz, and Lora Wildenthal. Lincoln: University of Nebraska Press, 2005.

Sippel, Harald. "Rechtspolitische Ansätze zur Vermeidung einer Mischlingsbevölkerung." In *Rassenmischehen – Mischlinge – Rassentrennung*, edited by Frank Becker. Stuttgart: Franz Steiner Verlag, 2004.

Slotkin, Richard. "Buffalo Bill's 'Wild West' and the Mythologization of the American Empire." In *Cultures of United States Imperialism*, edited by Amy Kaplan and Donald E. Pease. Durham: Duke University Press, 1993.

Smith, Helmut Walser. *The Continuities of German History: Nation, Religion, and Race Across the Long Nineteenth Century.* New York: Cambridge University Press, 2008.

———. "Jenseits der Sonderwegdebatte." In *Das Deutsche Kaiserreich in der Kontroverse*, edited by Sven Oliver Müller and Cornelius Torp. Göttingen: Vandenhoeck & Ruprecht, 2009.

———. "The Logic of Colonial Violence: Germany in Southwest Africa (1904–1907); the United States in the Philippines (1899–1902)." In *German and American Nationalism: A Comparative Perspective*, edited by Hartmut Lehmann and Hermann Wellenreuther. New York: Berg, 1999.

———. "The Talk of Genocide, the Rhetoric of Miscegenation: Notes on the Debates in the German Reichstag Concerning Southwest Africa, 1904–14." In *The Imperialist Imagination: German Colonialism and its Legacy*, edited by Sara Friedrichsmeyer, Sara Lennox, and Susanne Zantop. Ann Arbor: University of Michigan Press, 1998.

Smith, Neil. *American Empire: Roosevelt's Geographer and the Prelude to Globalization.* Berkeley: University of California Press, 2003.

Smith, William Benjamin. *The Color Line: A Brief on Behalf of the Unborn.* New York: McClure, Phillips & CO., 1905.

Smith, Woodruff D. "Friedrich Ratzel and the Origins of 'Lebensraum.'" *German Studies Review* 3, no. 1 (1980): 51–68.

———. *The Ideological Origins of Nazi Imperialism.* New York: Oxford University Press, 1986.

———. *Politics and the Sciences of Culture in Germany, 1840–1920.* New York: Oxford University Press, 1991.

———. "'Weltpolitik' und 'Lebensraum.'" In *Das Kaiserreich transnational: Deutschland in der Welt 1871–1914.* Göttingen: Vandenhoeck & Ruprecht, 2004.

Sobich, Frank Oliver. *"Schwarze Bestien, Rote Gefahr": Rassismus und Antisozialismus im Deutschen Kaiserreich.* Frankfurt a. M.: Campus Verlag, 2006.

Sperber, Jonathan. "Comments on Marcus Kreuzer's Article." *Central European History* 36, no. 3 (2003): 359–66.

Steenson, Gary. *"Not One Man! Not One Penny!" German Social Democracy, 1863–1914.* Pittsburgh: University of Pittsburgh Press, 1981.

Stehlin, Stewart A. "Introduction." In *Sketches of Urban and Cultural Life in North America.* New Brunswick: Rutgers University Press, 1988.

Steinberg, Hans-Josef. *Sozialismus und deutsche Sozialdemokratie.* Berlin: J. H. W. Dietz Nachf. GmbH, 1976.

Steinmetz, George. *The Devil's Handwriting: Precoloniality and the German Colonial State in Qingdao, Samoa, and Southwest Africa.* Chicago: University of Chicago Press, 2007.

———. "Return to Empire: The New U.S. Imperialism in Comparative-Historical Perspective." *Sociological Theory* 23, no. 4 (2005).

Steinwallner, Bruno. "Rassenhygienische Gesetzgebung und Maßnahmen im Ausland. 2. Teil. Rassenhygienische Gesetzgebung und Maßnahmen förderlicher Art." *Fortschritte der Erbpathologie, Rassenhygiene und ihrer Grenzgebiete* III (1939).

Steinweis, Alan E. "Eastern Europe and the Notion of the 'Frontier' in Germany to 1945." *Yearbook of European Studies* 13 (1999): 56–70.

Stocking Jr., George W. *Victorian Anthropology.* London: Collier Macmillan, 1987.

Stone, Dan, and Richard H. King. *Hannah Arendt and the Uses of History: Imperialism, Nation, Race, and Genocide.* New York: Berghahn Books, 2007.

Strandmann, H. Pogge von. "Domestic Origins of Germany's Colonial Expansion under Bismarck." *Past and Present* 42, no. 1 (1969): 140–59.

———. *Imperialismus vom grünen Tisch.* Berlin: Ch. Links Verlag, 2009.

———. "The Purpose of German Colonialism, or the Long Shadow of Bismarck's Colonial Policy." In *German Colonialism: Race, the Holocaust, and Postwar Germany*, edited by Volker Langbehn and Mohammad Salama. New York: Columbia University Press, 2011.

Stroever, Carl. "Treibende Kräfte amerikanischer Kolonialpolitik." *Beiträge zur Kolonialpolitik und Kolonialwirtschaft* (1900–01): 129–33.

Sullivan, Eileen P. "Liberalism and Imperialism: J. S. Mill's Defense of the British Empire." *Journal of the History of Ideas* 44, no. 4 (1983): 599–617.

Taylor, A. J. P. *Germany's First Bid for Colonies 1884–1885: A Move in Bismarck's European Policy.* New York: Norton, 1970.

Terra, Helmut de. "Alexander von Humboldt's Correspondence with Jefferson, Madison, and Gallatin." *Proceedings of the American Philosophical Society* 103, no. 6 (1959).

Thompson, David. *Europe since Napoleon.* New York: Alfred A. Knopf, 1962.

Thörner, Klaus. "'Der ganze Südosten ist unser Hinterland.' Deutsche Südosteuropapläne von 1840 bis 1945." Oldenburg: Carl von Ossietzky Universität, 1999.

Tocqueville, Alexis de. *Democracy in America.* New York: Random House, 1981.

Tooze, Adam. *The Wages of Destruction: The Making and Breaking of the Nazi Economy.* New York: Viking, 2007.

Torp, Cornelius. *Max Weber und die preußischen Junker.* Tübingen: J. C. B. Mohr, 1998.

Torp, Cornelius, and Sven Oliver Müller. *Das Deutsche Kaiserreich in der Kontroverse.* Göttingen: Vandenhoeck & Ruprecht, 2009.

———. *Imperial Germany Revisited: Continuing Debates and New Perspectives.* New York: Berghahn Books, 2011.

Trevor-Roper, Hugh R., ed. *Hitler's Table Talk, 1941–1944: His Private Conversations.* New York: Enigma Books, 1953.

Turner Bushnell, Amy. *Establishing Exceptionalism: Historiography and the Colonial Americas. Vol. 5: An Expanding World.* Aldershot: Variorum, 1995.

Turner, Frederick Jackson. "American Colonization." In *The Eloquence of Frederick Jackson Turner*, edited by Ronald H. Carpenter. San Marino: Huntington Library, [1893] 1983.

———. "Geographic Influences in American History (Book Review)." *Journal of Geography* 4 (1905): 34–37.

Van Alstyne, R.W. *The Rising American Empire*. Oxford: Basil Blackwell, 1960.

von Ruville, A. "Die Eingeborenen-Politik der großen Kolonialmächte."
Preußische Jahrbücher 104 (1901): 38–69.

von Unruh, Georg Christoph. "Nordamerikanische Einfluesse auf die
deutsche Verfassungentwicklung." *Deutsches Verwaltungsblatt* 91
(1976).

Walkenhorst, Peter. *Nation – Volk – Rasse. Radikaler Nationalismus
im Deutschen Kaiserreich 1890–1914*. Göttingen: Vandenhoeck &
Ruprecht, 2007.

Walker, Mack. *Germany and the Emigration, 1816–1885*. Cambridge,
Mass.: Harvard University Press, 1964.

Ward, Julie K., and Tommy Lee Lott. *Philosophers on Race: Critical
Essays*. Oxford: Blackwell, 2002.

Warneck, Gustav. *Die gegenwärtige Lage der deutschen evangelischen
Mission*. Berlin: Martin Warneck, 1905.

Washausen, H. *Hamburg und die Kolonialpolitik des Deutschen
Reiches, 1880 bis 1890*. Hamburg: Christians, 1968.

Weaver, Walter P. *The Historical Jesus in the Twentieth Century*. Harrisburg, PA: Trinity Press, 1999.

Weber, Marianne. *Max Weber: A Biography*. New Brunswick: Transaction Publishers, 1988.

Weber, Max. *Der Nationalstaat und die Volkswirtschaftspolitik:
Akademische Antrittsrede*. Freiburg: Akademische Verlagsbuchhandlung von J. C. B. Mohr, 1895.

Wehler, Hans Ulrich. *Bismarck und der Imperialismus*. Köln: Kiepenheuer u. Witsch, 1969.

———. "Bismarck's Imperialism." In *Imperial Germany*, edited by
James Sheehan. New York: Franklin Watts, 1976, 180–222.

———. "Ein Buch trifft ins Schwarze." *Die Zeit*, October 9, 2010.

———. *The German Empire, 1871–1918*. Dover, NH: Berg Publishers,
[1973] 1985.

———. *Imperialismus*. Köln: Kiepenheuer & Witsch, 1970.

———. *Sozialdemokratie und Nationalstaat: Nationalitätenfragen in
Deutschland 1840–1914*. Göttingen: Vandenhoeck & Ruprecht,
1971.

———. "Sozialimperialismus." In *Escape into War? The Foreign Policy
of Imperial Germany*, edited by Gregor Schöllgen. London: Berg,
1990.

Weikart, Richard. *From Darwin to Hitler: Evolutionary Ethics, Eugenics, and Racism in Germany*. New York: Palgrave Macmillan,
2004.

————. "Progress through Racial Extermination: Social Darwinism, Eugenics, and Pacifism in Germany, 1860–1918." *German Studies Review* 26, no. 2 (2003): 273–94.

Weinberg, Gerhard L. "Hitler's Image of the United States." *American Historical Review* 69, no. 4 (1964).

Weinberger, Gerda. "Die deutsche Sozialdemokratie und die Kolonialpolitik." *Zeitschrift für Geschichtswissenschaft* 15, no. 3 (1967): 402–23.

Wellenreuther, Hermann, and Elisabeth Gläser. *Bridging the Atlantic: Publications of the German Historical Institute.* New York: Cambridge University Press, 2000.

Wesseling, Hendrik L. *Teile und herrsche. Die Aufteilung Afrikas 1880–1914.* Stuttgart: Franz Steiner Verlag, 1999.

Wigard, Franz. *Stenographischer Bericht über die Verhandlungen der deutschen constituirenden Nationalversammlung zu Frankfurt am Main.* Frankfurt a. M.: 1848–49.

Wigger, Iris. *Die "Schwarze Schmach am Rhein": Rassistische Diskriminierung zwischen Geschlecht, Klasse, Nation und Rasse.* Münster: Westfälisches Dampfboot, 2007.

Winkler, Heinrich August. *Preussischer Liberalismus und deutscher Nationalstaat: Studien zur Geschichte der Deutschen Fortschrittspartei, 1861–1866.* Tubingen: Mohr, 1964.

Wildenthal, Lora. *German Women for Empire, 1884–1945.* Durham: Duke University Press, 2001.

————. "'She Is the Victor': Bourgeois Women, Nationalist Identities, and the Ideal of the Independent Woman Farmer in German Southwest Africa." In *Society, Culture, and the State in Germany 1870–1930*, edited by Geoff Eley. Ann Arbor: University of Michigan Press, 1997.

Wildenthal, Lora, Eric Ames, and Marcia Klotz, eds. *Germany's Colonial Pasts.* Lincoln: University of Nebraska Press, 2005.

Wilder, Gary. *The French Imperial Nation State: Negritude and Colonial Humanism between the Two World Wars.* Chicago: University of Chicago Press, 2005.

Williams, William Appleman. "The Frontier Thesis and American Foreign Policy." *Pacific Historical Review* 24 (1955): 379–95.

Winkler, Heinrich August. *Germany: The Long Road West.* New York: Oxford University Press, 2007.

Wirth, Albrecht. *Das Wachstum der Vereinigten Staaten von Nordamerika und ihre auswärtige Politik.* Bonn: Universitäts-Buchdruckerei von Carl Georgi, 1899.

Wirth, Eduard. "Die jüngste Entwicklung Nordamerikas." *Beiträge zur Kolonialpolitik und Kolonialwirtschaft* (1900–01): 609–11.

Wölky, Guido. "Roscher, Waitz, Bluntschli und Treitschke als Politikwissenschaftler. Spätblüte und Untergang eines klassischen Universitätsfaches in der zweiten Hälfte des 19. Jahrhunderts." Ph.D. dissertation, Ruhr Universität Bochum, 2006.

Wood, Gordon S. *Empire of Liberty: A History of the Early Republic, 1789–1815.* Oxford: Oxford University Press, 2010.

Woodward, C. Vann. *Origins of the New South, 1877–1913.* Baton Rouge: Louisiana State University Press, 1951.

Wrobel, David M. *The End of American Exceptionalism.* Lawrence: University Press of Kansas, 1993.

Zantop, Susanne. "The Beautiful, the Ugly, and the German: Race, Gender and Nationality in Eighteenth-Century Anthropological Discourse." In *Gender and Germanness*, edited by Patricia Herrringhouse. Providence: Berghahn, 1997.

———. *Colonial Fantasies: Conquest, Family, and Nation in Precolonial Germany, 1770–1870.* Durham: Duke University Press, 1997.

———. "Close Encounters: Deutsche and Indianer." In *Germans and Indians: Fantasies, Encounters, Projections* Edited by Colin G. Calloway, Gerd Gemünden, and Susanne Zantop. Lincoln: University of Nebraska Press, 2002.

———."'Der Indianer' im Rasse- und Geschlechterdiskurs der deutschen Spätaufklärung." In *Das Subjekt und die Anderen: Interkulturalität und Geschlechterdifferenz vom 18. Jahrhundert bis zur Gegenwart*, edited by Viktoria Schmidt-Linsenhoff. Berlin: Erich Schmidt, 2001.

Zimmerer, Jürgen. "The Birth of the Ostland out of the Spirit of Colonialism: A Postcolonial Perspective on the Nazi Policy of Conquest and Extermination." *Patterns of Prejudice* 39, no. 2 (2005): 197–219.

———. *Deutsche Herrschaft über Afrikaner.* Münster: Lit, 2001.

———. "Holocaust und Kolonialismus: Beitrag zu einer Archäologie des genozidalen Denkens." *Zeitschrift für Geschichtswissenschaft* 51, no. 12 (2003): 1098–119.

———. "Kein Sonderweg im 'Rassekrieg'. Der Genozid an den Herero und Nama 1904–08 zwischen deutschen Kontinuitäten und der Globalgeschichte der Massengewalt." In *Das Deutsche Kaiserreich in der Kontroverse*, edited by Sven Oliver Müller and Cornelius Torp. Göttingen: Vandenhoeck & Ruprecht, 2009.

———. "Krieg, KZ und Völkermord in Südwestafrika." In *Völkermord in Deutsch-Südwestafrika. Der Kolonialkrieg (1904–08) in Namibia und seine Folgen*, edited by Jürgen Zimmerer and Joachim Zeller. Berlin: Links, 2003.

———. "Von Windhuk nach Warschau. Die rassische Privilegiengesellschaft in Deutsch-Südwestafrika, ein Modell mit Zukunft?" In *Rassenmischehen – Mischlinge – Rassentrennung. Zur Politk der Rasse im deutschen Kolonialreich*, edited by Frank Becker. Stuttgart: Franz Steiner Verlag, 2004.

Zimmerman, Andrew. *Alabama in Africa: Booker T. Washington, the German Empire, and the Globalization of the New South*. Princeton: Princeton University Press, 2010.

———. *Anthropology and Antihumanism in Imperial Germany*. Chicago: University of Chicago Press, 2001.

———. "Decolonizing Weber." *Postcolonial Studies* 9, no. 1 (2006): 53–79.

———. "A German Alabama in Africa: The Tuskegee Expedition to German Togo and the Transnational Origins of West African Cotton Growers." *American Historical Review* 110 (2005): 1362–98.

———. "The German Empire, the Atlantic Revolutions of the Nineteenth Century, and the Colonial Construction of the Precolonial." Paper presented at the Conference: German Post-Colonial History in a Global Age, Free University Berlin 2011.

Zimmermann, Peter. "Kampf um den 'Lebensraum'. Ein Mythos der Kolonial- und der Blut-und-Boden-Literatur." In *Die deutsche Literatur im Dritten Reich*, edited by Horst Denkler and Karl Prumm. Stuttgart: Philipp Reclam, 1976.

Zitelmann, Rainer. *Nationalsozialismus und Modernisierung*. Darmstadt: Wissenschaftliche Buchgemeinschaft, 1994.

Zorn, Wolfgang, and Werner Conze. *Die Protokolle des Volkswirtschaftlichen Ausschusses der deutschen Nationalversammlung 1848/49*. Boppard am Rhein: Harald Boldt Verlag, 1992.

Index

Aboriginal peoples, 56, 80, 84, 86, 91, 121. *See also* Native Americans
Academics, 3, 161, 177–179, 182–184, 190, 202, 204, 206
Academy of Natural Sciences, 65
Adorno, Theodor, 33, 219, 223–224
Africa. *See also specific colony*
 colonization of, 88, 109, 187–188, 229
 German expansionism and, 192
 Nazi regime and, 187–188
African-Americans
 Allied occupation of Rhineland and, 176
 colonialism and, 48–50
 German views of, 60, 65, 89, 92, 215
 Jim Crow laws (*See* Jim Crow laws)
 liberalism and, 40
 miscegenation laws, 137, 142, 146, 148–149
 slavery (*See* Slavery)
Aimard, Gustave, 86
Alabama, 140
Alabama in Africa (Zimmerman), 10, 128
Albers, Hans, 169

Algeria, French expansionism in, 34, 46, 87
Algiers, 46
Alldeutscher Verband. *See* Pan-German League
American Civil War, 29
American exceptionalism, 6, 36, 87–88, 124
American Indians. *See* Native Americans
American Jewish Congress, 198
American Slavery, American Freedom (Morgan), 54
American South
 miscegenation laws in, 137, 142, 146, 148
 race codes in, 17, 129, 132, 134, 137, 142, 146, 148, 152, 154–155, 158
 segregation in, 232
American West
 Eastern Europe compared, 184, 207–216
 German Southwest Africa compared, 80–81, 86
 Nazi regime and, 207–216
 possibility of German colonization in, 57–58, 66–67, 70–76, 95, 192

American West (*cont.*)
  settler colonialism and, 57–59, 64,
    67, 112
  "Wild West" analogy, 16, 63–64,
    85, 101, 106, 164, 207–208
Amerika in Wort und Bild (Hellwald),
  92
Amerika und die großen Mächte
  (Oncken), 178
Anderson, Margaret Lavinia, 24–25,
  174
An die Kulturwelt (address), 183
Andrée, Karl, 12–13
Anglo-American colonization, 47, 72,
  86, 98–99, 107, 109, 135–136
Anglo-Saxons, 32
Anthropology, 34, 48
Anti-Corn Law movement (U.K.),
  60
Anti-Semitic Party, 102
Anti-Semitism
  generally, 23, 152–153
  expulsion of Jews from Prussia,
    164–165
  Holocaust, 22, 220, 224
  in Nazi regime, 195–196, 198,
    204–205, 212, 217, 219, 223
  Peters on, 37–38, 110, 168–169,
    172
Apache people, 92–93, 102
Arenberg, Franz von, 111
Arendt, Hannah, 35, 219, 228–232
Arizona, 92, 121
Arizona Miner (newspaper), 93
Asia, French expansionism in, 61
Association for Continuing Education
  in the Political Sciences, 153
Association for Social Policy, 173
Augsburger Allgemeine Zeitung
  (newspaper), 71
Das Ausland (journal), 42, 60, 62, 65,
  68, 74, 89–90, 93
Australia, colonization of, 88, 91,
  109, 120

Bamberger, Ludwig, 30, 168
Bebel, August, 107, 110–111, 115

Beer-Hall Putsch, 191
*Beiträge zur Kolonialpolitik und
  Kolonialwirtschaft* (journal), 42
Belgian Congo, 187
Belgium, loss of territory to, 6
*Bericht über eine Reise nach den
  westlichen Staaten
  Nord-Amerikas* (Duden), 59, 60
Berlin, University of, 103
Berliner Neueste Nachrichten
  (newspaper), 120
Berliner Staatsbibliotek, 41
Berlinische Monatsschrift (journal),
  54, 56
Bernhard (Duke), 43
Bethmann-Hollweg, Theobald von,
  23, 157, 184
Beveridge, Ray, 181–182
Billington, Ray Allen, 86, 92
Biology, 89, 91, 194, 204
Bismarck, Herbert von, 106
Bismarck, Otto von, 6, 30, 33, 68,
  77–78, 105–106, 138
Blackbourn, David, 15, 18, 24, 116,
  225
Blacks. *See* African-Americans
Blumenau, Hermann, 71–72
Blumenbach, Johann Friedrich, 64
Boers, 228
Bollmann, Dr., 54–56
Bourgeois morality, 36, 40, 77–78,
  102, 189, 193–194, 223, 225
Bourgeois utilitarianism, 50
Bourne, Randolph, 179
Bowman, Isaiah, 100
Boxer Rebellion, 187
Braband, Carl, 147
Brandenburg Gate, 231
Braun, Ernst Ludwig, 71
Brentano, Lorenz, 29–30, 190
Brentano, Lujo, 179–180
Brest-Litovsk Treaty, 164
Bülow, Albrecht von, 107
Bülow, Bernhard von, 113, 138
Bülow disaster, 107
Bundesarchiv, 41–42
Bundesrat, 132

Burnett, Peter, 93
"Bushmen," 120

California, 66–67, 72, 93, 203
Cameroon, 155
Canada, 63, 79
Cass, Lewis, 62, 65, 67, 76–77, 85,
        93
Center Party
    generally, 111, 139, 174
    miscegenation laws and, 131–132,
        151, 154–155, 157–158
    race codes and, 148–150
    representation in Reichstag,
        114–115, 147
    Rohrbach on, 185–186
    segregation and, 160
Central Europe, German hegemony
        in, 152–153, 177–178, 194
Césaire, Aimé, 224, 231
Chamberlain, Houston Stewart, 190
Chamberlain, Joseph, 104
Chamberlain, Neville, 104
Chartist movement (U.K.), 60
Cheyenne people, 101, 106
Chicago, 105, 146
Chickering, Roger, 20, 24
Christian-Social Party, 149, 152
Cincinnati, 46, 111
Civilization, 59–62, 67, 76, 90, 98,
        111, 117, 124–125
"Civilizing mission," 39
Civil War (U.S.), 29
Class, Heinrich, 23
Cody, "Buffalo Bill," 5, 101–102,
        106
Cold War, 9, 35, 224
Colonialism
    African-Americans and, 48–50
    Dernburg and, 1–2, 80, 84, 88,
        137–141, 169, 215–216
    de Tocqueville on, 40, 61, 63,
        98–99
    Hitler and, 186–188, 222
    labor question, 136–137
    Lebensraum as anti-colonialism,
        189–197

liberalism and, 39–41
liberty and, 44–55
Nazi regime, effect on, 218–223
    in Netherlands, 57
    Peters and, 79–80, 123, 135,
        165–169, 192, 207–208, 229
    post-World War II period, effect
        on, 224–232
    race and, 2, 4, 27–28, 31–35, 37,
        48–55
    Ratzel and, 73, 138–139, 169
    Rosenberg on, 188, 191–193, 222
    settler colonialism (*See* Settler
        colonialism)
    slavery and, 12–14, 49–56, 232
    Solf and, 116, 155–159, 169, 207,
        215–216
    in United Kingdom, 50–51, 57,
        77–78, 104
Colonization
    of Africa, 88, 109, 187–188, 229
    American West, possibility of
        German colonization in, 57–58,
        66–67, 70–76, 95, 192
    Anglo-American colonization, 47,
        72, 86, 98–99, 107, 109,
        135–136
    France, colonization in North
        America, 98
    "inner colonization," 63
    Prussia, possibility of colonization
        in, 17, 164–165, 170, 193, 227
    United Kingdom, colonization in
        North America, 98–99
Colorado, 123
*The Color Line: A Brief on Behalf
    of the Unborn* (Smith), 152–153
Confederacy, 141
Conrad, Sebastian, 10–12
Conservative Party, 114
Constitution (U.S.), 135, 213
Coolidge, Archibald Cary, 153–154,
        182
Cooper, James Fenimore, 85
Cotta (Baron), 71
Cotton, 141
Cronau, Rudolf, 92

Czechoslovakia
   annexation of, 198
   loss of territory to, 6

Dahrendorf, Ralf, 27–28, 220
Danzig, 168
Darré, Richard Walther, 20, 183,
   188, 192
Darwinism, 89–91, 119
Davis, David Brion, 54
Davis, William Morris, 100
The Decline of the West (Spengler),
   183
Decolonization, 26, 225–226
Decree on Preventing Hereditarily Ill
   Progeny, 203
Delbrück, Hans, 174, 184, 225
Democracy and expansionism, 44–55,
   96–97
Democracy in America (de
   Tocqueville), 61
Democratic Party (U.S.), 60
Denmark, loss of territory to, 6
Der deutsche Gedanke in der Welt
   (Rohrbach), 120
Dernburg, Bernhard
   generally, 131, 133, 144–145, 164,
      176, 190, 212
   colonialism and, 1–2, 80, 84, 88,
      137–141, 169, 215–216
   on German Southwest Africa,
      116–120, 125
   liberalism and, 16, 30, 37, 155,
      173–174, 206–207, 218, 225
   on Nazi regime, 185–187
"Dernburg turn," 139, 159, 221
Despotism, 52
*Deutsche Auswanderung und
   Colonisation* (Blumenau), 71
Deutsche Demokratische Partei, 131,
   185–188
Deutsche Fortschrittspartei, 30–31,
   68, 174
Deutsche Kolonialgesellschaft, 111
Deutsche Kolonialzeitung (journal),
   42, 111
Deutsche Reichspartei (National
   Party), 110–111, 114

Deutsche Vaterlandspartei. *See*
   Fatherland Party
Deutsche Volkspartei, 187
Deutschland schafft sich ab
   (Sarrazin), 226
The Dialectics of the Enlightenment
   (Adorno and Horkheimer), 219
Disraeli, Benjamin, 77
Dodd, William E., 178
Drang nach Osten, 15
Drechsler, Horst, 232
DuBois, W.E.B., 179
Duden, Gottfried, 12, 56, 59–60, 67

Eastern Europe. *See also Lebensraum*
   American West compared, 184,
      207–216
   Hitler and, 13–14
   Lebensraum and, 189–192
   Nazi regime and, 210–211
   occupation during World War I, 22
   "Ostreich," 210–211
   Pan-German League and, 164
   settler colonialism and, 162
   World War I, effect on German
      expansionism in, 161–174
Elbe River, 103
Eley, Geoff, 15, 18–20, 24, 31, 225
Eley, Richard T., 179
Emancipation Proclamation (U.S.),
   146, 155
Emigration to America, 59
Emin Pasha, 105
England. *See* United Kingdom
England und die Engländer (Peters),
   110
Enlightenment, 33, 39, 48, 52, 219
Epp, Franz Ritter von, 187–189
Equatoria (South Sudan), 105
*Erklärung der Hochschullehrer des
   Deutschen Reiches* (address),
   183
Erzberger, Matthias, 115, 131, 150
Estwick, Samuel, 49–50, 53
Ethnicism. *See* Race
Ethnography, 89
Eugenics, 100, 202–204
Evolution, 90

Expansionism
  Africa, German expansionism and, 192
  Algeria, French expansionism in, 34, 46, 87
  Asia, French expansionism in, 61
  democracy and, 44–55, 96–97
  de Tocqueville on, 34, 47, 53, 87–88
  Eastern Europe, effect of World War I on German expansionism in, 161–174
  France and, 77
  Hitler and, 19–20, 183
  industrialization and, 64
  liberalism and, 3, 6, 27–41
  national unity and, 69–78
  Nazi regime and, 6
  North Africa, French expansionism in, 46, 61, 107
  in Poland, 46–47, 169–174
  progress and, 55–69
  race and, 55–69
  Ratzel and, 2, 16, 124
  republicanism and, 44–55, 96–97
  Russia, German expansionism and, 162
  social control and, 55–69
  United Kingdom and, 50–51, 77–78
  Weber on, 97
  World War I, impact of, 18–27, 161–174
  World War II, German expansionism during, 22, 116, 162
Expulsion
  generally, 4, 80
  in German Southwest Africa, 120
  of Native Americans, 12, 34, 56, 68, 77
  of Poles and Russians, 165
Extinction, 4, 56, 68, 77, 81, 88, 117, 120, 220

Fascism. *See* Nazi regime
Fatherland Party (Deutsche Vaterlandspartei), 20, 38, 164,
165, 167, 172, 174, 175, 183, 184
Federal Council, 132
Federal Republic of Germany, 173, 225–228, 230–232
Feudalism, 33, 57, 179
Fifteenth Amendment (U.S.), 155
Filipino people, 102
First Morocco Crisis, 21
First Volunteer Cavalry (U.S.), 5
Fischer, Fritz, 220
Fitzpatrick, Matthew, 10, 25, 69–70
Florida (Prussian settlement), 46
Fortschritte der Erbpathologie, Rassenhygiene und ihrer Grenzgebiete (journal), 201
Fortschrittliche Volkspartei, 31, 147, 183, 185
The Foundations of the 19th Century (Chamberlain), 190–191
Fourteenth Amendment (U.S.), 155
France
  Algeria, expansionism in, 34, 46, 87
  Asia, expansionism in, 61
  colonialism in, 57
  decolonization and, 225
  ethnicism in, 32, 35
  expansionism and, 77
  Free French, 187
  French Revolution, 29, 51, 61
  impact of colonialism, 14
  imperialism in, 33–34
  July Revolution of 1830, 61
  liberalism in, 220, 230
  loss of territory to, 6
  miscegenation laws in, 133
  Native Americans, romanticization of, 83
  North Africa, expansionism in, 46, 61, 107
  North America, colonization in, 98
  tension with German Empire, 99
  Terror, 52, 61
  in World War I, 161, 167
Frank, Hans, 209
Frankfurt, University of, 202

Frankfurt Parliament, 57, 69–70, 72–73, 95
Frech, Stefan, 20
Frederick II (Prussia), 46
Frederickson, George M., 137
Free Corps, 168
Free French, 187
Freiburg, University of, 40, 153, 164
Freicorps, 202
Freisinnige Volkspartei, 110, 114–115, 183, 185
Freisler, Roland, 199
Frevert, Ute, 24–25
Friedrich-Wilhelm University, 153
"Frontier thesis," 94
Frymann, Daniel. See Class, Heinrich.
Furber, David, 22

Gagern, Hans Christoph von, 57–58, 71
Gagern, Heinrich von, 57
Games, Allison, 11
Die Gartenlaube (journal), 42, 73–75, 77–78, 91–93, 97
Gassert, Philipp, 197
Genocide
    in German Southwest Africa, 111, 113, 121, 232
    Holocaust, 22, 220, 224
    of Native Americans, 1–2
Geographical Interpretations of American History (Semple), 100
Geography, 89
German Association, 70
German Colonial Association, 111, 121, 125
German Colonial League, 188
German Democratic Party, 131, 185–188
German East Africa
    generally, 21, 140, 187
    miscegenation laws in, 130, 143, 145, 156
    Peters on, 105–107, 110
    race codes in, 4, 80
    sharecropping in, 128
    uprisings in, 144–145

German Empire. *See also specific colony*
    Africa, expansionism and, 192
    France, tension with, 99
    miscegenation laws, 130–133, 141–145, 150–152, 154–158, 177, 229–230
    race, 127–160
    segregation, 127–132, 140–145, 160, 229–230
    unification of Germany, 30, 32–33
German exceptionalism, 6, 15, 130. *See also Sonderweg*
"Germanization," 13, 72, 165
"German mind," 84
German Navy, 21
German People's Party, 187
German Progressive Party, 30–31, 68, 174
German Samoa, 4, 80, 130–131, 145, 151
German Southwest Africa
    generally, 99, 162
    American West compared, 80–81, 86
    Dernburg on, 116–120, 125
    expulsion in, 120
    genocide in, 111, 113, 121, 232
    Jim Crow laws, influence of, 13
    miscegenation laws in, 130–131, 144–145, 156
    Native Americans compared, 111–126, 184
    race codes in, 4, 80, 205–206
    Rohrbach on, 17, 120–121, 124–125
    segregation in, 143–144, 222
    settler colonialism, 4, 80, 119, 124
    Social Democratic Party and, 119
    uprisings in, 144–145
    war in, 109, 111–126, 141, 177, 187, 198
Germany. *See specific topic*
Gerstäcker, Friedrich, 66–67, 89
Gerwarth, Robert, 25
Gesellschaft für Deutsche Kolonisation (Peters), 105

Gesellschaft für Staatswissenschaftliche Fortbildung, 153
"Gesetz zur Verhütung erbkranken Nachwuchses." *See* Decree on Preventing Hereditarily Ill Progeny
Gilmore, Glenda, 127–128
Globalisierung und Nation (Conrad), 10
Globalism, 11–12
Globus (journal), 12, 42
Gobineau (Count), 149
Goebbels, Joseph, 197, 211–212, 217
Goerdeler, Carl, 189
Goethe, Johann Wolfgang von, 43
Gold Rush of 1849, 66
Göring, Hermann, 212, 215
Göttingen, University of, 12, 29, 49, 103, 152–153, 178, 180
Great Britain. *See* United Kingdom
Great Depression, 196
Great War
  changing attitudes toward United States following, 175–181
  Eastern Europe, effect on German expansionism in, 161–174
  effect on German views of United States, 161–162
  German nationalism during, 20
  impact on German expansionism, 18–27
  loss of German colonies following, 163–164
  occupation of Eastern Europe during, 22
Grey, Edward, 32
Grimm, Hans, 206
Grimmer-Solem, Erik, 117
Gröber, Adolf, 148
Großdeutscher Pressedienst (journal), 200
Grosse, Pascal, 25–26, 228
GSWA. *See* German Southwest Africa
Guam, American conquest of, 9, 101
Guest workers, 226
Guidelines for Colonial Propaganda (Goebbels), 197

Haeckel, Ernst, 91, 93
Hagenlücke, Heinz, 20
Hahl, Albert, 140
Hambacher Fest, 61
Hannover (Kingdom), 103
"Hänge-Peters," 111
Hartz, Louis, 35
Harvard University, 99–100, 153
Hasenclever, Adolf, 180, 190
Hasse, Ernst, 21, 97
Hecht, Günther, 204–206, 208
Hecker, Friedrich, 29–30
Hegel, George Friedrich Wilhelm, 56–57, 87
Hellwald, Friedrich, 89–90, 92
Henke, Alfred, 147
Herero people, 80, 112–113, 115, 117–119, 125, 131, 141, 232
Heuss, Theodor, 173
Heydrich, Reinhard, 199
Hildebrand, Klaus, 189
Hillgruber, Andreas, 194
Himmler, Heinrich, 20, 164, 183, 186, 188, 208–209, 211–212, 215
Hitler, Adolf
  generally, 24
  colonialism and, 186–188, 222
  Eastern Europe and, 13–14
  expansionism and, 19–20, 183
  on Jews, 195
  on *Lebensraum*, 190–199, 208–216
Hitler's Empire (Mazower), 22
Hobohm, Martin, 184
Hofstadter, Richard, 35
Hohenlohe-Langenburg, Ernst zu, 133, 143–144
Holocaust, 22, 220, 224
Holocaust Memorial, 231
Horkheimer, Max, 33, 219, 223–224
Hossbach Protocol, 196
Hottentot elections, 36–37, 113, 159, 176
Howe, Frederick C., 179
Hudson River, 79
Humboldt, Alexander von, 43, 45–47, 56, 58–60, 65–66, 76
Humboldt University, 153

The Ideological Origins of Nazi Imperialism (Smith), 19
"Ignoble savage" stereotype, 82–87
Immigration, 100, 226
Imperial Colonial Department (Reichskolonialamt [RKA])
  generally, 42, 137, 141, 176, 187
  lynchings and, 146–147
  miscegenation laws and, 144, 150–152
  race codes and, 130–134, 153–159
Imperial Colonial Office (Reichskolonialabteilung [RKA-B]), 1, 42, 117–118, 133, 143–144
Imperialism, 100–101
  in France, 33–34
  liberalism and, 39–41
  Nazi regime, effect on, 218–223
  "social imperialism," 6, 40
  in United Kingdom, 33–34, 104
  in United States, 177–178
  Weber on, 40–41
India, 210
Indiana, 203
Indians. *See* Native Americans
Individualism, 201, 207–208, 216.
  See also Liberalism
Industrialization and expansionism, 64
"Inner colonization," 63
Interracial marriage. *See* Miscegenation laws
Iroquois people, 46
Israel, 224

Jackson, Andrew, 60, 62, 85
Jefferson, Thomas, 28–29, 34, 40, 44–46, 51, 55–59, 64, 76
Jews
  anti-Semitism (*See* Anti-Semitism)
  expulsion from Prussia, 165
  Hitler on, 195
  Native Americans compared, 209
  Nuremberg race laws, 199–201, 204
  Peters on, 110
  pogroms, 196, 198

Rosenberg on, 191
United States seen by Nazi regime as controlled by, 196–206, 212, 217, 223
Jim Crow laws (U.S.)
  generally, 180–181, 209
  German colonies, influence on, 142, 146, 150–152, 154–155, 159
  German Southwest Africa, influence on, 13
  Nazi regime, influence on, 128–129, 199, 204, 222
July Revolution of 1830 (France), 61

Kant, Immanuel, 28–29, 34, 47–49, 54, 64
Kapp Putsch, 202
Kardorff, Wilhelm von, 110
Kartell der schaffenden Stände (Cartel of the Productive Estates), 19, 174
Kayser, Paul, 107, 169
Kenya, 224
Kershaw, Ian, 24–25
Kolonialfrage und Rassegedanke (Hecht), 205
Kolonialpolitischer Führer (Schmoller), 122–123
Kolonialpolitisches Aktionskomité, 116–117, 122, 173
Kolonialrecht und Kolonialwirtschaft (journal), 42
Die innere Kolonisation im östlichen Deutschland (Sering), 169, 170
Kramer, Paul, 32
Krieger, Heinrich, 200–201, 204, 208
Kuhn, Alexander, 121, 216
Kundrus, Birthe, 25
Kurlander, Eric, 31, 220

Labor and colonialism, 136–137
Lagarde, Anton Paul de, 152–153
Laissez-faire philosophy, 3, 81, 99, 107–109, 136, 138, 155–156, 159. *See also* Liberalism
Last of the Mohicans (Cooper), 85

Lebensraum
  generally, 94, 175
  as anti-colonialism, 189–197
  as anti-liberalism, 189–197
  Eastern Europe and, 189–192
  Hitler on, 190–199, 208–216
  Nazi regime and, 15, 19–21, 26–27,
    162, 189–197, 211, 214–215
  Ratzel on, 19, 175
  Rosenberg on, 20, 183, 186, 211
Der Lebensraum (Ratzel), 99
Ledebour, Georg, 111, 115, 147
Leers, Johann von, 204
Left-liberals in Germany, 30–31, 37,
  68, 120, 172–173, 176. *See also*
  specific Party
Le Havre, 70
Leipzig, University of, 93
"Leitkulturdebatte," 226
Lettenbaur, Josef, 111
Leutwein, Theodor Gotthiff von, 84,
  112, 122–124, 144
Liberal colonialism, 78–80, 102, 109,
  135, 137, 224–225
Liberale Kolonialpolitik, 78–80, 102,
  109, 135, 137, 224–225
Liberal Imperialism (Fitzpatrick), 10
Liberalism
  African-Americans and, 40
  changing views of United States in
    German liberalism, 175–181
  colonialism and, 39–41
  Dernburg and, 16, 30, 37, 155,
    173–174, 206–207, 218, 225
  expansionism and, 3, 6, 27–41
  in France, 220, 230
  imperialism and, 39–41
  Lebensraum as anti-liberalism,
    189–197
  in National-Liberal Party, 30–31
  Nazi regime and, 17, 26
  Peters and, 37–39, 217, 221, 223,
    225
  post-World War II period, effect
    on, 224–225
  race and, 167–168
  Ratzel and, 30, 108, 116, 207, 218,
    225

Revolutions of 1848 and, 29–30,
    68–69, 227
Rohrbach and, 225
slavery and, 28–29
Solf and, 37, 218, 225
in United Kingdom, 220, 230
in United States, 217–218
Weber and, 30, 35, 225
Liberal People's Party, 110, 114–115,
    183, 185
Liberty and colonialism, 44–55
Liebert, Eduard von, 21
Lincoln, Abraham, 146, 200
Lindequist, Friedrich von, 155
List, Friedrich, 16, 61, 63–64, 67–68,
    76
Literacy, 56
Lithuania, loss of territory to, 6
Little Big Horn, 92
Liulevicius, Vejas, 22–23
"Living space." *See Lebensraum*
Livingston, David, 103
Locke, John, 34
Long, Edward, 53
Longue dureé perspective, 218–219
Louisiana, 140
Lüderitz (city), 118
Lukács, Georg, 41
Lynchings, 146–147, 181, 199

Madley, Benjamin, 22
Mahan, Alfred Thayer, 178
Maharero, Samuel, 112
Mainzer Adelsverein, 73
Malinowski, Stefan, 25
Malthus, Thomas, 57
Marriage. *See* Miscegenation laws
Marx, Karl, 223
May, Karl, 82, 84–85, 92, 208–209
Mazower, Mark, 15, 22, 218, 224
Meinecke, Friedrich, 97
Meiners, Christoph, 12, 29, 39–40,
    47, 49–54, 64
Mein Kampf (Hitler), 193, 195–196,
    214
Mengele, Josef, 202
Mexicans, 32
Mill, John Stuart, 34, 40, 53, 168

Miquel, Johann von, 97
Miscegenation laws
  in American South, 137, 142, 146,
    148–149
  in British colonies, 142
  Center Party and, 131–132, 151,
    154–155, 157–158
  in German colonies, 130–133,
    141–145, 150–152, 154–158,
    177, 229–230
  National-Liberal Party and, 157
  Nazi regime and, 199
  Pan-German League and, 157
  Social Democratic Party and,
    131–132, 148–151, 154,
    157–158
  Solf on, 130–132, 144–147, 151,
    153
Mississippi River, 13, 62, 209
Mississippi (state), 140
Missouri, 59–60
Mixed-race marriage. *See*
  Miscegenation laws
Mommsen, Wolfgang J., 35, 227
Mongolian race, 49
Monroe Doctrine, 213–215, 217
Montgelas, Max von, 181
Morgan, Edmund, 54
Morton, Samuel George, 65–66, 68
Mount Kilimanjaro, 106–107, 169
Müller, Hermann, 84, 115–116, 216,
  222
Mumm, Reinhard, 121, 149, 206
Der Mythus des 20. Jahrhunderts
  (Rosenberg), 190–191

Nama people, 80, 112, 118, 125,
  131, 141, 232
Namibia. *See* German Southwest
  Africa
Napoleonic Wars, 47, 57–58, 63
National Assembly (Frankfurt), 57,
  69–70, 72–73, 95
"National Christianity," 152
"*Das nationale System der politischen
  Oekonomie*" (List), 63
Nationalism, 20, 192

Nationalliberale Partei. *See*
  National-Liberal Party
National-Liberal Party
  generally, 2, 138, 187
  divisions in, 183
  liberalism in, 30–31
  miscegenation laws and, 157
  Peters in, 38, 102
  Ratzel in, 95–97, 192
  representation in Reichstag, 37,
    114, 147–148
National Party. *See* Deutsche
  Reichspartei
National-Social Association, 173
National Socialist German Workers
  Party, 31, 185–189, 199, 205,
  220. *See also* Nazi regime
Nationalsozialer Verein, 173
Nationalsozialistische Deutsche
  Arbeiterpartei. *See* National
  Socialist German Workers Party
Nationalsozialistische Monatshefte
  (journal), 42, 199
National unity and expansionism,
  69–78
Nationalzeitung (newspaper), 137
Native Americans
  British romanticization of, 83
  change in German view of
    American policy toward, 161,
    176
  de Tocqueville on, 46
  expulsion of, 12, 34, 56, 68, 77
  French romanticization of, 83
  genocide of, 1–2
  German romanticization of, 82–87
  German Southwest Africa
    compared, 111–126, 184
  German views of, 1–2, 4–5, 12–14,
    48–49, 62, 65–68, 76–77, 89–93
  "ignoble savage" stereotype, 82–87
  Jefferson on, 45
  Jews compared, 209
  Nazi regime and, 116, 209
  Peters on, 79–81, 109
  removal of, 62, 65, 68, 76, 85, 87
  settler colonialism and, 84–85

westward American expansion and,
55–60
Nature and Man in America (Shaler),
99
Natürliche Schöpfungsgeschichte
(Haeckel), 91
Naumann, Friedrich, 30, 97,
173–174, 179, 184, 225
Naval League, 111
Nazi regime
African colonization and, 187–188
American West and, 207–216
anti-Semitism of, 195–196, 198,
204–205, 212, 217, 219, 223
colonialism, effect of, 218–223
Dernburg on, 185–187
Eastern Europe and, 210–211
expansionism and, 6
imperialism, effect of, 218–223
Jim Crow laws, influence of,
128–129, 199, 204, 222
Lebensraum and, 15, 19–21,
26–27, 162, 189–197, 211,
214–215
liberalism and, 17, 26
miscegenation laws and, 199
nationalism and, 192
Native Americans and, 116, 209
race and, 192, 221–223
Rohrbach on, 17, 185–186
seizure of power, 17
settler colonialism and, 188,
192–193
Solf on, 185–186
Soviet Union and, 25, 35
views of United States, 17–18,
25–26, 189–217, 223
Negroes. *See* African-Americans
Nelson, Robert L., 16, 22–23
Netherlands
colonialism in, 57
miscegenation laws in, 133
Neudeutschland in Westamerika
(Braun), 71
Neuhaus (city), 103
Nevada, 122
"New Atlantic History," 11

New Guinea, 140
New Mexico, 92
New Orleans, 133, 145
New York Times, 138
"Noble savage" stereotype, 85, 92,
131
Nordenflycht, Ferdinand von,
133–134
North Africa, French expansionism
in, 46
North American Review (journal), 62
NSDAP. *See* National Socialist
German Workers Party
Nuremberg race laws, 199–201, 204

Oklahoma, 141
Omaheke Desert, 113
Oncken, Hermann, 174, 178, 182,
190
The Origins of the New South
(Woodward), 127
The Origins of Totalitarianism
(Arendt), 219, 228, 230
"Ostreich," 210–211

Palestine, 152
Pan-Germanism, 19–21, 37–38, 183,
219, 229–231
Pan-German League
generally, 23, 111, 149, 227
Eastern Europe and, 164
ideology of, 19–21, 221
miscegenation laws and, 157
Peters on, 38, 110, 172, 227
Ratzel on, 172, 174, 227
Rohrbach on, 174, 184
Solf on, 174
Weber on, 172–174, 227
World War I, impact of, 171–174
Pan-Slavism, 219, 229–231
Papen, Franz von, 186
Peculiarities of German history, 15,
35, 86, 222
The Peculiarities of German History
(Blackbourn and Eley), 15
Pennsylvania, University of, 65
Penny, H. Glenn, 83

Peschel, Oscar, 89–91, 93
Petermann's Mittheilungen (journal),
    42, 74
Peters, Carl
    generally, 16–17, 47, 87, 137–139,
        212, 216
    on Anti-Semitism, 37–38, 110,
        168–169, 172
    colonialism and, 79–80, 123, 135,
        165–169, 192, 207–208, 229
    on German East Africa, 105–107,
        110
    on Jews, 110
    liberalism and, 37–39, 217, 221,
        223, 225
    in National-Liberal Party, 38, 102
    on Native Americans, 79–81, 109
    overview, 102–111
    on Pan-German League, 38, 110,
        172, 227
Philadelphia (Prussian settlement), 46
Philippines, American conquest of, 9,
    101
Pitts, Jennifer, 37, 53
Plains Wars, 101, 106–107
Pogroms, 196, 198
Poland
    expulsion of Poles from Prussia,
        165
    German expansionism and,
        169–174
    invasion of, 214
    loss of territory to, 6
    Prussian expansionism in, 46–47
    Weber, anti-Polish sentiment of,
        164, 168, 227
PolitischeGeographie (Ratzel), 94,
    96
*Politische Geographie der Vereinigten
    Staaten von Nord-Amerika*
    (Ratzel), 136–137
"Polonization," 164
Pomerania, 193
Posen province, 165, 170, 193
Die Post (newspaper), 139
*The Problem of Slavery in the Age of
    Revolution* (Davis), 54

Progress and expansionism, 55–69
Progressive People's Party, 31, 147,
    183, 185
Proletariat, 40
Pro-slavery arguments, 12, 34, 48, 50,
    53
Prussia
    acquisition of territory from
        Poland, 46–47
    expulsion from, 164–165
    literacy in, 56
    possibility of colonization in, 17,
        164–165, 170, 193, 227
    representation in Reichstag, 114
    unification of Germany and, 31–33,
        89
Puerto Rico, American conquest of, 9,
    101

Race
    Allied occupation of Rhineland
        and, 175–176, 180–181
    American South, race codes in, 17,
        129, 132, 134, 137, 142, 146,
        148, 152, 154–155, 158
    in British colonies, 151
    colonialism and, 2, 4, 27–28,
        31–35, 37, 48–55
    de Tocqueville on, 168
    European colonies and, 127–128
    expansionism and, 55–69
    German colonies and, 127–160
    German Southwest Africa, race
        codes in, 4, 80, 205–206
    Jim Crow laws (See Jim Crow
        laws)
    liberalism and, 167–168
    miscegenation laws (See
        Miscegenation laws)
    Nazi regime and, 192, 221–223
    Nuremberg race laws, 199–201,
        204
    during post-World War I period,
        182–183
    race consciousness, 150, 156
    racial purity, 149
    Rohrbach on, 220, 229

segregation (*See* Segregation)
settler colonialism and, 10, 17, 19, 129, 184
slavery (*See* Slavery)
Weber on, 229
"Race Relations in the United States" (Coolidge), 154
Das Rasserecht in den Vereinigten Staaten (Krieger), 200
Ratzel, Friedrich
generally, 80, 87, 89–90, 216, 229
colonialism and, 73, 138–139, 169
on economic development, 64
expansionism and, 2, 16, 124
on *Lebensraum,* 19, 175
liberalism and, 30, 108, 116, 207, 218, 225
in National-Liberal Party, 95–97, 192
overview, 93–102
on Pan-German League, 172, 174, 227
on Revolutions of 1848, 36
on science, 47
on slavery, 13
views of United States, 135–137, 210–212
Rechenberg, Georg Albrecht von, 140
Reconstruction Amendments (U.S.), 146, 155
"Redskins," 91
Reichskolonialabteilung. *See Imperial Colonial Office*
Reichskolonialamt. *See* Imperial Colonial Department
Reichstag. *See specific party*
Reismann-Grone, Theodor, 21
Republicanism and expansionism, 44–55, 96–97
Republican Party (U.S.), 29
Reshaping the German Right (Eley), 19
Revolutions of 1848
generally, 47, 232
Frankfurt Parliament, 57, 60, 64–65, 69–70, 72–73, 95

liberalism and, 29–30, 68–69, 227
Ratzel on, 36
United States and, 97, 162
Rhineland, Allied occupation of, 175–176, 180–181
Rhodes, Cecil, 37, 181
Richter, Eugen, 30, 109–110, 138–139, 168
Richthofen, Hartmann Freiherr von, 148–151, 181, 218
Right-wing politics in Germany, 18–20, 30–31, 37–38. *See also* Nazi regime; *specific Party*
Rockefeller Foundation, 202
Rohrbach, Paul
generally, 84, 116, 173, 190, 218
on Center Party, 185–186
on German Southwest Africa, 17, 120–121, 124–125
liberalism and, 225
on Nazi regime, 17, 185–186
on Pan-German League, 174, 184
on race, 220, 229
Roosevelt, Franklin D., 198, 213
Roosevelt, Theodore, 5, 32, 37, 85, 101–102, 178–179
Rosenberg, Alfred
generally, 6
on colonialism, 188, 191–193, 222
on Jews, 191
on *Lebensraum,* 20, 183, 186, 211
on United States, 198–199
"Rough Riders," 5, 101
Russia. *See also* Soviet Union
demise of empire, 38, 166
expulsion of Russians from Prussia, 165
German expansionism and, 162

Sagan (city), 115
Said, Edward, 33
St. John, Percy, 86
St. John's River, 79
St. Lawrence River, 79
Sammons, Jeffrey L., 84
Saratoga (Prussian settlement), 46
Sarrazin, Thilo, 226–227

Schacht, Hjalmar, 187–189
Scheidemann, Philipp, 187
Schmitt, Carl, 212–213, 215, 217
Schmoller, Gustav, 116–117, 122,
    173, 179, 216
Schnee, Heinrich, 187–189
Schopenhauer, Arthur, 104
Schubert, Günter, 193
Schulz, Friedrich, 72, 78
Schurz, Carl, 29
"Scientific racism," 65
Second Book (Hitler), 193–196, 214
Second Reich. *See* German Empire
Segregation
    in American South, 232
    Center Party and, 160
    in German colonies, 127–132,
        140–145, 160, 229–230
    in German Southwest Africa,
        143–144, 222
    Nuremberg race laws and, 199–201
    Social Democratic Party and,
        160
Self-government, 79, 141, 167
Semple, Ellen Churchill, 100
Sering, Max, 164, 169–171, 193,
    216, 225
Settler colonialism
    American West and, 57–59, 64, 67,
        112
    Eastern Europe and, 162
    German Southwest Africa, 4, 80,
        119, 124
    Native Americans and, 84–85
    Nazi regime and, 188, 192–193
    race and, 10, 17, 19, 129, 184
    social change and, 97
    Weber and, 173
Shaler, Nathaniel S., 99–100
Sharecropping, 141, 215
Shark Island concentration camp,
    118–119
Sheehan, James, 27
Simplicissimus (magazine), 161
*Sketches of Urban and Cultural Life
    in North America* (Ratzel), 93,
    95–96

Slavery
    civilization and, 59
    colonialism and, 12–14, 49–56,
        232
    German views of, 65, 68
    labor and, 136
    liberalism and, 28–29
    Ratzel on, 13
Smith, Helmut Walser, 117, 220
Smith, William Benjamin, 152–153,
    182
Smith, Woodruff, 19–20
Social control and expansionism,
    55–69
Social Darwinism, 89–91, 119
Social Democratic Party
    generally, 107, 110–111, 122, 139,
        174
    German Southwest Africa and, 119
    miscegenation laws and, 131–132,
        148–151, 154, 157–158
    representation in Reichstag,
        114–115, 130, 147
    segregation and, 160
"Social engineering," 179
"Social imperialism," 6, 40
"Social question," 57–58, 70
Society for German Colonization, 105
Solf, Wilhelm
    generally, 139, 164, 176, 190, 212
    change in views of United States,
        180–181
    colonialism and, 116, 155–159,
        169, 207, 215–216
    liberalism and, 37, 218, 225
    on miscegenation laws, 130–132,
        144–147, 151, 153
    on Nazi regime, 185–186
    on Pan-German League, 174
    on race codes, 134, 205–206
Sömmering, Samuel Thomas, 64
Sonderweg, 6, 15, 32, 130, 220,
    224
Sources, 41–42
South. *See* American South
South Africa, 128, 142, 151, 181
South Dakota, 101, 106

Southwest Africa. *See* German Southwest Africa
Soviet Union. *See also* Russia
    Cold War and, 9
    invasion of, 208–209
    Nazi regime and, 25, 35
    totalitarianism in, 219–220, 231
Sozialdemokratische Partei Deutschlands. *See* Social Democratic Party
Spanish-American War, 5, 101
Spengler, Oswald, 183
Springfield, Illinois, 147
Der Staat und sein Boden geographisch betrachtet (Ratzel), 99
"Stab-in-the-back" myth, 195
Stalingrad, 209
Stalinism, 219, 230
Stanley, Henry Morton, 105
Steinwallner, Bruno, 204
Sterilization laws, 203
Stocking, George W., Jr., 91
Stoecker, Adolf, 152
Stolle, Ferdinand, 74
Struve, Gustav, 29–30
Stübel, Oscar Wilhelm, 117

Table Talk (Hitler), 214
Tanganyika. *See* German East Africa
Tanzania. *See* German East Africa
Tasmania, 91
Tecklenburg, Hans, 130, 141–144
Tellkampf, Johann, 72, 76, 78
Texas, 73, 140
Third Reich. *See* Nazi regime
Thirteenth Amendment (U.S.), 146
Thomsen, Hans, 214
Tocqueville, Alexis de
    generally, 56
    on colonialism, 40, 61, 63, 98–99
    on expansionism, 34, 47, 53, 87–88
    on Native Americans, 46
    on race, 168
Togo, 80, 128, 215–216
Tooze, Adam, 194
Totalitarianism, 219, 231

To the Cultured World (address), 183
Transatlantic connections, 3, 11–12, 59, 75, 85–87, 182, 216, 222, 232
Transnationalism, 24
Transvaal province, 128, 142, 151
Triple Entente, 166, 172
Trotha, Lothar von, 80, 112–113, 115, 119–120
Tübingen, University of, 103
Tulane University, 152
Turkey, 225–226
Turner, Frederick Jackson, 2, 75, 94, 100–101, 178
Tuskegee Institute, 177, 209

"Über den Gebrauch teleologischer Prinzipien in der Philosophie" (Kant), 48
"Über die Rechtmässigkeit des Negern-Handelns" (Meiners), 49
Unification of Germany, 30, 32–33, 89
United Kingdom
    anti-Corn Law movement, 60
    British Navy, 187
    Chartist movement, 60
    colonialism in, 50–51, 57, 77–78, 104
    decolonization and, 225
    ethnicism in, 32, 35
    expansionism and, 50–51, 77–78
    impact of colonialism, 14
    imperialism in, 33–34, 104
    liberalism in, 220, 230
    miscegenation laws in, 133
    Native Americans, romanticization of, 83
    North America, colonization in, 98–99
    in War of 1812, 45
    in World War I, 161, 166–167
United States
    Civil War, 29
    Constitution, 135, 213

United States (*cont.*)
  Democratic Party, 60
  Emancipation Proclamation, 146,
    155
  Fifteenth Amendment, 155
  First Volunteer Cavalry, 5
  Fourteenth Amendment, 155
  imperialism in, 177–178
  Jews seen by Nazi regime as
    controlling, 196–206, 212, 217,
    223
  Jim Crow laws (*See* Jim Crow laws
    (U.S.))
  liberalism in, 217–218
  Nazi regime views of, 17–18,
    25–26, 189–217, 223
  Ratzel on, 135–137, 210–212
  Reconstruction Amendments, 146,
    155
  Republican Party, 29
  Revolutions of 1848 and, 97, 162
  Rosenberg on, 198–199
  Solf on, 180–181
  South (*See* American South)
  Thirteenth Amendment, 146
  West (*See* American West)
  World War I, changing German
    attitudes toward following,
    161–162, 175–181
University of. *See specific University*
Utilitarianism, 50, 179, 209

Vallaux, Camille, 99
"Vanishing native," 58, 117–118
Verein für Sozialpolitik, 173
Versailles Treaty, 6, 174, 190, 197,
  206
Verschuer, Otmar Freiherr von,
  201–202
Virginia, 122
Volga River, 13, 209
Völkerrechtliche Grossraumordnung
  (Schmitt), 212
Der Völkische Beobachter
  (newspaper), 17, 42, 199–203,
  207–208
Völkisch morality, 19, 21, 182, 194,
  206, 220

Volk ohne Raum (Grimm), 206
Vom Reich zum Weltreich
  (Hildebrand), 189

Wagner, Gerhard, 199
Waitz, Georg, 103
Walkenhorst, Peter, 20–21
War of 1812, 45
Washington, Booker T., 177
"Was ist Aufklärung" (Kant), 54
Waterberg, 113
Weber, Max
  generally, 169, 179, 216, 232
  anti-Polish sentiment of, 164, 168,
    227
  on expansionism, 97
  on imperialism, 40–41
  liberalism and, 30, 35, 225
  on Pan-German League, 172–174,
    227
  on race, 229
  settler colonialism and, 173
  West German views of, 227–229
Wehler, Hans-Ulrich, 6, 24, 32, 35,
  40, 220, 226–227
Wehrmacht, 208
Weimar Constitution, 168
Weimar Republic, 19–20, 24, 26, 131,
  182, 187, 190, 197, 202–203
Weltanschauung, 20
Weltmachtpolitik, 40–41
Wenn ich der Kaiser wär' (Class), 23
West. *See* American West
"The West as a Field for Historical
  Study" (Turner), 100
West Germany, 173, 225–228,
  230–232
Wildenthal, Lora, 25–26
"Wild West" analogy, 16, 63–64, 85,
  101, 106, 164, 207–208
Wilhelm II, 111, 113, 137
Willenswelt und Weltwille (Peters),
  104
Wilson, Woodrow, 130, 161
Windhoek, 112, 143
Winnetou (literary character), 92
Wood, Gordon, 55
Woodward, C. Vann, 127

Working class, 40, 104
World War I
    changing German attitudes toward
        United States following, 175–181
    Eastern Europe, effect on German
        expansionism in, 161–174
    effect on German views of United
        States, 161–162
    German nationalism during, 20
    impact on German expansionism,
        18–27
    loss of German colonies following,
        163–164
    occupation of Eastern Europe
        during, 22

Pan-German League, impact on,
    171–174
World War II
    defeat in, 13
    German expansionism during, 22,
        116, 162
    loss of territory following, 224–225
Wyoming, 123

Zantop, Susanne, 82, 84
Zeitschrift für Kolonialpolitik
    (journal), 42
Zimmerer, Jürgen, 22
Zimmerman, Andrew, 10, 117, 128,
    228